LOCAL PRODUCTION SYSTEMS IN EUROPE: RISE OR DEMISE?

Local Production Systems in Europe: Rise or Demise?

Colin Crouch, Patrick Le Galès,
Carlo Trigilia, and Helmut Voelzkow

OXFORD

UNIVERSITY PRESS

OXFORD

UNIVERSITY PRESS

Great Clarendon Street, Oxford OX2 6DP

Oxford University Press is a department of the University of Oxford.
It furthers the University's objective of excellence in research, scholarship,
and education by publishing worldwide in

Oxford New York

Athens Auckland Bangkok Bogotá Buenos Aires Cape Town
Chennai Dar es Salaam Delhi Florence Hong Kong Istanbul Karachi
Kolkata Kuala Lumpur Madrid Melbourne Mexico City Mumbai Nairobi
Paris São Paulo Shanghai Singapore Taipei Tokyo Toronto Warsaw

with associated companies in Berlin Ibadan

Oxford is a registered trade mark of Oxford University Press
in the UK and in certain other countries

Published in the United States
by Oxford University Press Inc., New York

British Library Cataloguing in Publication Data

Data available

Library of Congress Cataloging in Publication Data

Local production systems in Europe: rise or demise?/Colin Crouch . . . [et al.].
p.cm.
Includes bibliographical references and index.
1. Small business—Europe, Western. 2. Europe, Western–Economic conditions—1945–
3. Europe, Western–Economic policy. I. Crouch, Colin, 1944–
HD2346.E85 L63 2001   338.94–dc21   2001016334

ISBN 0-19-924251-8

1 3 5 7 9 10 8 6 4 2

Typeset by Newgen Imaging Systems (P) Ltd., Chennai, India
Printed in Great Britain
on acid-free paper by
Biddles Ltd., Guildford & King's Lynn

ACKNOWLEDGEMENTS

The research on which this volume is based was funded jointly by the European University Institute, Florence, and the Max-Planck Institute for Society Research, Cologne. The authors are grateful to both institutes for their support.

The authors also wish to thank Bruno Courault, Laurent Davezies, Juergen Grote, Bob Hancké, Gary Herrigel, Jonah Lévy, Fabio Sforzi, Marc Smyrl, Michael Storper, and Jonathan Zeitlin, who gave valuable advice at various points of our work, though of course none can be held responsible for anything we have written. Henry Farrell also deserves thanks for his work in constructing the References.

CONTENTS

LIST OF FIGURES

LIST OF TABLES

NOTES ON THE CONTRIBUTORS

Valeria Aniello is a researcher at the 'Federico II' University of Naples and at CEVIFOP (Institut d'Etudes Politiques—CNRS), Paris. She is engaged on research into the competitiveness of local production systems, particularly those emerging in southern Italy. Co-editor (with Luca Meldolesi) of *Un'Italia che non c'è: quant'è, dov'è, com'è?* (special issue of *Rivista di Politica Economica*, 1998).

Luigi Burroni is a researcher in the Department of Political Science and Sociology of the University of Florence, and lecturer for the course on Comparative Industrial Relations at the University of Florence. He has published two essays on small-firm development ('Mutamenti nell'organizzazione produttiva della Terza Italia' and 'La regolazione locale nelle regioni della Terza Italia', both in *Sviluppo Locale*, 1999). He is currently working on a book on *Networks of Firms or Networked Firms? New Models of Local Governance in Italy*.

Colin Crouch is a Professor in Sociology at the European University Institute, Florence. He is also an External Scientific Member of the Max Planck Institute for Society Research at Cologne. His recent books include *Industrial Relations and European State Traditions* (Oxford University Press, 1993); *Are Skills the Answer?* (with David Finegold and Mari Sako, Oxford University Press, 1999); and *Social Change in Western Europe* (Oxford University Press, 1999).

Henry Farrell is a Research Fellow at the Max Planck Project Group on the Law of Common Goods, Bonn. He was recently awarded his PhD thesis by Georgetown University for work on problems of institutional trust among small and medium-sized enterprises in Emiglia Romagna and Baden-Württemberg.

Ulrich Glassmann is a doctoral student at the Max Planck Institute for Society Research at Cologne, where he is working on the governance of local economies in the machinery industries of Emiglia Romagna and Baden-Württemberg. He has also been a teaching assistant at the Institute for Political Science at the University of Cologne and with the Open University at Hagen.

Patrick Le Galès is CNRS senior research fellow at CEVIPOF (Institut d'Etudes Politiques) and associate professor of sociology and politics at Sciences Po, Paris. He is the editor of the *International Journal of Urban and Regional Research*. His books include: *Politiques urbaines et développement local, une comparaison franco-britannique* (Paris, L'Harmattan, 1993); *Les réseaux de l'action publique* (ed. with M. Thatcher, Paris: L'Harmattan, 1995); *Regions in Europe, The Paradox of Power* (ed. with C. Lequesne, London: Routledge, 1998); *Cities in Contemporary Europe* (ed. with A. Bagnasco, Cambridge: Cambridge University Press). He is currently working on a book about cities as local societies and sites of governance in Europe.

Andrés Rodríguez-Pose is Senior Lecturer in Economic Geography and Director of the MSc in Local Economic Development at the London School of Economics and Political Science. His research deals with the connection between economic growth and social, institutional and political factors at a regional level in Europe and Latin America. He is the author of *Dynamics of Regional Growth in Europe* (Oxford University Press, 1998).

Carlo Trigilia is Professor of Economic Sociology in the University of Florence and editor of the journal *Stato e Mercato*. Among his works are 'Small-firm development and local political subcultures in Italy', *European Sociological Review*, 1986; 'The paradox of the region: economic regulation and the representation of interests', *Economy and Society*, 1991; *La construction sociale du marché. Le défi de la troisième Italie* (Paris: Editions de l'Ens, 1993, with A. Bagnasco); 'Italy: The Political Economy of a Regionalized Capitalism', *South European Society and Politics*, 1997; *Economic Sociology. State, Market and Society in Modern Capitalism* (Oxford: Blackwell, forthcoming).

Helmut Voelzkow is a wissenschaftlicher Mitarbeiter at the Max Planck Institute for Society Research at Cologne, where he works on economic sociology, economic structural change and policy, and technological development. He gained his Habilitation at the Ruhr-Universität Bochum, Fakultät für Sozialwissenschaft. His publications include *Mehr Technik in die Region* (Wiesbaden: DUV, 1990) and *Private Regierungen in der Techniksteuerung* (Frankfurt am Main: Campus, 1996).

1

Introduction: The Governance of Local Economies

PATRICK LE GALÈS AND HELMUT VOELZKOW

In this book we attempt systematically to examine the changes within local economies in four European countries by analysing their national contexts, their overall transformation, their modes of governance, and the production of their competitive advantages through what we call 'local collective competition goods'. This book is the first result of a cross-country comparative research project which has been carried out jointly by a number of research institutions and academics in four countries: Italy, Germany, France and the UK. Later contributions will concentrate on specific localities and economic sectors. Here however we offer a systematic comparison of various forms of local economies in their national contexts.

Fundamental for this project is the hypothesis that there are viable alternative forms of manufacturing in advanced societies beyond the model of large firms and classic cases of vertical integration. In order to develop and prosper, firms need to use all sorts of goods and services that are provided in different ways, from knowledge about foreign markets to specialized skills. When these are made available within a particular geographical context they become local collective competition goods. These constitute the advantages that geographical proximity and the density of communication it brings can yield for participating firms. Regional business networks arise, comprising small and medium-sized enterprises all working on complementary products and services. Together, these businesses take on the quality of a regional production system that, as a complex unity, can hold its own against the theoretical alternative of a vertically integrated conglomerate. Internal co-operation secures firms' external competitiveness. Moreover, local economies have at their disposal specific infrastructures which are available to all firms in the region and offer important services to those taking advantage of them (such as technology transfer, training and continuing education or joint marketing, and so on). The provision of such services is essential from the perspective of the firms involved, as they are too small to provide them on their own. The social and institutional foundations of innovation have usually been analysed as the key dimension. Without underestimating the importance of innovation and its diffusion, we want to consider a larger set of collective goods. Provision of such goods must be ensured by social or political arrangements, that is by forms of local governance.

Together with globalization processes, local economies have become a central focus of attention during the past two decades. By now, more than a thousand articles and books have been published. This explosion of literature goes beyond frontiers, including academic ones. The subject initially came to the fore with a wave of enthusiastic proponents, building on the amazing cases of the Third Italy, Baden-Württemberg and Silicon Valley. Piore and Sabel's famous book *The Second Industrial Divide* (1984) clearly set the tone and opened the way to thinking in terms of flexible specialization and post-Fordism. Local economies were back and a new world of possibilities was in the making. Unsurprisingly, together with a somewhat desperate search for industrial districts or the building of science parks all over the place, a second wave of sceptical work soon contested those findings and their more normative consequences. From different starting-points, all kinds of scholars expressed doubts concerning the rise of both local economies and post-Fordism (see for example the contributions in Benko and Lipietz (1992) and Amin (1994)). Now, over the past few years, a third wave of literature has emerged, which critically examines both theoretically and empirically the transformation of local economies, trying to avoid the excessive enthusiasm of the first wave and the undue scepticism of the second. Research is also moving beyond the classic cases to consider urban economies and the role of subcontractors.

Local Collective Competition Goods—A Missing Element of the Success of Local Economies?

How to make sense of the invisible factors of economic development related to geographic proximity is decisive in understanding the past strengths of some local economies and their evolution. A variety of terms and concepts has been associated with such regional or local economies, such as the 'industrial districts' (Piore and Sabel 1984; Sabel 1989), 'new industrial spaces' (Scott 1988a and b; Scott and Storper 1992a and b), 'learning regions' (Morgan 1997a; Maskell and Malmberg 1999), 'intelligent regions' (Cooke and Morgan 1990), 'innovative milieux' (Aydalot 1986), and so on.[1] Our purpose is more modest theoretically, but more ambitious as we aim to make a systematic comparison of local economies in four countries, and then to provide an analytical framework in terms of institutionalization; hence the need to rely upon robust categories that one can operationalize in different local and national contexts. That is the reason why, building upon our experience, discussion and existing literature, we have defined local collective competition goods in some detail.

---

[1] See also, for example, the contributions in Benko and Dunford (1991), Bergmann, Maier and Tödtling (1991), Storper and Scott (1992), Grabher (1993), Amin and Thrift (1994), Rhodes (1995), Staber, Schaefer and Sharma (1996) and Braczyk, Cooke and Heidenreich (1998). See also recent accounts in Storper (1997), Cooke and Morgan (1998), Perulli (1998), Scott (1999), and Trigilia (1998).

Local Collective Competition Goods

Networked forms of production made firms more dependent on the local environment in which they are located. Therefore, local contexts became important as providers of rich external economies. In particular one can distinguish between two basic kinds of such economies: intangible and tangible. The former have to do with cognitive and normative resources, such as tacit knowledge, specialized languages and conventions, and trust. The second include infrastructure and services. A short list of these collective goods is given in Figure 1.1. It is not exhaustive, and some items can be added from one country or region to the next. But it provides a useful starting-point both for some further conceptualization and for our comparative empirical survey.

Local economies as more or less integrated production systems may profit from the competitive advantages usually ascribed to small and medium-sized enterprises: flexibility, creativity, the high motivation of both management and workers, links with innovative firms and markets, and so on. But where there is light, there is also shadow. Small and medium-sized firms often lack the specific resources that could enable them to cash in on their advantages within the competitive marketplace, and they can be pushed out by large firms. They may lack, for example, specialized know-how regarding the introduction of new technologies; or they may need information regarding current developments on

- to equip a section of the workforce with new skills
- to access research and development to improve a product or product range
- to procure orders
- to acquire information on marketing in new foreign markets
- to acquire information on marketing in new markets in this country
- actually to establish marketing arrangements in new foreign markets
- to acquire information on changes in product costs and demand
- to acquire information on new developments in production methods or work organization
- to get help with new technology
- to research a patent
- to articulate a policy concern to central government
- to articulate a policy concern to local government
- to acquire expensive new equipment or technology
- to ensure quality and standards fulfilment of the firm's product
- to gain access to expensive services (e.g. quality testing)
- to find new employees of satisfactory quality
- to resolve a labour dispute
- to get help with management problems
- to raise capital
- to get legal advice

FIGURE 1.1. Local Collective Competition Goods—A List of Examples

sales or procurement markets; or they may be too small to afford the costs of setting up a differentiated marketing system. The central thesis asserts that the framework of a local economy can compensate for such deficits or shortages. As Pyke and Sengenberger (1992:4) put it:

The key problem of small firms appears not to be that of being small, but that of being isolated. Thus, what might be relevant are not the characteristics and resources of the single small firm but the characteristics of the industrial structure and context in which it is implanted. Consequently, much more emphasis, in this view, should be given to the creation of organizational forms under which the small firm can combine its advantages of flexibility with the support and stability that comes from larger networks.

The availability of qualified employees on the regional market is a typical collective good of this kind (Streeck *et al.* 1987). The supply of employees with 'appropriate' job skills benefits each and every company. And this is a collective good because it is available to companies regardless of whether or not they themselves may have contributed to providing education and training for the potential (regional) labour force. Thus where vocational skills are concerned there is a danger of falling into a rationality trap: for the individual firm the rational thing to do is not to make any contribution of its own towards providing the collective good of vocational training, but instead to woo skilled staff away from other companies. From the collective point of view, that is, the view of the local economy, on the other hand, it is this individual-rational behaviour that is irrational. If each firm dispenses with training to escape the risk of other companies wooing away qualified staff, the overall level of employees' skills will inevitably remain too low. Hence there is a need for some kind of institutional precaution to ensure that the collective good of professional training for employees found on the regional labour market is generated. That is why there are different variants of non-market production of the good of 'vocational training,' which extend from public provision via associative arrangements to co-operative solutions from company conglomerates. 'Vocational training networks' are also conceivable in which public, semi-public and private organizations are integrated, each taking responsibility for providing a service or product needed for vocational training.

The example of vocational training and further education concerns a collective good required by the labour market. There are other markets affecting companies that require comparable collective goods. Small and medium-sized firms, for instance, find it difficult to realize certain research and development projects on their own; they cannot afford to buy the necessary services and facilities. However, if several firms collaborate, R&D services can be developed that will improve the competitiveness of all companies involved. Here too the rationality trap can quickly unfold: the individual company wants to make use of all the advantages the research collaboration brings, while simultaneously bearing as few of the costs as possible. Only if adequate institutional safeguards are implemented can it be expected that the collective good of research and development will be provided. There again, strategic alliances formed by several companies are also conceivable, as are associative arrangements or the public provision of certain services. Research and development is an area the public sector feels particularly obliged to support, in the interest of promoting local trade and industry. Public or semi-public facilities can help local firms gain easy access to new knowledge and make commercial use of new knowledge. These too are collective goods serving to enhance regional competitiveness from the local economy's point of view.

There are many other examples. Providing information on the development of the relevant procurement or sales markets, or on the development of production costs and product quantities on the relevant markets would be one. Another would be articulating the collective interests of the local economy to governmental agencies. It is also possible to conceive of primary products or production technology being jointly procured or of technical systems being used collectively, say, for the purpose of quality evaluation. Likewise, specifying common product standards could be useful for the local economy, as could joint regional or product marketing. Establishing ground rules for fair competition should also be considered, as should developing strategies to open up new markets outside the region.

These collective goods do not appear at random. Our comparative project aims at showing the diversity and the dynamics of diverse institutional arrangements.

How to Produce Local Collective Competition Goods: The Governance Approach

Basically, one can assume that the procurement of these competition goods is indispensable for the competitiveness of small and medium-sized enterprises— whatever the manner of procuring them. As Staber (1996b: 4) puts it:

Firms are often not able to produce all necessary services in-house, and where these services involve transactional ambiguities (as technology research or labour training) and asset specificity (as in acquiring and using dedicated equipment) some form of public intervention may lead to more efficient solutions for firms.

However, government provision need not be considered the only option. Accordingly, it can be presumed that local economies are distinguished by the way they provide their local enterprises with collective competition goods, while there will probably be different institutional variants, initially to be regarded as 'equifunctional'.

The so-called 'governance approach' is useful for the explication of these differences. It was originally developed for application within comparative social research because it is especially well suited for making the specific qualities of the structure and development of modern societies recognizable in their respective national economies. 'Governance' refers to the entirety of institutions which co-ordinate or regulate action or transaction among (economic) subjects within an (economic) system (Streeck and Schmitter 1985; Hollingsworth, Schmitter and Streeck 1994a; Hollingsworth and Boyer 1997).

The approach can also be used for analysing the internal functioning of local economies. It assumes that every modern society can be described as a specific combination of modes of regulation. In order to be able to identify such combinations of patterns of social order, research following the governance approach selects from various models of social order (ideal types) which are then recognizable in real contexts in a more or less definite form or in particular combinations. The attempt is then made to find the best fit between the empirical cases and the ideal-typical models of social order, in the knowledge that this requires radical analytical simplifications.

Five ideal-typical models of social order have been identified. This differs from the transaction-cost theory of Williamson (1975, 1985), which typically positions economic institutions on a range between markets and (business) hierarchies only. Figure 1.2 shows the five as analysed by Hollingsworth and Boyer (1997:9). Each ideal-typical model is named after its respective central institution. Following this typology of possible models of social order, the components of a governance system can be identified as the market, the (business) organization, the state, the community, and the association. Accordingly, a distinction can be made between competition (the market), hierarchy (the business organization), coercion on the basis of a monopoly of the use of physical

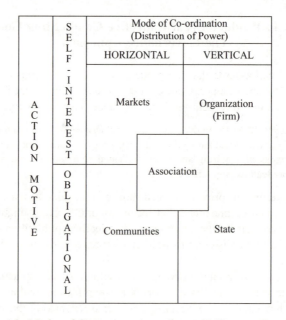

FIGURE 1.2. Modes of Governance According to Hollingsworth and Boyer
Source: Adapted from Hollingsworth and Boyer 1997: 9.

violence (the state), solidarity (the community) and negotiation (the association). Decisive for distinguishing among the models is the motivation that pushes actors to take up relations with other actors.

The market: The market model takes for granted the presence of rational actors whose goal is to increase individual utility via the exchange of private goods and services (utility maximization). The model is based on the assumption that individuals and collectivities (especially firms) are primarily concerned with profit. It serves to explain the allocation of private goods in a free market economy. Atomistic competition constitutes the ideal-typical leading principle guiding the co-ordination of actors. However, the theory states that the market mechanism frequently fails to provide collective goods (Olson 1971)—and thus also the collective competition goods of our main concern. But this is not inevitable. One could imagine a constellation in which an individually rational agent pays for a collective good—even though other individuals will act as 'free riders'—because the benefit to him exceeds the costs he incurs. (This qualification of the argument was made by Olson (1971) himself.) Applied to the production of collective competition goods for a local economy, it is conceivable that a (presumably larger) company would act accordingly and provide its regional environment with information, consulting or other services in order to realize its own economic benefits via the increased competitiveness of the other enterprises. A well-known example for such a 'strategic' network is offered by the Benetton company which provides regional textile and fashion industries in 'Third Italy' with common services (Belussi 1987).

The organization (vertical integration): The organization model is based on agents who—by means of fixed rights and responsibilities—are part of instruction-based relationships. In this model of social order, activities are co-ordinated by hierarchy. The production of a collective competition good will be realized by a vertical integration, that is, the merger of several companies of a region (which previously could have been regarded as a collective that would not have ensured the production of the collective good). In the process of vertical integration, the competition good will of course lose its collective characteristics; in a sense, the good or service will be transformed into a private good of the vertically integrated large enterprise where it could appear under the heading 'overheads'.

The state: The state model is also grounded in the co-ordination of actors through hierarchical control. The decisive motives are, on the part of those who occupy the higher positions in the hierarchy, the wish to further a career or to exercise power; on the part of all the others, it is the readiness to be obedient. This readiness follows from the fact of being in an inferior power position and need only be grounded in the fear of punishment. The state model ultimately rests on the application of force, even in the case of domination in the interests of the dominated. This has clear implications for local economies. In a context such as Italy where the state is ineffective, local economies are likely to be quite different from their equivalents in contexts with an effective national state. As far as the provision of collective competition goods is concerned, the state model suggests a co-operation of private companies with public institutions that provide information, consulting and other services via specialized administrative or other public institutions. These can be initiatives, local institutions (e.g., within the framework of promotion of economic development and trade), administrative units on the regional level, but also universities, other educational institutions and publicly funded sources of R&D.

The community: Here, the guiding principle of co-ordination among actors is informal, autonomous, and sometimes spontaneous solidarity among members of a social unit such as a family, a 'clan', a local authority area or a village 'community'. Not profit but rather the appreciation of the other members of the community or the desire to belong to a group constitute the characteristic motivation for individuals. Co-operation between several small and medium-sized enterprises that commonly fulfil certain operational functions and thus provide collective competition goods is also conceivable. In this case, the community context suspends the individually rational orientation which otherwise would have caused a market failure. A co-operation of exclusively private enterprises emerges on the basis of collective identities, and the conviction that the other enterprises will act just as collectively rational (a 'community' of enterprises, or a regional 'enterprise network'). This said, communities need not only work through common identity, and it is often difficult to disentangle what is due to gift exchange and reciprocity (in the sense of Maus) and what is due to community identity, as both are intimately linked in the case of local economies.

The association: At the centre of the model of associational order are organizations founded for the promotion of functionally defined interests (businesses, workers, professionals, and so on). Its leading principle is negotiation or 'concertation' of interests within and between various interest groups (as in wage setting, for example). As has been demonstrated in various studies, organized interests can in fact take the position of a 'private government'—they can work out collective agreements on behalf of their members and enforce them internally (Streeck and Schmitter 1985). Within such corporatist arrangements, organized interests can contribute to fulfilling public duties by their organizational potential. At the same time, these associations provide their members with diverse services. For instance, there are certain service organizations offering information and consulting to their members. It is also conceivable for there to be services rendered by organizations whose main objective is to represent their members' interests towards the state or other interest groups, but which also provide selective goods. These take the form of services, which contribute to providing small and medium-sized enterprises with resources that they would not have been able to produce on their own.

The country studies apply the above-introduced system of models of social order to the institutional variants producing collective competition goods for local economies. This reveals a quite differentiated picture of regionally and nationally specific solutions, and also demonstrates the existence of functional equivalents. Indeed, certain elements of the five models of order can be found in all local economies, but their respective weights are distributed quite unevenly. The governance approach puts great emphasis on this 'contingency of orders', that is, the variety of ways in which certain tasks (here: the production of collective competition goods) can be assigned to market, enterprise organization, community, government bureaucracy and association. What will be worked out through market exchanges in one local economy could be achieved by government entitlements in another. A collective competition good of a third local economy may be provided via a community context or associational forms of collective action.

Such a perspective that recognizes contingencies in social order and admits different institutional variants for the solution of collective problems, of course allows also combinations of the different models of social order. One example is the way in which the potential of the market model for the production of collective competition goods can be enhanced by tax incentives—political and administrative regulations. Private governments that want to ensure the production of collective competition goods in the framework of the association model but are not able to enforce collective agreements towards their members will be strengthened if government makes available its sanction apparatus for this purpose. It can be expected that, in practice, these combination solutions are rather the rule than the exception.

Thus the governance approach allows an unexpected range of theoretical possibilities and leaves it to empirical research to identify specific governance structures and analyse their functioning (in a horizontal comparison of case studies) as well as their development dynamics (in a comparison over time) in greater detail. Of course, this undertaking is not done for amusement but the attempt to systematize the comparison of local economies in the tradition of functional analysis. The analysis distinguishes structures and functions and takes the functional equivalence of different structures as a starting-point, even if the results and consequences of specific structures for fulfilling functions show differences. In other words, the production of collective competition goods (function) can be realized via different institutional variants (structures) at different levels; and it is significant for the results or consequences of governance which institutional variant has been chosen to ensure the production of collective competition goods.

The Search for Local 'Invisible Factors of Economic Development'

The hypothesis that local collective goods and the modes of local governance of the economies are the key to explain the successes of local economies is not a new one. It is the lowest common denominator of the literature of recent decades, the search for what Doeringer, Terkla, and Topakian (1987) have called the 'invisible factors of economic development'. In the following we use just some of this literature to stress the questions of local collective competition goods and governance of local economies.

Flexible Specialization

First, Piore and Sabel (1984) proposed the influential thesis that in the course of current structural changes regional or local economic structures will develop again and that these structures will resemble economic formations which had existed already at one time previously in the mid-nineteenth century. This is referred to as a 'regional production cluster', or a geographical concentration of functionally interdependent firms. 'Perhaps the most dramatic response to the continuing instability of international markets has been the formation or revitalization of regional economies that strongly resemble the nineteenth-century centres of flexible specialization' (Sabel 1989:9). Because of these arguments, the concept of industrial districts—in reference to early studies by Marshall (1919)—could once again achieve currency (Brusco 1989, 1990; Becattini 1990, 1991). The logic of diversification and specialization which underlies firms' responses to the diversification of markets leads to the formation and sharper definition of regional or local economies. This involves geographic clusters of firms or operational units with different areas of specialization, which work together in various combinations to deliver products to the same markets.

The best example of such 'new industrial districts' is the remarkably dynamic 'Third Italy', a case of embeddedness of the market within a local society. The uniqueness of these districts is rooted in a division of tasks in a single production process among specialized and functionally differentiated small and medium-sized enterprises whereby all are situated in geographical proximity to each other and together constitute something like a local community of production. Following the understanding of Brusco (1992:177), one can state:

that an industrial district is a set of companies located in a relatively small geographical area; that the said companies work, either directly or indirectly, for the same end market; that their shared range of values and body of knowledge is so important that they define a cultural environment; and that they are linked to one another by very specific relations in a complex mix of competition and co-operation.

As demonstrated by the Italians and by Piore and Sabel (1984), the success of Italian industrial districts characterized by 'flexible specialization' is owed principally to a social advantage of their location. The internal co-ordination of these local economies relies on a certain measure of trust and readiness to co-operate and a particular set of social relations (families, little hierarchy, social mobility). The thesis is that:

local agglomeration of the value-chain in an industry provides vital support for an industrial paradigm composed of loose confederations of specialist firms responding rapidly to changing market environments. Proximity is said to provide the social solidarity and trust, the face-to face contact, the pool of skills and know-how, the easy access to input and output markets that such a paradigm needs. (Sabel 1989)

This regional measure of trust and co-operation imparts itself to the relationship between companies' management and staff—relations within the companies—as well as the relationships between specialized and functionally differentiated companies as a whole. Trust and co-operation as indispensable foundations of specific organizational forms of industrial districts are founded on social rules, which preclude certain 'unfair' types of competition such as wage dumping or unacceptable working conditions.

Apart from the industrial districts of Third Italy, Charles Sabel and his colleagues have presented numerous further examples of regional flexible specialization economies in order to demonstrate that they are more than exotic exceptions from the rule. Furthermore, the ideal type perceptions of structure and inner functioning of flexibly specialized local economies have been adopted in many other research contexts (Sabel and Zeitlin 1989; Hirst and Zeitlin 1991; Pyke and Sengenberger 1992; Scott and Storper 1992a and b), with cases identified in Germany, the USA, Denmark, Sweden, Spain and even in France and the UK. In the meantime, a number of more or less differentiated analyses have been made which describe innovative growth regions and relate their success to changes in the global economy and the specific social organization of economic activities on a local level. The literature pointed to the role of local systems of small and medium-sized firms (or industrial districts) as a crucial resource for achieving economic development and offsetting the crisis of Fordist large firms.

Although Piore and Sabel (1984) placed strong emphasis on the role of small firms, even in that volume local economies were not strictly identified with them. In any case the ensuing literature made clear that the growing role of local economies could also be related to the restructuring of large firms and networked firms strongly connected to local systems of subcontractors. (See Sabel's (1989) idea of a 'double convergence' and his discussion of the re-emergence of regional economies.) The reason for this extension is that:

flexible specialization has been defined in two ways. It was introduced as the inverse of mass production: the manufacture of specialized goods by means of general-purpose resources rather than vice versa. Later it was defined as a system in which firms know that they do not know precisely what they will have to produce, and further that they must count on the collaboration of workers and subcontractors in meeting the market's eventual demand. (ibid.: 53)

The second definition includes the 'big firm model' embedded in a local economy of subcontractors, all working in the flexible specialization mode.

However, the important progress of the thesis can be seen in the findings on the institutional requirements for small and medium-sized enterprises that exist due to their dependence on particular resources. From this it can be concluded that the competitive advantage of small firms results not only from their flexible specialization, but also from their exogenous capacities. And if flexible specialization and vertical disintegration are connected, the relevance of the external environment even increases to the extent that vertical disintegration also increases:

The more specialized the firm became, the more it depended on the success of complementary products to sell its own, and hence, the pursuit of its particular interest required defence of those superordinate institutions—vocational schools and research institutes, marketing agencies—which safeguarded the industry as a whole. Here the industry is not a classification of independent entities, but rather a medium indispensable to the reproduction of symbiotic organism. (Sabel *et al.* 1989:388)

In this approach the idea of local collective competition goods is included.

Economic Geography and the California School of External Economies

Meanwhile, faced with the remarkable rise of the Californian economy, a group of scholars (e.g., Storper 1997; Scott 1999) developed a specific argument linking agglomeration to the reduction of transaction costs, that is, in close relation to neo-institutionalist economics (Williamson 1985). Their analysis rooted flexibility in the division of labour in production and linked that to agglomeration via an analysis of the transaction costs associated with inter-firm linkages. They accumulated research on the clothing industry, entertainment (Hollywood in particular), high tech, finance, and aeronautics; all cases where flexibility and complex disintegration in inter-firm linkages reinforced the attraction of the agglomeration. Allen Scott in particular, building on the work of economists such as Perroux and organization economists, has elaborated a theory of location that links various forms of integration, division of labour, innovations, and flexibility with the spatial dimension. He first concentrated on the externalities provided by an agglomeration, which is an outcome of the minimization of transaction costs. He has then gone further in bringing together different kinds of externalities and spatially dependent transaction costs in order to give an account of different types of location patterns, including agglomerations and districts. He therefore put forward a more historical economic geography perspective to take into account the dynamism of regional economics, path dependent process and historically constituted agglomerations.

For us, Scott's contribution is interesting, as his analysis of externalities is very similar to what we called collective competition goods, though the collective dimension we emphasize is not his concern. He does stress the territorial logic, that is, the extent to which those goods are available within the metropolis, and how these are central to the metropolization process and economic development. In contrast to us, however, he remains within the neo-classical paradigm (Williamson 1995). This literature emphasizes the various mechanisms for co-ordination to increase efficiency (their definition of governance). By focusing for instance on the time constraints in Just-in-Time organizations within major firms (for example in the motor industry), these authors have pointed to the territorial constraints and resources of firms. In different European countries, in the USA, and also increasingly in Asia, numerous studies have concentrated on the dynamics of inter-firm linkages and in particular on the increasingly complex relations between firms and subcontractors to structure modes of governance. And the external economies discussed in this literature are at least—in our view—(local) collective competition goods too.

Interestingly, the Californian group soon moved beyond the Williamson linkage-transaction costs model to analyse the agglomeration as such as a source of economic innovation:

... there was no assurance that markets alone, nor even various forms of contracts, could successfully co-ordinate the nexus of transactions in an industrial agglomeration. Such transactions—in labour markets, in inter-firm relations, in innovation and knowledge development—tended to have points of failure in the absence of appropriate institutions. In these two respects—evolution and institutions—we attempted to go beyond the initial Williamson framework to argue that the 'institutional arrangements' of agglomer-ations—that is, the nexus of transactions and their economic performance—were them-selves outcomes of broader institutional environments, and themselves generators of future choices for pathways of development. So we came 'full circle' to rejoin the initial authors of the flexible specialization thesis. (Storper 1997:11)

The more they worked with comparison, the more Scott and Storper were led to raise the question of institutional settings, and increasingly institutional struc-tures, for local economies and urban regions.

How Does Proximity Matter in Local Economies?

A dynamic and contested strand of research has emerged, including literature about innovative milieux, high-tech-school learning economies, associative economy, conventions, regulations, governance and untraded interdependencies (see for instance reviews in Krätke 1997; Storper 1997; and Amin 1999). Most of them address in a rather sophisticated way issues of local collective goods and governance. Various attempts have been made to try to define more specifically the dynamics between regions and firms and more importantly to try to explain the role played by territorial proximity (Amin and Thrift (1992) on institutional thickness; Cooke and Morgan (1998) on associative economy; and Storper (1997) on 'regional worlds' of production). They have worked within different per-spectives, from economic sociology, institutional economics, and evolutionary economics.[2]

[2] For present purposes let us just mention that evolutionary economics is well known for its analysis of path dependent processes (in particular in the field of technologies), trajectories (including

Both in the USA and in Europe, the resurgence of interest in local economies originated in issues of innovations and new technologies. Silicon Valley, route 128 near the Massachusetts Institute of Technology (MIT) and the subsequent science park fever fed a large amount of regional research. In Europe, the GREMI group in particular tried to conceptualize the role of innovative milieux, rooted in a territory as a socio-economic formation, that is, sets of networks which provide actors with forms of co-operation, resources, knowledge to engage in innovation. (See the contributions in Aydalot and Keeble (1988) and Camagni (1991) or the articles of Maillat and Perrin (1993) and Maillat, Quevit, and Senn (1993). For our purpose, an innovative milieu is characterized as an environment that produces collective competition goods (as outcomes), but there is not really an analysis of the conditions and the processes that allow this to take place or reasons for change.

That strand of work was particularly concerned with questions of innovation and the diffusion of innovations, hence the parallel with US research on regional socio-economic formations which have proved so economically successful, the 'high tech school' (Castells 1989; Saxenian 1994). There are elements of political construction here, including the role of defence programmes. Storper points to the fact that:

the new economics of technological change has suggested that there are knowledge or 'common practices' spillovers such that technological excellence comes in packages or ensembles. Since such excellence relies frequently on knowledge or practices that are not fully codifiable, the particular firms who master it are tied into various kinds of networks with other firms, through formal exchanges and untraded interdependencies. The latter include labor markets, public institutions and locally or nationally derived rules of action, customs, understanding or values. (Storper 1997:19)

For us, that literature points to the uncertainties, the potential impact of reflexive actors over time, and the dynamics of action frameworks, institution building and rules and norms setting. Economic development can therefore be analysed in terms of collective action. These authors stress, on the one hand, one particular type of local collective competition good which is rooted locally and not available on the market, and on the other hand, the importance of social and political processes for the use of such goods. They are useless if they are available but not used in dynamic and creative ways, hence the importance of networks, interactions within a cognitive frame,[3] and social and political processes.

Using in particular the so-called French 'school of conventions', Storper (together with Salais) moves away from the Williamson framework outlined

___

accidents, critical junctures). It underlines the interdependence of choice in the trajectories of technologies and the interactions between users and producers. See in particular Storper (1997: ch. 3).

[3] Storper and Salais's *Worlds of Production* (1998) and Storper's own synthesis in *The Regional World* is about those frameworks for economic actions and the territorial relational assets and untraded interdependencies. Both books constitute the most achieved and complete attempt to disentangle the logics of territorial development in a global environment.

before, and beyond the 'localist' explanation derived from the industrial district literature, to focus on regions as stocks of relational assets, at different levels. He suggests (1997:42–43):

The frameworks of action (ensembles of conventions) learned by actors constitute key forms of asset specificity in the economy, which are external to individual firms; and in turn, those persons caught up in such webs of conventions allow firms in situations of mutual interdependence to co-ordinate effectively with each other. This explanation of geographical concentration and territorial differentiation is now quite far from that which relies on linkages, input–output systems, and even economies of scale and scope in factor markets. While not excluding any of the latter, it suggests that the content of the linkages is shaped through convention and underlies the co-ordination of economic actors in production systems and gives rise to the level of economic efficiency they achieve and the specific qualities of products they are able to master. In sum [we] need refocusing...to the geography of untraded interdependencies and the dialectics of proximity and distance in them. This, in turn, is necessarily bound up with the geography of conventions and relations, which have cognitive, informational and psychological and cultural foundations.

This analysis in other words stresses the micro dynamics of the economy, the dynamics towards the institutionalization of meso 'worlds of production', and the ways in which co-ordination mechanisms are elaborated through interdependence and, in our language, modes of governance beyond the local level. Salais and Storper's (1993) analysis of the national conventions of economies and the limited impact of globalization is particularly useful for us to avoid the dangers of localism.

That analysis also underlines a key question for us: the governance of regional economies through a mix of different modes of governance and institutions (and/or conventions) at different levels and the logics of institution-building (Storper 1997). By contrast with their emphasis on conventions, we tend to focus on more classical analysis in terms of institutions (in the original sense of North 1990), social structures, public policies, exchanges. We do not give so much importance to psychological and cognitive aspects as the determinant factors, partly because these are quite difficult to apprehend within a comparative analysis.

By contrast with the micro-meso dynamics approaches, another kind of work has looked top down to the questions of local collective competition goods and governance. Building on the French *régulation* theory, those authors examine the role of local or regional partial regimes of regulation in providing conditions for economic development (Dunford and Kafkalas 1992; Benko and Lipietz 1999; Gilly and Pecqueur 1995; and Moulaert 1996). They try to articulate globalization processes, the dismantling of national regulation and the emergence of diverse regional regimes. It is in other words an attempt for some within the *régulation* school to go from the macro level to the meso level of analysis, and to take into account the diversity of local economies. In some cases this leads them to define the local dimension of the regulation, or

the constraints imposed by national regulation, hence a neo-Marxist function-
alist bias in our view, in particular within the British literature which has
followed this genre.

By contrast Krätke (1997) emphasizes three dimensions of local and regional
development: the structure of the production system; the regulation of the local
economy (closer to what we understand by governance) including institutions
and culture; and infrastructures and geographical location. His analysis and
typologies of local economies constitute a more successful attempt to take into
account both the structures of regulations and the diversity of local economies,
thus emphasizing the importance of institutional arrangements.

Three points are useful for us. First, these authors critically stress the diversity
of local and regional economies and the dynamics of inequalities. Crucially, they
underline the role of social conflicts and do not solely concentrate on economic
success analysed in isolation. This critical element remains quite fundamental
when too many authors analyse the 'good governance', the 'best practices' of
those economies. Second, in the classic *régulation* tradition, they stress the
importance of the institutional setting of regional economies. In the UK and
German case in particular, detailed analyses have been made of institutional
restructuring in relation to national political and economic restructuring. Third,
they are particularly concerned to articulate the different levels. Although one
may dispute the way they sometimes use the constraints associated with globalization (too much top down in our view), they never relinquish the importance
of the macro framework, an important methodological lesson for our work.
Exploring the tensions between the restructuring of large firms and European or
national public policies together with the dynamics of change of local economies
and their 'institutional fix' is crucial (Peck and Tickell 1994).

Another attempt to underline this reflexive collective action dimension of
local economies is encapsulated in the term 'learning economy'. Amin, in his
review of that literature, notes that:

...observers who note the difference between formal and informal knowledge for economic competitiveness (e.g. Becattini and Rullani 1993; Asheim 1997; Maskell *et al.* 1998)
suggest that geography plays a unique role in supplying informally constituted assets.
For instance, Maskell *et al.* (1998) argue that tacit forms of information and knowledge
are better consolidated through face to face contact, not only due to the transactional
advantages of proximity, but also because of their dependence upon a high degree of
mutual trust and understanding. This is often constructed around shared values and cultures...Those different scholars have distinguished between codified knowledge as a
feature of trans-local networks (e.g. business journals and courses, education and training
institutions, printed scientific knowledge (e.g. workplace skills and practical conventions) as aspects locked into the 'industrial atmosphere' of individual places. (Amin
1999:369)

That stimulating strand of research has made a whole series of complex claims
about the merits of proximity that often seemed to be rooted in particular

limited cases. This is another sophisticated approach towards what we named local collective competition goods, emphasizing innovation and the role of networks and values, pushing sometimes towards a more communitarian view of local economies. We try to be more systematic about the identity of the goods, and we do not try to identify such ideal cases but rather the overall dynamics of local economies in each country.

In a more critical vein, Veltz's (1996) major book *Mondialisation, villes et territoires* also constitutes an attempt to analyse local economies in relation to firms' strategies. Veltz is in sympathy with the work on flexible specialization and the re-emergence of regional economics (i.e., critical of under-socializing neo-classical economics). However Veltz, both in terms of macro economics and in terms of firms' strategies, underlines the risk of an 'over-socialized' view of the economy and the emphasis on local communities, the role of institutions, cognitive framework, set of conventions, but also public policies or social regulations (values, norms). He rather insists on the heterogeneity of the region and the multiplicity of flows. What is important in his mind is the capacity of the region to articulate that heterogeneity, to articulate external flows with the localities, to manage diverging and incoherent interactions (i.e. issues of local governance). This point is for us essential because it leads us away from the more communitarian account of regional governance, which tends to neglect, first conflicts and inequalities, and second the inherent heterogeneity of most localities in Europe. In other words, we are reluctant to concentrate too much on shared norms and values (or inherited social capital) and place more weight on conflicts, organized actions, strategies, public policies, that is, the world of politics and policies in governance within the very diverse world of local economies in Europe.

Veltz's analysis derives from the mounting pressure for competition, uncertainties, changing forms of competitiveness (Porter 1998), and productivity. *Inter alia*, he argues that productivity is more and more about the dynamic and creative combination of relations and resources. The growing complexity of organization relations within firms or systems of production gives a crucial role to interfaces and relations, that is, *la productivité des interfaces*, or productivity by co-ordination and organization. In territorial terms, Veltz points to the complex interpenetration between production, exchange, transaction spaces and the interdependence between processes. In this way, he also leans towards a sophisticated analysis of externalities related to some proximities, keeping in mind that there are various forms of social proximities which are far from always being structured and organized within a given territory. These are therefore in his view the most important local collective competition goods, which are crucially found within cities. Faced with uncertainties, feeling the pressure of constant changes and reluctant to stabilize long-term investment in local societies, firms however need more and more resources of this kind, which are produced slowly through rooted institutions. The more risks the firms perceive, the more diverse and secure the environment they need. Veltz develops the idea of cities as 'insurance flexibility' to explain the logic of risk reduction for firms (innovation diffusion, labour market, alliances and linkages with different partners—in our language, availability of local collective competition goods). Increased flexibility and risks for firms are therefore the dynamics that support metropolization logics. By focusing on firms' strategies (including large firms), Veltz has provided us with some key insights. What are now missing though are first a more complete operationalization of those *interfaces de proximité*, and second some analysis of the ways in which these are produced and used. He suggests as a hypothesis that 'urban governance' may become the most crucial variable for the development of local economies (Veltz 2000b).

Our research project is an attempt to go beyond, to operationalize theory on those interactions and to take into account at the same time both firms' strategies and their embeddedness in all kinds of local environment and network, and the governance of local economies. This raises key questions about institutions. Those are explored in detail in the Conclusions.

Challenges and Changes: Governance of Local Economies in a Dynamic Perspective

While industrial economists and geographers called attention to certain kinds of local collective competition goods—such as tacit knowledge, specialized know-how, training, services—economic sociologists, political scientists and experts in industrial relations called more attention to trust and local identities, and to industrial relations and local governments. One can say that the theme of local governance emerged as a crucial factor for explaining the ability to produce local collective competition goods. Actually, research showed the importance of co-operation between private and public local actors for the production of local collective competition goods, and therefore of governance as distinguished from government. But according to the premises which underlie our understanding of the governance of local economies, several implications follow and deadlocks should be avoided.

The first premise is rather obvious: globalization processes are not leading towards the end of differences, to a space of flows, a global economic order dismantling everything, in particular in Europe. These processes are multiple, conflicting, contested, limited and do not create a social and political *tabula rasa*. As economic sociologists or political economists, we take for granted the fact that there is not one best market way for economic development and we believe neither in the complete domination of market mechanisms nor in their inherent efficiency in capitalist societies. There is more than market domination, although we do recognize the need to analyse the rise of global capitalism and its implication in terms of domination or inequalities.

There are two rival starting hypotheses. One is that globalization may reinforce the role of new local economies—or indeed of old ones—as far as these local settings are able rapidly to adjust through the production of effective local collective competition goods. Local economies can still work as a success strategy to improve economic development in advanced countries. The second is that globalization may weaken certain local economies, especially those based on old industries. In order to demonstrate the difference in relevance and patterns of reaction, the country studies discuss two—strongly simplified—patterns of diagnosis to be found in the literature on the development of local economies. These patterns will help to explain why there are specific problems in adjustment or even crises in some local economies.

According to the first pattern, globalization causes the erosion of those specific elements of regional governance which have been identified as pillars of regional success by the analyses of the flexible specialization school. In this case, the previous inner functioning of the regional economy cannot be sustained in the 'cold wind' of globalization. There has for years been a controversial debate concerning the future potential of the Italian industrial districts: whether the social factors for their success, especially the often-described readiness to co-operate on the basis of communal relations, will be undermined by the process of globalization (for example, Harrison 1994a). It is argued that increasing external networking and internationalization will destroy community markets.

The second pattern maintains that, while specific regional or national forms of governance of local economies initially remain stable in the era of globalization, they will increasingly prove to be dysfunctional in meeting new challenges.

Our second premise is that local economies matter as such, but most importantly in relation to the erosion of national models of economic governance or regulation. Localities and regions are becoming more important in Europe as units of organization of social, political and economic life. If nation-states and national regulations carry less weight, it is not surprising to see in the European context the re-emergence of infra-national territories. The loosening of state constraints both opens opportunities and creates new constraints for cities and regions (Anderson 1992; Keating and Loughlin 1996; Bagnasco and Le Galès 2000a). In the economic sociology field, evidence of interesting regional and local economic development is not explained by classical economic theory. Perception of this has opened the way to a new research agenda on local economies.

Critics have rightly drawn attention to the political implication of 'vulgar new regionalism' (Lovering 1999), and have also pointed out the risks and the deadlocks of local research which would fail to take into account the basics of macro economics, continuing state power or globalized forms of capital. We recognize the force of these criticisms and the dangers of overgeneralization from a few cases. We do not pretend that regions are the only or the main unit of analysis for capitalism, and we acknowledge the implications of state restructuring. We are also fully aware of the fact that the multiplication of networks and some processes of globalization provide remarkable avenues for some actors, firms or social groups to avoid the constraints associated with a particular territory. That sometimes leads—and there are many examples in western Europe—to the complete fragmentation and disintegration of localities. There is no one way street towards the rise of a Europe of regions or whatever else.

We therefore hope to avoid the trap of 'vulgar new localism'. Nevertheless, most social research nowadays attempts to bridge gaps between micro, meso and macro level of explanations. We do think that territories play an important role in the restructuring of economy and society in Europe, but that is not the sole level of analysis. It should not be considered in isolation, and by no means all authors in the field are vulnerable to the criticisms, far from it. Comparative work on local economies has in particular led to the conclusion that their emergence and shape was often strongly related to the political economy of a particular country, not just the local governance of those economies. We must therefore consider their relations towards national models of capitalism, globalization processes, structure of firms, sectors, structure of organized interests, not to mention the state and public policies (Ganne 1990; Bagnasco and Sabel 1995; Storper and Salais 1998).

Our third premise is that these changing scales are not just the results of chance. Sociologists, economists, political scientists and geographers alike now emphasize the less central role of the nation-state as the locus of conflicts, as a site to accumulate power and wealth, to aggregate interests, to steer societies, to impose culture or policies, or to regulate the economy. We have now sufficient evidence of firms' strategies, organization of interest, production of innovation, investment flows, policy regulations, public policies, all operating at the local, regional, national, European, transnational and global levels (often at the same time) to suggest that variety of scale and articulation among levels is essential to contemporary economies (Brenner 1998). Hollingsworth and Boyer's (1997) phrase 'from national embeddedness to spatial and institutional nestedness' of the economy captures nicely that imbrication of different levels and the double shift (up and down) of governance modes. Changing scales of economic, political and social regulation leave some room of manoeuvre at the infra-national level, but we do not know exactly what. We do know that variation occurs among regions, among countries, among economic sectors. Analysing local economies in isolation does not make much sense. Beyond cases of pure local governance (the neo-regionalist regulation of Bagnasco (1977) and Trigilia (1986a)), there is large room for manoeuvre to explore the role of regions and localities in articulation with different levels, and the difficult construction of modes of governance and partial regulation (Trigilia 1990; Benko and Lipietz 1992; Gilly and Pecqueur 1995; Le Galès 1998).

Neo-Marxist writers have rightly suggested the importance of the 'spatial fix' in the accumulation process (Harvey 1985). There are different contributions usually written from a British perspective, which have suggested analysis of regionalization as the result of the crisis of Fordism and the search for a new 'institutional fix' (e.g., Peck and Tickell 1995). Regional and local modes of governance can be analysed in relation to what Jessop named the hollowing out of the national Keynesian welfare state. The so-called neo-Gramscian regulation school has emphasized the dynamics of new local and regional modes of governance in relation with globalization processes and the restructuring of the state. Although we would disagree with the functional and deterministic elements of their approach (however sophisticated it might be and however relevant for the UK and USA situation it appears), they point to the fact that these changing scales are contested, that some groups tend to develop hegemonic projects, and that there is nothing inherently good in decentralization or reforms of regional modes of governance.

These changing scales point to what one might call the 'paradoxes of territories'. Harvey (1985, 1989) was among the first to have signalled this. Economic globalization means increased mobility of capital and the ability for capitalists, to a certain extent, to overcome spatial constraints. Hence the domination of local economies by large firms. Paradoxically, this goes hand in hand with an increased sensitivity to territory, especially in the form of cities as possible sites for investment and living. Attention has been drawn to the same types of paradox in different ways in a different political economy tradition, and also in political scientists' analyses of local and regional governments in Europe: there is at the same time decreasing capacity to structure and regulate flux within territories, but an increasing salience of some regions and localities as sites for structuring relations and groups interactions, aggregating and representing interests. The same applies to the governance of local economies. In contrast to what 'vulgar globalization theory' suggests, regions, cities and localities are not just passive spaces where some localization takes place; they are more than just machines. In accordance with our economic sociology and political economy perspective, we want to suggest that regions (some of them) are structures of differentiated relations which tend to orientate the behaviours of different groups of actors (Storper 1997: ch. 6; Le Galès 1998).

According to our fourth premise, one of the advantages of the governance approach is its potential to cover development dynamics in the assignment of economic transactions over time. We make the general assumption that collective needs can be satisfied through different institutional variants attributable to the available analytical models of social order, thus allowing for a differentiation of solution patterns in community, market, organizational and hierarchical, state, and association forms. It remains an empirical question which specific shifts can be observed in the institutional order system. Thus, in a local economy, the production of a specific collective competition good (e.g., qualification or the transfer of knowledge and technology) may have been the responsibility of a community of some kind (families, clans, enterprises of a local economy).

But in the process of modernization, communities can erode or structural changes may bring up new challenges, which exceed the potential of existing community solutions. Such developments may then provoke some kind of substitute solution: for example, intervention and regulation by the political and administrative system. In this case, the matter shifts from the community model to that of state provision. However, for whatever reasons (e.g., information deficits, legitimation weaknesses, funding problems) these public solutions can also prove to be deficient. It is conceivable that the problem is subsequently 'shifted' into the market sector, due to the introduction of institutional reforms, which are then labelled 'privatization' or 'deregulation'. But markets can fail, too—especially as far as collective goods are concerned. A solution for both state and market failure could, for example, subsequently be offered by an associational solution through 'private government'. Naturally, neo-corporatist arrangements can also be subject to erosion, which would then undermine the capacity of this model of social order. It is also possible that those socio-political government institutions which were still operating as pillars of social order and compensation in the 1970s and 1980s become restricted in their potential to act as 'private governments' because of exogenous changes (the process of globalization). (See, for example, the contributions in Schmitter and Lehmbruch (1979), Lehmbruch and Schmitter (1982), Streeck and Schmitter (1985), and Streeck (1994).)

This finding echoes the work on the diversity of capitalism (Crouch and Streeck, 1997). Our contribution clearly relates to what Swedberg calls 'the new political economy'. This refers to political economists and economic sociologists who have concentrated on the analysis of diverse forms of national capitalism and the institutional embeddedness of the economy by stressing, not only the role of communities in the social construction of the economy (à la Polanyi or Bagnasco), but also that of institutions, systems of firms, social conflicts, organized interests, the state, political regulation and associations (Hollingsworth and Boyer 1997). An example is the analysis of corporatism and the political economy of capitalism, which has run in parallel with the French school of *régulation*, or the literature on institutionalized 'business systems' (Whitley and Kristensen 1996), and 'worlds of production' (Salais and Storper 1993). In that tradition, there is no such thing as one best model of capitalism, with exceptions bound to adapt or disappear. In European terms, globalization processes and the increase of trade may not lead to the making of a European economy aligned to the US model. By contrast, it may well be the case that distinct patterns of European capitalism, more territorialized and institutionalized, will take new forms, hence the importance of local economies.

The starting-point of such an analysis is the idea that, over recent years, the various local economies have been facing a changed competitive situation as globalization processes have affected them too. But, presumably, the impact varies, because institutional contexts were different at the outset (particularly because of the national economies in which they are integrated). There is not just one capitalism but several (national) versions of it which differ in the respective institutional setting of their economies (and thus their local economies) (Albert 1991; Crouch and Streeck 1997). This implies that the consequences of globalization and the relevant patterns of reaction are different as well. Therefore the application of the governance approach also demonstrates why different local economies react differently to the same economic challenge. Within the local economies, the challenges 'from the outside' will be perceived as specific internal problems or weaknesses because of the differences in the previous institutional context.

Further, there is no such thing as one model of local economy upon which one may base a grand theory. Diverse institutional settings and social embeddedness are particularly important. The methodological and theoretical limits and weaknesses of existing analyses of local economies are unmistakable (Sayer 1989a, 1989b; Amin and Robins 1990a, 1990b; Amin 1993; Staber 1996a). This is so despite the convincing case studies and examples explicitly and implicitly referring to the model of flexibly specialized industrial districts, innovative milieux or high-tech regions, not to mention old industrial areas revitalized through new networks of production clusters. The main weakness concerns the generalizing conclusions of this practice of research. These are usually based on qualitative case studies that tend to follow the mainstream of 'shining examples' and infer the general from the particular. In the face of manifold and often contradictory singular findings, overly simplifying and generalizing concepts are increasingly subject to criticism. With the increasing quantity of literature on different local economies in different countries, however, it became increasingly doubtful whether all the cases cited could be considered constituent parts of one and the same category. This scepticism mostly concerns the practice of throwing all the various success stories of regional development into one pot.

The Structure of This Volume

Therefore the country studies presented in this book re-examine the available literature on local economies' success stories in order to test the thesis that there was diversity in the structure of those regions, the success of which attracted so much attention in the 1970s and 1980s. The fact that some local economies which in the past were treated as cases of success have since had to deal with serious structural problems, while others are still performing relatively well, leads to the conclusion that the differences between them need to be examined more carefully than in the past. Specific characteristics of the respective countries and their national economies have never been denied; it was mainly the central common aspects of local economies in different countries that took centre stage in the discussion.

First, Chapter 2 offers an overview of regional development in Europe in recent decades, progressing through analyses at national, regional and local level, revealing ever-greater diversity of experience. Then follow the four countries. We begin with Italy, the heartland of the European debate over local economies, followed by Germany, the other main European country where local production systems have been observed. The remaining cases are of countries (France and the UK) normally regarded in the literature as lacking economic dynamism based on clusters of small and medium-sized firms. These studies follow a general broad pattern. They raise the question of whether and to what extent there are empirical indications for a renaissance of local economies within the country concerned; they explore significant features of the governance of the local economies they identify; and consider whether the last two decades have seen changes in the development of patterns of governance. The final chapter offers a comparative framework on current trends in local economies, and explores some wider implications for existing theories of economic development. In particular it confronts evolutionary models which would regard areas of geographical specialization as a stage due to be transcended by more universal forms of organization.

2

Local Production Systems and Economic Performance in France, Germany, Italy, and the United Kingdom

ANDRÉS RODRÍGUEZ-POSE

Recent decades have brought about a growing interest in the economic performance of regions and localities and, as a consequence, in the forms of sub-national governance which are associated with different levels of economic dynamism. The reasons behind this growing focus on meso- and micro-levels of economic performance and governance and on local production systems are manifold and come from different fields. First and foremost are the changes that certain researchers have identified in the evolution of the capitalist system. Aglietta (1977), Boyer (1986, 1989), and Scott and Storper (1986), to name but a few, have highlighted the profound transformation undergone by the traditional system of accumulation, based on mass-production and Taylorist principles, which is giving way to a post-industrial system in which flexibility seems to be the key word. Parallel to these structural changes, the dominant economic system of the post-war decades has been challenged from another angle. Advances in technology, information technology and deregulation have made movements of capital, information, goods, and services much easier than hitherto (Castells 1989 and 1996) and much more difficult to harness with traditional forms of governance. Economic globalization and the rise of the information society are creating a space of flows (Castells 1989) which is altering the traditional conception of space.

This combination of socio-economic restructuring and economic globalization is posing serious challenges—and also offering new opportunities—for the development of nations, regions, and localities. Advances in technology, free flows of capital and goods, and the almost universal access to codified knowledge, together with the need to respond rapidly to global competition, have put territories all over the world under considerable strain, facing the alternatives of adapting to the new environment or suffering economic decline.

Large metropolitan areas, because of their ability to attract and generate pools of capital, technology, and information, have been expected to perform better (Sassen 1991; Hall 1993). But beyond these, the economic dynamism of a series of regions whose basic common denominator is the presence of dense networks of small and medium-sized enterprises (SMEs) caught the eye of researchers, as has been summarized by Le Galès and Voelzkow in the Introduction. They also point out how, as these economies began to encounter difficulties in the second half of the 1980s, the enthusiasm of observers also waned. Then the perceived failure of attempts to develop imitative local production systems almost *ex nihilo* in places like Wales was the last straw for those who claim that the story behind learning regions 'is largely a fiction' (Lovering 1999:380).

These swings of the pendulum are however often based on short-term economic change. It needs only a couple of years of weak economic growth in certain key local systems for critics to dismiss them as an interlude, just as the earlier belief in them often relied on a decade of excellent economic performance in Emilia-Romagna during the late 1970s and early 1980s. Attempts properly to assess the economic dynamism of these areas are few and far between, and often only deal with one region or local economic system (Semlinger 1993; Dei Ottati 1996). The question that Trigilia asked himself at the beginning of the 1990s is thus still very much alive: are local production systems a myth based on real economic dynamism, or did they simply represent an interlude while large industries adapted to the conditions of a globalized economy (Trigilia 1992a)? This is the question that we address in this chapter, by analysing the economic performance of local production systems in Britain, France, Germany and Italy between 1977 and 1994. We do so in order to try to establish to what extent these changes may be related to the existence of local and regional production systems and, consequently, to the emergence of new regional and local forms of governance. We will first study the economic evolution of nations, regions, and local production systems since the late 1970s, before outlining the structural reasons behind differences in economic performance. The last section of the chapter will sketch the possible explanations of economic dynamism at the regional and local level, and whether they are related to the appearance of localized forms of economic governance. These explanations are developed in depth in the national chapters later in the volume.

The Russian Doll of Multiple Governance Levels and Economic Performance

Although different strands of research dealing with the processes of globalization and socio-economic restructuring have focused on different factors, there is one tenet which most seem to embrace: recent changes are challenging the capacity of the nation-state to shape economic trends and are leading to the emergence of regions and localities as more adequate units of economic analysis. In contrast to what was the norm in the 1960s and 1970s, most recent studies of economically successful areas focus on these rather than on nations. In addition to the Italian research, great attention has been paid to innovative high-tech (Cooke 1992; Malecki 1994; Saxenian 1994; Audretsch and Feldman 1996) and low-tech (Kristensen 1992; Maskell 1998) regions in Europe and the United States. Even authors who have stuck to the national framework as the basic unit of economic analysis have had to acknowledge that concentrations of economically dynamic industries and services increasingly tend to occur at the sub-national rather than at the national level (Porter 1998). Moreover, the economic dynamism of regions and localities is also increasingly considered to be at the root of the emergence of a new form of European regionalism (Keating 1998); a regionalism which is no longer exclusively rooted in questions of language, culture, history, or identity, but which is increasingly linked to the clustering of economic activity at sub-national levels.

However, the claim that the nation-state is losing relevance through a combination of globalization and regionalization is not uncontested. Borrás-Alomar *et al.* (1994), Quah (1996), Rodríguez-Pose (1998), and López-Bazo *et al.* (1999) have highlighted that regional growth patterns are still strongly embedded in national economic trajectories. These authors have stressed that the economic performance of the Third Italy is to a large extent determined by the overall economic performance of Italy. Likewise economic growth in Baden-Württemberg fluctuates within the range of other German regions.

In sum, recent changes have led to the creation of an economic, social and institutional panorama distinguished by greater complexity. Different territorial levels of economic and institutional governance are like a Russian *matriushka*, with local levels of governance embedded in regional, and these, in turn, in national and supranational levels. All are interdependent and interrelated. The economic dynamism of Italy, for example, is linked to the dynamism of the regions of the Third Italy, and the dynamism of these regions is, in turn, explained by how industrial districts have performed in the areas of Arezzo, Faenza, Forlì, Modena, Parma, or Prato and vice versa. Hence, in order to understand the economic performance of local production systems, we need to study the recent evolution of growth patterns at all levels. The main aim here is to try to identify whether, as has often been claimed, there has been a significant change in growth trends over the last two decades; and whether, as a result of the emergence of autonomous local production systems, local growth trends are becoming less constrained by national and regional growth patterns.

National Growth Patterns in the Post-industrial Era

The 1950s and 1960s were a period of strong catch-up across the whole of Europe. Countries with the lowest levels of GDP achieved the highest rates of growth. Convergence rates were in general close to the levels of 2 per cent a year predicted by the neo-classical theory of growth (Barro 1991; Barro and Sala-I-Martín 1991). France, Germany, Italy and the UK were not exceptions. During the 1950s and early 1960s the highest rate was achieved in Germany, a country which was quickly recovering in the aftermath of the Second World War. Growth rates of 7 per cent during the 'German miracle' were almost matched by those of

TABLE 2.1. National Real Growth Rates in France, Germany, Italy, and the UK, 1950–99

	France	Germany	Italy	UK	OECD
1950–65	4.96	7.02	6.00	2.85	4.74
1965–75	4.33	3.13	4.24	2.27	4.02
1975–85	2.34	2.20	3.07	1.92	2.99
1985–94	2.03	2.73	2.09	2.13	2.46
1995–99*	2.21	1.45	1.18	2.48	2.74

Source: Own elaboration using Maddison (1995) and *OECD National accounts data.

Italy, where growth averaged 6 per cent (Table 2.1).[1] In contrast, the two richest countries at the time, France and, above all, the UK experienced lower growth. The late 1960s and early 1970s followed a similar trend. The highest growth was achieved in the countries that had the lowest GDP per capita, France and Italy, whereas Germany, which had already become the richest country in the group, had lower growth. Britain was again the poorest performer, with growth rates that were almost half those of France (Table 2.1).

As a result of these trends, the economic gap between the United Kingdom, on the one hand, and Germany, France and Italy, on the other, quickly dwindled between 1950 and 1975. Germany, whose economy was approximately two-thirds the size of the British economy in 1950, caught up and overtook the UK as the biggest economy in Europe by 1958. The French economy, which was roughly the same size as the German economy in 1950, did it by 1971. And Italy—which had an economy half the size of that of the UK in 1950—caught up with Britain in 1980 (Figure 2.1).

The general trend towards convergence and a reduction of national disparities of the post-war decades came however to a halt after 1975. Italy, which continued its catch-up until the late 1970s, has not been able to reduce the gap with Germany and France since. Britain, despite becoming the poorest nation in the group in 1980, has also not managed to converge to the levels of GDP of Germany and France. It has kept up with Italy, but both countries have been outpaced by Germany (Table 2.1 and Figure 2.1). France has also not performed particularly well, especially since 1985. The greatest levels of growth since 1975 have been achieved in Germany, the richest country in the group, marking a break with the convergence of previous decades.

The outcome of this change in patterns is that between 1975 and 1994 national economic disparities have remained more or less stable. Overall only relatively minor changes can be reported. Germany and Italy have increased their share of

---

[1] National data used in this chapter—with the exception of the period 1995/99—stem from the Maddison database (1995). Data represent GDP measured in 1990 US dollars. The source of the data for the period 1995–9 are the OECD National Accounts. GDP data for this period is measured at 1995 prices and 1995 exchange rates.

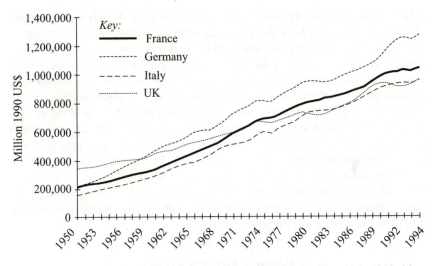

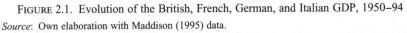

FIGURE 2.1. Evolution of the British, French, German, and Italian GDP, 1950–94
Source: Own elaboration with Maddison (1995) data.

the EU's GDP by 5 and 4.4 per cent, whereas the share of the UK and France has decreased by 3.2 and 2.2 per cent respectively. The last few years of the twentieth century have however witnessed a light reversal of the trend. Between 1995 and 1999 the two worst performers of the previous period regained greater dynamism. The UK and France, with growth rates of 2.48 and 2.21 per cent per annum respectively, have outpaced Germany (1.45 per cent) and Italy (1.18 per cent).

Many authors trace the shift in growth patterns in Europe to the oil shocks of the 1970s. It has been claimed that the change in long-term growth rates may have been related to the capacity of individual countries to cope with the sudden rises in oil prices. However, such an explanation—popular in the 1980s (Jackman 1987)—does not stand in light of the fact that the only country with substantial oil reserves in the group, the UK, was also until very recently the worst performer. A more plausible explanation might be linked to the twin challenges of socio-economic restructuring and globalization, and to the greater capacity of economic structures in Germany and Italy to adapt to them. There are several indications that point in that direction. First of all, most of the cases of clusters of dynamic industries that constitute the bulk of the literature on flexible production have been identified in Italy and in Germany. There are fewer examples of similar local production systems in Britain and France, and, especially in the case of France, many of these have to do with direct government planning (Sophia-Antipolis, Toulouse), rather than with the autonomous development of regional and local networks of firms.

A second possible explanation is the more balanced urban systems of Germany and Italy, which have allowed for greater territorial competition among cities

(Cheshire and Gordon 1996 and 1998). Last but not least, the territorial structure of those countries may have also played an important role in the development of new forms of economic governance, which may have encouraged higher economic performance. Germany has been a federal state since the end of the Second World War, and regions in Italy achieved autonomy in 1970. This has allowed regional governments to foster in some cases, and to collaborate in others, in the setting up of regional institutions and policies which are at the base of the success of some of the local systems of governance. In contrast, Britain remained a centralized state until 1999, and although regions in France have enjoyed some level of regional autonomy since the early 1980s, the powers granted to regional governments cannot be compared to those in Germany and Italy. In these relatively centralized national contexts, the possibilities of developing and supporting alternative forms of economic governance at the regional and local level have thus been more limited (Rodríguez-Pose 1998).

Regional Growth Trends

The similarities between long-term growth trajectories at the national and at the regional level are numerous. As in the case of national economies, the decades before 1975 had seen a strong process of regional convergence. Most studies of European regional growth which cover these periods report rates of convergence varying between 3.6 per cent[2] and 0.9 per cent,[3] with overall rates close to the neo-classical average of 2 per cent a year (Barro and Sala-I-Martín 1991; Armstrong 1995; Sala-I-Martín 1996). However, since 1975 convergence at the regional level has almost come to a stand still (Molle and Boeckhout 1995; Champion, Mønnesland and Vandermotten 1996; López-Bazo *et al.* 1999). Most research on the topic reports rates of convergence of only 1 per cent (Armstrong 1995) or lower (Cheshire and Carbonaro 1995; Rodríguez-Pose 1999a). It could be claimed that during this period the convergence observed until 1975 has been substituted by simultaneous processes of convergence and divergence which are in reality hiding the capacity of different types of region to cope with the new challenges related to socio-economic restructuring, globalization and increasing competition (Rodríguez-Pose 1999a). However, similar overall trends in long-term growth rates at the national and regional levels do not hide a much greater variation in regional patterns since 1977. If we take the change in the level of participation of individual regions in their respective national GDP as an indicator of regional dynamism, regional changes exceed those observed at the national level. Figure 2.2 maps these changes.[4]

---

[2] Barro and Sala-I-Martín (1991) for seventy-three European regions between 1960 and 1970.

[3] Armstrong (1995) for seventy-five European regions in the period between 1950 and 1960.

[4] Regional data used in this chapter stem from the Eurostat Regio database. Data refer to changes in the regional share of national GDP between 1977 and 1994, for France, Italy and the UK, and between 1978 and 1994 for Germany. Data are only available for the period between 1979 and 1994

As can be seen, the regional panorama emerging from the last twenty years is more complicated and variegated than the one suggested by national growth patterns. The greatest relative growth was achieved in the former East German regions, which, with the exception of Mecklenburg-Vorpommern, have experienced an increase of more than 50 per cent in their share of the German GDP in a period of only four years. East Germany represents an exceptional case, in which high growth is determined both by a very low starting-point in terms of GDP, as well as by a massive level of state intervention since reunification.

Even if East Germany is not taken into account, the variation in regional growth is still much greater than national. If we take levels of change of ±3 per cent in the regional share of the national GDP between 1977 and 1994 as the threshold dividing rising and declining regions, and of ±10 per cent in order to identify highly dynamic and strongly declining regions, significant regional contrasts come to light. Strongly dynamic regions are scattered evenly across the four countries, with a north–south axis between Germany and Italy which extends from Hesse in the north, across Bavaria, along Trentino-Alto Adige and Veneto, and ends up in Molise (Figure 2.2). Outside this axis, signs of dynamism are evident in southern England and southern France. East Anglia is the most dynamic region in the four countries considered in the analysis—outside the former Eastern German *Länder*—with an increase of its share in national GDP of almost 23 per cent. South-West England follows closely. Midi-Pyrénées and the Languedoc have also significantly improved their position within the French context.

Moderate dynamism is observed in other regions in southern Italy (Campania, Sardinia, and Sicily) and especially along the Adriatic coast (Marche and Puglia); southern England (East Midlands and the South-East) and Northern Ireland; and in the Île-de-France and Pays de la Loire (France).

The other side of the coin basically comprises old industrial regions. Northern England (the North and North-West), north-eastern France (Champagne-Ardenne, Franche-Comté, Lorraine, Nord-Pas de Calais, Picardie), north-western Italy (Liguria and Piedmont) and North Rhine-Westphalia suffered relative declines of more than 10 per cent (Figure 2.2). Moderate decline is evident in other manufacturing regions (Yorkshire and Humberside, West Midlands, Wales, Upper Normandy, Saarland, Lombardy), and in traditionally lagging agricultural regions (Rhineland-Palatinate, Schleswig-Holstein, Auvergne, Burgundy, Corsica, Limousin, and Basilicata).

for Berlin; 1982 and 1994 for Corsica; and only between 1991 and 1994 for the former East German *Länder*.

 The reasons behind the use of nationally weighted instead of raw data relate to the distortions created by the national dimension and geographical proximity when comparing regional growth cross-nationally (Button and Pentecost 1995; Quah 1996; Rodríguez-Pose 1999a). These distortions—in the form of spatial autocorrelation—are linked to the strong connection between national and regional economic trajectories. Despite the fact that many researchers have emphasized that the processes of globalization and socio-economic restructuring are putting the role of the nation-state in jeopardy, from an economic point of view regional growth is still strongly determined by the national context, and by geographical proximity (Quah 1996).

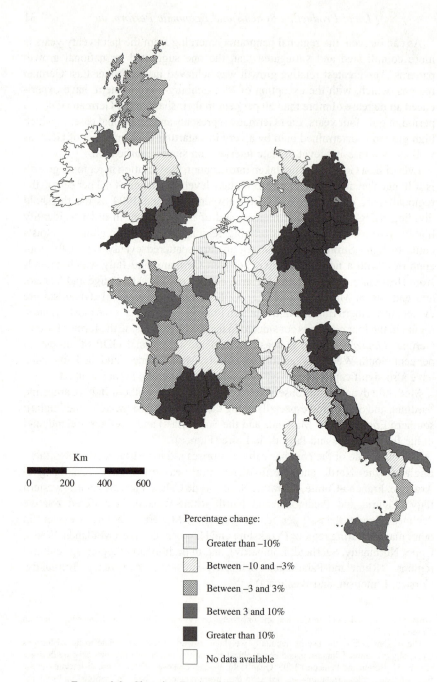

Km

| 0 | 200 | 400 | 600 |

Percentage change:

Greater than −10%

Between −10 and −3%

Between −3 and 3%

Between 3 and 10%

Greater than 10%

No data available

Figure 2.2. Changing Regional Shares in National GDP, 1977–94

The picture emerging in three of the four countries is one of greater polarization. This is clearly the case in the UK, where the gap between a relatively poor North and a rich South has widened over the last two decades. In Germany, the North and the Rhine valley have continued their decline, while most economic dynamism has been concentrated in the Centre and South, mainly in Hesse and Bavaria. In France, the most dynamic poles emerge around Paris and in the south. Italy seems to be the only exception. The rich North-West and Lombardy have been caught up by regions in the North-East, and many regions in the Mezzogiorno have performed rather well in comparative terms (Figure 2.2).

From a European perspective, the rising zones tend to be found, with few exceptions, outside the traditional European core. The much heralded Blue Banana is among the worst performing areas. (The European Commission often used the expression 'Blue Banana' during the late 1980s and early 1990s to describe a banana-shaped area expanding from the English midlands along the Rhine Valley to central Italy, where traditionally a large percentage of European industry was concentrated.) The strongest decline is located along a line that extends from the North of England to Corsica, covering north-eastern France, the Rhine valley and north-western Italy. This axis is only broken by the South of England, which represents an oasis of dynamism stuck in the declining European spine. Symptoms of economic dynamism are evident to the east, west, and south of this imaginary line.

The regions which witnessed the strongest economic rise since 1977 (those whose share in the European GDP has risen by more than 10 per cent) tend to be either regions dominated by a large urban agglomeration or regions with a high concentration of industrial districts and other analogous forms of local production systems. Lazio and Hesse belong to the former group; Bavaria, Trentino-Alto Adige, Veneto, and, to a lesser extent, Abruzzo and Molise to the latter. East Anglia and South-West England are a combination of both, since the presence of local industrial clusters of SMEs is complemented by dynamism linked to the economic expansion of London beyond the administrative boundaries of the South-East region. The French regions of Midi-Pyrénées and Languedoc-Roussillon owe their economic élan to the location of high-tech industries. As a group, these regions tend to grow 0.8 points above the average of the regions included in the analysis. The greatest differences in growth rates were achieved in the late 1970s and early 1980s. The growth gap has declined steadily since the mid-1980s and the average growth in the beginning of the 1990s is only 0.3 percentage points above the mean (Figure 2.3).

The remaining rising regions (those which have seen their relative position improve by between 3 and 10 per cent) form a more heterogeneous group. The large urban agglomerations of London, Paris and Berlin share similar levels of dynamism with the intermediate regions of the East Midlands and Northern Ireland, Pays de la Loire, and Marche, Campania, Puglia, Sardinia and Sicily. Growth rates in these regions have remained constant at levels of 0.3 percentage

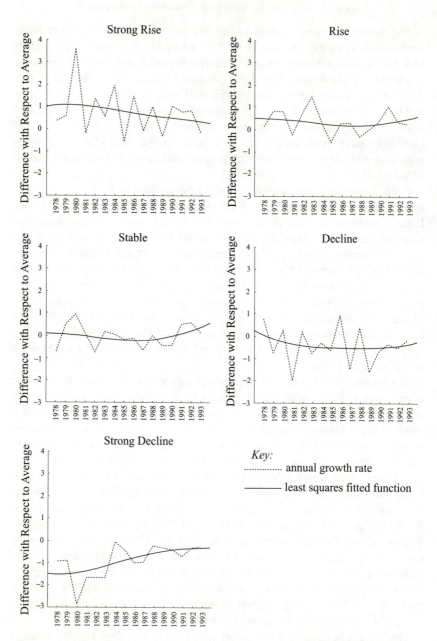

FIGURE 2.3. Growth Trajectories of Rising, Stable and Declining Regions during the Period of Analysis

points above the average rate of growth, with no significant changes throughout the period of analysis. As the least squares fitted function in Figure 2.3 indicates, the only serious dent in their growth performance was during the period of economic expansion of the second half of the 1980s.

Most regions in the stable category (those whose level of change is limited to ±3 per cent around the four country average) tend to be intermediate regions, that is regions which started from intermediate levels of GDP, did not belong to the industrial core, and had no clearly dominant sector. Calabria is probably the only exception to the rule. Emilia-Romagna, Baden-Württemberg, Friuli-Venezia-Giulia, and Rhône-Alpes are also host to considerable concentrations of industrial districts and similar forms of local productive systems. Yet, in contrast with some other regions with comparable economic structures (Veneto or Bavaria), their growth performance remains close to the mean throughout the period of analysis. Relatively low levels in the mid- and late-1980s coincide with what Trigilia (1992a), Semlinger (1993), and Dei Ottati (1996) have identified as a thorough restructuring of some of the industrial districts in these areas (Figure 2.3). Their recovery during the early 1990s may be linked to the end of the restructuring process and/or to the greater capacity of local production systems to respond to changes in the economic environment during periods of economic recession.

Declining regions (those whose relative contribution to their respective national GDP has declined between 3 and 10 per cent) are geographically scattered and include some of the old industrial havens (Yorkshire and Humberside, Wales, Saarland), traditionally agricultural regions in their respective national contexts (Schleswig-Holstein, Rheinland-Pfalz, Auvergne, Limousin), core regions (Lombardy), and outright peripheral ones (Basilicata). Their annual growth rate is on average 0.3 percentage points below the mean of all the regions included in the analysis. The least squares fitted function in Figure 2.3 also depicts a declining trend, more pronounced during the end of the 1980s and which has not been fully corrected by a better economic performance at the beginning of the 1990s.

Finally, the regions that suffer the strongest level of decline (those losing more than 10 per cent of their share) are almost exclusively old industrial regions. The share of the economy of Piedmont in the Italian GDP and that of Lorraine in French GDP have shrunk by more than 17 per cent in a period of less than twenty years. Liguria, Champagne-Ardenne, Nord-Pas de Calais, North-West England and Franche-Comté have suffered declines of 12 per cent or more. The high point of decline was during the late 1970s and early 1980s, when the process of industrial restructuring was fully under way. In those years the regions belonging to this group were on average growing 1.5 percentage points below the French, German, Italian and British averages (Figure 2.3). The promotion of active development policies in most of these regions, together with the emergence of alternative economic structures reduced the growth gap with the rest of the regions. However, despite significant improvement in the early 1990s, strongly declining regions still grew as a group 0.5 percentage points below the average of the four countries analysed.

Local Growth Trends

The last layer in the Russian doll of economic governance in Europe is that of the local production systems. Comparable data at this level for Britain, France, Germany and Italy are not available. Therefore we have had to resort to county (Britain), department (France), *Bezirke* (Germany), and province (Italy) data as proxies to measure the performance of local production systems since 1980.[5] At this territorial level, contrasts in economic dynamism become even more evident than at the regional.

The more dynamic local production systems tend to be associated with large metropolitan areas. The greatest dynamism in Britain is linked to the Greater London functional urban region. Although the core of this region stagnated during the period of analysis, the whole area surrounding it experienced considerable dynamism. Buckinghamshire (the most dynamic administrative entity at this level in the four countries analysed), Berkshire, Surrey, Suffolk and West Sussex are among the fastest growing counties in Britain. More distant ones such as Dorset, Wiltshire, Oxfordshire, Northamptonshire and Cambridgeshire have also benefited from the decentralization of economic activity from London, as well as from the development of relatively autonomous local production systems (Figure 2.4). In France, the suburbs of Paris grew fastest. Departments such as Essone, Val d'Oise, and Yvelines have taken advantage of the dynamism of Paris as an economic centre. Equally, in Germany and Italy, economic growth is increasingly connected to large metropolitan areas. That is the case of Berlin, Frankfurt, or Munich (expanding towards Upper Bavaria and Upper Palatinate) in Germany, and of Milan and Rome in Italy (Figure 2.4).

However, many of the districts where local systems of governance have been identified also rank among the fastest growing areas. This is the case of the provinces of Bolzano, Padua, Pescara, Treviso, or Vincenza, and, to a lesser

---

[5] The main source of data at the sub-regional level has once again been the Regio database of Eurostat. This is the source of the German *Bezirke* data between 1980 and 1994, the British county data, and the French *département* data during the same period, as well as the Italian province data for 1980. Italian province level data for the end of the period of analysis stem from the Istituto Tagliacarne. No data are available for East Germany, and the French regions of Provence-Alpes-Côte d'Azur and Corsica. In the latter cases regional data have been used. Because of lack of data for the beginning of the period of analysis, none of the new Italian provinces created since 1980 has been included in the analysis. Their 1995 GDP data have been added to the provinces from which they seceded: Biella to Vercelli; Crotone and Vibo Valentia to Catanzaro; Lecco to Como; Lodi to Milan; Prato to Florence; Rimini to Forlì; and Verbania-Cusio-Ossola to Novara. In order to avoid distortions due to the special circumstances of Berlin, the city's growth rates since German reunification have been applied to West Berlin's data in 1990.

Lack of data at this level prior to 1980 prevents us from covering the same period in the local (1980–94) as in the regional analysis (1977–94). This time difference explains some of the discrepancies in economic dynamism between Figure 2.4 and Figure 2.2. These mainly refer to the Italian regions of Val d'Aosta and Molise.

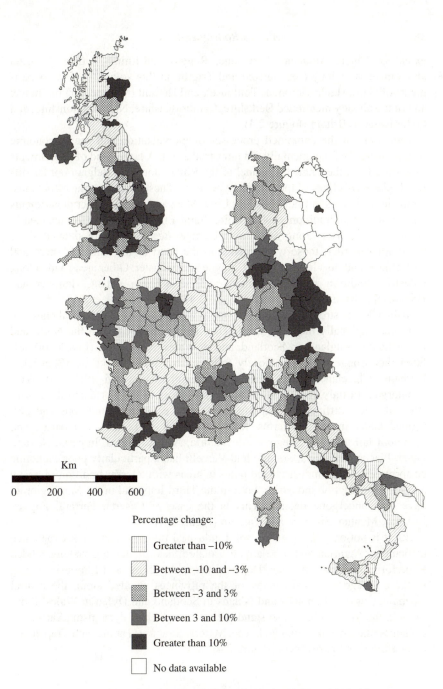

Percentage change:

Greater than –10%

Between –10 and –3%

Between –3 and 3%

Between 3 and 10%

Greater than 10%

No data available

FIGURE 2.4. Changing Local Shares in National GDP, 1977–94

extent of Chieti, Modena, Pordenone, Reggio nell'Emilia, Udine, Venezia and Vincenza in Italy (see Burroni and Trigilia in this volume); of the departments of Gard, Haute-Garonne (Toulouse), and Hérault (Montpellier) in France; and of the already mentioned Berkshire, Cambridgeshire, Northamptonshire, and Oxfordshire in Britain (Figure 2.4).

The losers in the combined processes of globalization and socio-economic restructuring are fundamentally old industrial areas. A large band of departments extending from the English Channel to the Rhine along the Belgian border suffered relative declines of more than 10 per cent. These include some of the most industrialized cities in France such as Lille, Metz and Nancy. Other departments with an industrial tradition, such as Loire (Saint-Étienne), also performed clearly below average. The strongly declining German *Bezirke* also are situated along the Belgian border: those which make up the heart of the Ruhr (Ansberg and Düsseldorf) and, to a lesser extent, Cologne and Münster. Other areas with a long industrial tradition such as Bremen, and, to a lesser extent, Hanover and Brunswick, also under-performed (Figure 2.4).

In the UK, the strongly declining counties were also the old industrial ones, but were geographically more scattered. They tend to be located in the North and North-East of England, in Scotland, and in Wales. Merseyside (Liverpool) suffered the strongest decline, closely followed by South Yorkshire (Sheffield), Durham, Cleveland, Fife, Stirling, Northumberland, and Mid and West Glamorgan. In Italy, many industrialized provinces of the North and the North-West also had difficulties adapting to the new economic conditions and performed badly in relative terms. Many provinces in Liguria, Lombardy, and Piedmont fall into this category: Alessandria, Asti, Cremona, Imperia, Novara, Pavia, Piacenza, Savona, Sondrio and Vercelli had a particularly poor economic performance. Other industrialized poles in areas with a lesser tradition of heavy and mass-production industries, both in the Third Italy and in the Mezzogiorno, have also undergone decline. This is the case of Caserta, Ferrara, Foggia, Livorno, Mantua, Siracuse and Taranto (Figure 2.4).

But it is not only areas with a solid industrial tradition that often experience difficulties. Agrarian and/or relatively isolated local production systems tended to perform below the average. Departments in Auvergne and Limousin belong to these categories, as do many of the provinces situated along the central Apennines or the Highlands and Islands in Scotland and Dyfed in Wales. Provinces in the Mezzogiorno also stand out for their lack of dynamism: Agrigento, Caltanissetta, Cosenza, Foggia, Lecce, Matera, Siracuse, Taranto and Trapani are among the worst performers (Figure 2.4).

Structural Change and Economic Performance

Why are there such strong differences in economic performance among regions and local production systems, when disparities in national growth rates have been

TABLE 2.2. Regional Growth Regressed on Initial Employment and
Employment Change

	Situation in 1977[a]	Change 1977–94[a]
Agriculture, forestry and fishery	0.217 (0.088)	−0.342** (0.006)
Industry:	−0.368** (0.003)	0.454** (0.000)
Fuel and power products	−0.281* (0.025)	0.219 (0.085)
Manufactured products	−0.328** (0.009)	0.535** (0.000)
Building and construction	0.163 (0.202)	−0.313* (0.012)
Services:	0.150 (0.239)	−0.149 (0.243)
Market services	−0.031 (0.825)	0.080 (0.574)
Non-market services	0.251 (0.073)	−0.189 (0.181)

Note: Standardized β-coefficients reported. Probability levels in parenthesis, alongside coefficients.
Degrees of freedom 1.62.
Statistical significance at the 0.01/0.05 level is denoted by **/*
[a]Data cover the period 1977–94 for Germany; 1977–92 for France; 1980–95 for Italy; and 1977–91
for the United Kingdom.
Source: Own elaboration using Eurostat data.

relatively stable? As the previous analysis highlights, differences in growth rates among regions and localities in Britain, France, Germany and Italy in the last decades are closely linked to the initial economic structure of each region and to the changes in this structure during the period of analysis. Whereas large service-oriented economies seemed to perform well, old industrial areas experienced economic decline.

In this section we study the connection between the sectoral structure of regions[6] and their economic performance during the period of analysis.[7] Tables 2.2 and 2.3 report the results of regressing regional growth rates in the four countries on initial employment and employment change, and on initial value added and change in value added. The results highlight the robust association between changes in sector (especially in manufacturing) and economic performance. Whereas high initial industrial employment and value added are connected to low growth rates, the strongest positive coefficients are those which reflect increases in manufacturing employment and in gross value added throughout the period of analysis. Hence, regions which have managed to generate manufacturing employment and greater manufacturing value added have outperformed regions which have created employment in other sectors, and most notably in the service sector (Tables 2.2 and 2.3). These regions coincide with many of the areas

[6] Lack of available data for *Bezirke*, counties, departments and provinces precludes us from carrying out such analysis at the local level.
[7] Regional data refer to the NACE-CLIO R6 branch nomenclatures used by Eurostat in the Regio database. The sub-sectoral groups include agriculture, forestry and fishery; fuel and power products; manufactured products; building and construction; market services; and non-market services. Data for German regions cover the period 1977–94; 1977–92 for French regions; 1980–95 for Italian regions; and 1977–91 for British regions.

TABLE 2.3. Regional Growth Regressed on Initial Gross Value Added and
Value Added Change

	Situation in 1977[a]	Change 1977–94[a]
Agriculture, forestry and fishery	0.233 (0.064)	−0.316* (0.012)
Industry:	−0.258* (0.039)	0.291* (0.021)
Fuel and power products	−0.185 (0.143)	0.116 (0.366)
Manufactured products	−0.272* (0.030)	0.324** (0.010)
Building and construction	0.231 (0.067)	−0.255* (0.043)
Services:	0.170 (0.178)	−0.115 (0.371)
Market services	0.151 (0.232)	0.147 (0.249)
Non-market services	0.081 (0.523)	−0.364** (0.003)

Note: Standardized β-coefficients reported. Probability levels in parenthesis, alongside coefficients.
Degrees of freedom 1.62.
Statistical significance at the 0.01/0.05 level is denoted by **/*
[a]Data cover the period 1977–94 for Germany; 1977–92 for France; 1980–95 for Italy; and 1977–91
for the United Kingdom.
Source: Own elaboration using Eurostat data.

where local production systems based on networks of SMEs have been identified.
While large industries, under strong pressure to restructure and rationalize, have
been shedding jobs, SMEs are responsible for most new jobs generated in
manufacturing (Keeble 1997).

Building and construction is the only sub-sector within the secondary sector
that behaves in an opposite way to manufacturing. The results indicate that the
higher the initial level of employment and of value added generated in building
and construction, the higher the level of growth during the 1980s and early
1990s. However, the connection between both factors is not particularly robust
(Tables 2.2 and 2.3). When changes in building and construction are taken into
consideration, the relationship becomes statistically significant. In this case both
relative increases in employment and value added are associated with below
average economic performance.

Despite the fact that services are often regarded as the motor of economic
growth in a post-industrial society, the results of regressing economic growth
between 1979 and 1994 on service employment and value added are much less
significant than in the case of industry. A high initial service employment rate has
a slightly positive association with economic growth in the following period. But
none of the coefficients reported is statistically significant. The only exception is
the relationship between change in gross value added in non-market services and
economic performance: regions that have seen their value added in non-market
services grow have not been particularly dynamic in economic terms. The relationship between growth in employment in non-market services and growth is
equally negative, although not statistically significant (Tables 2.2 and 2.3).
Finally, there is a significant negative connection between changes in the primary
sector and economic growth. Regions that have retained employment and value

added in agriculture, forestry and fishery throughout the period of analysis grew at a lower rate than those areas where the decline of the agricultural sector has been strongest (Tables 2.2 and 2.3).

Possible Explanations of Regional Dynamism

What are the reasons behind regional growth and decline in France, Germany, Italy and the UK over the last two decades? To what extent are these changes in regional dynamics the result of socio-economic restructuring and globalization and of the emergence of new forms of economic governance at the regional and local levels? At first sight there seems to be a strong association between economic performance and changes in the production system highlighted by the literature on socio-economic restructuring. The strongest economic decline occurs precisely in regions that had originally been the motors of the industrial revolution and the havens of heavy and mass-production industry. Not a single old industrial region escapes this declining trend. The rigidity of their economic and political structure and their reliance on large industrial complexes have made them less able to adapt to the changing economic context.

In contrast, the greatest economic dynamism is found precisely in some of the areas with the highest concentration of clusters of SMEs. South-East England is an example of this. In contrast to the overall lack of clusters in northern and South-West England, Wales, and Scotland, South-East England displays a large concentration of them (Bennett *et al.* 1999; Crouch and Farrell, this volume). Clusters of dynamic sectors and university spin-offs in the Cambridge area and around the M25 motorway, together with the process of economic decentralization from London, have propelled growth in the rest of the South-East, and parts of East Anglia and the South-West (Crouch and Farrell in this volume). The existence and/or emergence of service clusters in and around the metropolitan area of London, such as the financial or the media districts (Pratt 1997), are contributing further to the growth of the South-East. The emergence of new clusters, such as the motor sports valley (Henry, Pinch and Russell 1996; Pinch and Henry 1999a and b), is another symptom of the vigour of local production systems in the South of England.

Economic growth in Italy is also closely related to the presence of industrial districts. Veneto and Trentino-Alto Adige have excelled because of the performance of some of their districts located in and around some of the medium-sized cities in both regions, most notably Bolzano, Padua, Treviso and Vincenza (Burroni and Trigilia, this volume). Equally, the economic vitality of the southern Adriatic regions has been linked by several authors to the emergence of clusters of SMEs during the 1980s and early 1990s (Bottazzi 1990; Trigilia 1992b; Bodo and Viesti 1997). And the dynamic southern German regions also host the majority of the economic clusters that have been identified by the literature on the topic (Glassmann and Voelzkow, this volume).

There is less connection between the territorial distribution of economic clusters in France and regional growth. A possible explanation is the relative absence of what can be considered local productive systems outside the Paris region (Aniello and Le Galès, this volume). Although numerous economic micro-clusters can be identified across France, they are too small in size and too scattered territorially to have any significant influence on regional economic performance. Hence, regional dynamism is more related to long-term centralized planning strategies, such as the development of the aerospace and scientific pole of Toulouse in Midi-Pyrénées, and to the location of large industrial complexes and dynamic services, than to any specific forms of local economic networks in the Italian industrial district sense.

Despite the above-mentioned positive relationship between local economic clusters and regional economic dynamism in the UK, Italy and Germany, the correlation between the presence of local production systems and regional economic dynamism is less than perfect. The lacklustre performance of certain regions considered as hubs of flexible production cast doubt about the capacity of networks of SMEs alone to generate economic dynamism in a world in continuous change. This is the case in Italy, where regions that concentrate some of what have been described as the main examples of industrial districts have undergone relative economic decline. The restructuring of the industrial districts in Empoli, Poggibonsi, Prato, Monsummano and Santa Croce in Tuscany is connected to the poor economic performance of the region (Dei Ottati 1996), which lost 3.5 per cent of its share of total Italian GDP during the period of analysis. Also in Tuscany, Pisa and Livorno (a province affected by the economic restructuring of old industrial plants) saw serious decline, while there was high relative growth in Florence. Slow growth in the province of Belluno contrasts with that of the rest of Veneto; and that of Trento with the dynamism of Bolzano in Trentino-Alto Adige. The same could be said for Emilia-Romagna and Umbria, whose economies have remained relatively stable, in spite of high concentrations of industrial districts. Recent signs of recovery in some of the Emilian districts (Bologna, Modena and Reggio nell'Emilia) are nowhere to be seen in the Romagna (decline in Ferrara, Forlì and Ravenna) or in Piacenza.

The poor economic performance of Baden-Württemberg, especially since the beginning of the 1990s, is also paradoxical. Rhône-Alpes represents a similar case in the French context.

In addition, the emergence of dynamic industrial districts in some traditional industrial regions has also made little difference to their economic decline. The dynamic textile district of Biella (Locke 1996) or silk and metal-working districts in and around Turin (Giaccaria 1999) have not been able to curb the strong decline of the Piedmontese economy. Here too there are internal contrasts. In Baden-Württemberg growth in Tübingen outstrips that elsewhere; and in Rhône-Alpes, the departments closer to the Alps (Isère and Upper and Lower Savoy) perform better than the rest of the region.

In brief, regional and local evidence suggests a positive association between the density of local production systems and growth, but that the presence of industrial districts and/or clusters and networks of SMEs is not in itself a guarantee of greater economic dynamism. Conversely, the opposite relationship does hold in all cases: regions dominated by heavy and/or mass-production enterprises have undergone economic decline—and, in some cases, serious economic decline—since the mid-1970s.

It is therefore necessary to complement the account of causes of regional economic dynamism in the post-industrial period by looking in other directions. Possible explanations of the dynamism, or lack of it, of certain regions point to factors which have little to do with the presence or absence of local production systems. First, there is a tendency for economic growth to be increasingly concentrated in large urban agglomerations (Krätke 1991; Sassen 1991; Hall 1993; Taylor 2000), and particularly in those where economic and financial power is combined with political power (Rodríguez-Pose 1998). The strong performance of regions such as Lazio, Hesse, Île de France, and South-East England is related to the rapid insertion of cities like Rome, Frankfurt, Paris and London in world economic circuits and their increasing detachment—especially in the case of London—from national economies. This urban dynamism, which affects above all global ('alpha') cities (Sassen 1991; Hall 1993; Taylor 2000) and, to a lesser extent, European (Hall 1993) and 'beta' or 'gamma' (Taylor 2000) cities, is at the root of the emergence of an 'archipelago economy' (Veltz 1997). According to this model these cities are more connected to one another than to their traditional national economic backgrounds. Berlin represents another example of how political and economic power come hand in hand. The city, which during the 1970s and 1980s had struggled to keep up with the economic pace of the rest of Germany, witnessed a sudden economic boost connected to German reunification and with the prospects of its becoming the new capital.

The tendency of growth to be associated with large urban centres is reproduced at the level of medium-sized cities, many of which show signs of greater economic dynamism than surrounding areas. This is evident in Emilia-Romagna or Tuscany, where Bologna and Florence perform better than neighbouring provinces, and in the cases of Grenoble, Montpellier, Nantes, Strasbourg and Toulouse, which also grow at a greater pace than smaller cities in neighbouring departments. Even in lagging areas of the Italian Mezzogiorno a similar pattern seems to emerge: Bari, Cagliari, Naples, Palermo and Potenza grow faster than their respective regions.

The dynamism of regions also seems to be related to innovative capacity. Regions which experienced the greatest economic rise over the past two decades also tend to be those with greater resources devoted to R&D. Bavaria is second only to Baden-Württemberg in R&D in Germany, with important concentrations of R&D facilities in the public, private and university sectors in the area around Munich. Île de France and Midi-Pyrénées also concentrate most of the French R&D effort, with levels of investment which in 1994 were equivalent to 3.7 and

3.1 per cent of their respective GDPs. This represents in the case of Midi-Pyrénées a level of relative expenditure 40 per cent above that of Rhône-Alpes, the third French region in this category (Rodríguez-Pose 1999b). Likewise, R&D facilities were heavily concentrated in South-East England and East Anglia, and in Lazio and Lombardy in Italy. In some regions, such as East Anglia, Bavaria, South-East England and Île de France, innovative capacity linked to the R&D effort is enhanced by the presence of networks and inter-firm linkages (Dosi 1988; Malecki 1994; Cooke 1996). The collaboration between research bodies, such as advanced universities, and local systems of enterprises has been considered to be at the origin of the spillovers which underlie the innovative capacity of many local production systems (Audretsch and Feldman 1996; Audretsch and Vivarelli 1996). And the connection between local productive systems and research bodies, together with several other regional institutions and policies, further promote the formation of regional innovation systems and dynamic spaces (Cooke 1992; Storper 1995a).

Conclusions

In this chapter we have tried to address the question of the dynamism of local production systems since the mid-1970s by looking at the performance of regions and sub-regional territorial units in France, Germany, Italy and the UK. Are local production systems the panacea that some have tried to suggest? The economic performance of areas with a high density of local production systems is too diverse to permit sweeping conclusions. Some regions with high densities of SME networks and local collective competition goods are among the best performers (Bavaria, East Anglia, Midi-Pyrénées, Veneto, or Trentino-Alto Adige), whereas others—and perhaps the most well-known cases—have rather disappointing rates of growth (Baden-Württemberg, Emilia-Romagna and Tuscany). At the local level, the panorama is not very different. Strong dynamism in Bologna, Cambridge, Lower Bavaria, Toulouse, or Treviso contrasts with average economic performances in Brescia, Karlsruhe, Parma, Pisa or Stuttgart. Hence, the development of local production systems based on networks of SMEs does not seem to be a panacea for achieving high growth: there are many local production systems which have not been able to exploit any competitive advantage in an increasingly globalized economy and therefore do not perform better or worse than neighbouring areas.

However, local production systems should not be easily dismissed as nine-day wonders. The presence of clusters of SMEs in a certain area seems to be almost a vaccine against economic decline. The few local production systems that perform badly during the period of analysis (Cremona, Forlì, Novara, Mantua or Ravenna) are the exception and not the rule. Most other local production systems tend to grow over a period of almost twenty years at least at the same rate as their respective national economies, if not at a faster or even much faster pace.

In contrast, areas deprived of the features that have been associated with local production systems almost inevitably suffer greater decline. Old industrial regions belong to such a group. The large heavy and mass-production industrial complexes located in them have proved difficult to restructure, and few alternatives have emerged. As a result, large areas of northern France, north and north-west England and Scotland, north-east Italy and west Germany have been unable to adapt to the new economic environment and endured strong decline. Many lagging areas deprived of networks of SMEs have suffered a similar fate.

High growth in the post-industrial era in western Europe seems to be first and foremost an urban phenomenon, but local production systems—despite their heterogeneity—do not lag far behind. And the best economic performances occur when metropolitan spaces and local production systems meet, as in the case of the outer London green belt or the Paris basin. The capacity of local production systems to cope with and adapt to new challenges, together with their flexibility and ability to generate high value added manufacturing jobs, have thus made them a suitable and viable alternative in an ever-changing economic setting.

3

Italy: Economic Development through Local Economies

LUIGI BURRONI AND CARLO TRIGILIA

The role of small-firm systems—especially in the form of industrial districts—has attracted attention as a distinctive feature of Italian economic development. The aim of this chapter is to analyse the most recent changes in local economies. Are these productive structures still growing? Or are they facing a decline? Has there been a change in the organization of production and in governance models? We shall show that local production systems continued to grow in the 1990s and increased their role in the Italian economy. However, this process has entailed an increasing variety of organizational models. Traditional industrial districts are still important, especially in the regions of the Third Italy (central and north-east Italy). At the same time new models of networks have grown: local production systems based on the role of a leading large firm (networked firm) or of a few medium-sized firms.

From the territorial point of view, three trends will be stressed. First, we shall show a process of diversification of local production systems in the Third Italy. Second, we shall focus our attention on the growth of local systems in the North-West—the former home of Italian Fordism and large firms. Third, we shall emphasize the emergence of local production systems in the South—though still weak and unstable, and largely based on forms of hidden economy.

Before dealing with the most recent changes, we shall briefly review the main trends of the past decade, focusing on the industrial district model. We shall then outline the important role that local production systems still play in the Italian economy. Finally, we analyse the productive organization and the governance models which characterize the different regions of Italy, stressing the emergence of different patterns in the Third Italy, the processes of economic restructuring in the old Fordist model of north-western regions, and the rise of new regions of economic dynamism and local development in the South.

Economic Restructuring and Industrial Districts in the 1980s

As is well known, at the beginning of the 1970s a serious crisis of the Fordist model occurred. Several conditions influenced this outcome: the saturation of final markets and their increasing instability and segmentation, together with other conjunctural factors, such as the end of the Bretton Woods system, and the oil crisis of 1973–74. They created strong rigidities, which proved an obstacle to competitive strategies based on containment of costs. In addition, the diffusion of flexible, low-cost technology, along with other factors, undermined the foundation of a model characterized by limited flexibility and high volumes of production. As discussed in the Introduction, following these changes, intensive restructuring of large-scale enterprises began and new opportunities emerged for the development of competitive models other than Fordism, capable of combining considerable flexibility with diversification of products and with a different price–quality relationship. As also noted in the Introduction, Piore and Sabel (1984), and Sabel (1989) in particular, later pointed to a process of 'double convergence'. Systems of small and medium-sized enterprises (SMEs) developed stronger inter-firm links, while large-scale firms reorganized themselves in networks of such firms. Italy was a privileged point from which to observe these new trends based on flexible specialization. This form of economic organization had already developed in Italy while Fordism was in its golden age, and continued to grow when this model showed the first signs of crisis.

A strong link with the local institutional context characterized the areas of flexible specialization. They were mainly concentrated in the central regions (Emilia-Romagna, Toscana, Marche and Umbria) and in the North-East (Friuli V. G., Trentino A. A., Veneto). Thus, this important pattern of local development led Italian scholars to design a different map of the Italian economy. There was a shift from a dualistic conception (the developed and industrialized North versus the backward and rural South), to the idea of a 'Third Italy'.[1] Therefore, three main areas were identified. First, the North-West primarily characterized by large firms, with a Fordist organizational model, where intensive restructuring processes began. Second, the South where an undeveloped industrial structure co-existed with large firms, often state-owned and specialized in heavy industries. Finally, the Centre and North-East, characterized by local networks of small firms specialized in both traditional (textiles, clothing, footwear, and so on) and modern (mechanical engineering, machinery, and so on) sectors.

This research stressed the importance of geographical concentration of manufacturing activities, especially for SMEs. Many studies focused their attention on those local economies characterized by a high degree of employment in manufacture—here defined as local production systems.[2] It was showed that a specific type of local production system, the industrial district,[3] was very widespread in

---

[1] According to this definition, proposed by Bagnasco (1977), the Third Italy was composed of Friuli Venezia Giulia, Trentino Alto Adige, Veneto, Emilia-Romagna, Tuscany, Umbria and Marche. The regions of the North-West were Piemonte, Liguria, Lombardy and Valle d'Aosta. Those remaining are part of the South.

[2] As we shall see, a local production system is a Travel to Work Area which has a percentage of persons employed in manufacturing activities higher than the national average.

[3] We define as industrial district a local production system with a high concentration of small and medium-sized firms, characterized by a high level of productive specialization and by horizontal integration among small firms.

the regions of the Third Italy since the early 1980s (Table 3.1). ISTAT identified 199 industrial districts in 1991, where more than two million people were employed in manufacturing activities.

Given the importance of industrial districts in the local production systems, an extensive literature has tried to interpret the organizational features of this model, as well as its institutional conditions (Bagnasco 1977, 1988; Trigilia 1986a and b, 1992a; Becattini 1987; Brusco 1989). We shall not go into the details of this well-known literature, but it is worth mentioning some basic aspects of the industrial district model. The productive structure of industrial districts is based on a highly specialized division of labour among SMEs. Only a limited number of firms have access to final markets; most of them are specialized in a single stage of production. Districts are specialized in the production of particular kinds of goods; the most represented sectors are the traditional ones (textiles, clothing, footwear, furniture, ceramics, and so on), but there were also significant development in the more 'modern' sectors, particularly mechanical engineering and the machine tools sector.

Therefore, we can define the industrial district as the network of firms model: it is characterized by a low level of hierarchy, by horizontal linkages among small firms, by inter-organizational networks (Bellandi 1987). External economies support this model of productive organization especially in two ways: on the one hand, the high density of firms and a widespread interpersonal trust favour the spreading of information about technological innovation, organizational problems and the production of a specific know-how ('tacit knowledge'). Marshall referred to this kind of collective competition goods when he emphasized the role of the 'industrial atmosphere' as a peculiar component of the industrial district model (Becattini 1987, 1989). On the other hand, as is well known, these firms are not large enough to produce internally the services they need. Thus, successful production of collective goods is dependent on the formal and informal processes that supply such goods (training, technological information, export promotion, information on market trends, and so on). This production is supported by the complex institutional setting and by the particular governance structures of

TABLE 3.1. Local Production Systems and Industrial Districts in Italy, 1991

	Number of travel to work areas	Manufacturing workforce in TTWAs	Number of local production systems	Manufacturing workforce in LPSs	Number of local industrial districts	Manufacturing workforce in industrial districts
North-West	140	2,096,636	96	1,937,426	59	922,140
North-East	143	1,378,683	80	1,017,308	65	835,521
Centre	136	928,079	73	544,655	60	405,613
South	365	824,151	30	157,602	15	58,970
Italy	784	5,227,549	279	3,656,991	199	2,222,244

Source: ISTAT, 1996.

this kind of local economy. We can distinguish between communitarian, informal mechanisms and more institutionalized and formalized procedures.

The combination of three institutional elements has been crucial for the growth of a social system of production based on districts of small firms. These are present in a typical form in the so-called Third Italy (Trigilia 1986a; Bagnasco 1988). First, a network of small and medium centres exists which can be traced back to medieval communes. They enjoyed widespread traditions of crafts and commerce, which were not eroded by industrialization, urbanization and immigration. The entrepreneurship of small firms came mainly from these centres. Second, the presence of self-employment in agriculture (sharecroppers or small peasants) was also important in supporting the formation of a flexible, low-cost, workforce with appropriate training and a particular work ethic. A third significant factor was the strong influence of both local political traditions and institutions tied to the Catholic Church or to the socialist and communist movements. Thus, these regions were characterized by a 'white' or 'red' regional political subculture.

Political subcultures, although in a different way, contributed historically to preserving the particular socio-economic fabric already mentioned, characterized by a peculiar mixture of modern and traditional elements, and a high level of social integration. As a result, subcultures helped to strengthen a network of trust and models of social relations, which fostered the growth of small firms. Secondly, the rooting of both Catholic and socialist and communist cultures in these regions has historically favoured the emancipation of the local political system from civil society. Politics became more orientated to the provision of collective goods, and hence influenced industrial relations and local government activities in such a way as to help the growth of small firms (provision of infrastructure, economic services, local welfare, and so on).

As we noted, an important source for the provision of collective competition goods are informal reciprocity arrangements, which rely on trust and on strong local community ties. However, in addition to informal regulation it is necessary to take into account the role played by local institutions. In fact, trade unions, employers' associations and local governments favour more formalized co-operation between both workers and small entrepreneurs. A co-operative model of industrial relations strengthens co-operation within firms, which compensates for labour flexibility and redistributes local income through local collective bargaining and social policies. On the other hand, co-operation among trade unions, employers' associations and local governments is important for the production of other kinds of competition goods, through the establishment of specific institutions (*centri di servizi*) which provided training, export promotion and other services. Finally, there is a third mechanism for the production of these goods—the market. In these areas, private firms play an important role in providing and selling of strategic goods and services, which, thus, have no value as 'collective' goods.

Summing up, the local institutional setting represented an important competitive advantage for these local systems: local government, interest associations and trade unions played an important role in the provision of collective competition goods which strengthened the competitiveness of the small-firms systems. The importance of local concertation has been recently recognized also by the central government, which adopted new policies to sustain local economic growth: territorial pacts. These are an instrument which has the aim of supporting local development through local concertation, and 'area contracts', which are promoted by an agreement between local employers associations and trade unions with the aims of raising labour flexibility and reducing labour costs.

Organizational and Territorial Changes in the 1990s

As mentioned above, the research on industrial districts and the Third Italy showed the existence of competitive models that are an alternative to Fordism. Attention was focused on networks of small firms strongly rooted in local context, and able to adjust rapidly and respond in a flexible way to the demands of increasingly unstable final markets. From the beginning of the 1990s, research interests have gradually shifted to other directions, seeking to respond to new questions, such as how local networks deal with global pressures (Pyke, Sengenberger, and Cossentino 1996). In particular, it is important to assess whether globalization is bringing about a de-regionalization of productive activities.

The study of the readjustment processes led to identification of three possible outcomes. First, a number of local production systems have lost their productive character due to a strong de-localization towards those countries where production costs are lower. However, as some studies have shown (Unioncamere 1995; Censis 1998), this phenomenon only affected a minority of local production systems. A second path has been more common. It is also based on de-localization, but only of a few stages of production, less important for the quality of the final product, but in which significant reductions in labour costs are possible. Finally, there is a third form of adjustment: some 'mature' industrial districts become 'tertiary districts', which keep the most important stages of production (designing and conception of products, marketing, and so on) (Sforzi 1993, 1995a and b) while the most labour-intensive phases are de-localized.

Therefore, these studies suggest that globalizing trends are not necessarily undermining the role of local production systems. We can test more precisely this hypothesis by asking three questions. Has territorial concentration of productive activity increased, and if so, to what degree? What is the nature, in organizational terms, of local production systems? What are the main productive specializations that characterize them? As we shall see, the answers to these questions show that territorial concentration of productive activity continues to be important, and that this phenomenon has in fact increased in recent years. It seems, thus, that where certain institutional conditions pertain, for some areas globalization can prove to be an opportunity rather than a constraint. However, the growing importance of

TABLE 3.2. Local Production Systems in the Italy, 1990s

Year	Number of local production systems	Manufacturing employees in LPSs as a percentage of the national total	Average value of the LQ index for local production systems
1991	280	60.7	1.335
1996	292	61.2	1.385

Source: Processed data of ISTAT database (1999).

territorial concentration is not bringing about a convergence between the various organizational models present at the local level. Rather, as we shall see, models of productive organization are heterogeneous and differences seem to grow over time.

The first step in response to our questions is the identification of the most appropriate territorial units of analysis. We need to find areas that are homogeneous from a socio-economic point of view. We decided to use 'Travel to Work Areas', for their socio-economic definition of micro labour markets, since we are interested in the territorial concentration of productive activities. We shall define these local systems as local production systems (LPSs). This can be done using an indicator—the Location Quotient (LQ)[4]—that measures the territorial concentration of manufacturing activity compared to the national average.[5] Has the relative weight of local production systems increased? As Table 3.2 shows, the weight of local production systems grew between 1991 and 1996, in absolute terms, and, albeit marginally, as a percentage of the total number employed in the manufacturing sector. There were 280 systems in 1991, in 1996 we find 292 (37.2 per cent of total amount of Italian local systems) with a concentration in manufacturing activities higher than the national average (the value of 1.385 for the index LQ refers to a percentage of workers in manufacturing activities of 48.7 per cent). Even if only 36 per cent of national population live in these local production systems, they actually employ more than 60 per cent of total national manufacturing employment. At the national level from 1991 to 1996 there was a

[4] The index LQ has the following algorithm:

$$Lq \text{ for the Local System } A = \frac{Employment\ 1}{Employment\ 3} : \frac{Employment\ 2}{Employment\ 4}$$

Employment 1: employment in manufacturing activities in the local system A
Employment 2: employment in manufacturing activities in Italy
Employment 3: total employment in the local system A
Employment 4: total employment in Italy

[5] When a Travel to Work Area has a value on the LQ index higher than 1, then the concentration of manufacturing activities in this local system will be above the national average, thus identifying a local production system. In 1996 35.2 per cent of the total number of employees worked in manufacturing firms: this means that a local system which can be defined as local production system has at least 35.2 per cent of employed in manufacturing activities.

Luigi Burroni and Carlo Trigilia

TABLE 3.3. New Local Production Systems in Italy[1]

	Number of local production systems formed between 1991 and 1996	Number of manufacturing employees
North-West	6	23,414
North-East	5	12,316
Centre	10	32,375
South	16	57,017
Italy	37	125,122

Note: [1]The territorial division adopted in this chapter refers to the Bagnasco's definition of the three 'Italy'; the North-West is composed of Valle d'Aosta, Piemonte, Lombardia, and Liguria. The North-East Friuli V. G., Trentino A. A., Veneto. The Centre: Emilia-Romagna, Tuscany, Marche and Umbria. And finally the South, thus, Lazio, Abruzzo, Molise, Campania, Basilicata, Puglia, Calabria, Sicilia and Sardegna.

Source: Processed data of ISTAT database (1999).

decrease in employment in manufacturing of −6.8 per cent, but in the LPSs it was only −3.3 per cent. Furthermore, it is interesting to note that during the 1990s in the 280 'old' local production systems there was a widespread strengthening of manufacturing employment: the relative weight of manufacturing activities[6] grew in more than 70 per cent of local production systems. This trend shows that during the period 1991–96 there was a reinforcement of those systems already characterized by a high degree of sectoral specialization.

The strengthening and diffusion of this model of LPSs affected practically the whole country, including some areas of the South. Most of the thirty-seven new local production systems were in the South (Table 3.3).[7] One should also note that these new systems represented a significant part of manufacturing employment, more than 25,000 employees.

The figures presented above suggest a preliminary response: territorial concentration of productive activity grew at the beginning of the 1990s, and this is true, although to varying degrees, for the entire country. As Table 3.4 shows, the majority of local production systems are to be found in the North-West and the Centre, confirming the importance of these areas in the Italian productive system. Regarding the North-East and the South, these areas have about the same number of local production systems, but it should be noted that there is a huge difference between the two, the density of local production systems being much higher in the former. While in the South there are 52 LPSs out of a total of 392 local systems (12.7 per cent), in the North-East there are 52 out of a total of 95 (54 per cent).

---

[6] Here measured by the index of territorial concentration LQ: an increase in the value of the index LQ in manufacturing corresponds to a strengthening of employment in this sector compared to others.

[7] The difference between the overall number of local production systems in 1991 and in 1996 is just twelve. This is however due to the fact that some local systems (25) that specialized in manufacturing in 1991 lost this characteristic in the period 1991–96. For this reason the number of new local production systems in 1996 was thirty-seven.

TABLE 3.4. Territorial Concentration of Local Systems and
Local Production Systems in Italy

	North-West	North-East	Centre	South
Local systems as a percentage of the national total	17.9	12.1	20.0	50.0
Local production systems as a percentage of the national total	31.8	17.8	33.2	17.1

Source: Processed data of ISTAT database (1999).

The majority of new LPSs (about 70 per cent) border on areas which by 1991 were already characterized by a high concentration of manufacturing activity (Figure 3.1). This suggests a possible territorial diffusion of this model of productive organization into the areas that were geographically adjacent. Finally, as we have already said, the relative weight of LPSs is particularly important in all areas of the north and central regions, whereas it is found far less in the South.

Previous figures confirm the importance to the Italian economy of local production systems, but they tell us nothing about the organizational models that characterize them. Using the coefficient of local concentration, it is possible to show the organizational specialization of each LPS in comparison to the national average.[8]

The majority of LPSs (almost 70 per cent) are characterized by the presence of a large number of firms with fewer than 250 employees. Given the particular importance of small and medium-sized firms, it could be useful to divide the LPSs into three groups: local systems with a large number of small firms (compared to the national average); those with a large number of small and medium-sized firms; and those where large firms prevail.[9] Thus, it becomes possible better to identify the productive organization of each local system.[10] Different types of LPS characterize the various regions (Table 3.5). LPSs of small firms are more concentrated in central regions, while in the North-West, and also in the North-East, local production systems with small and medium-sized firms prevail. In the South, LPSs with large firms are more widespread.

---

[8] In this case the index LQ is also used, referring however to the size of firms: an LPS that has a value greater than 1 on the LQ index in the class with 1–249 workers will thus be considered specialized in this particular organizational model.

[9] This definition is drawn from the sub-division used by other authors including Sforzi (1995a) and ISTAT (1997). In LPSs of small firms there is a percentage higher than national average of workers in firms that have 1 to 50 workers. Small-medium firms are LPS that have a percentage higher than the national average of workers in firms with 50–250 employees. Finally, systems of large firms are those with a percentage above the national average of employees in firms with more than 250 employees. In the case in which a local system has a percentage of employment above the national average in the class 1–49 and 50–249, it will be classified as a small/medium-sized firm system.

[10] The threshold of 250 employees for the definition of a large firm was due to the dominant type of productive specialization often found in these areas. This is primarily light industry and mechanical engineering, for which a firm with 300 employees is relatively large.

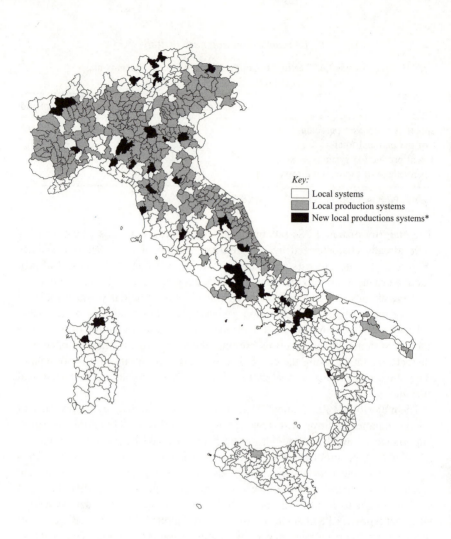

FIGURE 3.1. Local Production Systems in Italy, 1996

Note: *Local Production Systems that emerged during the period 1991–6.

TABLE 3.5. Local Production Systems in Italy by Type of Firm

	Local production systems of small firms	Local production systems of small/medium firms	Local production systems of large firms
North-West	14.0	51.6	34.4
North-East	19.2	51.9	28.8
Centre	42.3	39.2	18.6
South	30.0	24.0	46.0

Source: Processed data of ISTAT database (1999).

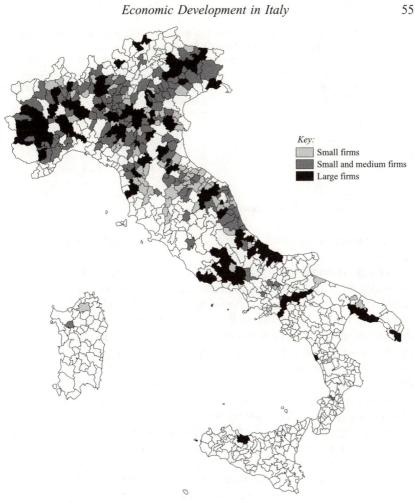

FIGURE 3.2. Local Production Systems and Organizational Specialisms in Italy, 1996
Source: Processed data of ISTAT database (1999).

Therefore, the model of the 'Three Italies' seems confirmed, with the North-West characterized by large firms and the Centre and North-East by small and medium-sized firms (Figure 3.2). However, it is also possible to identify a new axis that runs from eastern Lombardy to Veneto. This is characterized by local production systems of small and medium firms, while in central Italy, and especially in Tuscany and Marche, local systems based on small-scale firms prevail. The local production systems of the South are based on large

TABLE 3.6. Percentage of Italian LPSs that Recorded a Growth in Manufacturing
Employment by Type of Local System, 1991–6

	Local production systems of small firms	Local production systems of small/ medium firms	Local production systems of large firms
North-West	6.5	64.5	29.0
North-East	13.3	53.4	33.3
Centre	32.4	35.1	32.4
South	22.2	25.9	51.9
Italy	19.2	44.8	36.0

Source: Processed data of ISTAT database (1999).

firms, although, as we shall see later, systems with small-scale firms are also growing.

As far as the dynamism of these types of LPS is concerned, at the national level the majority of the 269 systems that registered a growth in manufacturing employment consists of those systems characterized by both small and medium-sized firms (Table 3.6). It seems thus that the presence of medium-sized firms fostered dynamism, at least in terms of employment. Once again, however, there are differences between the various regions of the country, as shown in Table 3.6. Local systems with small or medium-sized firms experienced growth in the North (both east and west). In the Centre, however, there are a significant number of systems of small firms that also recorded good performances. In the South, the systems of large firms have had relative success.

During the period 1990–6, the added value for the entire Italian economy had a growth of about 47 per cent, whilst industrial activities increased at a lower rate (33 per cent). It is also notable that the growth rate of those specializations in which SMEs predominate (machinery and more traditional productions such as textiles and clothing) was lower than that of industrial activities in general (Figure 3.3).

Nevertheless, these specializations continue to play an important role in the Italian economy. In 1998 they were responsible for about 40 per cent of total national exports, and they employed more than 40 per cent of total manufacturing employment (Figure 3.4).

In focusing on productive specialization, it may be useful to adopt the following classification: heavy industry, light industry, food production and mechanical engineering.[11] Then, proceeding with the method adopted for

---

[11] The distinction used here is that between light industry, heavy industry, mechanical engineering and food industry, as suggested by ISTAT (1997). Light industry comprises textiles and clothing, fur, decorating products, jewellery, musical instruments, and so on. Mechanical engineering comprises manufacturing, installation, repair and maintenance of machines and mechanical equipment, manufacture of electrical and electronic machines and equipment, and manufacture of metallic products. Heavy industry includes metalwork, production of petrochemicals and means of transport.

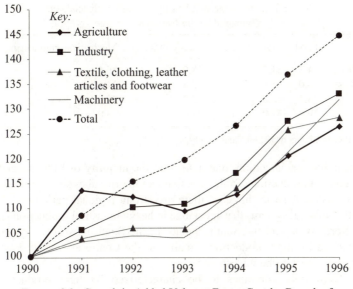

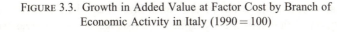

FIGURE 3.3. Growth in Added Value at Factor Cost by Branch of
Economic Activity in Italy (1990 = 100)

Source: Processed data of ISTAT database (1999).

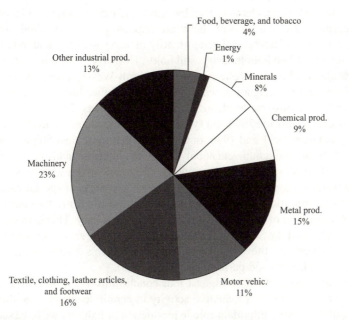

FIGURE 3.4. Percentage of Export by Productive Specialization in Italy, 1998

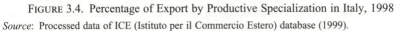

Source: Processed data of ICE (Istituto per il Commercio Estero) database (1999).

TABLE 3.7. Percentage of LPSs by Prevailing Specialization
Compared to the National Average

	Food	Light industry	Heavy industry	Mechanical engineering	Total
North-West	4.3	31.2	28.0	36.6	100
North-East	0.0	61.5	3.8	34.6	100
Centre	3.1	66.0	5.2	25.8	100
South	10.0	54.0	28.0	8.0	100

Source: Processed data of ISTAT database (1999).

organizational specialization, one notes that the majority of LPSs specialize in light industrial production (Table 3.7). Only a minority does so in engineering or heavy industry. Also in this case there are strong regional variations. A large proportion of local systems that specialize in heavy industrial production is found in the North-West and the South, though in the South most local systems are characterized by light production. Finally, in the Centre and North-East, light industry continues to be widespread.

The Third Italy continues to be characterized by light production and mechanical engineering, while in the North-West there is a concentration of heavy industry with engineering, despite the existence of certain areas (such as Biella) which specialize in light production. East Lombardy (Bergamo, Lecco, and Brescia) seems rather to constitute a type of border area between North-West and North-East, being characterized by heavy and light industry, and mechanical engineering. The sub-division between regions of the so-called 'industrial triangle' (North-West) specialized primarily in heavy industry, and regions of the Third Italy based on light industry, still holds. However, it should be stressed that it holds above all for the western part of the North-West (the area around Torino, Avigliana, and Carmagnola), while in the rest of Piedmont, and especially in Lombardy, it is possible to identify many 'hybrid' areas (Figure 3.5).

Considering now the 269 local systems that recorded growth in manufacturing activity between 1991 and 1996, one can note that more than 50 per cent are in light industrial production, and about 10 per cent in heavy industry. A significant number of local systems with growing employment are also specialized in mechanical engineering. These figures confirm that areas of specialization often defined as traditional—characteristic of industrial districts—constitute an important element of the dynamism of production in Italy. This is true above all of the Centre and the South, and, though to a lesser degree, of the North-East. In the North-West, on the other hand, the local systems characterized by engineering have had a good performance (Table 3.8).

The data presented above suggest four conclusions. First, they show that territorial concentration of productive activity in certain local systems, that is, the LPSs, still has a very important role in production in Italy. As we have seen, both the total number of LPSs (in all areas of the country) and the concentration of manufacturing activity within them have grown. Second, we saw that LPSs are

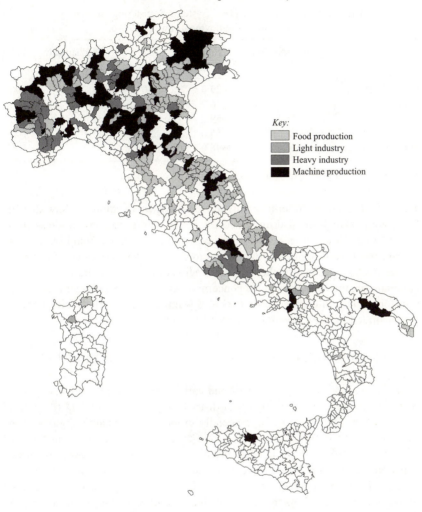

FIGURE 3.5. Local Production Systems and Productive Specializations in Italy
Source: Processed data of ISTAT database (1999).

heterogeneous, in terms of organizational model and productive specialization. However, the majority of local production systems are characterized by small and medium-sized firms, with a dominant specialization linked to light industry and mechanical engineering, confirming that this type of firm continues to have a specific geographical location. Third, one notes that light industry and engineering have performed best, though to different degrees in the different

TABLE 3.8. Percentage of Local Systems Registering Growth in
Manufacturing Employment, Italy, 1991–6

	Food	Light industry	Heavy industry	Mechanical engineering	Total
North-West	3.2	29.0	29.0	38.7	100
North-East	0.0	46.7	3.3	50.0	100
Centre	2.7	59.5	5.4	32.4	100
South	11.1	55.6	22.2	11.1	100
Percentage of local systems	4.0	48.0	14.4	33.6	100

Source: Processed data of ISTAT database (1999).

areas of the country. In terms of organizational specialization, we saw that the LPSs with small firms had more success in the central regions, whereas those with medium-sized firms had more success in the North-West and North-East. Fourth, what we described above seems to confirm that processes of diversification are taking place in the different regions of the Third Italy, as far as a dominant organizational model is concerned. Also, in the South there has been a transformation, with processes of local dynamism and local development, as demonstrated by the formation of new LPSs in this area.

The Diversification of Local Economies in the Third Italy

As we said above, during the 1970s and early 1980s attention was mainly concentrated on the concept of industrial districts as a main instrument to interpret the growth of small-firm LPSs, especially in the highly dynamic regions of the Third Italy. We defined this path of industrial organization as the network of firms model. However, in the last decade a more clear-cut process of differentiation has occurred in the central and north-eastern regions, and a new organizational formula has emerged. This is a more hierarchical model centred on medium or large firms that organize and control a number of subcontracting firms. In this case, the level of hierarchy is quite high, and the leader firm usually provides competition goods (information on new technology and markets, financial assistance, and so on) necessary to the competitiveness of the network. Thus, this system provides club rather than collective goods: the leader firm provides them only to the suppliers which are part of its network, and these goods are not to be used by the entire local community of firms. We shall define this model as that of the networked firm.

The main features of these two organizational models can be evaluated analysing two important regions of the Third Italy, Tuscany and Veneto. In fact, notable examples of these two different trends could be found in Tuscany[12] for

---

[12] The organizational model of the network of firms, closer to the model of industrial districts, is also particularly important in Emilia-Romagna and Marche.

the traditional industrial district and in Veneto for what could be called the networked firms model. To analyse this process of diversification of productive organization we refer to the overall proportion of LPSs by type of firm and number of employees. As Table 3.9 shows, at the beginning of the 1990s most employees in the manufacturing sector were concentrated in LPSs: SMEs in Veneto, and LPSs with only small firms in Tuscany. One should note also that the differences stressed above were reinforced in the period 1991–96: in this period there was in Veneto a large increase in the percentage of employees in systems of SMEs, and also large-scale firms, while in Tuscany there was an increase in the percentage of employees in systems of small firms.

This confirms the existence of a diversification of models of productive organization in the LPSs in the two regions. In addition to these differences in productive structure there are differences in the regulation of local economies. As research carried out during the 1980s has shown (Trigilia 1986a), there were already large differences between the models of regulation in the two regions. However, the initial differences appear to have further increased, again following a clear process of diversification.

This diversification can be assessed through the degree of political inter- vention in the local economy. In Veneto, local governments have delegated important aspect of regulation to large firms and to associations. On the one hand, delegation of political responsibility to firms was facilitated by the presence of large-scale enterprises, but on the other it probably also helped to reinforce them. Furthermore, business associations play an important role in the provision of competition goods such as professional training, information on markets, diffusion of innovation. Moreover, in Veneto trade unions allowed great flexibility in labour and wage regulation, which supported the compe- titiveness of local firms. Since the beginning of the 1990s there has been a high growth of 'atypical' labour contracts, and wage levels were lower than those of Tuscany, for both small and large industrial firms. This model of governance and of provision of collective competition goods, based on representative associations and networked firms, contributed to the industrial expansion of LPSs in Veneto, which registered in the 1990s the highest growth rate in Italy.

However, there are also some shortcomings in this model, especially a low capacity to produce collective competition goods, which are necessary to the long-term reproduction of this type of organization. In the case of the networked firm, for example, the club goods can only be used by the members of each specific network, and directed mainly towards the specific needs of the leading firm. On the other hand, the production of strategic resources by associations has to respond to the pressure and needs of the membership, and is mainly directed to short-term problems. In this case, we can speak of 'categorical goods' suited to specific actors and with a short-term focus. Furthermore, there are goods that cannot be produced either by associations or individual firms without the assistance of local governments. For example, urban planning and transport,

TABLE 3.9. Number of Local Production Systems in the Two Regions and Percentage of Employees*

Year	Veneto			Tuscany		
	Number of local production systems of small firms (% employees)	Number of local production systems of small/medium firms (% employees)	Number of local production systems of large firms (% employees)	Number of local production systems of small firms (% employees)	Number of local production systems of small/medium firms (% employees)	Number of local production systems of large firms (% employees)
1991	35.0 (23.8)	50.0 (57.5)	15.0 (18.7)	45.5 (63.1)	40.9 (24.3)	13.6 (12.5)
1996	25.6 (15.4)	48.8 (64.3)	25.6 (20.3)	56.5 (75.5)	34.8 (14.9)	8.7 (9.6)

Note: *The figure is calculated as a percentage of the total number of employees in local production systems.
Source: Processed data of ISTAT database (1999).

infrastructures, social services. Thus, although a low degree of political regulation, weak industrial relations and the delegation to private actors may have contributed to the development and the performance of local systems in Veneto, it could also endanger success in the long-term (Burroni 1999b).

In Tuscany, public institutions—in particular local and regional governments—continue to be key actors in the regulation of local economies. In this region, in fact, local administrations have contributed to the creation of collective goods aimed at improving the competitiveness, not of single firms, but rather of the overall LPS. At the same time, trade unions adopted more traditional strategies, and maintained a higher rate of membership. Higher labour costs and standard labour contracts were more widespread in Tuscany (Burroni 1999b). However, this model has some shortcomings too. First, it is not easy to provide an adequate supply of collective competition goods and to overcome political failures. Second, the strong ties between local government and voters, and the need of political consensus, can also hinder the production of collective goods with a long-term orientation.

We can better appreciate the contrast between these two models of productive organization and governance by looking at two polar examples: the local production system of Prato for Tuscany and the Benetton Group, which is based in Treviso, for Veneto.

The Prato District and the Benetton Model

The main differences in the type of productive structure between the local system in Treviso (Benetton) and that in Prato are summarized in Table 3.10. In Prato almost all employees in manufacturing (almost 90 per cent) are to be found in firms with fewer than 50 employees. In Treviso, however, in addition to the large number of medium-sized firms, a large proportion of employees work in large-scale firms. As we shall see, this initial difference in productive structure is tightly connected to other important differences, related to the relationship between firms and the mode of regulation of the economy.

Prato is located in central Tuscany, and has a population of about 240,000 with almost 50,000 employees in the manufacturing sector. This is one of the most important Italian industrial districts. The textile industry accounts for 80 per cent of manufacturing firms and employs 83 per cent of employment in manufacturing

TABLE 3.10. Percentage of Employees in Local Manufacturing Units in the Local Systems of Prato and Treviso, 1996

	Firms with 1–49 employees	Firms with 50–249 employees	Firms with more than 250 employees
Prato	87.9	12.1	0.0
Treviso	62.9	19.1	18.0

Source: Processed data of ISTAT database (1999).

activities, and it accounts for 10.8 per cent of national textile exports. Production is highly fragmented in its various stages with many firms specialized in each stage of production. Linkages between firms are in fact multiple (that is to say that each supplier refers to a wide number of customer firms and each customer firm has in turn a wide number of suppliers), with wide possibilities of exit both for suppliers as well as for customer firms (and consequently a low level of external hierarchy). Recently, there has been a growth in business services, tied to the de-localization of the more labour-intensive stages of production. Notwithstanding this homogeneity in size of firms, one can identify different models of competition within the district. Some of these are based on innovation and diversification, while others compete within largely 'traditional' sectors (Bellandi and Trigilia 1991). The relationship between firms in this area remains close to the traditional industrial district model (Becattini 1997).

The governance of this productive structure has been both of the communitarian type as well as formalized: in fact, the behaviour of the economic actors has often been regulated by 'implicit' rules. People who behave as opportunists are excluded from the group; this mechanism of living up to one's own reputation has been and still is of considerable importance in regulating inter-firm activity (Dei Ottati 1992, 1995). It has also been emphasized that agreements between suppliers and customers are informal, and that any disagreements should be settled by mutual accord, informally and by 'meeting each other half way'. Yet, alongside these processes of informal reciprocity, a strong formal role is played by local political institutions and associations. Union density is particularly high, employers' associations (both *artigianato* and industrial) provide services for their members, and local government is active in sustaining local economic development. This phenomenon is already well known in the literature (Trigilia 1990).

An important agreement signed in 1997 by the employers' associations (Unione Industriale, CNA and Confartigianato), represents a good example of this tendency. It aims at improving the relations between customers and suppliers, and at preventing opportunistic behaviour by both sides. The agreement provides a replacement for the so-called 'oral contracts' with a standard written document in which quantity, price and terms of payment are well specified, establishing a model that has been generally adopted in national law 192/98, which regulates customer and supplier relations. This agreement substantially followed two objectives (Alacevich 1999). First, institutionalization of social partnership, as the regulation agreed on by the social partners, should reduce disputes and stabilize prices. Second, the agreement attempts to raise the quality of production in the area through greater co-ordination between the partners, which should improve the quality of the production system. It is thus an agreement that confirms a collective involvement in the creation of local collective competition goods, and the gradual co-ordination of relations between individual and collective actors. Another interesting example of a competition good provided by local institutions through more formalized regulation is the constitution of the joint company, FIL. Local government together with employers' associations and trade unions supported the creation of a privately owned company, which is the vehicle for the funds for training of the European Social Fund. In this way, the company could immediately dispose of resources to arrange professional training projects. Thanks to this joint venture, Prato is one of the few local systems able to use the entire amount of European funds for training activities.

These are just two of the recent examples of mechanisms of regulation introduced in this area; many more could be found. However these two show the lively collective activity which characterizes this local production system. One should not ignore the role played by political institutions and industrial relations in facilitating the adoption of competitive models characterized by a high level of flexibility. At the same time, it is important to stress the rise of private business services firms, in some cases directly supported by local public institutions. As a result, in Prato the percentage of employees working in firms in the service sector is higher than the national average.

The Benetton case is quite different. Here a cluster of small firms concentrated near Treviso work exclusively for a customer firm. The latter decentralizes most production, relying on a stable network of sub-suppliers. Although many of the firms working to produce components for the leader firm are small, the situation is quite different from that of the industrial district: here we face a productive monocentric network[13] and strong hierarchical ties, albeit through external relations (Belussi 1992). The leader firm decides the quality and quantity of goods to be produced and maintains strong ties with commercial outlets through the franchising system. The low value-added stages of production are therefore external, while the leader firm internalizes the more tertiary and strategic stages.

To a certain extent this system is close to a Japanese model of just in time, with a sort of flexible mass production characterized by a high level of diversification (Belussi 1992; Storper and Harrison 1992). In fact, the commercial network 'consists of roughly 80 agency offices (each responsible for a precise geographical area), with over 800 staff who constitute the group's interface with the plethora of independent shops selling Benetton goods throughout the world' (Benetton 1996). These agencies send orders to the central system in Ponzano (Treviso), which, in turn transmits them to production plants. The mechanism of governance and the production of collective competition goods are different from that prevailing in the district of Prato. A dominant player organizes and co-ordinates the production and marketing of goods; it controls the quality of production; and it provides technological innovation through top-down links. Therefore, competition goods maintain a strong club character, and are more targeted to the specific needs of the leader firm. Local policies play only a limited role of indirect support to the system (for example through urban development plans which allow the agglomeration of subcontractors in particular areas), while regional policies mainly provide financial help (Freschi 1993).

---

[13] By monocentric network we mean a network which has a leader with a high level of contractual power.

The networked firm is not the only model of organization that characterizes this area. An important role is also played by interest associations in providing services to smaller firms, according to the model that applies to most LPSs in Veneto (Anastasia and Corò 1996; Diamanti 1996; Rullani and Romano 1998; Burroni 1999a and 1999b). The main difference with the case of Prato is that this model of local governance is less dependent on direct political intervention. We could say that stable and hierarchical networks among firms and interests associations occupy the space left free by political institutions.

Summarizing, there are three possible conclusions to this brief analysis of governance models in Tuscany and Veneto. First, a process of productive and organizational diversification is taking place between different regions of the Third Italy. As for organizational specialization, in Veneto local systems with medium-sized and large firms have become more important, while in Tuscany local systems are mainly composed of small firms. Second, there are important differences in the processes of economic regulation, and in particular in the role of local administrations. In Tuscany 'politics' and industrial relations play a leading role in local regulation and the production of competition goods, while in Veneto local governments delegate economic regulation to employers' organizations and to firms themselves. Finally, networks of firms in the two regions are different. The two cases presented above—the network of firms in Prato and the networked firm of Benetton—constitute two poles of a continuum with many intermediate cases.

Local Economies in the North-West

North-western regions (especially Lombardy, Piedmont, and Liguria) have been the home of Italian Fordism, which developed in the 1950s and 1960s and entered a serious crisis in the 1970s. Starting with the 1980s, remarkable processes of industrial restructuring have occurred in this area, and employment in large firms dramatically shrank (Regini and Sabel 1989). However, this trend has been partly compensated for by the growth of local production systems of SMEs. In some cases this trend is linked to the reorganization of old large firms, in other situations more autonomous patterns of development can be found. However, local concentration of manufacturing activities is also extremely important in this part of Italy: in the North-West there are 93 local production systems out of a total of 140 which have a high concentration of manufacturing activities (LQ > 1), and 72.6 of the total manufacturing workforce is concentrated in these. Furthermore, these local economies had a good performance in the period 1991–96: the relative weight of manufacturing activities[14] grew in more than 70 per cent of cases. Finally, almost 65 per cent of LPSs that recorded growth are those of SMEs. The figure for LPSs of large firms is lower than the national average (29 per cent for the North-West, compared to 36 per cent for the country as a whole).

---

[14] Measured as the index of territorial concentration LQ.

If LPSs of large firms continue to be important in these areas, a process of readjustment is taking place, which recalls the 'double convergence' suggested by Sabel (1989). Local systems of SMEs are emerging; there is a reorganization with an increase in the chance of diversification, together with a reduction in volume of production, supported by the use of new models of organization. The transition is from the model of the large, vertically integrated firm to one of medium-sized firms linked to a network of external suppliers (of varying size).

The organizational model, thus, comes closer to the one we presented above as the networked firm. This seems to be confirmed by the findings of recent research (Unioncamere 1995; Censis 1998). The data we presented above also confirm these conclusions: we underlined the presence of many local systems in eastern Lombardy that constitute a border area between the North-West of large-scale firms, specialized in heavy industry, and the North-East of small and medium-sized firms and industrial districts.

Nevertheless, it is also possible to identify several industrial districts such as those that are more widespread in Tuscany and in other central regions, some of them with a long historical tradition: for example, the district of Castel Goffredo, between Mantova and Brescia, where around 70 per cent of national production and 40 per cent of European production of women's stockings takes place. In this area 61.6 per cent of the firms operate in just one phase of the production cycle. Or there is the LPS of Lumezzane, which has almost 20,000 employees in manufacturing, and specializes in household goods, and where 70 per cent of production is exported. Another is Olgiate (Como) with around 30,000 employees, which exports almost 70 per cent of its textile production (Censis 1998). It is also possible to identify examples in Piedmont, where there are LPSs characterized by SMEs and intermediary mechanisms of local governance similar to those of the Third Italy. This is the case of Casale Monferrato, for example, for the production of electronic goods, and of Biella, which we shall discuss in more detail below. The National Statistical Institute (ISTAT) has estimated that 11 per cent of national export of mechanical products, 4.2 per cent of domestic products, and 19 per cent of textiles are concentrated in districts of Lombardy and Piedmont.

Alongside these systems with long traditions, there are also new productive agglomerations. Censis (1998) identified in the North-West seven recently formed areas with a high concentration of productive activity. In these areas there were 9,000 firms with a total number of around 150,000 employees. These are LPSs with small and more especially medium-sized firms, characterized by a high level of exports (about 40 per cent of production). An example is the area of Valle Varaita, in Piedmont, where there are 150 firms specializing in the production of furniture, or Asse del Sempione in Lombardy, an area specializing in textile production where there are around 3,900 firms.

Overall, with the decline of the Fordist model, new opportunities emerged for other organizational models, more rooted in the local context. The old LPSs have been strengthened and new ones have emerged, leading to an intermediary form of governance. In these cases the productive structure is more based on the role of a leading group of medium-sized firms, which sometimes have the same organization as the networked model found in Veneto. But in this kind of local system, local collective actors (trade unions, employers associations, chambers of commerce, and so on) and local public institutions provide collective competition goods according to a model of governance similar to Tuscany's: 'The capacity for interaction between politics and economics is being created, and in a number of cases one has the impression of an organized mobilization of resources' (Bagnasco 1997). For example, in 1998, the regional institutions of Piedmont identified twenty-five areas with high sectoral specialization, and set out specific policies to support them. Again, in 1998 the region of Lombardy identified twenty-one areas defined as industrial districts where it specified local economic policies which created investment of more than 70 billion lire (*Il Sole 24 Ore*, 17 February 1998). Also in this case, we can try better to illustrate these features analysing briefly a well-known case, the industrial district of Biella.

The Local Production System of Biella

Biella is an industrial district with a long history. It is therefore not representative of recently formed local systems. However, analysis of it is of prime importance for more than one reason. It is one of the biggest LPSs in the entire North-West, with around 2,000 manufacturing firms that employ around 20,000 workers. Also, it is a local area found in the heart of a region considered the home of Italian Fordism, Piedmont.

It is characterized by a particularly low unemployment rate (*c.* 5 per cent), by a high rate of employment in the industrial sector (*c.* 54.2 per cent of total employment), by a strong productive specialization (*c.* 64 per cent of the total employees in the industrial sector working in the textile and clothing industries), and by a strong export capacity (9.8 per cent of national exports of knitting yarn). Furthermore, in this area there are some leading firms whose trademarks are known world wide. Processes of integration among firms seem to be in place in this local system (Paolazzi and Moussanet 1992). Thus, in comparison with the traditional industrial district model, this productive organization shows more structured inter-firm relationships.

The average size of firms in Biella is closer to those in Veneto, rather than to the highly fragmented Tuscan model. Nonetheless, in Biella there is not a single networked system as in the Benetton case, but a kind of intermediate model. For instance, a high percentage of employees work in business services, a feature which is far from that prevailing in the Benetton area and closer to that found in Prato. In Biella 13.1 per cent of the total workforce worked in this sector in 1991, compared with a national average of 12.4 per cent. These data confirm that, despite the larger average size of the firms, part of the services is produced by outside suppliers. This growth in tertiary activity linked to businesses constitutes a process started in Biella at the end of the 1980s, and has also occurred in other LPSs with a long industrial tradition (ISTAT 1997).

Since the 1980s local institutions seem to have promoted the development of this district (Locke 1995), following a serious industrial reorganization. Thus, it is not a mere coincidence that an institution such as the Città Studi was founded in Biella. The Città Studi is a centre where bodies like the Università Tecnica (branch of the University of Turin specializing in textile technologies), the Centro Studi Rivetti (sponsored by the National Research Council and specializing in research on wool) and the Assist (an agency that supports innovation and diffusion of new technologies and services) are active. Furthermore, Biella, together with Prato, is one of the founding members of the Club Italiano dei Distretti. The aim of this association, promoted by industrial associations, chambers of commerce and other bodies from several Italian industrial districts, is to organize and represent the interest of industrial districts both to central government and at the European level.

Finally, an equally important indicator of public–private co-operation comes from the Institute of Textile Tradition and Technology, Texilia Spa, an educational centre for workers in the textile sector initiated in 1984. Three-quarters of the organization is owned by the regional government, and among the other members, public and private, there is the Biella Industrial Union. As Locke pointed out, in this LPS industry 'has been able to count on the existence of well-structured structural networks of socio-political groups and associations capable of co-ordinating strategies, diffusing information, and mediating in conflicts, between small and medium-sized firms and between entrepreneurs and local trade unions' (1995:54).

In conclusion, we can say that some local production systems based on the model of networked economies have developed in the previously Fordist area: their organizational model is more structured and hierarchical than the traditional industrial district, but it is less dependent on a leader firm than in the paradigmatic Benetton case. With regard to governance mechanisms, local collective actors (chambers of commerce, employers' associations and trade unions) seem to foster local development, even if the action of local governments is weaker in comparison to other areas (such as Tuscany). However, the role played by local public bodies to promote the productions of these collective goods has recently increased.

New Local Industrial Systems in the South

The South is the most economically backward area of Italy. In 1991 the area had 36 per cent of national population but only 25.3 per cent of national GDP; by 1998 this had decreased to 24.2 per cent (Svimez 1999). During the same period, employment fell by, on average, 1.3 per cent per year, a rate three times that of the Centre and North, with an overall loss of 617,000 jobs. By 1998 the unemployment rate had reached 22.8 per cent, a growth of 7 per cent since the end of 1992, while in the Centre and North it had increased by less than 1 per cent (from 6.5 per cent to 7.4 per cent).

Despite these aggregate characteristics, even in these areas it is possible to identify some trends of dynamism and local development (Trigilia 1992a; Viesti and Bodo 1997; Meldolesi 1998). In fact, in the South one finds 44 per cent of all the local systems that have registered a growth in the number of employees in the manufacturing sector and 58 per cent local systems where there has been a growth in the number of manufacturing firms.

It is therefore worthwhile identifying the areas of the South that constitute important areas of manufacturing activity, even if they do not have the density of productive activity which characterizes the LPSs in the Centre and North. This can be done by using the LQ index again, but calculated on the southern average, as opposed to the national criteria used until now. This allows us to identify those LPSs with the largest concentration of manufacturing activity, which can be defined as southern local production systems (SLPS). In this way 145 SLPSs can be identified, of which 37 were formed between 1991 and 1996 (Figure 3.6). Of the new SLPSs 68.4 per cent are small firms, 23.7 per cent medium-sized and 7.9 per cent are large firms. As far as productive specialization is concerned, 71.1 per cent of new SLPSs specialize in light industry, compared to 15.8 per cent specializing in heavy productions. Of all local systems that recorded growth in the period under consideration 47 per cent were small firms, while 23.9 per cent were medium-sized, and 28.9 per cent large-scale firms.

These figures demonstrate the existence of local production systems of small firms that are dynamic and co-exist with local systems of traditional large firms. As Figure 3.7 shows, it is possible to identify a considerable number of SLPSs based on small firms in both Puglia and Campania, together with an important group of local systems based on larger firms (above all the areas of Rieti, L'Aquila, Avezzano, and Frosinone). In terms of productive specialization (Figure 3.8) there is also a dualistic structure: 57.5 per cent of SLPSs specialize in light production, which co-exist with a considerable proportion of those specializing in heavy industry (25.3 per cent). The SLPSs remaining specialize in mechanical industry (8.2 per cent) and food industry (8.9 per cent).

Even if local production systems of small firms are spreading, the model of productive organization based on traditional large firms continues to play a strategic role in the South. They make notable investments thanks to particular incentives such as those provided by the law regulating investment in backward areas (Law 488/92). Another example are the *Contratti di Programma* (programme contracts) between private and public actors on specific economic projects, which are mainly directed at large firms (or large consortia of SMEs), and which promote and support consistent investment. Between 1993 and 1996 several of these contracts were signed by important firms such as Texas Instruments, SGS Thomson, IPM, Natuzzi and others. The overall investment was about 5 billion lire, with creation of about 9,000 jobs.

Key:
■ New local production systems
▨ Southern local production systems

FIGURE 3.6. Southern Italian Local Production Systems, 1996
Source: Processed data of ISTAT database (1999).

In all these cases, exogenous investments may trigger endogenous development. This contrasts with what happened in the past, when there was a tendency to build the so-called 'cathedrals in the desert', large plants which mainly aimed to benefit from state funding. Some of these recent investments have well-defined programmes and business plans, which expect to be profitable in the long term. The establishment of large plants may therefore have some positive effects on

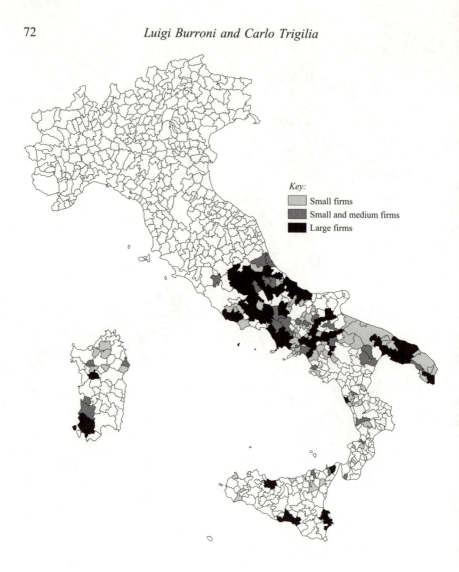

FIGURE 3.7. Southern Italian Local Production Systems and
Organizational Specializations, 1996

Source: Processed Data of ISTAT Database (1999).

local development processes and on the endogenous growth of some areas. Thus,
increasing differences are emerging within the South. The areas of industrial
decline are contrasted with areas showing new local dynamism. Among the latter
it is worth while analysing cases of local autonomous development and situations
in which economic dynamism has been triggered by external investments.

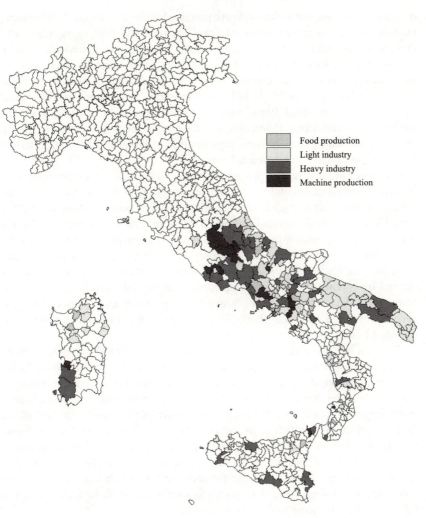

FIGURE 3.8. Southern Italian Local Production Systems and
Productive Specializations, 1996

Source: Processed data of ISTAT database (1999).

Autonomous Local Systems

It is important to distinguish southern autonomous local systems based on
networks of firms from those in the North. In many situations, these 'proto-
industrial districts' or industrial clusters benefit from evasion of fiscal and labour

regulations, and use old technologies to produce low-quality goods. Furthermore, most firms work as external subcontractors for northern firms especially in traditional sectors such as textiles and clothing. Despite this some authors have identified a core of local systems of small firms which compete directly in the final markets, with a good export capacity and production of medium to high-quality goods (Viesti and Bodo 1997). For example, the shoe-making district of Barletta, based on small firms, some of which specialize in producing such quality goods as trekking shoes, and with a strong export capacity (Viesti 1995). There are similar systems of quality production in Putignano, Barletta, Martina Franca, Solofra and San Giuseppe Vesuviano.

Another example of a solid process of local growth, with interesting innovation in organizational model and in relations among firms, is the so-called *triangolo del salotto* (the sofa triangle), between Matera, Santeramo and Altamura (at the border between Basilicata and Puglia). This is an area with a high productive specialization in sofas (60 per cent of national production of leather sofas). By the 1970s, there were already many *artigiano* firms specialized in upholstery and carpentry, and during the 1980s there was a process of economic growth, mainly centred on export. Today this sector consists of around forty firms with 6,000 employees. The strategy is to supply quality goods at competitive prices, trying to penetrate foreign markets; about 70 per cent of the district's production is exported (Viesti 1995).

The area has a strong leader firm, Natuzzi, which directly employs around 2,000 people, with external employment in subcontracting firms of about 2,000. The consolidation of the area is connected to the history of a local entrepreneur, Pasquale Natuzzi, the Italian prototype of the self-made man. He began with a small firm and today he is at the head of one of the world's most important plants for the production of leather sofas, with a turnover of 1,063 billion lire (the figure was just 465 billion in 1993). The presence of a large firm led to important spin-off processes: today, besides this leader enterprise, there is also a considerable group of other firms specializing in the same sector, which were created in the 1980s and are still growing. Two previous employees at Natuzzi, Nicoletti and Calia, founded the other two major firms in the area.

In this case too we find an intermediate situation between the networked firm and the network of firms. On the one hand, we can find in the sofa triangle some features typical of the industrial district such as, for example, an established cluster of small firms, with high productive specialization, widespread innovative capacity, a high diffusion of information about technology and products, and a high level of participation in the labour market. On the other hand, other features show the importance of a leader firm (Natuzzi), which plays an important role in local governance and to whose destiny the success of the entire area is bound.

The effects induced by Natuzzi are a clear example of the role played by the leader firm. Contrary to trends of productive de-localization, this region has evolved a network of local sub-suppliers, which developed into the pre-existing productive fabric, and which now produces the majority of intermediate products, previously purchased from northern enterprises (Belussi 1997). Natuzzi has promoted this local agglomeration of sub-suppliers that had grown out of the previous craft structures. In fact, the Natuzzi group used a *contratto di pro-gramma* with the aim of concentrating the entire production process within the sofa triangle, from raw material procurement to the end product. Furthermore, as pointed out by recent studies (Viesti 1995), the role of Natuzzi is also essential to the governance of the productive process. On the one hand, it controls the quality of the goods produced by sub-suppliers; on the other, it promotes, directly and indirectly, technical innovation in the entire area.

Thus, for the networked firm, the production of collective competition goods is partially linked to the action of the leader firm. Nevertheless, important contributions to technological innovation and diffusion of information are supported by the interaction of firms active in the same local setting. As we said above, the production of competition goods by a large firm alone can be insufficient to sustain long-term local development. In fact, local entrepreneurs complain about the inadequacy of local services (for instance, professional training) and local infrastructure (for instance, transport and communications). The weak action of local governments and the lack of solid ties among the various local collective actors (unions and industrial associations) seem to hinder the provision of these collective goods.

Summing up, we find a situation of local development characterized by growth, not only in terms of turnover and employment, but also of knowledge and know-how. It is a system where a leading actor (and now more than one) played a key role, and where the production stages are now performed within the area. Thus, economic development is strongly embedded in the local territory, even if there is the risk, well perceived by local actors, that weak local institutions cannot support long-term competitiveness.

External Investments and Large Firms

Notwithstanding a general situation of economic backwardness, the last few years have seen a certain growth of investment in the southern part of Italy, by large Italian and foreign firms. These investments have favoured the growth of local dynamism, with a decrease in unemployment and the growth of per capita income.

Where these investments support processes of spin-off and creation of a large network of sub-suppliers, stimulating local entrepreneurship, and where a local reservoir of competencies and skills emerge, the local system may shift from local dynamism to a kind of local autonomous development. Local development can thus be measured in terms of entrenchment of widespread know-how, including technical and organizational knowledge and tendencies favourable to entrepreneurship. When these resources are deeply embedded in the local system, the economic development of an area becomes independent of the results of the single external initiative (Trigilia 1997:77). In this case, exogenous investments may trigger endogenous development.

The new Fiat plant in Melfi represents an interesting example. In this case, we have a large northern firm investing massively in a 'green field' area. The project accomplished in Melfi had deep effects on employment—8,020 people employed directly by Fiat, and more than 1,800 employed by the ACM (see below). The number of employees increased three and a half times between 1991 and 1996. The entire project covers an area of 2,700 square km, and the plant has a productive capacity of around 450,000 cars per year.

The organization of the plant follows the model of the integrated firm, which adopts some features of the Japanese model. One of these features is reliance on a network of suppliers located close to the plant. These first-level suppliers are usually branches of northern enterprises. There is also a large network of minor suppliers. In some cases, these second-level suppliers are local firms, specialized in lower quality production phases. Therefore, this is a case of hierarchical relations among enterprises, characterized by strong ties between the plant and the first-level suppliers, but at the same time by high decentralization of responsibilities and by partial autonomy of the suppliers (Bonazzi 1995). Thanks to the tight linkage between the final firm and the suppliers, functions such as production co-ordination, quality and process control are driven by Fiat. However, there are also collective and co-operative actions arising among the sub-suppliers themselves, such as the creation of a consortium (called ACM). This consortium was formed by thirty-two sub-suppliers, 80 per cent of which are from Piedmont and Lombardy. It developed a *contratto di programma* that has mobilized investment of 560 billion lire, with an increase in employment of around 1,800 employees. However, also this case of local dynamism runs risks. Most important is the difficulty of triggering local autonomous development. As already mentioned, most first-level suppliers are not local, and second-level phases delegated to local firms are low-quality ones. The result is that an endogenous network of local suppliers is not well developed, and the local economic setting is not increasing its autonomy from the large leading firm. If the situation does not change, the local economy will continue to depend on external factors.

Conclusions

At the beginning of this chapter we asked whether the process of globalization is bringing about a de-territorialization of productive activities, and a consequent decline of local economies in Italy. In the 1990s two processes can be observed. On the one hand there is the change and growth of old local production systems; on the other, this model of territorial organization has also spread outside its traditional homeland in the Third Italy. We saw, however, that the growth of local systems is accompanied by a large differentiation in productive organization and governance models. In the North-East and the North-West the local production systems that performed best in the 1990s are those with both small and medium-sized firms. The dynamism of this type of local system was lower in the centre, where systems of small firms continued to play an important role. At the same time, systems of medium-sized firms did not perform well in the South, where most of the new local systems are of small firms, and the old systems that performed best were also of small firms. These differences in performance suggest that the new competitive models of firms are based on network systems, but at the same time it shows that there are different kinds of networks. The type of tie between firms varies, as do external hierarchy, the degree of reciprocal dependency and, finally, the degree of co-ordination among the different actors that belong to the network.

Together with this diversity of models of productive organization, it is possible to identify a large variety of governance mechanisms in the different local economies. We tried to synthesize this heterogeneity through identification of a continuum between two poles. At one end there is the model that can be defined as the networked firm, characterized by the presence of a medium or large leader firm which organizes and controls the local industrial system and which provides competition goods with a club character. Here, local government plays only a limited role, providing indirect support to the local economic system. The ability to combine flexibility, diversification and high volumes of production, together with strong direct ties with the market, explains the high performance of this model during the 1990s.

Nevertheless, there are two potential problems for local development based on this model: first, smaller firms tend to be more dependent on the large ones and this could weaken the re-production of redundant resources which are indispensable for the processes of economic restructuring. Second, the action of the leader firm and of associations (trade union and employers' associations) can partially compensate for the less active role of local government. Therefore, this setting may be unable to provide for collective competition goods.

At the other end of the continuum, we have the network of firms model, characterized by the prevalence of small firms tied together by horizontal linkages, where local government directly, or through co-operation with local associations, provides some competition goods. Also in this case, changes are emerging: the consolidation of medium-size firms, which tend to organize relations with sub-suppliers in a more structured way, and the de-localization of the more labour-intensive stages of production. Naturally, as we said above, these cases represent the two poles of a continuum, and many different intermediate situations—as empirical clusters—can be found.

We saw that local production systems of small and medium firms are growing in the North-West, under pressures from autonomous development and from the restructuring of large firms. Here, the prevailing organizational model is more structured and hierarchical than in the traditional industrial districts, but it is less dependent on a leader firm as in the paradigmatic Benetton case in Veneto. Moreover, in these areas, governance mechanisms also seem to be in an intermediate position between the two above-mentioned models: collective actors and local governments contribute to the production of competition goods.

Finally, intermediate settings can also be found in the South. Here, several areas of local dynamism are emerging. In some cases, this trend is linked to the establishment of new plants by large northern firms (Melfi), while in others we can find local autonomous development (such as the sofa triangle). In all these cases, however, the action of local associations and local governments seems weaker than in other parts of the country, and the provision of competition goods has to rely more on the action of the single large firm, with clear shortcomings.

In conclusion, therefore, two points may be mentioned. Global pressures have not reduced the importance of local economies in Italy and have led to a convergence neither of organizational models, nor of governance models. There is not one best model that reacts to new pressures; rather, there are different answers in different contexts. We can expect that the growing importance of local institutional context will probably have the effect of increasing competition among different areas, and, certainly, the capability of producing collective competition goods will constitute a competitive advantage.

4

The Governance of Local Economies in Germany

ULRICH GLASSMANN AND HELMUT VOELZKOW

This chapter asks whether local economies actually exist in Germany. We show that they do, but that they are subject to other governance mechanisms than those associated with the term 'industrial district'. The collective competition goods that are produced via inter-firm co-operation and diverse local or regional providers evolve from a distinct institutional arrangement.

We examine first the structure of local economies in Germany, and show that there is spatial concentration of specific branches, albeit to a lesser extent than in some other countries. Typically this is due not to the sectoral specialization of small and medium-sized firms (SMEs), but to the presence of flagship enterprises around which smaller firms agglomerate. Concentration may also result from the natural environment in which firms act, as for example in the shipbuilding industry in coastal areas or the mining industry in the Ruhr area.[1] In the following section, Baden-Württemberg (and especially Stuttgart) is taken as a *pars pro toto* to explain the competitive strengths (and weaknesses) of the German model. These results hold for other *Länder* than Baden-Württemberg, because of a national homogeneity in how collective competition goods are provided in Germany. We go on to discuss the new challenges facing the economy since the beginning of the 1990s. Again, we use Stuttgart as an example of how the globalization process is affecting the governance of the economy. The final section comments on the particularities of the governance of local economies in Germany.

Local Economies in Germany

Following Schmitz, an industrial district can be defined:

by more than geographical proximity and sectoral specialisation. Additional attributes are: the predominance of small firms, close inter-firm collaboration, inter-firm competition through innovation rather than through wage squeeze, high degree of trust between employers and skilled workers, provision of collective services through self-help organisation and active regional and municipal government strengthening the innovative capacity of local industry. (Schmitz 1992:88)

[1] However, political decisions have also influenced the concentration of firms, for instance in the mining industry (Abelshauser 1984).

This definition has at least three aspects. First, it involves economic structure (spatial concentration, sectoral specialization, craft-based production and size of firms). Second, it speaks to relations between the actors (entrepreneurs and other decision-makers) belonging to an industrial district. Finally, it makes claims about the institutional environment (associational, regional or local politics).

If we look only at spatial concentration and sectoral specialization, it is certainly possible to identify regional clusters of production in Germany. In his national report on (West) Germany, Porter (1991: 178ff., 203ff.) lists the following clusters: the steel industry in Dortmund, Essen and Düsseldorf; locksmith goods in Velbert; cutlery in Solingen; chemicals in Leverkusen, Frankfurt and Ludwigshafen; jewellery in Pforzheim; surgical instruments in Tuttlingen; cars in Stuttgart, Munich, Ingolstadt, Neckarsulm and Regensburg; machine tools in Stuttgart; pens and pencils in Nuremberg; printing presses in Heidelberg, Würzburg and Offenbach; optical instruments in Wetzlar; and tools in Remscheid.

This list could no doubt be extended to include other examples. Both traditional industries, such as the production of ceramics in the Palatinate, and newer industries, such as environmental technology, which can be found in the Ruhr area, are sometimes concentrated in a particular locality. Clusters also exist in the service sector, such as the so-called health region of Ostwestfalen-Lippe, in the media industry around Cologne, or in the Frankfurt financial sector (Ronneberger 1995). Nevertheless, one should note that even Porter's study does not clearly classify industries or delimit local entities; furthermore, some of the industries he identifies only show a local concentration because of the presence of large firms in the area concerned (e.g., car manufacturing, chemicals and steel production).

Other studies which try to outline the structure and development of spatially concentrated firms on the basis of employment statistics face the same problem. The most impressive so far is that of Helmstädter (1996). This study uses employment statistics and the regional database of the Wissenschaftszentrum Berlin für Sozialforschung. These data relate to the period 1970–94. We have drawn heavily on them for our analysis. The main findings are summarized in Table 4.1. This shows the spatial concentration of firms in travel to work areas (*Arbeitsamtsbezirke*) of (West) Germany. The maximum localization coefficient referred to relates to the situation in 1980, while the Gini coefficients refer to 1980 and 1994. Helmstädter concludes on the basis of his analysis that industrial specialization within local confines is increasing over time in Germany. However, there are some exceptions to this rule, including Stuttgart, which shows the opposite trend in recent years.

Above all, these specialization processes are taking place on the basis of a rather low level of concentration. This finding confirms our thesis that the local clustering of industry in Germany does not on the whole follow any pattern implying local variation in the provision of collective competition goods. Local clustering to secure competitive advantages does not appear to be a dominant strategy for German enterprises. The Gini coefficients in Table 4.1 express the

TABLE 4.1. Spatial Concentration of 50 Industrial Branches, West Germany, 1980–94

Branch of industry[1]	Gini coefficient 1980[2]	Gini coefficient 1994	Maximal localization coefficient[3]	Travel to work areas with highest localization coefficient (Arbeitsantbezirke)
22 Locksmiths, blacksmiths	0.215	0.206	4.623	Brühl, Essen, Recklinghausen
25 Environmental engineering	0.244	0.221	2.977	Bremerhaven, Flensburg, Heide
30 Car repair	0.26	0.228	3.98	Flensburg, Münster, Uelzen
56 Slaughtering, meat processing	0.285	0.311	5.015	Vechta, Flensburg
54 Food production	0.318	0.295	5.654	Stade, Bremerhaven, Verden
26 Machinery industry	0.327	0.322	2.85	Ahlen, Göppingen, Offenbach, Aalen
44 Printing, duplication	0.344	0.31	3.641	Bad Oldesloe, Offenburg, Essen
14 Production of rock, stone, and related mineral products	0.346	0.351	5.246	Mayen, Montabaur
34 Electronics	0.359	0.32	3.204	Nuremberg, Berlin, Soest
57 Drinks manufacturing	0.36	0.398	6.363	Koblenz, Mainz, Mayen
27 Manufacturing of cogwheels and gears	0.381	0.333	7.088	Schweinfurt, Passau, Cologne
12 Processing of man-made materials	0.384	0.375	4.092	Korbach, Ansbach, Mannheim
23 Steel, light metals, and manufacturing of reservoirs, tanks, and other sheet-metal containers	0.424	0.375	7.086	Korbach, Oberhausen, Wesel
35 Precision and instrument engineering	0.433	0.389	5.544	Lübeck, Wetzlar, Göttingen
43 Paper production and processing	0.433	0.45	14.054	Düren, Rastatt, Landau
53 Upholstery	0.437	0.435	8.687	Herford, Nagold, Nienburg
52 Clothing trade, sewing industry	0.438	0.475	8.31	Aschaffenburg, Passau, Herford
37 Manufacturing of hardware, cutlery, tools, and locks	0.441	0.426	7.653	Solingen, Wuppertal, Iserlohn
41 Carpentry products	0.447	0.402	5.639	Detmold, Paderborn, Coburg
42 Other wood processing	0.496	0.464	10.507	Ansbach, Coburg, Korbach

TABLE 4.1. (Continued)

Branch of industry[1]	Gini coefficient 1980[2]	Gini coefficient 1994	Maximal localization coefficient[3]	Travel to work areas with highest localization coefficient (Arbeitsantbezirke)
40 Timber processing	0.563	0.577	7.394	Leer, Detmold, Passau
21 Secondary transformation, treatment, and coating of metals	0.577	0.539	8.297	Iserlohn, Hagen, Solingen
9 Chemicals industry	0.59	0.575	8.856	Ludwigshafen, Recklinghausen, Bergisch-Gladbach, Pfarrkirchen, Frankfurt
19 Foundries	0.595	0.588	8.977	Marburg, Meschede, Brilon, Wetzlar
51 Other textile processing	0.633	0.64	17.504	Balingen, Reutlingen, Rheine
45 Tanning, refining of leather	0.644	0.637	33.802	Offenbach, Bad Kreuznach
28 Car construction	0.664	0.656	10.605	Helmstedt, Emden, Landshut, Ingolstadt, Stuttgart
55 Production of confectionery	0.674	0.681	10.746	Marburg, Aachen, Hanover
13 Rubber and asbestos processing	0.686	0.683	13.096	Korbach, Hanau, Hanover
38 Manufacturing of musical instruments and toys	0.7	0.69	14.808	Coburg, Weissenburg, Ansbach
46 Repair and manufacturing of leather goods	0.709	0.655	70.559	Pirmasens
16 Manufacturing and processing of glass	0.728	0.722	18.61	Weiden, Mainz, Deggendorf
20 Drawing plants and cold-rolling mills	0.754	0.683	19.679	Hamm, Mayen, Paderborn, Soest
18 Production of non-precious metals	0.76	0.763	12.482	Constance, Iserlohn, Goslar
33 Repair and manufacturing of data-processing and office equipment	0.788	0.757	33.023	Wilhelmshaven, Villingen, Paderborn, Augsburg
29 Motorcycle manufacturing	0.793	0.819	26.348	Vechta, Osnabrück, Kiel

		Gini coefficient	Localization coefficient	Localities
15	Whiteware	0.803	24.732	Hof, Weiden, Montabaur, Saarlouis, Coburg
47	Wool processing	0.816	16.672	Wilhelmshaven, Mönchengladbach
24	Wagon building	0.834	30.148	Donauwörth, Braunschweig, Kassel
17	Manufacturing of iron and steel	0.843	17.787	Duisburg, Dortmund, Oberhausen, Saarbrücken
11	Processing of mineral oil	0.856	18.852	Heide, Brühl, Hamburg, Nordhorn
58	Tobacco processing	0.856	14.455	Bremen, Herford, Bad Oldesloe
48	Cotton processing	0.857	23.629	Nordhorn, Rheine
32	Aerospace equipment manufacturing	0.875	11.286	Oldenburg, Bremen, Munich, Wilhelmshaven, Constance
39	Jewellery production	0.885	70.643	Pforzheim, Bad Kreuznach, Kempten
50	Linen processing	0.894	19.48	Ulm, Coesfeld, Fulda
49	Silk processing	0.896	24.717	Krefeld, Trier, Wuppertal
36	Clock-making industry and clock repair	0.906	46.564	Villingen, Rottweil, Pforzheim
10	Production of man-made fibres	0.923	23.98	Aschaffenburg, Bad Hersfeld, Aachen, Hamm, Neumünster
31	Shipbuilding industry	0.932	43.218	Bremerhaven, Kiel, Emden, Leer, Lübeck

Note: [1]Numbers according to the directory of the Bundesanstalt für Arbeit (Federal Institute of Labour).
[2]The Gini coefficients express the degree to which a particular branch is unequally dispersed over localities.
[3]The localization coefficient (in the table referring to the situation in 1980) expresses the degree of specialization of a locality according to employment. It is obtained by dividing employment in a branch in a particular locality by the average employment in this branch.

Source: Helmstädter (1996).

degree to which industries are unequally dispersed over localities. Some branches, like linen processing and clock-making show a relatively high degree of unequal dispersion and concentration. These are traditional or old industrial branches, which had been concentrated before and remain relatively concentrated in few spots. One cannot infer the degree of concentration of particular branches from the total number of employees, given the effects of firm size on the statistics. For instance, while the machinery industry is comparable to the chemicals industry in terms of the total number of employees, the latter seems much more concentrated because of the importance of large firms.

It comes as no surprise that, on the basis of such data, sectors which are dominated by large firms show a high degree of spatial concentration (e.g., chemicals, iron and steel production, car and aircraft manufacturing). In addition, the data show a comparatively high degree of spatial concentration when production depends on specific resources in the area. Examples of this include the oil-processing industry, iron and steel production, and the shipbuilding industry. It is also striking that the rates of spatial concentration appear to be rather low in those sectors that are dominated by small enterprises. This is especially true for sectors where firms are not only small but depend on spatial proximity to their clients (e.g., car repair, parts of the food industry, as well as printing and duplicating businesses). However, some (although not many) sectors show a high degree of concentration despite the small size of the firms concerned. Such concentrated sectors include traditional fields of production, for example, jewellery making, textiles and clock-making, but there has been a tremendous loss of employment in the latter two industries in recent decades. Export-oriented and technology-intensive sectors such as the machinery industry, electronics, precision engineering and optical instruments show a comparably low degree of concentration.[2]

This supports the conclusion that sectorally specialized clusters are the exception rather than the rule in Germany. However, sceptics could reply that the employment statistics used to reach this conclusion are not disaggregated enough with respect to individual economic sectors. Spatial concentration of firms might occur at the sub-sectoral level, and not be well captured by sectoral data. For example, the production of pens and pencils in Nuremberg cannot be captured using these statistics. Unfortunately, it is extremely difficult to disaggregate data sectorally in order to identify the local concentration of firms in Germany. Combining sectorally and locally disaggregated data might allow the identification of individual firms, which would contravene German data protection law.[3] It has therefore not been possible to replicate Helmstädter's work,

---

[2] The machinery industry is concentrated more in Baden-Württemberg, Bavaria and North Rhine Westphalia than in other parts of Germany. Nevertheless, it cannot a priori be inferred that higher sectoral concentration there leads to a different form of governance within these agglomerations, making them comparable to industrial districts.

[3] The problem here is that the spatial concentration of particular sectors and sub-sectors in the manufacturing industry is not comparable across countries; the official German statistics differentiate

which was carried out under special circumstances, for a more recent period. This is one reason why research in Germany is characterized by case studies, which explore the spatial concentration of firms in a particular (sub) sector by taking obvious examples.

This said, there are still reasons to believe that the degree of spatial concentration of sectorally specialized enterprises is lower in Germany than in Italy (Lau 1997). Even the impressive case studies illustrating the sectoral concentration of firms in localities such as Solingen cannot contradict more general findings that German entrepreneurs do not seek spatial proximity in business relations connected with the value chain of their product. The cutlery industry in Solingen, for instance, is long established and historically gained competitive advantages from inter-firm co-operation during the golden age (1870–1914) of flexible specialization in the area (Boch 1997:155). Shared forges were 'a kind of common institution for the whole cutlery district, creating a huge rationalization effect without losing the ability for flexible specialisation which, together with many other forms of co-operation, allowed Solingen successfully to compete with Sheffield, despite the relatively high wages and minimum piece rates' (ibid.: 157).

The whole production system changed towards mass production at a later stage, because of the lack of craft-based skilled labour before and after the Second World War. Boch claims that it was the destruction of the apprenticeship system in the 1920s and the breakdown of the guilds that caused this development. Mass production, although less attractive than the craft-based production system, was pursued because skills were dying out. It is interesting to note that this development went hand in hand with the construction of the new general apprenticeship system, out of which the much-praised model of the dual system later evolved, a model that provided competitive advantages in other branches such as machinery. However, it remains doubtful whether this development can adequately be described as a move from flexible specialization to diversified quality production. The distinction between the two paradigms no longer seems to be as clear as it may have been in the past.

It is clear that local economies are not only shaped by firms, and a high concentration of sectorally specialized firms in a particular area may be nothing more than a cluster of firms, which is not a priori the same as a local economy. According to the definition in the beginning of this chapter, local subcultures may underpin co-operation between firms, while political institutions and associations (which may themselves be locally based) may also contribute to co-operation between firms in an area as well as providing collective goods for them. In such instances, one has to take account of relevant public actors in order to understand the sources of competitive advantages for local economies. In Germany, the most important public actors are often the Landesregierung and the

either between sectors or regions, but there is no combination of the two, making the Italian approach to identifying industrial districts (Burroni and Trigilia, this volume) impossible.

Landeswirtschaftsministerium (the government and Ministry of Economics of the *Land*, respectively). In general, public actors are important in German economies, and *Länder* authorities are particularly relevant because of the federalist political system (Engel 1993; Grote 1997).

This helps to explain why German firms can, to a certain extent, neglect spatial proximity. It only makes sense for specialized firms to cluster together if this leads to competitive advantage. We argue that the German economy is provided homogeneously with collective competition goods via its political and associational institutions. To the extent that this is so, firms can expect no unique competitive advantage from local differences in institutions that would lead them to set up in one place rather than another. Many important collective goods, such as training and technology transfer, are provided across the country with no extraordinary differences between *Länder*. If political and associational institutions provide these goods, homogeneous performance capability must therefore be expected of them.

We cannot deny that the southern *Länder* appear to perform better economically than the northern ones (Friedrichs, Häußermann and Siebel 1986). But, for example, Baden-Württemberg, unlike North Rhine Westphalia, does not have a declining old industrial sector. Research has shown that, if one were to distinguish between the Ruhr area and the rest of the *Land*, the performance of the industrial sector of North Rhine Westphalia would not deviate significantly from the average performance of the industrial sector as a whole (Heinze, Voelzkow, and Hilbert 1992:30ff.). Here, differences in economic performance can be explained by economic geography. The existence of natural resources, especially coal, in northern Germany gave these areas a competitive advantage during the first phase of industrialization. In contrast, Stuttgart, which is now one of Germany's major industrial cities, did not have such resources, and was not easily accessible in terms of transport. While Württemberg then relied strongly on agriculture, it later industrialized through high skill manufacturing, its only possible route to success given its dearth of natural resources: in particular it specialized in machinery, electronics and car production.

We do not wish to imply by using the *Land* as our primary level of analysis that the *Länder* are culturally determined entities. Their creation resulted from the federal constitution of the German political system (Rudzio 1996), and *Länder* governments are key actors developing support strategies for the economy. However, it would be short-sighted to claim that, since federalism empowers German sub-national actors *vis-à-vis* the federal government more than, say, Italian regions *vis-à-vis* their central state authorities, German actors face totally different institutional environments and political frameworks for economic action. The co-operative structure of German federalism leaves a great deal of executive power at the level of the *Land*, whereas Art. 70 of the Basic Law concedes only restricted legislative power to the *Länder* authorities alone (Ismayr 1997). Moreover, in Art. 91a of the Basic Law, systematic (financial) aid by the federal government was agreed even in areas which had originally been the responsibility of the *Land* alone. Differences in the economic performance of the *Länder* after the Second World War prompted federal government financial intervention better to equalize living conditions. This led to the *Gemeinschafts-aufgabe*, which defines the support of regional economic structures as a joint task to be assumed by the federal and the *Land* authorities (Hoppe and Voelzkow 1999). As a result of this, many projects that are carried out by regional or local institutions are initiated by the federal government and are co-financed by the federal level. The production of collective goods by public institutions therefore is a joint task, which can only be understood if the principle of co-operative federalism is taken into account (Scharpf, Reissert, and Schnabel 1976; Kilper and Lhotta 1995).

We shall now take three *Länder*: Lower Saxony, North Rhine Westphalia and Baden-Württemberg, examining whether local economies exist in them and how political institutions support innovation and restructuring processes. These three cases present comparable industrial activities, which is not to say that one would find a different industrial order in other *Länder*.

Between Agriculture and Industry: Enterprises in Lower Saxony[4]

With about 8 million inhabitants at the end of 1996, Lower Saxony has a territory of 47,612.24 sq. km. It is characterized by a large number of SMEs employing almost 80 per cent of all workers subject to compulsory insurance (*sozialversicherungspflichtig Beschäftigte*). Nevertheless, large firms are also based there, including Volkswagen in Wolfsburg, Preussag and others. Policy initiatives in Lower Saxony have often been aimed at structural change, because of the importance of declining sectors such as mining and shipbuilding (Krafft and Ullrich 1993).

The most important sector for employment is the car industry, which provides more than 100,000 jobs in the *Land* if the production of parts and components is included. Volkswagen is important, but supplier firms also provide many jobs. It is well known that Volkswagen pursued internationalization long before it became important for companies such as Mercedes-Benz. As a result, supplier firms in the region had the same problems as many others in the 1990s in struggling to adapt to international standards and the challenges of modern supply chain management, so as to become system partners and survive as global suppliers. For example, Heidemann Automobiltechnik in Einbeck faced a crisis as early as 1986, but seems to have recovered in the 1990s. Between 1993 and 1997, the firm's sales increased by 96 per cent, reaching DM 134 million. The financial crisis was overcome by an influx of venture capital from abroad,

---

[4] Some of the information on the development of firms and statistics on employment in Lower Saxony and the presentation of the institutional infrastructure is taken from a report by the Niedersächsisches Ministerium für Wirtschaft, Technologie und Verkehr, February 1998. Employment figures given for Lower Saxony always refer to the average for 1997.

especially from Great Britain, while production was concentrated in car parts. The final element in the firm's success was its restructuring to become an international system partner with plants in Spain and probably soon in Mexico and Brazil. This restructuring was supported by the *Land* government and its Department of Economics. In this context, one should note that Lower Saxony policies attracted more new investors from abroad in the 1990s than before, with an increase in foreign direct investment in Lower Saxony of more than 50 per cent between 1991 and 1995. The *Land* government actively helps to shape the conditions for innovation and organizational adaptation: the region does not differ from the more often cited case of Baden-Württemberg in its resolve to create regional support networks.

Other important sectors in Lower Saxony include rubber and plastics (more than 40,000 workers), the machinery industry (in which more than 50,000 people are employed), chemicals (in which firms employ about 25,000 workers) and paper and publishing (accounting for some 35,000 employees). One of the best-known firms in rubber and plastics, Continental, is another example of regional policy intervention. In this case, the *Land* government helped the firm to remain independent via an investor consortium. However, in general, Lower Saxony is clearly one of those *Länder* that have found it difficult to catch up with industrial production. Its middle and northern regions, in particular, are dominated by agriculture. Research and development (R&D) for industrial production must be promoted more than they have been in the past, and the 1990s have seen public actors taking a more active role in this (Knodt 1998). Incentives to help specialized firms survive on the international market face the problem that some sectors, such as the machinery and packaging industry, are too oriented towards traditional (agricultural) production (Lompe 1996). Firms in related industries such as precision engineering could not be rescued, despite government intervention. Some local economies therefore experienced a permanent and lasting decline involving de-industrialization. Lompe claims that traditional industries were not adequately sustained, which is one reason why the car industry came to dominate in the south-east part of Lower Saxony (ibid.: 93).

Before turning to this region, it may be helpful to draw attention to local economies in Lower Saxony identified in Table 4.1. A number of localities with a high localization coefficient can be seen: for example, Nordhorn for the manufacture of oil and cotton, Vechta for meat, Emden for the car and shipbuilding industries, Leer for wood, Hanover for rubber and plastics. The high localization coefficient of rubber and plastics in Hanover is partly due to the presence of Continental and other large firms, which applies to many other localities too, for example, in the chemicals industry or car production.

The data confirm the more general impression that Lower Saxony is dominated by traditional industries, as well as the argument that de-industrialization continues to increase over time in already de-industrialized localities, such as Hanover, where the specialization of particular industrial branches is already low. The opposite seems to be true for industrialized centres whose degree of industrial specialization is already high. While in both these types of local economy employment in the respective industrial branches decreases in absolute terms, it increases in more peripheral regions, where industrial specialization is growing at the same time.

South-East Lower Saxony: An Environment for Growth in Local Economies? The literature on Lower Saxony, unlike that for Baden-Württemberg or North Rhine Westphalia, has not produced very many examples of local economies, despite employing both regional policy perspectives and network analysis. (For a network analysis, see Grote 1998).

Does this mean that Baden-Württemberg was able to arrange a support environment that was worth studying, while Lower Saxony cannot claim to have established similar forms of co-operation among social and economic actors? According to Bruch-Krumbein, Hellmer and Krumbein (1997), many regions in Germany can be seen as *Normalregionen* (normal regions), which are characterized by a heterogeneous industrial landscape and because of this do not differ very much from each other regarding sectoral specialization and spatial concentration. Nevertheless, firms in normal regions have developed distinct strategies for innovation, regional and national co-operation, and so on. From this perspective, local economic dynamism results not from networked co-operation, but rather from bilateral arrangements where the co-operation of firms is not especially linked to their immediate localities. While networks may emerge in social institutions that aim to support industry, economic actors are not very involved in these networks. The argument that the region is increasing in importance as a level of decision-making is seen as wishful thinking (Bruch-Krumbein, Hellmer and Krumbein 1997; Hellmer *et al.* 1999). From our perspective, this argument rightly points to the importance of nation-wide co-operation between firms and institutions, but fails to acknowledge that this form of co-operation is part of the specific variant by which existing local economies are provided with collective competition goods in Germany.

The eastern part of Lower Saxony is a good example of this. As a region famous for car manufacturing, it is enclosed by the industrial triangle consisting of Wolfsburg, Salzgitter and Peine, as well as the surrounding areas Helmstedt, Wolfenbüttel and Gifhorn. The data show that Helmstedt is one of the German industrial cities with the greatest localization coefficient for car manufacturing, while Braunschweig, also located in this region, has a comparable position in railway wagon building. The whole east of Lower Saxony consists of local economies specialized in particular niches of cars and transport business. Specialization is again partly due to large firms such as Volkswagen. More than 30 per cent of the region's added value was generated in the car industry at the beginning of the 1990s, while one in four employees works in a firm directly belonging to that branch (Lompe and Blöcker 1997:275).

Local economies in this region differ from those in North Rhine Westphalia or Baden-Württemberg in that there are no inter-sectoral links between this branch and the machinery industry. The transport business (including rail transport) is the dominant regional production system, but as such it remains relatively isolated. However, a development plan has been formulated to strengthen the comparative advantage of the industry in the local economies of this region, through the concept of the transport competence region (*Verkehrskompetenzregion*). The idea is that the existing industry should pursue R&D beyond product improvement, and achieve broader competence in issues generally connected with modern transport solutions. This includes ecological problems, such as recycling strategies and processes for cars, but it is not limited to technical and material advances. The region seeks more generally to finance and implement projects on alternative transportation technologies and the social dimension of transport. This is split into five categories: 1. motor, car and security technology, 2. new material, 3. car recycling, 4. traffic and transport management, and 5. concepts for (public) transport and logistics (Lompe 1996). While it is the *Land* government that initiates projects, firms such as Volkswagen also co-operate with institutions of higher education (e.g., polytechnics) to realize projects such as the eco car. Although many of these activities started in the 1990s, and are emblematic of the need for change in local economies, they still highlight the principal actors strengthening local economies in Germany. These are: large firms; the *Land* government; organizations such as IG-Metall (the metalworkers union, which helped to develop the concept in collaboration with a social science research group); and the classical institutions of R&D or higher education. Preussag and Volkswagen co-founded the regional development agency 'Reson', which helped attract public actors to become involved too. Researchers who have interviewed the actors involved in implementation find that although bottom-up initiatives were not totally irrelevant in the transport competence region project, their success largely depended on their compatibility with the official goals of the *Land* Ministry of Economics and environmental politics.

North Rhine Westphalia: Old Declining Industries and New Local Dynamism[5]

North Rhine Westphalia covers an area of 34,077.70 sq. km., and is densely populated, with more than 17 million inhabitants in 1996, more than twice as many as Lower Saxony (Statistisches Bundesamt 1998). The most important economic sectors are machinery, chemicals, again cars, and food. Traditionally, the *Land* was an important steel and mining region, but as in Lower Saxony, this sector has been hit by a structural crisis that led to decline, especially in the Ruhr area. A major challenge for the political authorities has been to encourage necessary structural changes in the former coal and steel areas. Businesses in this industry are heavily subsidized, to help them survive international competition.

---

[5] The statistical material is taken from the NRW Lexikon available at http://www.nrw.de.

The Federal government and the respective *Länder* are jointly responsible for providing these monies, which amounted to DM 7.5 billion for mining in 1996 alone. Because this state aid is only a short-term solution to the problems of these industries, subsidies will be cut in the future. The *Land* government has increasingly argued that any long-run solution to restructuring must involve active support for SMEs and government-led stimulation of new entrepreneurial activities in other sectors. The decline of coal and steel businesses has already caused a tremendous loss of jobs; of 180,000 jobs in the mining industry in North Rhine Westphalia in 1980, there were only 102,000 in 1994. The loss has been even more dramatic in steel: while about 200,000 people were still employed in this sector in 1980, this had fallen to as few as 85,000 by 1994.

It is not only these older industries that have undergone decline. The machinery industry, the largest source of employment in the *Land*, also faced serious trouble in the 1990s. This crisis was the result of problems in export markets stemming from disadvantageous rates of exchange and weakness in demand for capital goods. North Rhine Westphalia is strongly dependent on the machinery industry and was badly hit; almost 30 per cent of national turnover in this industry is generated in North Rhine Westphalia, and about 25 per cent of total German employment in it is in the region. With more than 240,000 jobs, the industry still dominates the industrial structure of the *Land*. Table 4.1 shows that Ahlen is the locality with the highest localization coefficient for the machinery industry in this *Land*, but it also reveals that the maximum localization coefficient for the machinery industry in general is relatively low.

While it comes as no surprise that the machinery industry is dominated by small firms (41.1 per cent) with fewer than 50 employees, it is striking that they provide no more than 8.8 per cent of all jobs in the *Land*. Only 2 per cent of all these firms are large companies (more than 1,000 employees), but they account for 23.1 per cent of all the jobs in the industry in North Rhine Westphalia.[6] Six of the large machinery plants belong to the ten largest firms in Germany: Thyssen AG in Düsseldorf, Mannesmann AG in Düsseldorf, Friedrich Krupp AG in Essen, Deutsche Babcock AG in Oberhausen, Thysssen Industrie AG in Essen and Klöckner Werke in Duisburg. Vertical co-operation between such firms, smaller machinery firms and enterprises in the mining and machinery industries has been a common means to collective good provision in the past. However, the specialization of these firms is often a problem: many machinery firms are linked to the coal and mining sector, and are currently threatened by declining demand, even when they are world technological leaders in their niches. Changes in specialization are being actively supported by programmes implemented by the *Land* government (Heinze, Voelzkow and Hilbert 1992).

The supply of collective goods through vertical co-operation can also be seen as one of the outstanding patterns in the many firms that provide systems and parts for the large car producers in North Rhine Westphalia: Ford in Cologne,

---

[6] The numbers given refer to September 1994; see Neitzel and Schauerte (1998).

Opel in Bochum and Mercedes-Benz in Düsseldorf. There are 240,000 workers employed in this branch (if the supply industry is also taken into account). About 40,000 employees work for the large car firms. Again, there is regional concentration. For instance, the manufacturing of metal parts for the car industry is concentrated in southern cities in the Ruhr area, while glass and tyres are produced in the south-western area near Aachen. Car electronics are made in Dortmund, Essen, Wuppertal, Cologne and the Märkischer Kreis, and finally lighting engineering and metal-forming machines are produced in the more north-eastern cities. The clustering of these firms can again be explained by the presence of flagship enterprises.

The economic structure of North Rhine Westphalia is heterogeneous, with, for example, a furniture industry, concentrated in northern and eastern Westphalia. Some of these industries provide evidence that local clustering is branch dependent, and that the more artisan (*handwerklich*) production becomes, the more there are opportunities for small enterprises to survive and to co-operate horizontally. It cannot be denied that the underlying social structure of localities, and the willingness (often absent in Germany) of individuals to set up their own businesses, affect small production units. However, it seems to be administratively easier for public actors to shape a local economy according to the needs of the powerful few in the locality instead of underpinning co-operation in entrepreneurial networks whose interests may be rather atomistic. In 1995, the ten largest firms were Bayer in Leverkusen (chemicals industry), RWE in Essen (public utilities, construction), Thyssen in Duisburg (plants, steel), Veba in Düsseldorf (energy, trade), Mannesmann in Düsseldorf (capital equipment), Ruhrkohle in Essen (mining), Krupp-Hoesch in Essen (machines, plants, steel), Ford in Cologne (car industry), Henkel in Düsseldorf (chemicals industry) and Deutsche Babcock in Oberhausen (plant industry) (see http://www.idan.org/german/p01/region/indcomp.htm). Nevertheless, other forms of co-operation, including informal ones, are perhaps easier to establish in new industries, such as the media, where traditional forms did not exist.

Adjusting Informal Networks to Managed Capitalism: The Media Industry in Cologne. The city of Cologne is situated in the Rhineland and is famous for its media sector. The city council decided in the 1980s to support this sector through a number of infrastructural initiatives. Today, almost 50 per cent of all businesses connected to this flourishing industry in North Rhine Westphalia are located in Cologne. One in every ten jobs in the city is related to the media branch, and about 45,000 people work for radio stations, television companies, and so on. Firms in this sector are highly specialized. They often work for large broadcasting companies that spend money on short-term projects. Employees therefore very often experience unstable market conditions in which contracts are short term, unless a new product is to be evaluated, produced or designed. According to a report by the Deutsches Institut für Wirtschaftsforschung (DIW; German Institute of Economic Research), the number of media firms in Cologne increased by approximately 24.2 per cent between 1992 and 1996, while turnover in the same period increased by approximately 18.2 per cent. (See http://www.BerliNews.de/archiv/135.shtml.)

The music branch provides much of the impetus for this. Cologne is well known for its music production, attracting famous choirs and orchestras, and bands who try to start their careers in the local club scene, which supports various niches in popular and electronic music. EMI Electrola and other labels located in Cologne benefit from this diversity. While it was initially the WDR orchestra and other classical music institutions that made music an important part of the local economy, a very lively youth culture has allowed music channels such as VIVA and VIVA2 to be established. Cologne is trying to create an infrastructure to support both these cultures. It has built a new concert hall where performances are recorded by the WDR, which is one of the largest broadcasting companies and belongs to the many stations that produce programmes for the ARD, one of two state-run television channels in Germany. It also set up the Media Park, where the new music channels, the local radio station and service firms are located. The WDR leads in promoting the media branch in general; it has the status of a public institution, runs five radio channels and one television channel. The WDR alone employs 4,600 people in Cologne, while the Deutsche Welle has 1,500 employees. Smaller broadcasting companies include Deutschland Radio, Radio Köln, RPR and VOX. RTL, which has been successful since the liberalization of the television market and which recently launched its second television channel, is also based in Cologne.

There is no universal skills profile for employees in the branch. The smaller service companies very often only ask for skills in data processing, but do not hire experts; instead they take on younger people whose background is the artificially created youth culture of the time, but not the specific subculture of the town or the region. Many jobs may be taken by students who hear about them in the cafeteria at Cologne University. This is one of the largest universities in Germany, and it seems to create its own labour market. People whose university qualification gives them poor job prospects at least have the opportunity of a small income from Cologne's media firms. Conversely, many of these firms would not be able to exist without this source of cheap labour. Many students who have passed their final examinations but have not found a job other than in the media branch often enrol again *pro forma* to retain the benefits of the student status.

This sort of transfer of human resources, which is untypical for Germany and occurs because the media sector is relatively unregulated, would be impossible in a traditional industrial sector with dual system training. Nevertheless, students can now obtain official qualifications for the media industry in Cologne, and the dual system has begun to adopt occupational profiles for this branch. Whether these initial attempts to adapt an unregulated but growing sector to the norms of managed capitalism will eliminate or further strengthen the competitive advantage of local economies such as Cologne remains to be seen.

Local Economies in Baden-Württemberg: Still an Example of Flexible Specialization?

Baden-Württemberg is intermediate between Lower Saxony and North Rhine Westphalia in population, with 10 million inhabitants, and covers an area of 35,751.76 sq. km. It has been prominent on account of its extraordinary economic performance in the 1980s. This changed dramatically in the 1990s, though the *Land* still has a rate of unemployment lower than the national average. This suggests that the performance of the economy in the 1990s was not altogether disastrous, though there has been relative decline in certain sectors. The *Land* government has responded through a number of initiatives, including the Future Commission Economy 2000, which has drawn up a report on the reasons for the recent economic decline. Among the major issues discussed in this report are the already familiar weaknesses resulting from specialization in export-dependent industries such as machinery, which dominates eight of the twelve regions of the *Land*. Stuttgart, Schwarzwald-Baar-Heuberg, Mittlerer Oberrhein and Hochrhein-Bodensee are the only regions where the machinery industry is not the most important economic sector. (Statistical information is available at http://www.business.germany-southwest.de.) This is not to say that the mechanical engineering sector is weak even in these regions; it is the third most important industry in three of them, and the second most important in one. About 293,000 workers were employed in the machinery industry in Baden-Württemberg in 1991, but by 1994 this figure had declined by 50,000, prompting alarm (Statistisches Landesamt 1994).

The most economically prominent region is Stuttgart; which is interestingly one of the exceptional regions in which the machinery industry ranks after the car and electronics industries. Twenty of the 50 largest enterprises are located in the Stuttgart area, including large car firms such as DaimlerChrysler (cf. Table 4.1). The presence of these firms explains how cluster-like concentrations of enterprises shape the local economic structure in the car and machinery industries. The region's many well-known successful firms supplying components to the car industry are not necessarily SMEs. Indeed many of them are growing as the large car firms increasingly reduce their process range in manufacturing. More than 60,000 people work in the supply business, and this part of the car industry alone has an annual turnover of more than DM 10 billion. Well-known supplier firms include Behr, Bosch, Eberspächer, Knecht and Mahle. Below we discuss the problems that increasing competition on international markets in the 1990s caused for suppliers in the car industry and for this region.

Bosch, Daimler, Maybach and other important engineers and inventors of the late nineteenth and early twentieth century had a decisive impact on the (somewhat late) industrialization of Stuttgart and Württemberg, which lessened its earlier heavy reliance on agriculture. The particular mixture of inventions in the field of mechanical engineering, electronics and later car production helped maintain a relatively integrated economy with a high degree of inter-firm co-operation. This again raises the question of the importance of large firms. The first machinery firm in Stuttgart was founded in the mid-nineteenth century, at a time when only small and medium-sized production units were viable. However, it is important to note that industrial development as a whole took much longer in Württemberg than in other kingdoms and (later) parts of the Reich. The literature often refers to these early days, when Württemberg stood at the threshold of industrialization, but the relevance of large firms was already apparent by 1925, when, despite the strong tradition of small production units, more than 50 per cent of industrial employment was in large firms (with more than 1,000 employees (Sauer 1991)).

Political decisions taken long before, such as Ferdinand Steinbeis's initiative to develop adequate training institutions, no doubt improved the framework underpinning regional growth, but did not create the basis for an *exceptional* economy. The national dual system of training has its roots in the achievements of Steinbeis and others responsible for Württemberg's leading role in training. However, this system started to become nationally regulated during the Weimar era, with the 1925 decision of the German Committee for Technical Education to develop a uniform national regulatory instrument for apprenticeship training which was partially implemented in 1935 and 1938 (CEDEFOP 1995:34). Vocational training in all branches became fully regulated with the Vocational Training Act in 1969. At the end of the first quarter of the twentieth century, the majority of training workshops were in metalworking, Stuttgart's growth sector. While Württemberg was indeed a model region, the process of adjustment to this model started long before the institutions of German federalism began to implement the principle of homogeneity of living conditions.

Observers such as Gary Herrigel would probably reply that we are speaking of the establishment of a new industrial order and the abandonment of the old one as one and the same thing, while in reality they continued to co-exist (Herrigel 1996b). While we would accept that, for instance, associations like the Verein Deutscher Ingenieure (VDI) remain as relics of an earlier epoch, these organizations have adapted themselves to the rules of a national governance system for collective goods provision. This national system now obtains despite previous disparities between German territories, and their different economic specializations and performances. It is notable that the empirical data show higher specialization in old and traditional branches, many of which came into being before there was a nationally regulated system of collective goods provision. But today, as the history of Solingen for instance illustrates, these historically rooted local economies too are structured by the national system of collective goods provision, not always to their advantage.

The region that ranks directly after Stuttgart in terms of the density of its industrial activity is Schwarzwald-Baar-Heuberg, where about 20,000 enterprises are officially registered. While the machinery industry is not dominant in this part of Baden-Württemberg, it is still very important. Besides electronics, other major branches include clock-making and medical instruments. Another unusual area in

Baden-Württemberg is Hochrhein-Bodensee, where the textile industry dominates. This region is very closely linked to Swiss business and culture, with many Swiss subsidiaries.

Apart from these regions and Mittlerer Oberrhein, where electronics is the most important branch, all the others are strongest in mechanical engineering. Employment in this industry accounts for as much as 25 per cent of industrial employment in some regions. This high concentration of businesses in one branch throughout the whole *Land* explains why many social scientists interested in industrial districts have been attracted to Baden-Württemberg. The industrial district model was the most popular explanation for the *Land*'s comparative advantage in the 1980s, and was congruent with the official vision promulgated by Chief Minister Lothar Späth, of a consensus society, where state, employers and employees joined forces. This image of the model region was closely linked to the goal of encouraging intensive investment on the part of the *Land* and principal economic actors to create a knowledge base in high-technology production (Knodt 1998).

The eventual reality looked rather different from these rosy visions, as was accurately predicted at the end of the 1980s by a study commissioned by IG Metall in Stuttgart on the Baden-Württemberg economy in the coming decade (Richter 1987). This predicted the crisis of the 1990s with uncanny precision, but the decline was not perceived as a real trend, because of the initial boost which unification provided to Stuttgart's industry. The recession became visible in 1992–93, when domestic demand failed to be sustained. The major problem seemed to be the dependence of the economy on three branches, prompting various initiatives to increase diversity by attracting media firms, and so on. There has also been considerable interest in environmental technology, which provides more than 100,000 jobs in the *Land*, while biotechnology received support in the 1990s and is now particularly strong in the Rhein-Neckar region around Heidelberg, Mannheim and Ludwigshafen.

Can Stuttgart Be Viewed as a Local Economy in the Orthodox Sense? Stuttgart has already been mentioned as one of the major industrial cities in Germany, and the characteristics of the Baden-Württemberg economy have frequently been illustrated using the city as an example for the spatial concentration of three branches. However, one can easily show that these branches also dominate elsewhere in the *Land*, so that the economic cluster is not specific to Stuttgart. Nevertheless, one can ask whether, in addition to the spatial concentration of specialized firms, community structures and decentralized support systems create local economic structures that provide competitive advantages to Stuttgart in comparison to other German cities. Baden-Württemberg is probably the closest example in Germany to the industrial district model, and it is tempting to point to the well-developed educational infrastructure, the innovative technology transfer institutions and so on to draw a picture of a self-sustaining and well-embedded economy. This view can be rejected out of hand for the large firms, but can it be rejected for the *Mittelstand* and the small firms of the machinery industry? Here, one has to refer to Herrigel's fascinating and extensive study (1996b), which claims that an industrial order exists in Germany that is distinct from the large firm model.

We argue against this view (to which we return in the next section) and claim that the local economies identified and described in the first section are not characterized by the decentralized provision of collective goods, but are (in most cases) sustained by large firms and the national regulations and institutions of managed capitalism. We thus strongly emphasize the existence of local econ-omies in Germany, not as deviant forms of economic or social interaction, but as locally concentrated and specialized industries which are patterned by the ways in which collective goods are provided in Germany. Where this is not yet the case, as in Cologne, adjustment processes are well in train. Stuttgart is no exception to this; it shows a high degree of concentration, especially in the car industry, but on the whole it has not generated different forms of collective goods provision than other local economies in Germany.

However, all this leads us to a question we have not yet answered, that of the differences between the paradigmatic industrial district or local economy, and what we find in Germany. To answer this, one has to explore the governance of local economies in more detail. Because of the emphasis on comparisons between Baden-Württemberg and other regions in the literature, we will begin by looking at the orthodox literature and will necessarily restrict our analysis to this part of the German economy.

The Governance of Local Economies in Germany

There has been extensive debate on how local economies in Germany (to the extent that they exist) have been institutionally structured (Streeck 1991:22). Two competing concepts have been applied to explain prevailing production methods and their institutional governance. The first of these concepts is flexible specialization, while the other has been termed diversified quality production (DQP) and reflects the German experience, emphasizing the relevance of formal institutions as opposed to what has been called a softer institutional variant of governance (ibid.).

Diversified quality production was positioned between flexible specialization and mass production, because it was thought to contain elements of both: large-scale production on the one hand and quality competitive, flexible and customer-specific production on the other. This mixture of the two concepts implied a different perspective on historical trajectories to that originally associated with flexible specialization. According to the perspective of DQP, production systems could not switch from mass production to flexible specialization in the sense of a linear historical development. Instead, DQP was seen as an option for growing craft-based systems and mass production systems that aimed to gain competitive advantages via quality rather than price. The German experience of large-scale quality production meant a stress on firm hierarchy in this concept. However, the difference between flexible specialization and DQP is now blurred, because hierarchy and formal institutions are oriented towards local economic governance and also are important in flexibly organized, craft-based local economies. Flexible specialization can therefore no longer be regarded as the soft variant of economic governance. In addition, the advocates of the flexible specialization school have stressed that history opens up a variety of possibilities for economic actors. It provides many interesting examples of how local production systems shape inter-firm co-operation and production methods (Sabel and Zeitlin 1997a), and the concept does not imply any linear historical development (Hirst and Zeitlin 1997).

Nevertheless, these two schools were once considered as rival interpretations of the same phenomenon, and both sides used the local economies of Baden-Württemberg to support their hypotheses. For the advocates of the flexible specialization school, Baden-Württemberg possessed numerous flexible industrial districts:

In West Germany, industrial districts in the Land of Baden-Württemberg are flourishing in textiles, garments, textile machine tools, and automobile components. The metalworking firms there are doing substantially better than similar firms in northern Länder that dominated the national economy during the heyday of mass production. (Sabel 1989:22)

Baden-Württemberg was thus seen as a model of successful local development for small business-based local economies. (See Herrigel 1989, 1993a and b, 1994; Maier 1989; Sabel 1989; Sabel, Herrigel, Deeg, and Kazis 1989; Cooke and Morgan 1990, 1994b; Semlinger 1993, 1996; and, taking a critical stance, Heidenreich 1996; and Heidenreich and Kraus 1998.) The keys to success were seen in four characteristics of the production system: 1. specialized firms had been flexibly organized and made use of a highly skilled workforce; 2. firms created networks in which they could share the risk of development and the particular knowledge of each collaborator of products in their niche; 3. firms were supported by services from external providers, such as associations fostering this kind of collaboration; 4. government helped to meet the demand for infrastructural provision, in particular with regard to innovation.

Proponents of DQP also saw Baden-Württemberg as an illustration of their arguments (Streeck 1991:26). Both schools agreed, *contra* neo-classical economics, that the success of the *Land* could partly be attributed to its institutional support infrastructure.

We too consider institutional support to be indispensable to local economies competing in high-quality market segments, and will therefore outline the institutional particularities of Baden-Württemberg. However, we postulate that the economy in Baden-Württemberg (and in Germany in general) is organized quite differently from the model of an institutionally decentralized industrial district, because regional or national innovation regimes are more important than decentralized support institutions. Herrigel has claimed that there are two distinct industrial orders in Baden-Württemberg, namely the decentralized one and that of large firms: '[a]n industrial order is not a governance mechanism, such as market or hierarchy; it is the social world within which these and other governance mechanisms are utilized' (Herrigel 1993a:228). But we consider these worlds to be quite interconnected and similar: the same system for collective goods provision, which was established in Germany after the War, is used in both. And in this sense, the historical development of social institutions has clearly made the formerly existing social and economic diversity of German territories irrelevant.

Herrigel's discussion of the difference between these worlds refers to the industrial district model, but the governance approach makes it clear that Baden-Württemberg operates according to a quite different form of social order (Voelzkow 1999). Further empirical evidence is obviously required, especially for the operation of SMEs, but there have been other accounts also critical of Herrigel (Braczyk, Schienstock, and Steffensen 1996:33ff. and 43ff.).

Recent studies of the structure and development of local economies in the *Land* can be used to outline these differences. The local economy we refer to is primarily Stuttgart; however, the literature presents Baden-Württemberg as the level of reference following the same logic that we used in the first section of this chapter.

Community

The idea that community can be a form of governance suggests that a particular kind of social order creates business networks quite different from simple market relationships, which may operate as business communities on the basis of trust and solidarity. They can turn the disadvantages of small firms into advantages, fostering flexible local production systems. Thus close relations between participating firms are the basis of the new industrial districts.

The level and importance of co-operation in Baden-Württemberg appears quite different from this. Previous research has not succeeded in identifying comparable forms of co-operative relations between small and medium-sized enterprises. Where horizontal co-operation between firms has succeeded, it has typically been with some institutional backing. Cooke and Morgan (1998) cite a keyboard manufacturer from Weingarten who sought technological improvements, and asked a competitor to collaborate in the required innovation. When they finally succeeded, a network of firms followed their example. However, the authors concede that the associative mechanism here was that the chief executive of the lead firm was at the time *Mittelstand* representative on the board of the Steinbeis Foundation (ibid.: 105).

Another example that is frequently referred to in the literature is the Committee of Suppliers or AKZ partnership (ibid.; Semlinger 1993). The AKZ can be described as a loose network for horizontal collaboration and system integration, consisting of about 20 SMEs. The participating firms hope thus to gain a competitive advantage over other companies that concentrate on producing components. However, such networking is atypical among SMEs in Baden-Württemberg and has been problematic even within the AKZ. Many entrepreneurs fear that co-operation would allow their competitors to take advantage of their well-protected know-how. Regional associations have been given more authority in the 1990s, and it will be interesting to see whether they are more successful in encouraging horizontal co-operation. One recent initiative has involved co-operation between car industry suppliers (discussed in more detail below). Institutional support seems to be usually necessary for horizontal co-operation: it is becoming increasingly important, so the ability of regional institutions to foster it will be crucial to regional economic success in the future.

Corporate Hierarchy

Small and medium-sized enterprises (the *Mittelstand*) are of great importance for the local economy of Stuttgart and other production systems in Baden-Würt-temberg. Nevertheless, small firms with fewer than 20 employees are less significant for the *Land* in general. If we compare the share of employment accounted for by such firms with Emilia-Romagna, for instance, it becomes clear that firm hierarchy is very significant for local economies in Germany and thus also for collective good production. According to data compiled by Heidenreich (1996:406), 42 per cent of the workforce was employed by small firms (fewer than 20 employees) in Emilia-Romagna (in 1991). In contrast, only 15 per cent of the workforce was employed by enterprises with fewer than 20 employees in Baden-Württemberg (in 1987). Workers in firms with more than 500 employees accounted for 47.5 per cent of the workforce in Baden-Württemberg (in 1992). We have already mentioned some of the large companies in Baden-Württemberg, in particular in Stuttgart, including the large car firms such as DaimlerChrysler. Other well-known names include Bosch, IBM, Alcatel SEL, Hewlett Packard and Sony. In contrast to Emilia-Romagna, their importance is quite obvious (DiGiovanna 1996:378), and '[s]ince the sectoral composition of industry is different, large firms play a greater role in Baden-Württemberg' (Schmitz 1992: 115). The degree of vertical integration is very high, regardless of firm size.

Consequently, firms' collective competition good requirements in Stuttgart are not those of an economy based on a network of firms. In Stuttgart, where large firms dominate the local economy, they can be provided in-house. DaimlerChrysler, for instance, has invested DM 1.3 billion in its centre for R&D; about 10,000 workers and engineers are to be employed there (*VDI nachrichten*, no. 40 (October 1998), p. 27).

The centre is designed to overcome the problems of conventional organizational structures, which hindered co-operation on R&D between different groups. The product is no longer made by craftsmen at the development stage, but is directly created by production lines according to the principles of mass production. Despite a trend of the 1990s towards reducing in-house production and shifting responsibilities to system partners, this concentration of R&D work in two places illustrates the enormous extent to which competition goods such as R&D are produced in-house in a large company such as DaimlerChrysler. The same is true of training. In addition to regular apprentice training, the firm has a corporate university to teach management skills.

A similar approach can be found in firms in the machinery industry. Machinery firms in Stuttgart acting in a global environment run their own training academy, and many other firms also have the necessary resources to produce competition goods in-house. Workers looking for further training options may participate in seminars offered by these larger companies. However, competition goods remain private if there is no interaction between actors to transform them into collective goods. This leads us to the significance of the market.

The Market

When examining collective competition good provision to SMEs, one should note that in Baden-Württemberg large producers often dictate the terms of the subcontracting agreement. In addition, they often insist that their supplier adopt new technology or production methods (DiGiovanna 1996:379). Despite the large number of small and medium-sized enterprises, they are often little more than subordinated units of the conglomerates for which they function as suppliers. In general, the inter-firm relationships tend to be more vertical than horizontal (ibid.; see also Schmitz 1992).

There is debate on whether one may classify the strong vertical relations between large firms and the German *Mittelstand* as market relations. Sabel (1989) and Herrigel (1996a) deny that such vertical relations follow the market model, while Cooke and Morgan (1998) disagree with this assessment. Empirical analysis of Baden-Württemberg suggests that we should be cautious in asserting that vertical co-operation involves more than the market model (and market power). Semlinger notes:

However, one should be careful in applying the term co-operation to vertical (subcontracting or other customer–supplier) relationships without thorough specification of what is meant by using it. Much of what happens here is simply market-kind exchange and if there is more interaction in a lasting relationship it can be very different from a consensual and balanced exchange, which is implied in the common meaning of co-operation. (Semlinger 1993:460)

Thus, if co-operation occurs in vertical relations, this is only when large companies support their supplier firms with specific services because they have an interest in their improved performance. On an abstract level, one might claim that market relations should be classified as horizontal ones (see the table presented in the Introduction), because both partners of the assumed transaction have something to gain if the deal is seen as motivated by economic principles.

To some extent this requires equal opportunities for both enterprises, as a supplier firm would otherwise stop contracting with a larger firm. Nevertheless, market relations can also be asymmetrical. Because of this, vertical subcontracting relations may also be included in the market mode of governance.

DaimlerChrysler shows how vertical relations may be market relations; 80 per cent of the value added in motor production comes from supplier firms. When the new V6 and V8 motors were developed, R&D aimed to improve the crankcases construction, thus decreasing pollution and fuel consumption. Supplier firms such as Heller, Gehring and Peak made a considerable contribution to this innovation (*VDI nachrichten*, no. 13 (April 1999), p. 5).

R&D, in particular, is a competition good where supplier relations not distinct from pure market relations are important for the wider economy. However, we should add once again that many of these companies are themselves larger firms operating as system partners. It should also be noted that supplier relations may change over time and are structured according to the necessities evolving from increasing global competition in the 1990s.

The State

Economic and technology policies in Baden-Württemberg are set via tripartite alliances between the *Land* government, leading conglomerates and diverse scientific institutions, with towns and cities playing only a marginal role. The importance of the *Land* government in creating frameworks to supply local small and medium-sized firms with collective competition goods extends back into the previous century, as shown by the example of the Steinbeis Foundation. This can trace its roots back to a state-sponsored institution, which was entrusted with the task of promoting the economy of the region through technology transfer and worker qualification in 1848. Such state-arranged infrastructures are still characteristic (Cooke and Morgan 1990; Schmitz 1992; Semlinger 1993).

Baden-Württemberg supports nine universities, many of which are strong in the technical disciplines, and thirty-eight technical colleges, which frequently co-operate closely with businesses. It is also home to fourteen Max Planck Institutes, fourteen Fraunhofer Institutes and three large research institutions. In addition, there are ten research institutes of the Arbeitsgemeinschaft industrieller Forschungsvereinigungen as well as numerous research centres operating in a non-university setting. This dense institutional network is soon to be expanded even further through the creation of technology centres.[7]

The Steinbeis Foundation is a good and frequently cited example of successful technology transfer, but it is not only a state-sponsored organization. It operates as a foundation and as such runs transfer centres, which are very often located in polytechnics. Their aim is to transfer know-how generated in the academic field to the world of business. Professors who have a chair in the relevant field usually

---

[7] For technology centres in Germany see Sternberg *et al.* (1996).

assume responsibility for the centres. The services include directly implemented R&D projects, entrepreneurial advice, information on technology transfer via the Steinbeis network, further training and help in acquiring funding from the federal or the *Land* government or the European Union. The foundation earned a total of DM 125.7 million from its advisory activities, R&D projects and training programmes in 1997 (Steinbeis-Stiftung 1997). However, it no longer acts only as a regional institution.

The reason why the Steinbeis Foundation falls within the state mode of governance is its origin in public institutions, namely the polytechnics, and foundation by the *Land* government. These roots are still visible today. The head of the foundation is also Commissioner for Technology Transfer and as such responsible to the Ministry of Economics of Baden-Württemberg, while many representatives on the Foundation's Board come from the *Land* parliament, the ministries and other public organs (in addition to representatives from industry, universities, and so on). Nevertheless, it is now a public–private partnership: it still receives money from the Ministry of Economics in order to set up new transfer centres and so forth, but is increasingly acting independently as a quasi-private organization. It therefore now partly fits into the market form of governance.

These changes were part of the Späth government's reforms of support programmes in 1984, which sought to combine regional and innovation support in a single programme. The government intended actively to intervene in technological innovation, creating incentives for firms to follow through on Späth's vision of Baden-Württemberg as a high-technology region. The emphasis on new technological development was such that it gave the impression that all firms had to do to receive financial aid from the state for R&D activities was to fill in a form. The instruments that were supposed to implement this process and structure it according to the needs of the market and the potential of the regional scientific base included the Steinbeis network. The foundation's capital fund was raised from DM 68,000 to DM 18 million by the *Land* government (Knodt 1998:233).

Land support became particularly important when the success of the Baden-Württemberg economy almost completely excluded it from receiving *Gemeinschaftsaufgabe* financial support in the 1980s. However, the European Commission saw some *Land* interventions as distorting competition, and objected. Since 1986 these measures have been implemented by the Landeskreditbank. Non-firm-specific measures are implemented by the Landesgewerbeamt (LGA), which is responsible for the provision of collective competition goods, especially to SMEs. Institutionally linked to the Ministry of Economics, the LGA also implements measures for firms that require specific information on Baden-Württemberg's market conditions or support in terms of motivation and finance. It also performs other advisory tasks and offers direct help on training issues.

It is interesting that in the 1980s, just when advocates of flexible specialization were trying to persuade the scientific community that regional policy in Baden-Württemberg was representative of more general patterns, the representatives of

Baden-Württemberg's policy-making system were simultaneously trying to persuade state and market actors all over the world that Baden-Württemberg could enjoy the success of Silicon Valley and other such regions. It is difficult to know now whether the discourse on Baden-Württemberg as a distinct region originated in politics or science.[8] This is not intended as a cynical remark on the literature, which has probably contributed to this image. Instead, we wish to emphasize that while Späth may have wanted to develop new economic instruments for the state, researchers should have taken more account of the fact that his policy was also determined by existing patterns of collective goods provision and would therefore never transform the *Land* into what we have seen in those local economies with a different governance structure.

Associations

Industrial relations in Baden-Württemberg are characteristic of Germany as a whole. The principle of co-determination ensures the strong presence of trade unions in both the bargaining process and shop-floor decision-making. There is 'a high rate of unionisation in both large and small firms; thus, wage discrepancy is kept to a minimum' (DiGiovanna 1996:378). It is important to understand that unions in Baden-Württemberg owe their strength to a model of industrial relations which is characteristic of the entire country, and thus to pay some attention to this model, which is sometimes neglected by students of local economies (Gertler and Rutherford 1996).

The German model is characterized by the dual system of industrial relations, consisting of autonomy in wage setting (at the level of the association) and of shop-floor participation rights (at the level of the individual factories) (Keller 1993; Müller-Jentsch 1986, 1995). The institutions of co-determination on the shop floor and at the level of firm management are relevant aspects of the model, as is the regulation of the labour market by umbrella associations of employers and employees. Regularly negotiated sectoral wage agreements in particular are far more important than in many other countries. The dual structure allows employee and employer interests to be balanced, which conforms to the basic underlying conditions set by macro-economic policy and also ensures social integration in the face of lasting socio-economic change and all its concomitant social problems.

The system opens up two functionally separate decision-making arenas, each with its own actors and specific forms of conflict resolution. At the level of the association, wage bargains are uniformly applied to all member firms operating in the same sector (wage levels, rules regarding working hours and the basic underlying conditions of employment relationships).[9] At the factory level, the

---

[8] The theory that Baden-Württemberg is an exceptional case has lost support due to the crisis of the economy in the 1990s (Naschold 1996). On the homogeneity of technology and innovation management with firms from other parts of Germany, see Lay (1996).

[9] For the structure and function of associations in Germany see Ronit and Schneider (1997).

Betriebsrat (works council) negotiates with management over factory-specific aspects of the employment relationship. The division of labour in this structure relieves union representatives at the level of the association from having to deal with factory-specific problems, and at the same time relieves the representatives on the shop floor from having to deal with subjects related to national agreements.

Germany differs from many other countries not only in its high wages, but also in relatively low wage differentials. It is exactly these levelling effects of the wage-bargaining system that are valued as social-welfare achievements. In short, the German model combines a high-technology orientation with a highly qualified and highly paid workforce. While these positive welfare effects of the model have a downside—a higher level of unemployment (which can also be seen as the deliberate renunciation of bad jobs)—this is considered a reasonable trade-off. Characteristic of this version of a regulated high-wage economy (Vitols 1996) is the belief that institutionalized class conflict creates a positive-sum game that serves to boost economic growth. The core element of this model is the specific manner in which sectoral wage agreements are arranged, as this is thought to assume beneficial regulatory and cartelization functions. Wages and working hours are standardized by the relevant associations of unions and businesses guided by the macro-economic and sectoral levels (and thus insensitive to the situation of individual plants). The regulatory and cartelization function of the wage-agreement system results from the fact that it standardizes and levels working conditions and pay (Streeck 1997). German unions adopt wage moderation, taking macro-economic factors into account. Wage increases are subject to economic practicalities, so that unions are orientated to stability and moderate in their demands (Bahnmüller and Bispinck 1995). This of course depends on firms' productivity being high enough to sustain minimum pay levels legally agreed upon and set for their branch. If a firm is unable to achieve the average level of productivity in its branch, its only course of action is to abandon the market or to file for bankruptcy. At the same time, those firms that are able to realize higher than average productivity gains are rewarded in that the profits thereby made possible are not taken into account in wage negotiations; or, if they are, this is done on the basis of a voluntary supplementary agreement at the factory level.

According to its proponents, the economic advantage of this corporatist wage-bargaining system lies in the pressures it puts on enterprises to increase productivity and to innovate. As long as labour costs are rigid across the whole branch, the only way that firms can stay in the black is to increase productivity and innovation. Wage dumping is practically impossible. As a regionally differentiated but ultimately centrally controlled instrument, collective bargaining provides an income policy that helps to increase productivity. Comparatively high levels of wages mean that price-competitive markets are relatively unattractive for German companies (Streeck 1997). The institutional framework forces them to concentrate primarily on quality-competitive markets. However, this applies to the whole of Germany and not just to Baden-Württemberg.

This general argument can also be applied to the role of associations in specific policy areas. As in the other *Länder*, the organizations of employees and of employers in Baden-Württemberg produce important collective competition goods for the local economies. One can see this in vocational training:

[B]oth organisations have been indispensable in the development of the extensive worker training programmes that exist in Baden-Württemberg. The fact that training is such an important part of the Baden-Württemberg system is often cited as one of the major reasons for the regions success. The extensive vocational training system has developed, in large part, with the input and support of the unions. (DiGiovanna 1996:378)

But here, too, in comparison with other European countries, vocational training is highly regulated, and even more so at the national than at the regional or local level (Streeck *et al.* 1987).

Local Economies under Pressure: Challenges and Changes in the 1990s

In this section we shall explore the development of German local economies in the 1990s, again using Baden-Württemberg and Stuttgart as *pars pro toto*. However, we do not only want to look at firm responses to the challenges of increased competition but at policy changes. What are the challenges? The literature on globalization (if it is indeed a unitary phenomenon) is characterized by decreasing consensus as academics try to investigate it in more detail (Hirst and Thompson 1996; Scharpf 1997; Garrett 1998). We shall leave aside the broader question of whether globalization adequately describes the changes taking place; as long as we restrict our analysis to the factors changing and threatening the internal functioning of local economies, we do not need to address this question directly.

The Crisis in Baden-Württemberg

One of the reasons why Baden-Württemberg was viewed as a model region in the 1980s was that the growth of its GDP after 1983 continuously exceeded the German average (Semlinger 1993). This trend was reversed in 1991. Although industry recovered slightly in 1994, varying from branch to branch, the region had suffered a shock. For the first time it appeared to be as vulnerable as any other region in Germany. Despite new growth in the second half of the 1990s, Baden-Württemberg and Germany as a whole continued to suffer from high unemployment. The major recession of 1992 and 1993 saw a decrease in Baden-Württemberg's contribution to Germany's GDP (from 15.0 per cent in 1993 to 14.4 per cent in 1997).

At the beginning of the 1990s, reunification created hopes of a new boost for the German economy, and turnover did actually increase on the German market for some products, including machinery. However, entrepreneurs were lulled and did not pay enough attention to dangerous developments on the export markets, especially in core sectors such as car machinery. When the bubble burst, the full extent of the crisis became obvious. Apart from the aforementioned job losses in the machinery industry, Daimler-Benz made 13,700 workers redundant in 1992–93, and Bosch laid off 7,500 workers (*Frankfurter Allgemeine Zeitung*, 23 December 1993:14). Investment declined, and orders were lacking in the core branches.

Unfavourable currency rates exacerbated this decline, and firms sought desperately to cope by beginning organizational restructuring, but for many firms in the capital goods industry this came too late. Some went bankrupt, while others were taken over by larger firms in the region. An additional factor leading to decline, at least in the capital goods industry, was the anti-inflationary policy of the German Bundesbank. Furthermore, as well-known firms in the machinery industry ran into problems, banks started to lose confidence in the future success of firms in this branch, and were hesitant to provide new capital or credits for investment in new machines or restructuring strategies. While much attention has been paid to the external factors of this crisis, there is not yet enough systematic examination of the actual competitiveness of Baden-Württemberg firms. For example, it is unclear whether lock-in effects can be made responsible to the extent claimed by Cooke and Morgan (1998).

One may ask whether these problems arose from globalization, but there is no easy answer. The emergence of new Japanese competitors in high-cost market niches of the machinery industry certainly presented a challenge to local economies in Baden-Württemberg (Braczyk, Schienstock and Steffensen 1996: 47). These challenges may have arisen from globalization, but the responses to these changes too have put pressure on local economies (Herrigel forthcoming).

The Threat to the Collectivity of Competition Goods Posed by the Further Internationalization of Large Firms

There are four basic challenges to vertical relations between firms in the Baden-Württemberg economy, which we examine here in the case of Mercedes-Benz supplier relations (Glassmann 1999). The first aspect concerns foreign direct investment. Mercedes-Benz has sought to open up foreign markets through new plants, as seen in the production of the All-Activity Vehicle in Alabama. Here, the firm has avoided transplanting German patterns of production and organization abroad. Instead, it seeks to adapt itself to the specific industrial environment abroad and relies on regional supplier firms in Alabama. This may be the exemplar of a future trend; according to its official statements on foreign direct investment, Mercedes hopes to increase production in foreign markets from 5–10 per cent in 1995 to 25 per cent in the year 2003 (*Süddeutsche Zeitung*, 14 May 1995:32).

Further internationalization of the company will lead to an increase in production abroad, and a declining role for regional and local supplier firms. An increase in foreign direct investment does not necessarily have a negative impact on the competitive advantage of the local economy. Indeed, this strategy might even have positive effects if the local economy benefits from the large firm's ability to maintain its competitiveness on the international market by concentrating on core areas of competence. While Mercedes has been transformed from a German car firm into an international motor company—and not only because of the DaimlerChrysler merger—it is possible to show that those firms in Stuttgart that have been investing more abroad have been laying off fewer workers than others (Holwegler and Trautwein 1998). Although this points to an interesting causal relation, the overall trend in the 1990s (both at Mercedes and at other prominent firms in Baden-Württemberg and Germany as a whole) has been a drop in employment. One may assume that the same is true for regionally and locally added value. While concentrating on core areas of competence may strengthen a firm's competitive position, the decision to open up new markets primarily increases the value added of these firms, not necessarily the local economy.[10]

The internal restructuring of Mercedes-Benz, which largely took place between 1995 and 1997 (not including the later merger between Daimler and Chrysler), brought about this new emphasis on core competences. This was seen as an indispensable restructuring strategy that involved abandoning the concept of the integrated technology company, according to which peripheral market activities that were associated with the existing product line, were integrated by the company. These activities were supposed to subsidize the main line when it was not doing well; the concept was doomed to failure (Töpfer 1998). Competitive pressures forced the company to define the markets where it wanted to maintain and increase its shares. This was primarily the car industry, which had been identified as the most competitive unit. Mercedes-Benz fused with Daimler-Benz AG again in 1997, probably also in preparation for the later merger.

This strategy obviously meant major changes for the supplier firms. Concentration among car industry suppliers in the 1990s was linked to a shift of responsibilities from large firms to their business partners. While this development completely changed large firms' bargaining power, demand for human resources and the organization of work, it also changed their responsibility for the production of competition goods. Many such goods are still produced in-house, but the large firm may have adapted depending on which competences have been

---

[10] It might be argued that this development is compensated for by the investment of foreign firms in Baden-Württemberg. However, the figures on foreign direct investment in Baden-Württemberg suggest otherwise: investment (current stock) in Baden-Württemberg from abroad has only increased from DM 29.8 billion in 1991 to DM 32.2 billion in 1995, while foreign direct investment (current stock) from Baden-Württemberg abroad has increased from DM 37.8 billion to DM 63.3 billion in the same period of time (Puhlmann, Bechinka and Wolf 1996; Statistisches Landesamt Baden-Württemberg 1997).

delegated to supplier firms. In addition, new vertical relations have been established when large firms have gone abroad. The Mercedes-Benz Alabama plant is a case in point. One of the few German firms that were able to benefit from the new plant was Zahnradfabrik Friedrichshafen, which was already a large supplier company and could fulfil the criteria to be a global supplier (logistics, capital, foreign market contacts, qualified personnel, and so on). While only a few of the system partners connected with the Mercedes plant in Alabama are originally German firms, suppliers create 80–85 per cent of value added in the production process of the All-Activity Vehicle (Büchtemann and Kuhlmann 1996).

The second factor is the new role that supplier firms (at least in the car industry) may play on the international market. Vertical relations may not really be endangered if such firms in the region grow as the flagship enterprise reduces its capacities. However, the tendency of supplier firms to become global companies, going abroad with the large firm and also opening up new markets for their products, is not likely to help employment in the region. Although well-known system partners (e.g., Zahnradfabrik Friedrichshafen) began to employ more workers at a time when 9.9 per cent of the 330,551 employees at Daimler-Benz had been made redundant (1994), this is a more general effect of the growing importance of those suppliers that successfully compete on the international market (Heidenreich 1996). An increase in the numbers employed by these firms probably reflects their increasing activities abroad rather than the growing importance of their home base. While successful suppliers benefit from this development, many small firms in the regional and local production base are excluded from the reorganized value chain, which now (from the perspective of both the large firm and the global suppliers) involves more business partners from abroad. The principal agents in this context are the large firms. Mercedes-Benz, for example, has transformed its strategy from a substantial reliance on regional and local sourcing to global sourcing with the expectation that international firms or those located abroad will be able to ensure a more efficient supply of components and parts. This trend is likely to accelerate with Business-to-Business auctioning of car parts on the Internet.

Global sourcing is pursued when a specialized firm abroad is able to produce more innovatively or cost-effectively than local firms. Mercedes-Benz began to reconsider its supplier relations in the early 1990s, and to emphasize the cost-effectiveness of supplier firms in the subsequent restructuring, focusing, as it did internally, on the return on capital employed. Still, poor performance by suppliers did not lead to an automatic break in relations: Mercedes had already implemented its dialogue-orientated supplier partnership concept. However, even this concept poses a threat to the collectivity of competition goods.

The attractions of global sourcing for large firms can be explained by their difficulties at the beginning of the 1990s. Accountants at Daimler-Benz calculated a net loss of DM 1.56 billion for the first six months of 1995, and in 1996 the company did not pay dividends for the first time in forty-five years. Fokker went bankrupt. Dornier suffered a loss of DM 553 million and was sold to Fairchild

Aircraft Inc., while AEG Electrocom was taken over by Siemens. Other parts of AEG had already been sold off. Organizational restructuring to focus on car manufacturing was absolutely essential, but conventional supplier relations could not be maintained either; even if, according to Heidenreich and Krauss (1998:226):

In the age of internationalized production structures, Baden-Württemberg's manufacturing industry has retained a surprisingly high degree of regional sourcing. Of the required input factors, some 53% of supplies are procured regionally, 26.7% from other German states and 20.4% from abroad.

Recent developments suggest that such vertical co-operation will not be maintained in the region. Local collective competition goods will be under-supplied to the extent that core firms shift to a strategy of global sourcing, neglecting firms that were formerly part of the value chain, as suppliers either for large firms or for system partners.

The third factor is ambivalent—the reorganization of the supplier–buyer relationship can strengthen vertical ties, but again, in the first place with system partners, not with the small suppliers from the region. In the 1990s, Mercedes-Benz developed the TANDEM programme to reorganize supplier links and announced that this would result in a new era of intensified co-operation. TANDEM seeks to take further advantage of established forms of co-operation, creating transparency in the supply chain and making it easier for the large firm to manage information flows, product innovation, and so on. However, Mercedes claimed that this intensified form of vertical co-operation would also be in the interest of suppliers, since both had to face global competition together, searching co-operatively for improvements in efficiency in supply chains, minimizing costs, and improving quality.

The TANDEM concept is based on three pillars, Events, Organization and Information. Each of these pillars has three components regulating future relations between Mercedes and its suppliers. The first pillar establishes rules for meetings between actors from both sides, setting up workshops, defining common projects with specific suppliers, and organizing more general meetings with suppliers to exchange information on the car industry. The organizational pillar provides institutionalized channels of information on product improvement—Mercedes employs people in purchasing who are directly responsible for the suppliers in order to provide information exchange. Mercedes also has a programme called TANDEM Support which offers assistance to suppliers trying to realize ideas in line with the Mercedes concept or who simply have a good idea for quality improvement or cost reduction. If the supplier firm does not have the know-how required, Mercedes uses TANDEM Support to provide the firm with the necessary skills, technology, and so on. This kind of co-operation transforms collective goods into club goods and thus provides advantages for those still in the value chain; however, other firms may be excluded. TANDEM Information provides information (journals, documents, and so on) to those involved and therefore makes co-operation a more efficient system for those who are part of it. The ambiguity of this concept is that it challenges suppliers to adapt to new standards of global competition. Close forms of co-operation may work for both sides as long as the individual firm can keep pace with recent technological developments, but sanctions can be more easily imposed when this becomes a problem. While system partners may benefit from intensified co-operation with the large firm, smaller suppliers to the system partners may lack adequate support and experience increased pressure.

The fourth factor is the use of information technology such as SAP R 3, a software product designed for managing human resources, accounting, production planning, sales and purchasing, which can also be applied to machines on the shop floor. This information system covers all facets of production, not only managing information, but also providing detailed descriptions of efficiency problems in a real-time environment. Such software, which is used in Mercedes-Benz plants, provides a technical instrument to achieve increased and precise control of costs and efficiency within the value chain. These networks are extended to cover supplier firms, which means that geographical proximity is no longer necessary for effective communication. In general, communication processes are shifting to Internet and Extranet solutions.[11] This again excludes firms that cannot adapt to these technological standards, increases the ability to impose sanctions and contributes to the erosion of local production patterns in which competition goods were accessible and thus formed the basis for transforming private goods into collective goods.

Strengthening Social Institutions and Regionalizing Political Support

The need to respond to the economic crisis in Baden-Württemberg not only meant that the *Land* government pursued new policies supporting new industries such as biotechnology or the media, it also created new organizations which aimed to improve co-operation between local firms and produce collective competition goods for the new branches. This is most obvious in Stuttgart, where the first regional assembly (a quasi-parliament with limited responsibilities) was elected in 1994. But there has been a long-running debate about regionalization in general in all *Länder* (Garlichs, Maier, and Semlinger 1983; Hilpert 1991; Hassink 1992, 1993).

The regional parliament in Stuttgart operates as an organ of the regional association, which, together with banks, some hundred other communes, chambers of industry and commerce, and the Landesentwicklungsgesellschaft, founded a new organization to support firms located in the region (Wirtschaftsförderung Region Stuttgart GmbH, WRS). The regional association and the WRS get funding from both the Federal and *Land* governments to support firms in the new branches.

---

[11] The Extranet is a system of electronically based connections between a leader firm and its suppliers.

They are also responsible for monitoring venture capital, marketing, information on the development of enterprises and the employment situation in specific branches, and so on. Older organizations, such as the former regional association of Stuttgart and similar organizations, did not establish such communication networks. The grand coalition in Baden-Württemberg has allowed consensus on granting further powers to regional organizations. Moreover, the crisis has underlined the need for active regional support for horizontal co-operation, which requires a decentralized support structure. The WRS has made initial attempts to establish a forum for car industry suppliers in Stuttgart, but has run into problems. Because this new initiative is financed by the Wirtschaftsministerium of the *Land*, it was not politically possible to regionalize conventional policy instruments excluding other regions of the *Land*. Applying ideas at the local or regional level may therefore be blocked sometimes by political actors on the *Land* level.

But these effects are not a result of *Politikverflechtung*; in Baden-Württemberg they occur because the *Land* government has not attempted to elaborate a common framework for regionalizing policies, but has only supported single initiatives which aim to better the performance of certain regions. Given this, it is difficult to avoid the disproportionate participation of certain regions and social actors. The latter problem is articulated by the unions, while the former is illustrated by the region of Karlsruhe, which has created its own development agency. In this context the region now articulates specific demands directed to the *Land* government. These new regional initiatives have to be co-ordinated at the *Land* level, as this is where the financial resources for strategies to improve firm co-operation remain. The decisive point is that the principle of equal living conditions should not be corrupted on the regional level, while it is strictly maintained between the *Länder*. Because of this and because of government control, one cannot yet observe a shift of formal competences towards the regions. The regionalization of support strategies is not a substitute for *Länder* action, but an additional instrument which itself demands *Land* level co-ordination.

Interestingly, Lower Saxony and North Rhine Westphalia show a similar trend to regionalization of policies. North Rhine Westphalia began to elaborate regionalized support initiatives much earlier, starting in 1987, so as to meet the very particular need for structural change in old industrial regions. In the beginning, decentralization was implemented to define the need for structural fund support more accurately, but in the late 1980s it was extended to the whole *Land*. Fifteen regions were defined for North Rhine Westphalia, and newly established regional conferences were supposed to develop support programmes with the participation of political, economic and social actors. In contrast to Baden-Württemberg, regionalization in other *Länder* is connected to the rationalization of structural fund allocation. An evaluation of this process has shown that regionalization did not, as expected, lead to the adequate participation of local firms (Heinze and Voelzkow 1997). Also, the more general programmes of the regional conferences tend to neglect particular regional industrial profiles in favour of the general problems of different policies.

However, there also exist comparable instruments, such as initiatives to support car suppliers in the early 1990s, which represent identical attempts in all *Länder* to start co-operation between (local) firms, not using the classical instrument of the *Förderprogramm*, but stimulating firm initiatives and monitoring co-operation. In all three *Länder* the state still operates according to conventional wisdom on supporting local firms, although political actors are now concerned that services are more effective to enterprises. This has meant that implementation has increasingly been delegated to private institutions; initiatives like the car supplier initiative in NRW have been out-sourced to external providers.

Conclusions

How may the governance approach be applied to the comparative analysis of local economies? One would like to explain why some are doing well, while others are declining or in crisis. Before tackling this we should present two hypotheses about the relationship between governance and economic structure in the analysed regions. The first hypothesis suggests that the governance approach helps to explain why the size of firms diverges between local economies in different national settings, while the second hypothesis suggests that the analysis of country-specific governance helps to explain differences in the spatial concentration of firms between countries. Finally, we draw some conclusions about how the further internationalization of markets affects the German system of collective goods provision.

Governance and Firm Size

Progress in understanding how local economies work can be seen in the findings on how the dependence of SMEs on particular resources affects their institutional requirements. One may conclude that the competitive advantage of small firms does not solely come from flexible specialization, and hence endogenous capacities. If flexible specialization and vertical disintegration are connected, as Sabel and others claim, the relevance of the external environment should increase to the same extent that vertical disintegration increases (Sabel *et al.* 1989). The governance approach provides an additional hypothesis, which we only outline very briefly here, as empirical evidence is not yet available to confirm or reject it. According to this hypothesis, the clear differences in average firm size between local economies in Germany and some other countries result from the predominant form of governance in these localities.

In Germany, medium-sized and large production units prevail in many branches, with a high degree of vertical integration. Any attempt to explain this on the basis of sectoral structure, which may also determine firm size, can only have limited validity, as there are within-branch differences in size between Germany and other countries. One may conclude that important production-orientated services, which are provided in-house in German enterprises, have to be produced by and transferred from public or private institutions that maintain an external infrastructure. If this hypothesis is confirmed, then one may reasonably assume a causal relationship between the size of firms in regional production systems and their governance framework. According to this interpretation of the structural distinctness of local economies, the higher degree of vertical dis-integration of enterprises in some other countries is possible because they are institutionally embedded. This allows these economies to create functional equivalents for those services that can be produced in-house in German enter-prises. They have to be produced in this way in Germany because it is impossible to ensure their provision through a network of spatially concentrated, horizontally co-operating firms. However, our arguments on internationalization suggest that exactly this kind of co-operation may be required much more in the future as vertical relations in local economies are threatened. Since German local econo-mies cannot rely on community-based co-operation, we suggest that other institutions—in particular the state and the association—will play a key role in assisting firms to create horizontal co-operation in the near future.

This means that the German system of collective goods provision may be endangered by internationalization on the firm side, and therefore needs to be stabilized by state and associational actors. Those associations involved in the industrial relations system which we described above are also under pressure, because of processes of decentralization which threaten the central collective bargaining structure, and because fewer firms are covered by works councils (Hassel 1999). This is a result of increased demands for worker and cost flexibility. So far it has not led to a complete erosion of the industrial relations system, but rather to solutions which aim at introducing flexibility within the existing order. It remains to be seen whether these measures will be sufficient to rescue the asso-ciational framework for production in Germany and thereby help to transform these associations into actors who may help solve emerging collective goods problems.

How the state can fulfil the increasing demand for collective goods provision with diminishing resources is a crucial question for the future of German capitalism. The solution here seems to be the establishment of public–private partnerships, in which the state may influence the provision of a collective good, while private organizations may secure its effective provision on the market. Despite current pessimism about whether the German model of capitalism can meet new conditions of increasing global competition, we believe that it is more likely than not that it can. The national system of collective goods provision may undergo reforms, but in doing so it can secure the competitiveness of hitherto vibrant local economies. Even Baden-Württemberg may therefore recover much earlier than expected.

Governance and Local Clustering: The Geography of Local Economies

A second aspect is that of economic geography. The pressure for SMEs to gain competitive advantage through spatial agglomeration differs in intensity between countries. If local economies comparable to industrial districts can be found at all in Germany, they are the exceptions. And if we take the marginal relevance of these economies into account, even these exceptions illustrate the more general rule that Germany's economy on the whole has a different structure of spatial concentration of enterprises. Given the difficulty of obtaining empirical data for Germany, it remains difficult to judge whether or not industrial districts are unique entities. The empirical data presented here nevertheless confirm that spatially concentrated specialization is not particularly strong. One cannot deny a trend towards further industrial specialization, but it is indispensable to distinguish between sectors or sub-sectors, in order to learn more about tendencies towards lower or higher concentration in general. First one may conclude that traditional industries are more concentrated than others. Second, the level of concentration depends on the size of firms in particular sectors, which is probably why machinery is less concentrated than, for instance, chemicals. There is little pressure on German firms to cluster because the system providing collective competition goods for SMEs exists at national or *Länder* levels.

Governance and the Performance of Local Economies

We shall now move on to our final point: whether a detailed analysis of the governance of local economies can help explain differences in local economic strength. We suggest that the governance approach can indeed improve our knowledge. As mentioned, attempts were made in the 1980s to use the district model to explain the surprising performance of local economies in Italy, Germany and other leading industrial countries. Economic performance was mainly attributed to 1. the intensive (non-market) inter-firm co-operation between vertically unconnected small and medium-sized enterprises; and 2. a shared local infrastructure for diverse services.

In the language of this book, both explanatory variables are ultimately related to a high level of availability of collective competition goods for small and medium-sized enterprises. However, success is always relative. The local economies of Baden-Württemberg were supposed to perform better than the average level of national economic development. The Third Italy was considered strong in comparison to the southern and northern parts of Italy, and Baden-Württemberg was compared with the traditionally industrialized regions in the North-West and on the coast of Germany. However, this last comparison is of doubtful value if we consider the fact that the institutional basis of the provision of collective competition goods largely reflects national patterns in Germany.

It cannot be denied that Baden-Württemberg has at its disposal an impressive range of public and semi-public infrastructures that provide local small and medium-sized enterprises with collective competition goods (Semlinger 1995; Cooke 1997). However, caution is called for, as the economic crisis in the region demonstrates. An institutional wealth of local infrastructures does not necessarily mean economic success. Moreover, other regions in Germany have comparable infrastructures (Klönne, Borowzcak and Voelzkow 1991).

The ability of the secondary literature to explain the economic performance of local economies is somewhat disappointing. The current state of research precludes identifying best methods of flexible specialization which explain why one region is more successful than another. While it is clear that the economic performance of local economies is connected to the supply of collective competition goods, there is no single way of providing these goods. Instead, we see a whole range of models of social order that deliver the indispensable collective competition goods to small and medium-sized enterprises via various paths.

5

Between Large Firms and Marginal Local Economies: The Making of Systems of Local Governance in France

VALERIA ANIELLO AND PATRICK LE GALÈS

Once upon a time the French model of capitalism and its economic success were either despised or hailed as the state-centred French exception. In that post-war period, the modernization of the economy was led by the state and its elites, which organized economic development and ran most of the national champions. Local economies were not an issue. Some disappeared, some remained hidden, and a dozen interesting cases remained rather strong.

As is the case in the rest of Europe, French industry is today going through a rapid restructuring process, and the state is less directly in charge. The near collapse of national champions in the late 1970s and early 1980s went hand in hand with the rediscovery of small and medium industrial enterprises (SMEs) due to their growing contribution to economic development, together with the discovery of success stories in Silicon Valley or in Italian industrial districts. Policy-makers and academics alike therefore led many inquiries to discover or rediscover SMEs and local economies.

Bernard Ganne (1990, 1992a and b, 1995) in particular gave the most persuasive interpretation of the relationship between SMEs, the state and politics. When he compared French local economies and the role of medium-size firms with the Italian situation he was of course struck by the difference. In the late 1980s, at a time when many were looking for industrial districts or for French flexible modernization, Ganne had started research on the political economy of local production systems. His comparison with the neo-localist regulation identified by Bagnasco and Trigilia in the Third Italy was essential to underline the fact that by contrast industrial districts were very rare in France. Ganne (1995) suggested analysing changes in the fortunes of local industrial systems in relation to the structure of politics and in particular centre–periphery relations. He suggested that the relationship between the state and the periphery was a mix that associated in interdependence political and economic governance. He identified four periods in France: 1. the state as mediator and the social model of family enterprises during the inter-war period; 2. state emphasis on planning and consequent fall from favour experienced by SMEs in the post-war period; 3. reinstatement of SMEs through a policy of co-ordinated action in the 1970s; 4. decentralization and mobilization around SMEs in the 1980s.

These findings constitute the starting-point of our attempt to understand local economies in relation to the political economy of France and its transformation.

The economic modernization policy conducted by the state and major industrial groups has contributed to the liquidation of local economic systems, but some observers also point to the decline of traditional sectors and purely economic causes: from 1951 to 1963 alone, 80,000 SMEs disappeared (Lescure 1999). Starting from an analysis of the fragmentation of local economic systems by branches of industry and by institutions, most authors stressed the role of influential local figures and of vertical integration, each branch or sector having a direct relation to the state. This is a complete contrast with Italy. Thus one can understand how an anti-investment pre-war state allowed these rigid local industrial systems to prosper, while the post-war state precipitated their ruin. However, Lescure, who has done the most extensive research on SMEs (though not local economies), shows that some dynamic SMEs were also successful during the 1960s.

The point of departure for this book is the national political economy of local economies. Both economic changes and the restructuring of the state (however related they may be) are producing both new constraints and new opportunities. The emerging picture is not very clear. French local economies are currently showing signs of moving beyond the large firm and subcontractor model. SME business leaders, restructuring large firms, state, and local public or semi-public agencies are engaged in a large process of collective action to support them. This new dynamism is messy, unco-ordinated, and will lead to many failures.

The chapter has two main aims. First, it provides a story of local economies in France and their transformation from the post-war period to the last two decades, when both decentralization reforms and the 'small is beautiful' economic fashion brought them back to prominence. Second, the chapter tries, more tentatively, to argue that several systems of local economic governance are either already in place or currently being constructed to nurture small-scale enterprises with less hierarchical relations with large firms.

The Demise of French Local Economies, 1945–75

The initial transformation and decline is related to the reorganization of economic space under the command of Paris and state industrial policies. French policy was hostile to SMEs and local economies. Bigger was better, and Parisian was better still.

SMEs as Symbols of French Industrial Backwardness:
The Legacy of the 1930s

Before the industrial revolution, local economies organized around craftsmen were to be found in most regions of France; they constituted the bulk of the economy. Fernand Braudel, in his classic history of France, has shown at length the dual structure of France: great diversity among regions that fed the dynamics of centralization and nation-state building. Until the late 1930s, different kinds of local economies were widespread all over the country (Sabel and Zeitlin 1989).

From that time onwards, local economies and SMEs became blamed for France's lack of modernization and industrial development in comparison with Germany or the UK.[1] In brief, economic historians (for instance Kuisel 1984) have shown the very slow rise of vertically integrated corporations in the aftermath of the First World War and late industrialization, though certain economists (e.g., Levy-Leboyer 1996) dispute this view. By contrast, networks of familial SME firms have maintained or even strengthened their position. Classic economic historians argue that this occurred despite limited modernization and limited dependence upon the banks, because of deep roots within localities until the 1930s. Ganne (1990) suggests it could only be maintained thanks to the Malthusian ideology of the state and the protection it organized, plus the power of local *notables* and local industrial families (for example, Marseilles business families (Zalio 1999)).

Due to the strong vertical fragmentation of both state and industry, some *notables* representing a sector or a locality mediated the relationship with the state. They promoted a conservative political and economic order, which favoured the maintenance (but not the modernization) of local productive systems. Economic historians have analysed the quasi-institutionalization of many semi-rural industrial districts in Lodève, Cholet, Bretagne and Lyon, either through the role of *notables* (in municipalities, chambers of commerce, local industrial courts) or familial strategies. They have also noted in many places the lack of intermediary institutions to strengthen their environment, a direct impact of *le Loi le Chapelier* (Hirsch and Minard 1998).

However, Lescure (1996, 1999) has shown that French SMEs were not backward. Apart from the very small firms, many were quite innovative and developed successful competition strategies in terms of specialization, and their economic performance over the 1920s was quite good (despite huge differences among sectors and regions). Lescure concludes that there were many successful

---

[1] This theme of backwardness, the *retard*, has ever since provoked a heated debate in France between right and left (or rather market-friendly and state-friendly historians and economists), and also between some Anglophone writers and their French counterparts. Basically some blame the state, protectionist policies, the political republican alliance between peasantry and bourgeoisie, and the intervention of the state for the slow industrial development of those two periods. Others by contrast would blame the conservatism of business and banking elites, the lack of innovation among the *grandes familles*, and the lack of coherent industrial policies due to the orthodoxy of the economic bureaucracy.

SMEs in the 1920s, well embedded in local and regional contexts, and together with the most dynamic large firms, at the time central to French economic development (Levy-Leboyer 1996). Interestingly, he stresses that SMEs were seriously handicapped in several ways: lack of capital and difficult access to capital, lack of labour in the late 1920s, and an erratic economic conjuncture which provoked a high rate of mortality. Dynamic SMEs, the youngest ones in particular, seriously suffered in the 1920s, which undermined their contribution to economic development. But, on the other hand, the systematic defence of very small firms both fiscally and by limiting imports did not accelerate the modernization of French capitalism. The ideology of '*Laissez-nous faire et protégez-nous beaucoup'*, as Hirsch and Minard (1998:135) put it, also explains the curious mix of liberalism and protectionism which characterized French political economy for a long time and under which SMEs could survive. At the end of the day, however, SMEs were blamed for the poor performances of the French economy.

Hierarchies, the State and French Capitalism against Hidden Local Economies

The story of the French economic miracle from 1945 to 1975 has been told many times.[2] It led to the marginalization of SMEs and of local economies in particular for both economic and political reasons. Although our concern is mainly with state policy, that does not mean that general social and economic changes (in particular urbanization) have not played a role in the rise of large corporations and decline of SMEs (Levy-Leboyer 1996; Lescure 1999).

The Centralization of French Economic Space under the Control of Paris: Vertical Integration within a Fordist Economy (Veltz 1996). In the past, most French industrialization took place on the eastern side of the diagonal Le Havre/Geneva, that is, mainly in Paris, Lyon, Marseille, the north-east of the country and some areas such as Le Creusot/Saint-Etienne. Heavy industries such as steel, coal, motor vehicles and metal production were heavily concentrated in those areas, for instance in Lorraine and the mining region, the Nord (Lille Roubaix Tourcoing) and in Saint-Etienne/Le Creusot, the Seine Valley. Those areas, which have been suffering serious reorganization and closures since the 1960s, have all the social and economic characteristics of old industrial areas in decline. In particular, economic centralization within the Paris region was early one of the key structural characteristics of French economic space: centralization of capital, of firms, elites, and the transport system.

From the 1950s onwards, at the height of the Fordist period (and France was heavily Fordist (Boyer 1998)), firms' strategies combined with indicative regional policies *(politique d'aménagement du territoire)*, to organize economic

---

[2] The role of the state in industrial development and the *exception française* elicited a remarkable series of writings in the Anglo-American world: Zysman 1977; Hall 1986; Hayward 1986. On the French side, see Fridenson and Strauss 1987; Stoffaës 1991; Boyer 1998.

development. This entailed the late industrialization of the West and South-West of France, which contributed to the dismantling of local economies. The economic concentration of the Paris region was sustained, but industrial firms left Paris itself. Large firms in the 1950s and 1960s had a twofold strategy, well identified for instance by Savy and Veltz (1993) and Alvergne (1997). On the one hand they used cheap, low-qualified, non-unionized labour leaving rural areas in the West, but on the other hand they located in traditional industrial areas. Restructuring sectors such as coal and textiles released some labour, which was then used for instance in the motor vehicle and chemicals sectors.

Under the guidance of local state representatives, *zones industrielles* were created all over the country (far too many), often in relation to the newly established *comités départementaux d'expansion économique* and the chambers of commerce and industry. In the 1950s and 1960s, aeronautics were relocated in Toulouse and Bordeaux, vehicles in Bordeaux, Rennes, Le Mans, Rouen and the Seine valley. These firms still often constitute the bulk of a city's industrial base. The same logic applied to foreign investment, which was encouraged to locate outside Paris: IBM in Montpellier, Motorola in Toulouse and Hewlett Packard in Grenoble have played a key role in the transformation of the image and the base of the local economy. Each region was given a specialized sector, such as electronics and computers in Brittany. This policy (*déconcentration industrielle*) supposedly contributed to the creation of about 400,000 jobs outside Paris (DATAR 1986). It had an impact as some regions in the West and South-West, Brittany and Normandy in particular, faced a rapid late industrialization.

This new trend of industrial decentralization was not spontaneous and was rigidly organized in hierarchical terms. Most major French corporations kept their headquarters in Paris. Lyon and Grenoble for instance, where many industrial firms started and developed, lost most of the headquarters and the commanding elites decade after decade.

Important for our purpose is the fact that the state at the same time invested massively in public services, including some competitive collective goods. In Toulouse, Lille, Strasbourg, Grenoble, Bordeaux, Montpellier, Rennes and Nantes (i.e. the second level in the urban hierarchy, regional capitals far enough from Parisian influence) new infrastructures were created: universities, research centres, technology centres, *grandes écoles*, hospitals, cultural centres. In many respects, that period (in particular the 1960s) was the golden age of urban planning. State-led modernization contributed to the creation of collective goods, which proved so essential to the rise of these regional capitals some twenty years later. Supported nationally by the technocratic modernizing elites and locally by active groups, firms, politicians and entrepreneurs, it gave rise to urban economic integration and the gradual development during the 1970s and early 1980s of networks of firms in most regional capitals. In some cases, networks of towns also benefited from the move. To a large extent, it was this which produced the remarkable economic development of many of these regional capitals in the

1980s (especially Toulouse, Montpellier, Rennes, Strasbourg, Grenoble, Nantes). Local actors used those opportunities to create and reinforce local economic development, and to support firms in various ways (see for instance Grossetti 1995 for Toulouse; Le Galès 1993 for Rennes; Borraz 1997 for Besançon in a completely different context). The collective dimension of local economies was therefore first rooted in state intervention, and then in relation to local (often urban) public strategies.

Some local and regional lobbies and political movements were also building and reinforcing that dynamic, in Alsace and Brittany in particular. Regional economic and political elites required the support of the state to promote the economic development of their regions, but also demanded some control. The state responded with the creation of various instruments and policies, from the *Sociétés de Développement Régional (SDR)*, financial institutions in charge of supporting regional economic development and SMEs, to some sort of institutionalized regional governments, though this took twenty years.

State-led Industrial Meccano and Soft Planning to Enhance Extensive Growth. After 1945, while France was still in part a rural country, a relatively small elite, politically structured by 'la Résistance' or professionally trained in *Grandes Écoles* (Polytechnique and ENA), was able to run financial institutions, industrial business and the civil service. They viewed small business and local initiatives as archaic, symbols of the failures of the past. During the post-war period, political and institutional processes confirmed the concentration of resources that allowed this elite to shape production systems. The nationalization of credit funding (*économie de financements administrés*), expanding public expenditure, and contracts from national champions enabled them to persuade a number of large employers to follow their views and projects. They were able to use a mix of incentives and coercion. Industrialization, mergers, modernization and innovation primarily followed a top-down logic.

The so-called French miracle tells the story of a large-scale rapid industrialization obtained through the organization of a national division of labour. If the state played a key role, the French indicative planning system also built on the support of major interest groups and agencies all over the country. This process relied on several elements: the emergence of a powerful technocracy that led both administrations and major companies; the role of *dirigiste* and then indicative planning; the vision of modernization as a technical problem that could only be driven by national champions; grand projects; sectorialized diagnosis; and programmes which either ignored existing industrial relationships and corporate strategies or denied private actors' ability to perform on their own—especially when they were local and provincial. Heroic public policies imposed grand views over supposedly mean private interests (Hayward 1986). A state-led industrial Meccano organized production systems around a limited number of leading firms, which drove the technical and commercial evolution of their suppliers.

For example, banks played an important role. The centralization of the banking system started in the nineteenth century, and soon financial institutions from Lyon, Lille and Bordeaux were integrated with national banks. The nationalization of banks after 1945 gave rise to a powerful centralized public banking system. As in the rest of the economy, the managers from these banks came overwhelmingly from the Ministry of Finance and started their careers as civil servants. Banks' priorities were therefore very much in tune with the economic priorities of governments: there was an obsession with economic modernization. Until the 1980s, the provision of finance was tightly controlled by the state: thanks to both bank nationalization and the creation of budgeted funds, the Ministry of Finance was able to set the price and the quantity of credit. However, the making of industrial national champions was not primarily supported by large deposit-banks, such as Crédit Lyonnais, the Banque Nationale de Paris or Société Générale. Although all three were state-owned, and had been built through nationalizations and mergers of regional banks, they were not called upon to finance the modernization of the French industry, either by providing long-term loans or by taking equity stakes. Instead, this function was given to specialized institutions, at least partly state-owned, which were able to deliver subsidized loans to priority sectors: *Fonds de développement économique et social, Institut de Développement Industriel, Comptoir des Entrepreneurs, Crédit Foncier de France.* With the exception of mutual regional banks (in particular in Alsace and Brittany), there was little banking support for SMEs or local networks of firms.

As Jobert and Muller have shown (1987), French elites' understanding of the world relied upon sectorial macro-economic diagnosis. In such a context, the content of structuring programmes primarily relied upon formal rationality principles: mergers were required to create big corporate actors, that is, national champions, which were supposed to be the only actors who could implement standardization and productivity improvements, who could make technological breakthroughs, and who could cope with international competition. Through supply contracts, 'large firms *à la française*' (Cohen 1992; Salais and Storper 1993; Levy-Leboyer 1996) would be able to drive the technical and commercial development of the whole country (Jenny and Weber 1976). Planning was seen as a distinctive pattern of French capitalism (Boyer 1998).

This extremely centralized method was not bound to sector-related distribution of activities, but also inspired the first *aménagement du territoire* policies: as specialized activities were allocated to a limited number of corporate actors in a *co-dirigiste* fashion involving senior civil servants and top executives, they were granted to under-industrialized and declining provinces. This structured some regions around new plants. Thus, local economies were involved in a top-down process, resembling a nation-wide *Meccano industriel* game (Bauer and Cohen 1981), with a majority of decision-makers and innovators (the players) in Paris.

The story of French local economies is thus one of gradual decline, faced with market forces, an unfriendly state, and local *notables* who rarely engaged in autonomous regional development despite the existence of SMEs. In that process SMEs lost their impetus: some declined, as they could not face the competition from large national firms; others were entangled as subsidiaries and were integrated within vertical organizations; others again survived. In most cases, however, what remained lost its local dimension and was integrated within the national economy.

When Local and Small Become Beautiful: The Restructuring of French SMEs

From the 1970s onwards, SMEs were rediscovered in France as elsewhere through a combination of objective indicators (including the crisis of large firms) and ideological turn, in particular in the industrial sector. This section attempts first to provide an overview of SMEs in France and their transformation; second to analyse the metropolization process and the dislocation of the periphery as opportunities for local economies; third, to analyse how, within the public policy sphere, SMEs are targeted by a large range of weakly co-ordinated programmes.

SMEs: Going through a Large-Scale Renewal

French productive space became organized within a Fordist division of labour between Paris and the regions. Local economies emerged therefore within that specialization, apart from the exception of some that had been forgotten by policy-makers and academics alike.

The French economy is well known for its relatively low level of both specialization and territorial concentration (Coriat and Taddéi 1993). When they compared Italy, France and the USA in the early 1990s, Storper and Salais (1998), using in particular trade statistics, emphasized once again the fact that France performs moderately well in a great number of sectors but well in very few. Their own calculations show that 'France is specialized in only a few clusters and sub-clusters of products: beverages and food products; inputs to the transportation industry (automobile components, tyres and so on); production of energy and turbines; health care (including pharmaceutics)' (ibid.: 102). In most cases, those sectors are dominated by large firms and have often benefited from economies of scale which used to be related to state modernization policies, to the defence industry (back in the 1920s), or directly constructed by the state for mass consumption.

But the role of SMEs in the industrial sector has been on the increase for the last two decades, a time when major firms reorganized their operations and shed labour. The rise of just-in-time production systems has had a lasting impact on the relationship between large firms and their subcontractors (Gorgeu and Mathieu 1996). As in other countries, some industrial SMEs have engaged in dynamic processes of innovation and reorganization, in part in close relation with large firms. However, foreign investment also played a dynamic role.

After a long period when foreign firms were not always welcome, France became in the 1990s the third country in the world in attracting foreign direct investment. This relatively new phenomenon has long-term implications: the massive, mostly European, foreign investment in the 1990s limited the steep decline of French industrial jobs, particularly spectacularly in the East: Alsace, Provence Côtes d'Azur, Rhône-Alpes. Foreign-owned firms now account for 32 per cent of manufacturing turnover and 27 per cent of the labour force, the highest proportion in the western world (Dupont and François 1998). Interestingly, those investments are made in medium-size firms (mainly from 100 to 2,000) with strong technological components. Nearly half the jobs in industrial firms with between 500 and 2,000 employees now belong to foreign capital. Those dynamic industrial firms are usually well integrated within their milieu (ibid.). Also, their investments are not made so much in the traditionally strong sectors of French industry (vehicles or aeronautics), but rather in chemicals, electronics, machine tools, machine construction, and new technologies.

Overall, there are now 20,300 small and middle-size industrial firms (between 20 and 499 employees) in France (SESSI 1999a), 36,000 if we take ten employees as the lower limit. They represent 53 per cent of jobs in the manufacturing sector (about 1.5 million employees), 39 per cent of investment, and 26 per cent of exports. More than 80 per cent of them are small (under 100 employees). The data reveal important movements: large firms down-sizing to become SMEs, SMEs collapsing or growing—and most importantly the strengthening of large SMEs. Their strong development over the past few years is related to both the vigorous development of some firms and the support of large firms. They deserve close attention.

About 7,000 of these SMEs are subsidiaries (French or foreign capital) of a larger industrial group or firm, and others are independent, usually relying upon local and familial capital. There is clearly a trend towards the progressive integration of larger SMEs within holdings or industrial groups. Those involved tend to be more high-tech and to export more. This trend is particularly important for motor vehicles (see below), chemicals, machinery, steel, metalwork and paper.

Independent firms represent 37 per cent of SMEs with between 200 and 499 employees, that is, they tend to be smaller and relatively less oriented towards export (11 per cent of exports) (see various reports from the Centre d'Études de l'Emploi, in particular Ardenti and Vrain 1995). However, they are still an important element of the economy, often as subcontractors. Some are involved in small niches for basic goods with limited competition. There is still a large number of rather small familial SMEs whose markets remain local or regional. They represent a non-spectacular part of many local and regional economies and are often forgotten. According to Ardenti and Vrain (ibid.), these firms suffered particularly in the late 1980s and early 1990s from increasing imports and price competition. That has led, even among traditional SMEs, to a new generation of diverse strategies (going upscale, including high-tech, exports, reduction of activities, associations within networks or integration within a larger group) which are central to the question of collective competitive goods.

The question of resources and access to collective goods has emerged as a central issue for business leaders and policy-makers alike, hence a mobilization outside Paris. According to the Ministry of Industry and various reports, the main problems of French industrial SMEs are the following: heavy concentration within traditional sectors; increasing but weak research and development; low number involved in exports; problems of qualifications of the labour force.

Metropolization and Dislocation of the Periphery: Some Opportunities for Reinforcing Surviving Local Economies

Metropolization has been a dominant process of the organization of economic space in the past fifteen years (see Rodriguez-Posé in this volume). Since the 1980s the Paris region has captured most of the economic growth in France, in particular in terms of jobs and productivity, which has followed the internationalization of the French economy (Davezies 1995; Veltz 1996, 2000a and b). Paris has become the main entrance point of various exchanges between the rest of the world and France. It accounts for more than 30 per cent of GNP. Productivity gaps are increasing, and Paris plays a role as a filtering pump attracting the most qualified labour force and firms in dynamic economic sectors.

In her major book on industry location patterns in France, Alvergne (1997) shows clearly the three dynamics involved: inheritance of industrialization and slow convergence in the 1960s and 1970s due to the declining industries of the North-East; industrialization of the West and limited rise of the South (sunbelt effect); and accelerated metropolization in the 1980s. At the end of the growth period industry was located in different regions of France, and the Paris region remained dominant. Her conclusion leads her to emphasize path dependent processes and the relatively slow change of industrial characteristics of French regions.

Over the past twenty-five years that specialization has collapsed, and the dislocation of any notion of integrated regional economies (region in the institutional sense) went hand in hand with political decentralization. Local systems were actively researched and sought after. The French economy had to face major transformation like others in Europe and beyond, among which were: de-industrialization, rise of services, processes of globalization for firms, increased competition, decline of state capacity to organize and control the economy, technological change.

On the other hand, in the French sense of region as a level of regional government, regional economies have lost part of their limited coherence. As Veltz and his colleagues put it, the hierarchical integrated economic space is gradually being replaced by the *Economie d'Archipels*, some growth centres (in general cities) with fewer and fewer connections with the rest of the country. Archipel-agoes, metropolization, disintegration of regional economies, fragmentation: all this also gives more opportunities in some territories, either to maintain and develop the existing local productive system, or to develop some clusters.

We must now identify more precisely industrial areas in France and sites of dynamic industrial SMEs (Figure 5.1a,b). As in other parts of Europe, old industrial regions today face considerable difficulties (social, economic, cultural) in becoming competitive. After the large restructuring and job losses in the steel industry and textiles, recent restructuring in the defence sector is raising difficulties for the large number of SMEs in the region Centre, not far from Paris, and in Bordeaux. Regions close to Paris have either also suffered extended disintegration or have been absorbed in the dynamics of the Paris region. Most cities, regional

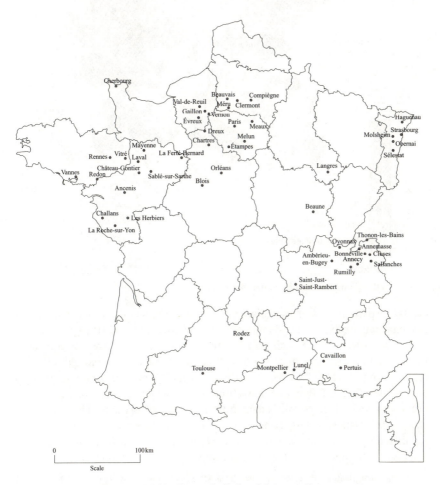

FIGURE 5.1(a). Dynamic Industrial Areas, France

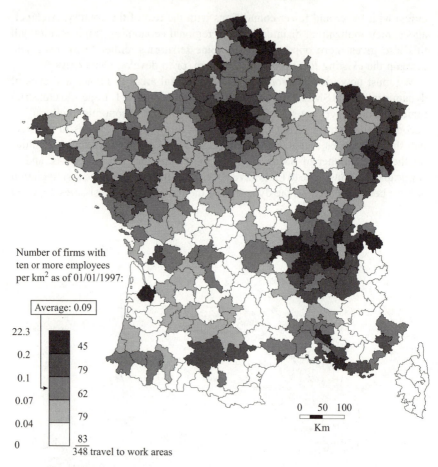

Number of firms with
ten or more employees
per km² as of 01/01/1997:

Average: 0.09

22.3
0.2
0.1
0.07
0.04
0

45
79
62
79
83

348 travel to work areas

FIGURE 5.1(b). Density of Manufacturing Firms by TTWA, France, 1997
Source: Authors' own elaborations of data presented in Table 5.1.

capitals in particular, are not specialized and they disappear from the list because of
the importance of services. The same applies to areas in the Paris region.[3]

The statistics include both large firms and SMEs, which are usually more
important in recent industrial regions (South and West). In some old industrial
regions—in particular Picardie, Nord Pas de Calais, and Normandy—there is an
emerging milieu of dynamic industrial SMEs which is escaping from subordination and which is fully adapted to international markets. Those firms (in
chemicals, plastics, metals, even more traditional sectors sometimes), often work
for different clients and not just large French firms, which in any case have
sometimes disappeared. Others just get integrated within foreign owned groups

[3] In the identification of sectors we use the NAP classification (NACE in English), which is
standardized at the European level.

as mentioned before. In newly industrialized regions, around Nantes in particular, but also in Brittany or within the Rhône-Alpes region, organized networks of industrial SMEs are growing, increasing their exports significantly, and playing an increasing role.

We have tried to select travel to work areas (TTWAs) where there was some economic development in the manufacturing sector. In doing this several indicators have been combined. The mix includes indicators of growth in private sector employment and some attempt to identify industrial firms (i.e., UNEDIC Industry). We have tried to aggregate diverse indicators (and changes since the 1980s), in particular. The full list includes: tax base (*taxe professionnelle*); employment in the private sector (UNEDIC); share of wages; manual employment (a distinctive sign of an industrial area); population growth; women in the labour market.[4] Once aggregated in a simple way, a list of dynamic TTWAs emerges (Figure 5.1(a)).

Different cases appear:

1. Dynamic clusters, highly specialized industrial districts well researched in the literature: in Savoy (in the Alps), Cluses, Annemasse, Annecy (Rhône-Alpes); in the Catholic West of France (Les Herbiers in Vendée); and to a lesser extent, that is less specialized or including large firms investments, in Haguenau, Molsheim near Strasbourg (Alsace), and in Vitré near Rennes. Most of these are in small towns.
2. Regional capitals enjoying strong economic development including large firms and subcontractors: Rennes, Toulouse, Strasbourg. These include important forms of business co-operation and subcontracting.
3. Places on the outskirts of the Paris region, usually dominated by major firms: Val de Reuil (a new town near Rouen), Evreux, Melun.

Regions that have accumulated two conditions are more interesting in terms of regional dynamics and structures of governance. These include localities far from Paris which have kept some cultural identity, which is likely to be reinterpreted and mobilized in favour of economic development, and regions that have not been transformed by the forces of the old industrialization. Both economists and sociologists have pointed to these regions which, despite being heavily fragmented, tend to have relatively large proportions of dynamics SMEs. In the North by contrast there is a rather high proportion of large firms and less diversity.

The data suggest that many regional economies are not so specialized, and are structured around regional capitals (metropolization model), but also that there is a diversity of models. It can be argued that centralization and homogenization (in terms of labour costs, qualifications, infrastructures, utilities) do not constitute a dynamic force to sustain specialized local economies. These are either specialized or diversified within and around a regional capital. Pressure for

---

[4] The statistical analysis of various data was done in co-operation with ŒIL (University Paris XII). We acknowledge the support of B.H. Nicot.

specialization does not derive from the production of competitive collective goods, which is more and more widespread, and to some extent, territorialized.

Local and Regional Institutional Mobilization: Extensive Revival of Local Economies within Policy Spheres

There is no space here to consider the extensive restructuring of industrial and economic policy in France over the past fifteen years. One should however keep in mind not only the industrial policy change (Cohen 1989; Schmidt 1996; Cohen, Hart, and Simmie 1997; Levy 1999)—particularly the impact of various waves of privatization and the growing autonomy of firms—but also the change of parameters of the macro-economic framework. These include the liberalization of the economy, tying the franc to the German mark, inflation targets, and more broadly acceptance and adaptation to the rules of the European market. This framework has created serious constraints for firms. It structured the conditions for large firms' reorganization, and its impact, for instance in terms of job losses, was not neutral.

Beyond those general conditions, we must consider changes specific to local economies. The French literature has usually emphasized the importance of the decentralization reforms, and many have looked for some sort of regional economic policy going hand in hand with the coming of age of regional government (Morvan and Marchand 1994). That view has been contested, it being argued that there is no such thing as a regionalization of the governance of the French economy, with a limited exception in the case of training (Mériaux 1999). The French case is interesting because of the large mobilization of a whole range of agencies at different levels. Focusing on the regions is therefore misleading.

As stated before, we argue that in the past production of collective goods for firms by national and public policy was a major factor to explain the lack of local industrial productive systems. Once political priorities changed and SMEs came back on the agenda, organizations and policies were explicitly restructured to suit their needs, or supposedly so—though this does not mean that policies and finances towards large firms were abandoned.

The Double Turn of Industrial Policy: Towards Local Economies and SMEs. In the 1970s state officials rediscovered the virtues of SMEs and had to respond to increasing pressure from the periphery for some local and regional intervention. To a large extent, the difficulties of regional economies were explained by sector crisis. However, financial resources remained concentrated in the hands of central authorities, and were mostly dedicated to large firms and classic *filières*. This was partly because the state could not easily withdraw from the scene it had set up, and partly because it still intended to rely upon them. During this period the main feature of industrial policy was the way the state managed industrial decline in emergency. Unable to avoid local crises and their national impact, the CIASI (the arm of *L'Etat brancardier*) dealt with a number of provincial SMEs

(Cohen 1989), but kept on playing 'industrial Meccano' to a certain extent, 'in order to save what could be saved' (Levy 1999). Interventionist policies still relied on large firms, and were revived by the left government after 1981: *grands projets* for technological developments were maintained (telecommunications, energy, transport) (Cohen 1992), and export boosting was implemented through *grands contrats*.

The first signs of interest in SMEs showed in the *Institut du Développement Industrie* (IOD). This was launched to support innovative, exporting and expanding SMEs. However, in both emergency and development programmes, SMEs were still the last served in the credit rationing system administered by the state: national champions and newly nationalized firms benefited from the bulk of support.

Since the mid-1980s celebrating and fostering enterprise have remained at the forefront of public policy, no matter the majority in Parliament. A number of measures have been implemented to respond to traditional weaknesses of SMEs, and local offices of ministries have been significantly reinforced. The Ministry of Industry delivers measures through regional and local offices of the Directions Régionales de l'Industrie, de la Recherche et de l'Environnement (DRIRE) and l'Agence Nationale pour la Valorisation de la Recherche (ANVAR), with the help of the chambers of commerce and industry. The Ministry of Labour delivers training. There are also the DATAR regional offices, and the Ministry of Trade has structured more or less formalized co-operation networks, which aim at transferring state-of-the-art technologies and management methods to small firms. Generally speaking, in addition to their function of legal control of business practices (regarding environment, security, working conditions), the mission of ministry provincial offices is twofold. First, they are supposed to shape the business environment in order to increase technical and financial resources available to SMEs and to facilitate implementation of management projects. Second, on their own or with help from the chambers or from employers' organizations, they intervene directly in the companies to spread modern management practices and to stimulate initiatives.

For instance, DRIRE local offices and ANVAR focus on technological improvements in SMEs. Their intervention has shifted from sectors to the local economies as such: in 1994–95, some 75 per cent of subsidized projects came from companies employing fewer than 50 people. ANVAR and DRIRE administer financial instruments, and have organized co-operation networks in each region (Réseaux de Diffusion Technologique (RDTs)).[5] Financial instruments

---

[5] For example: the organization of local trade fairs that gather firms with similar or complementary activities; quality certification programmes involving several entrepreneurs and other forms of partnerships; training. In 1995 the number of projects supported, both individual and collective, reached roughly 7,600. Although ANVAR is smaller than DRIRE, it relies on RDTs to mobilize some 1,000 proposals. In 1997 more than 4,600 industrial projects were supported, for a total amount of FRF 1.35 Bn. Whereas DRIRE supports acquisitions of resources (management forces, recent technologies and production methods), ANVAR offices focus on technological break-through, that is on industrialization and/or acceleration of R&D advances.

support investment projects, whether on a single firm or a collective basis. RDTs involve research laboratories, scientific and technical colleges of universities, graduate schools of engineering and subsidized technical centres. They support inter-firm co-operation links and the chambers of commerce. In his book elo-quently entitled *Tocqueville's Revenge*, Levy (1999: ch. 6) gives a coherent account of the profound transformation of these organizations towards localities and firms, DRIRE in particular. In total, if we include the ANVAR measures and financing from regional governments, budgeted subsidies devoted to industrial SMEs amounted to FF 2,850 million per year during the period 1994–98, of which almost 80 per cent consisted of state funds.

The socialist government elected in 1997 has also adopted the language and policies of supporting SMEs. In 1998, a new fund for business creations, the *Fond National de Développement des Enterprises* (FNDE), was set up, amounting to FF 200 million in its first year. It was launched in order to grant 0 per cent interest-rate loans to start-ups to favour interventions from venture capital. Part of firms' expenses resulting from risk assessment studies and administration of projects are reimbursed. A FF 90 million guarantee fund is administered by the BDPME (the SME bank).

Overall, the state apparatus has been reorganized (another evidence of the making of a regional level of the state in France), and there has been a multi-plication of schemes to support SMEs in various ways, or in other words to produce collective competitive goods. Those schemes have been completed by the mobilization of local and regional actors to support SMEs.

Local and Regional Institutions. This local and regional mobilization has been particularly important, but assessing its impact is difficult. After the crisis of the 1970s local and regional economic development was very much on the cards, a trend reinforced by decentralization reforms. A regional public policy aiming at promoting economic development seemed to consist of: 1. building and devel-oping SMEs collectively, whatever form it took, including working on the environment of firms; and 2. playing a role of regulation between various eco-nomic interests in order to deliver collective goods (for instance non-economic factors of economic development), or to prevent unintended consequences such as ecological disasters.

In France the state is usually very badly equipped to do such things. The region thus emerged as a sort of natural level to try to promote that sort of economic development because the regions were closer to small firms than the state. Although that led to a dramatic rise in local governments' initiatives, the legal and financial frameworks of interventions have not led to a regionalization of economic policies so far. Regional councils have been relatively weak and unable to take the lead on economic policies, their initiatives being squeezed between state authorities and a tough competition among all sub-national governments (Le Galès 1994; Levy 1999). Furthermore, although it has often been argued that local governments were in a better position than the central state to reach SMEs and to respond to their needs, a major part of investment has consisted of ambitious real estate operations, which were primarily designed to improve local attractiveness (Levy 1999).

Local and regional government's new policies turned to SMEs and start-ups. A great number of initiatives came from existing organizations (primarily the chambers of commerce, and previously state-owned large firms), or from purpose-built ones. These initiatives have aimed at producing all kinds of goods, or at easing access to them: subsidies, loans and capital financing, consulting, training, technology transfers, labour force recruitment. Although direct grants are no longer popular, local authorities still have a variety of schemes to support firms. Many regions still have schemes for loan guarantees (or a fund where firms can borrow money that they will repay on a longer term), which are managed by other organized business networks, CCI, public–private partnership, or even state external services. Local authorities (especially regions) have invested in financial institutions: stake in venture-capital companies, in *sociétés de développement régional* (SDR) for instance.

The decentralization process paved the way for increasing efforts from local authorities to promote the economy, though figures are to be taken with caution, since the meaning of 'economic intervention' is open to dispute. A survey made by the *Chambres régionales des Comptes* (Cour des Comptes 1995:24) shows that local authorities' budgets devoted to business promotion increased by 11.2 per cent between 1986 and 1993—that is twice as much as the rise in total expenditure (6.2 per cent)—to reach an annual FF 15 billion in 1993.

In government terms, the governance of regional economies in France seem to have been more structured by the regionalization of state agencies and schemes than by the rise of interventionist local and regional governments policies.

Organizations Involved in Local Economic Development. Besides initiatives from all government levels, many private organizations have been involved in supporting local business and their number is increasing. Some already existed but followed this path recently, such as the chambers of commerce, banking networks and large firms. Chambers are drastically restructured to provide services and collective competition goods (information, law, marketing, trade fairs). They play an increasing role in the governance of local economies and now build local strategies, though these are not as institutionalized as in Germany. Similarly, the transformation of the main business organization (CNPF) to MEDEF goes hand in hand with the reinforcement of the local and regional level of the organization. *Le Patronat* is now encouraged to play an active role in local and regional strategies.

What can be made of this brief review of organizational changes and disorganized, incoherent, massive mobilization towards the production of competitive goods for SMEs? First, something is going on. This kind of mobilization would have been unthinkable twenty years ago. For instance, for many years, *fonds de capital-risque* were non-existent for French SMEs, in particular in the industrial sector. There have now been all kinds of badly organized initiatives and failures with little impact. This has led to some nostalgia for a centralist state. However, in the past three years French risk capital investment has risen and is now the highest in Europe. Three major actors are in play and are successful: national funds within a new agency working closely with DRIRE and ANVAR, regional funds in some regions bringing together local public and private money, and funds arranged by business organization either at the national or the local level.

For instance, investment in risk capital has risen from FF 274 million in 1994 to FF 3 billion in 1998 in order to support start-up in the so-called 'new economy'. A similar change is occurring for classic investment in SMEs. It may well be the case that the mobilization that has been described is now sufficiently organized in structures of governance (either national networks or territorialized forms) to produce effective results and promising outcomes. In dynamic economic areas such as Rhône-Alpes (see Dunford 1991; Picchieri 1998) those forms of governance and collective goods provision seem to have a positive effect on economic development.

Second, such an optimistic interpretation is unlikely to take place in every region and every locality. Some places tend to demonstrate strong capacity for collective action, effectiveness, integrated modes of governance (or attempts to do so, see Morvan 1996 for Brittany), while in others fragmentation and disintegration are getting worse.

Another interesting finding is the change in relations with existing institutions. Together with a new generation of policy-makers, a new generation of business leaders has emerged in industrial SMEs in most of France: less dependent on the state, less rooted in conservative familial traditions, and more aware of the potential and collective benefits from that kind of organization within a given region. This is a trend not unrelated to the new challenges facing SMEs. Active involvement of SMEs in their local area is also evidence of growing territorial mobilization for economic development. Evidence of this appears in most case studies (Courault and Parat 2000), but we lack systematic data. A recent survey by the business journal *L'usine nouvelle* identified 120 business networks outside the Paris region which were all active in organizing projects and generating competitive collective goods. Broadly speaking, and again there is a lack of systematic evidence, there seems to be an increasing commitment of SMEs' chief executives to their locality, and less interest in the large firm model.

If that makes sense beyond case studies and approximative surveys, it would constitute a major change. Levy (1999), in his critique of the failure of local and regional economic policy after the decentralization reforms in two declining regions (Besançon and Saint-Etienne) makes it clear that 'the underdevelopment of employer associations has weighed heavily upon local economic strategies . . . affecting the conception, substance, and implementation of policy . . . In a sense, a vibrant tissue of employer associations constitutes another piece of local associational puzzle that France does not possess'.

It is also interesting to learn from various case studies that these clubs often benefit, and work with some indirect support, from established institutions, CCI or local authorities. Also, although these business networks sometimes organize themselves along one industrial sector (aeronautics subcontractors in Toulouse for instance, or SIPAREX in the Alps), it is rarely the case. Most often, they are the dynamic industrial SMEs organized along a territorial logic (commune, pays, urban region, half a *département*, whatever). At first, that may seem disappointing: the lack of sectorial specialization of these networks or clubs does not reveal the emergence of specialized local productive systems; but is that surprising in the French economy? Is regional concentration so much an issue when the production of competitive collective goods is not so much a regional problem?

Diverse Models of Local Governance of the Economy

There seems to be a dynamic combination of factors in the French context: opportunities for local economies, dynamic SMEs and a weakly co-ordinated but diverse and dynamic institutional support. We now turn to the question: has France been able to create a system of local economic governance to nurture these remnants and new developments of SMEs?

There is no simple answer. In a country where the centralization process was so powerful for so long, and where national champions were so dominant, it would be an analytical mistake to focus on local economies alone, or to analyse SMEs only in their local dimension. In terms of governance, two cases are rather clear. The first concerns surviving local productive systems, former industrial districts. The second concerns large firms and subcontractors in a hierarchical model with little horizontal co-ordination. Beyond these there is a large number of cases that combine different kinds of regulations, different kinds of firms and different kinds of mix between vertical and horizontal integration. This should not come as a surprise. Large firms try to combine economies of scale and proximity to particular regional markets.

Veltz (2000b), concluding research on the restructuring of large firms in France, insists that this is reinforced by their need to innovate, to react quickly, to anticipate changes. That leads to a whole set of different strategies by which firms try to deal with these tensions, the more so as they restructure to deal more and more closely with clients' needs (hence the current emphasis on knowledge management and logistics). Within that model, the distinction between large firms and SMEs tends to be blurred. Large firms can take different forms from the financial holding to the classic hierarchical case, to the centre of a network of partners and subcontractors, linked through all sorts of contracts. Veltz and his colleagues insist that in most cases, basic units (the plant, the subcontractors, the partners) tend to acquire more autonomy, but under standardized parameters of control and contracts. Even in the case of networked firms providing different services, including finance, hierarchies tend to be blurred with more mutual interdependence, though not in all sectors.

This sheds some light on the figures and trends presented above. The rise of SMEs in France, including dynamic, high-tech, export-oriented, rather large SMEs (a new phenomenon by French standards) is related to their inclusion within larger firms or holdings which provide capital, but also all sorts of collective competition goods. Second, large firms' internal differentiation and restructuring strategies (including more complex links and relations with SMEs) also make possible different plant locations. This enables their dependent SMEs to try to get the best of both worlds: securing collective goods from both professional networks and vertical links from large firms, as well as from the locality or region. At the same time they try to avoid constraints and controls. Third, even independent SMEs have to face new competitors and bound to be organized collectively either locally or externally to get the competition goods they need. Fourth, there is no such thing as a unique model of governance of local economies in France, even if large firms have played a key role in the restructuring process. Both large firms and SMEs are faced with the paradox of territory, gaining more opportunity to escape from the local but needing more of the collective goods produced locally (or in some locality) to increase their performance. There is an ongoing process of trial and error, and that redefinition of the links between firms and locality is still going on. In that context, modes of governance (never purely local) are in the making in different ways. Some will fail, some may work. We can provide some examples of interesting dynamics; they cannot be exhaustive at this stage.

The Restructuring of France's Few Local Productive Systems

As mentioned before, local economies did not disappear.[6] They were not that prosperous; they were discrete, hidden at times, but some survived, at least until the 1970s. Some have since disappeared or nearly so, such as the shoe-making districts in Fougères and Romans sur Isère, the watch industry in Besançon and Franche-Comté (Lévy 1999), or the textile local productive system in the Vosges, and the paper mills in Annonay (Ganne 1983). The list of survivors includes first Cholet, Oyonnax and the Vallée de l'Arve, but also cutlery in Thiers, and clothing in Roanne. Those cases were remote from the state; they were good examples of community governance.

Building upon interesting cases in the Rhône-Alpes region and the Italian literature, Ganne and his group (1992a and b) and Courlet and Pecqueur (1992)

---

[6] We here make use of the work of the research network on local productive systems which worked in the late 1980s, in particular in GLYSI in Lyon, and within the IRPED group in Grenoble (Courlet and Pecqueur 1992; Pecqueur 1996a and b, 2000; Courault, Pecqueur, and Soulage 1994). We also use the work of Courault (1992) and Courault and Parat (2000) in connection with Cholet, and Minguet (1985) and Rerat (1990) and Rerat and Courault (1992) for Roanne. Ganne was the main figure, both to co-ordinate various local research projects, and to make comparisons with Italy (1990).

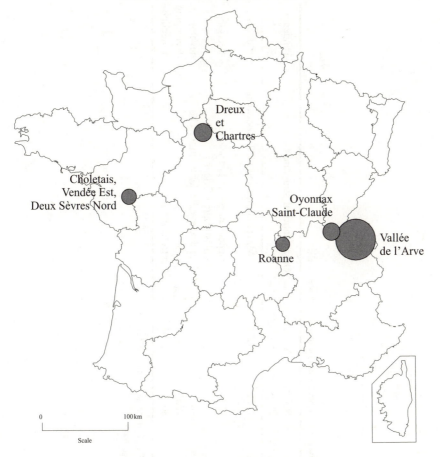

FIGURE 5.2. Surviving Industrial Districts, France

Source: Authors' own elaborations of data presented in Table 5.1.

carried out various surveys to identify remaining local economies and their characteristics. They demonstrated the existence of a small group of them, fewer than a dozen overall. The main cases, which have been well researched, are presented in Figure 5.2 and Table 5.1.

These are, or rather were, similar to some Italian districts, though there is no single model. What is immediately remarkable is the fact they are localized in the periphery, far away first from Paris, second from main cities, and third from the main communication systems. These areas share several characteristics. They are rural or semi-rural, where the chances of finding alternative forms of employment are very remote (weak public sector or even opposition to the state, and no major firms). This provides support for Ganne's thesis that they survived despite national policies, and because they were culturally and politically in the periphery. These are localities where it is possible to identify the kind of neo-localist autonomous

TABLE 5.1. Local Economies in France, c.1994

Sector	Areas	No. of firms	No. of employees	Organizational structure	Tendency
Clothing and footwear	Choletais, Vendée Est, Deux Sèvres Nord	100	11,500	CAMI (clothing) and GPT (footwear)	in decline
Plastic materials	Dreux, Chartres	150		Groupement des industriels de la plasturgie à Orléans	emerging
Precision plastics	Oyonnax, Saint Claude	80		Chambre syndicale; training schools	developing
Specialized metal parts	Vallée de l'Arve	130*	9,700**		developing
Textiles	Roanne	80*	9,300***	Centre d'Infographie	in decline

Abbreviations: CAMI: Centre d'Affaire pour la Mode; GPT: Groupe de Promotion Territoriale.

Sources: *DATAR; **Courault 1992; ***Courault and Parat 2000.

regulations based upon some key elements (social structures, autonomy or opposition to the state as in Vendée or Oyonnax). In all those local economies, researchers have identified forms of collective action and political life very close to the interests of the entrepreneur and related to familial structures. The evidence that such economies only exist on the margin of the national political, social and economic space are very similar to the early Italian findings, that is, the peripheral dimension enhances the strength and coherence of the locality. However, the Italian situation was subsequently discovered to be more diverse.

The evidence also suggests that the state could not be held responsible for every failure (GLYSI 1992). Sad stories of decline and disappearance of local economies have also much to do with failures to change and to adapt to new market conditions, and to the lack of response in face of changing markets (textiles and shoe-making). Of course, one could argue that the state did not provide incentives and policies to help organize a transition. However, it is also possible to argue that local industrial systems also benefited from state protection for a while.

Within the group of marginalized industrial districts a distinction should be made between the prosperous cases of the Alps (Oyonnax and Vallée de l'Arve) and the others.

Most surviving local economies that are identified in the literature are found in traditional sectors: shoe-making, clothing in Cholet, textiles and knitted goods in Roanne, paper in Annonay, cutlery in Thiers. Here, most surviving local economies still face uncertain and difficult conditions. In textiles, Roanne and Le Choletais have developed different strategies to survive, including for Cholet some interesting forms of institutionalization of co-operation between different actors to adapt and change collectively (Parat and Courault 2000). In contrast to the prosperous Italian districts in those sectors, French local economies do not enjoy favourable cost structures or image.

In those cases, therefore, survival is related to two factors. First is local capacity and production of collective competition goods through non-market and non-state relations. Second is the dense set of relations that have been created between them and national industrial groups able to provide some collective goods: investment, marketing, information about markets, technological innovations. Sophisticated and changing forms of co-ordination with Parisian groups (for instance in the textile and shoe-making sectors) have proved essential for the survival of some of those local economies together with strong cultural identity and peculiar entrepreneurial elites (Minguet 1985). The cases of le Choletais and Roanne are probably the most interesting in that regard (Rerat 1990; Courault 1992; Courault and Parat 2000). Courault and Parat stress that external investors in Cholet have not managed to halt the decline of the old system. They give a fascinating account of recent restructuring of the local productive system under the leadership of the *distributeurs*, who are closer to consumers and competitors. Cholet SMEs have learned the hard lesson of increased competition and have lost some of their room for autonomy.

By contrast, Courlet and the IRPEPD in Grenoble have emphasized the strength and development of the local economies in the Alps, close to the Italian border in Oyonnax and Vallée de l'Arve in particular. They are involved in heavier industries (plastics, specialized metal parts, metals), which require more capital, and include a higher proportion of new technologies. They are organized around middle-sized firms. These successful local economies signal once more the contrast with Italy. Ganne (2000) updated his research on Oyonnax, and gives a remarkable account of the institutionalization of an industrial district. The once integrated so-called 'plastic valley' had to face competition, and it changed. Ganne describes the 'triple institutionalization' of Oyonnax, that is, the professional institutionalization to develop sophisticated plastics for the motor industry. Large SMEs, major motor industry subcontractors, have invested in the valley; other firms have merged; horizontal co-operation between firms has increased and has become more formal. New training organizations are a good example of the outcome of this professionalization. Second, local firms have developed systematic links with banks and financial partners who have played a decisive rôle in the restructuring process. Third, Ganne shows how the professionals have made links with local authorities to develop the industry beyond the Valley in a larger zone, including the creation of a kind of plastics science park. Local authorities (*départements* and the regional council) have responded to the dynamics of business leaders to develop the industry on a larger scale and to contribute to the collective action of that small region.

Oyonnax is therefore a good case of openness towards the outside (firms, banks, local and regional authorities, world markets), but which built on the inheritance of the industrial district to develop institutionalized forms of collective action. The whole movement of institutionalization has been led and controlled, as Ganne rightly stresses, by local business leaders and the community, sometimes against classic public policy logics.

In such cases, local economies were governed through a combination of community (locality and family) and market regulation (Courault and Trouvé 2000). Changing economic conditions and competition in particular have led to more external market relations (investments from large external firms) and local processes of institutionalization where state organizations, local authorities and employers' association have been active. In the Cholet case, that seems to lead to a less local mode of governance, where market relations and quasi-vertical integration tend to become dominant. In Oyonnax, another local mode of governance of the local economy has been organized, combining community, market, large firms and some local authorities under the leadership of business leaders (families and associations).

Large Firms and Subcontractors. Few would dispute the claim that large firms have by and large been the major actors in the restructuring of the French economy since the 1980s. The relationship between major firms and their subcontractors changed. The economic and political legitimacy of big firms had an impact on subcontracting:

French big firms have been very slow to experiment with a strategy of structural sub-contracting, that is to say, a strategy characterized by some degree of planning in the orders and of stability in the relations between principal firms and sub-contractors. (Lescure 1999:152–53)

Despised SMEs were used only to deal with business fluctuations. This has changed in the 1980s—but not the subordination of SMEs. After much delay (Cohen 1989; Boyer 1998) and near collapse, large French industrial firms have engaged in a radical restructuring process involving subcontractors. An analysis by the Ministry of Industry has shown a marked transfer of added value from SMEs to large firms (SESSI 1998b) at a time when the importance of sub-contracting is rising. The success of large French firms in the second part of the 1990s has a lot to do, not only with the relatively good performances of the French economy in terms of growth, but also with this new division of labour and control between them and their subcontractors (see Figure 5.3).

Large firms have controlled their reorganization and have mobilized sub-contractors with their strategic objective in order to increase their competitiveness. This move has in particular been successful in the case of aeronautics (Gilly and Pecqueur 1995) and the motor industry (Gorgeu and Mathieu 1995a), but less so for Moulinex for instance. Beyond the question of price, large firms have increased their pressure on SMEs in terms of quality control, innovation and size. According to research done by the Centre d'Etude de l'Emploi, in classic successful cases of national champions (defence, vehicles, aeronautics), large firms have organized in the 1980s a quasi-integration of groups of SMEs, close to the model of lean production.

In a series of papers, Hancké has shown the logic of this restructuring process. His thesis is that large firms were able to:

reorganize precisely because there was no dynamic small firm sector; this allowed them to avoid being pushed into an adjustment path which took into account the interests of small firms, as in many ways large firms in Germany were. Yet this also implied that the large firms could force the smaller ones into reorganising in ways that would fit their own needs. (Hancké 1997:1–2)

That story is confirmed for the major industrial sectors in the 1980s. To some extent, Hancké argues, large firms became the step-parents of French SMEs, dominating them but providing expertise, capital, new technology developments and other collective competitive goods. They also developed a large set of quality controls and imposed goals (Gorgeu and Mathieu 1995b). In some cases there were

attempts by the large firms to merge their suppliers into larger firms, capable of taking over product development and providing training alone without help from the large firms . . . instead of relying on arm's length contracts with under financed, technologically backward suppliers. (Hancké 1997:11)

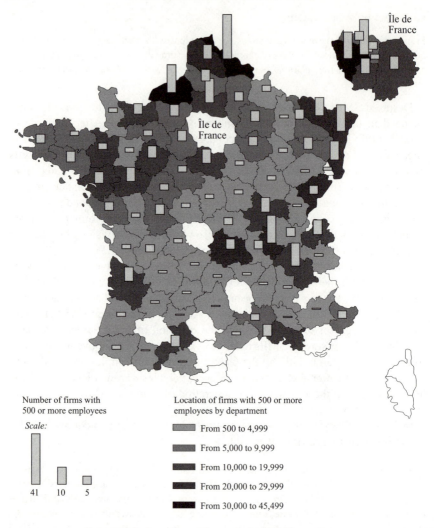

FIGURE 5.3. Location of Large Industrial Firms, France

Source: SESSI.

They also force them to adapt to international markets.

Hancké suggests therefore that 'previously existing unused regional production structures were mobilized in support of the large firms' adjustment
path...what emerged were autarchic regional production networks hierarchically organized around large firms'. Examples can be found in the motor
industry (Citroën in Rennes, Scania in Angers, Renault in the Seine valley),
electrical household appliances (Moulinex in Normandy), chemicals in Lyon,
aeronautics in Toulouse and Bordeaux, Michelin in Clermont-Ferrand. Last but

not least, working mostly from the case of vehicles, Hancké shows how large firms 'hijacked government policies...because the large firms became the interface between the regional policy apparatus and the SMEs who were supposed to be served by the regionalization' (ibid.: 17). In other words, not only did large firms integrate SMEs, but they also took advantage of the weaknesses of regional policy to manipulate the production of some competitive collective goods (training in particular) to their own advantage.

Hancké's powerful argument gives us a clear second model of governance of local economies in France: a hierarchical regional mode of governance led by large firms integrating captive regional suppliers with the support of local and regional policies: hierarchy and market governance combined with some local public support.[7]

Dynamic Areas and Modes of Governance of Local Economies in the Making

Our main argument so far in this section is that there is not one model of governance of local economies in France but several. We have identified two clear, nearly opposite models. We should also make it clear that in a large number of areas, there is not much beyond decline and de-territorialization. However, we also mentioned in the previous section the dynamism and diversity of SMEs on the one hand, and a widespread and messy mobilization of public agencies and business associations on the other. The objective is therefore to provide examples of interesting dynamics in terms of local economic development and governance. The hierarchical integration of large firms is not the whole story of local governance of the economy in France, and any generalization about autarchic regional industrial systems dominated at the local level by one or two firms can be disputed.

Fewer Hierarchies and More Horizontal Integration (in Relative Terms). First, there is a different trend of innovative SMEs, which used to be integrated in the old model and which are now under threat because large firms are involved in globalization processes (see below the cases of Bordeaux and Toulouse). Those dynamic industrial SMEs were under a lot of constraint in the early 1990s. At a time of very slow growth and recession in some sectors, large firms used their power to increase their own gains rather than being partners. SMEs faced severe difficulties; some were abandoned by the large firms, some had faced more constraints related to the centralization of subcontractors on a European or global scale (Veltz 1996). Many innovative industrial SMEs therefore tried to

---

[7] Hancké thus shows how large French firms did not follow the previous institutional past; it is not a case of path dependency which locked the national adjustment trajectory. By contrast, he argues (2001:3) that 'instead of being a helpless victim of its own industrial past, French industry appeared to have freed itself from that straightjacket'.

adapt, to develop new strategies and in particular to develop more collective strategies more or less independently from the large firms.

Second, Gorgeu and Mathieu (1995b:245) have shown how:

the former sub-contractor areas which had spread around leading firms have been dismantled as a result of increasingly internationalized delivery and ever more numerous technical imperatives. On the other hand, because of the increasing demand of the French car industry for just in time delivery, new equipment factories have been set up within reach of PSA and Renault assembly plants, usually in rural areas.

Under the impact of firms' globalization processes, hierarchically organized networks of subcontractors are seriously in doubt. As mentioned before, there is a large group of dynamic SMEs, now foreign owned, which has not been completely integrated in that process and which has a more complex strategy. Many SMEs were not so clearly integrated; some have remained familial or local, some have already escaped from the domination of large groups.

Third, the rise of SMEs and the impact of globalization processes on major French firms have led to some decline in terms of hierarchical co-ordination. Large firms have not taken the role of the state to any great extent. There are some attempts to provide flexible forms of quasi-integration dominated by the large firms. But in some cases those large firms have less interest or incentive to retain that structure of local subcontractors. Local SMEs, after some adaptation, then tend to look for new clients, to diversify their products, and to build local and regional alliances. Forms of collective action and local mobilization for economic development are taking concrete forms, and seem to lead to the structuration of modes of governance of local economies which are less dependent upon integration with one firm and are more organized horizontally.

Building upon the finding of Veltz (2000a and b), one may suggest that hierarchies are rather replaced by networks and different kind of regulations and/or governance. Related to this one would examine the case of regional capitals which explicitly aimed at creating networks among firms and at producing collective goods for the industrial sector. As mentioned before, although dynamic local productive systems have emerged in some regional capitals (such as Bordeaux, Strasbourg, Nantes, Toulouse, Grenoble), the figures are not so clear for two reasons. First, the degree of concentration (within France) is not so high, because there is always a significant part of the industry which is located in the Paris region. Second, regional capitals are by nature very diverse in economic terms; the relative diversity of their economic basis is a major asset in terms of economic growth, which supports the idea of complementarity and agglomeration effects between different sectors.

For example, networks of firms usually mean a relationship between a major firm and a series of subcontractors. This has been clearly identified in the case of Toulouse and Bordeaux, and Grenoble to a lesser extent. In the 1960s (sometimes earlier than that), some industries close to the state and seen as strategic were decentralized from Paris to the provinces. The aeronautic sector for instance, a flagship to France's voluntarist industrial policy, was either created or reinforced, far away from the German border, in Toulouse and Bordeaux (Grossetti and Gilly 1993; Jalabert *et al*. 1993; Beslay *et al*. 1998). In all those cases, the restructuring of French large firms, in particular but non-exclusively in high-tech and military sectors, and in particular in relation to the globalization of firms and mergers, has signalled a new area. Less protected by the state or large firms in the 1990s, many SMEs were in trouble. More than one middle-size town is now facing very serious industrial decline. This is however leading to structures of governance of the urban economy, a move which had been started a decade or two earlier in Grenoble and Rennes.

In Toulouse, for instance, the CNES (*Centre National d'Études Spatiales*) was decentralized in 1961 together with *grandes écoles d'ingénieurs* in order to create the *Pôle spatial toulousain*, which became a reality some twenty years later. From the mid-1970s onwards, the CNES and Aérospatiale (another national champion) have developed a local policy to structure relations with a large variety of subcontractors, to encourage local engineers to create firms in relation to them, and to finance research within the university in order to create a local system. The strategy became really successful when in the late 1970s, supported by the state, two leading firms established large plants in Toulouse: Matra and Thomson, in relation to the development of aerospace industries (Airbus, Ariane). This attracted local branches of specialized firms, leaders in their sector. About 5,000 persons work in the sector. Jalabert *et al*. (1993) have shown in detail the making of different networks, the social dynamics of the engineering communities (constituted as real local classes), the long-term slow development of the relationship between public and private institutions, the strategies of large firms, and the remarkable dynamic development of Toulouse as a high-tech growth centre.

Over the 1980s, as Gilly and Wallet have also shown (2001), the governance of the area was organized around the territorialization of national public institutions, public and private, enhanced by strong collective representation and homogeneous culture among technicians and engineers. A whole series of local and regional collaborative organizations was created specifically to enhance co-operation between different actors and to prepare new projects, in particular in terms of relations between subcontractors and the major firm (more pressure on quality and costs), and between science (research) and industry. Following the crisis of the early 1990s, the Toulouse aerospace centre has become more territorialized and integrated, but is now in direct competition with similar centres in Europe (Bristol, Hamburg or even Paris). Gilly and Wallet (ibid.), using a different kind of governance analysis, point to the structuring of collective action and the territorialization of governance over the 1980s in order to produce collective goods and to be competitive. This territorialization is paradoxically on the increase at a time when many dynamic local SMEs are being bought by outside firms, and when the structuring centre–periphery relationship dominated by large firms and state organization is being dismantled by globalization and state restructuring. The local productive system and the city seem to be brought together in a more coherent way to play the competition. It is an excellent example of the making of a governance structure over twenty-five years and the changing role of public institutions.

In the 1950s and 1960s, when the Mayor of Bordeaux was the leading Gaullist Jacques Chaban-Delmas (the then Prime Minister), the port of Bordeaux went through a serious crisis in the aftermath of decolonization and lost several thousand jobs. The state decided to create a *complexe aéronautique et militaire* in the city, in accordance with the regional policy of the time, which aimed at industrializing the west of France (and in particular cities). Several major firms in that field, mainly Dassault and SNPE, were located there. From the 1970s onwards, a myriad of subcontractors started to grow. In a context of continuous growth, that trend was accelerated when major firms increased externalization and worked systematically with more subcontractors. Up to 5,000 small and middle-sized firms worked in this area and sector at the end of the 1980s, about 20,000 jobs. The crisis started in 1991 with the gradual dismantling of the *French complexe militaro-industriel*. In Bordeaux 1,200 jobs were lost in that sector alone (Beslay *et al.* 1998). As Gilly and Wallet (2001) have shown, the mode of governance of the economy in that area used to be very clear and under the hierarchical control of the dominant firms (also Fringant 1997): there were three major branch plants, two belonging to the state (Ministry of Defence). They were vertically integrated with the national complex (of national champions), and weakly territorialized. Within a pyramidal structure, their room for manoeuvre was limited.

They then developed close relations with a whole range of local sub-contractors. These were very dependent upon the major branch, but there was not much competition for them; they were both dependent and protected. Until the 1991 crisis, their environment appeared very secure. In the *logique d'arsenal* (Muller 1989), the hierarchical mode of governance was very stable over time. The governance of that industrial system was organized around the state's national priorities and organization. Local autonomy and initiative was minimal.

More recently, that integrated local system has been severely restructured, and this has provoked a whole range of local initiatives and the creation of institutions to support economic development. After the initial shock many small and medium-size industrial firms seemed to recover and to adapt to market logic, with processes of a different kind of territorialization (but also de-territorialization) in the making. For instance, a localized system of actors is emerging to deal with economic development. In our language, the role of the local state in co-operation with the private sector is emerging in order to produce some collective good. There is therefore a new mode of governance in the making. However, at the same time, from the firms' point of view, logics of de-territorialization seem to be dominant and networks of firms are more and more fragmented. That may be a case, not so rare in France, of territorialized governance in the making at a time of fragmentation and de-territorialization of firms.

Another exception to the quasi-disappearance of local productive system is the Paris region as such. It has become a vast urban region in the sense of Scott (1999). Apart from the headquarters of major French and foreign corporations, between 50 and 70 per cent of French public and private research and development is located there. It has the most varied and elitist groups of *Grandes Écoles*, which produce business and political elites. It encompasses the largest set of industrial SMEs, in particular in the high-tech sectors which want to benefit from proximity of the public research centres and major corporations, including electronics, computers, telecommunications. The vast public financing of *grands projets de l'État high tech* (Cohen 1989) have benefited massively this complex of innovative firms, large traditional French corporations, public research centres and private services to firms, which are all highly concentrated in the region. It has become far and away the innovation centre of the French economy (Muller 1989; Cohen 1992).

Beckouche (1996) has shown the importance of this concentration for the aeronautics industry. Storper and Salais (1998) develop what they call the Île de France 'Economy of splendours'. The authors stress first the concentration of resources and competitive goods in the Paris region organized through a close integration between state ministries, large firms, research centres, state agencies, and small and medium-size firms: 'France's high technology industries are specialized in systems engineering and construction of large scale applied technological systems such as military and civilian aircraft and space hardware, and large-scale electronics and communication systems' (ibid.: 131).

This concentration has one major consequence: there is not so much left for the rest of the country, hence the relatively low level of territorial specialization. The rigid hierarchical pyramidal economic, social and political order has however benefited the second tier of the pyramid: regional capitals.

Several other sectors are also largely concentrated in the Paris region: printing, pharmaceuticals, specialized equipment, electronics, precision machinery. A particularly well-known case is that of the clothing industrial district, '*Le sentier*', combining prestigious *haute couture* with young people's clothing (Salais and Storper 1997; Bergeron 1998; Green 1998).

Recent research on the Paris region (Veltz 1996; Davezies 1998; Beckouche 1999) shows interesting developments. On the one hand the productivity of the Île de France region is increasing sharply, and its share of national GDP keeps growing. On the other hand, both public policies and firms' strategies are tending to change the structure of its economy. First, industrial production is disappearing from the region; it is in absolute decline, particularly in traditional sectors (Beckouche 1999). Second, decentralization policies and sometimes voluntarist ones have led to some decrease in the research that is concentrated there. The region is restructuring towards being even more the command centre of the French economy, with more internationalization, expertise, and services to firms.

In that environment there is not much co-ordination between firms beyond market relationship. Davezies' survey of Île de France SMEs revealed very few local relations. Most firms worked with others outside their TTWA, and often outside the urban region. Also, as already noted above, there is a high-tech complex associating state agencies, large firms in the electronics/telecom/ military complex, and a vast network of subcontractors, largely SMEs (Cohen 1989). Those two types of co-ordination between firms are very typical of the French governance of the economy. The two together make a large and dynamic metropolitan milieu.

However, more recently a different pattern seems to be emerging. Globalization processes, increasing competition and the restructuring of the military–industrial complex, seem to lead to profound reorganization of firms in the Paris region. Decoster's research tends to show in particular two major points (Decoster and Tabaries 1997; also Cohen 1996). First is the structuring of research and innovation networks bringing together SMEs, large firms and the dynamic and important research centres concentrated around Orsay—the '*Cité scientifique Île de France sud*'. That project is now about ten years old. It aimed at concentrating not only CNRS research centres but also elitist business schools and the prestigious *École Polytechnique* (and its research centres) in order to give easy access to large and small enterprises, and to promote R&D in order to help the restructuring and development of the high-tech core of the French economy. Information on new technologies and their diffusion seems to associate all these actors in formal and dynamic networks. Second is the structuring of specialized innovation milieux, which bring together networks of SMEs, organized around public institutions, such as the group around optical technologies.

Those more fragile micro-milieux of innovation are mainly organized at the level of the Île de France region. However, more surprisingly, Decoster and her colleagues suggest the making of more localized micro-milieux in the old traditional sector to the north and east of Paris, specifically organized around some centres for the diffusion of one type of innovation supported by local authorities. As in other French cities, there is therefore also some fragile, very local territorialization taking place. The whole range of disorganized institution mobilization for economic development to produce collective competitive goods for firms may therefore sometimes work in a more or less territorialized way.

Micro-Clusters and Networks: A Rising Tide, but How Significant Is It? Encouraged by the apparent trend towards more flexible forms of production, the development of SMEs, and a new interest from policy-makers (see below), different groups have started a detailed search for various kinds of clusters and networks of firms in France.[8]

---

[8] The following section therefore mainly relies upon work undertaken in particular by Courlet in Grenoble, with the state agency DATAR TECSA.

Having in mind the decline of national industrial and regional policies and the Italian example, the French government has developed new policy initiatives to identify and strengthen inter-firm co-operation, possibly leading to the development of local economies. This recent concern and policy response has had two consequences. First, it has led to detailed empirical surveys to identify various kinds of spatial concentration and networks of firms. Second, a side effect has been to call anything that would remotely resemble some territorial concentration an 'industrial district' or 'local economy'. An initial survey sought TTWAs having: 1. at least ten SMEs within a specialism; 2. at least 5 per cent of overall employment within the specialism; and 3. employment in the specialism representing at least 5 per cent of national employment in that sector. This analysis identified seventy-four local economies. A more qualitative research identified eighty-five.

France is not Italy. The indicators that are used rather demonstrate once again the low level of territorial concentration and specialization. However, two points have to be emphasized. First is the multiplication of micro-concentration on a very small scale (AIMVER and DATAR 1998). In particular, business associations of 50 to 100 SMEs, organized within a locality, are booming. That point had been noticed in case studies about local economic development in both cities and rural areas. By contrast with the isolated family SME, which had been the common feature of French local economies, localized networks of firms associated with various forms of specialization and co-ordination are in the making or developing all over the country.

Science Parks. A final example of territorial specialization within urban areas concerns the numerous attempts to create science parks. The fever spread in the early 1980s, and more than sixty science parks were created all over the country after the model set by Grenoble and Sophia Antipolis (near Nice, wholly created by the state). Most were established in imitation of the Silicon Valley miracle, and as justification for local public intervention, a key political issue in the aftermath of decentralization reforms (Le Galès 1994; Eberlein 1996).

In a few cases they proved to be useful tools in the competition to attract outside investment, sometimes in relation with the local research and productive capacity and competence. Other cases are hardly worth mentioning. For our purposes we should notice first that the level of co-operation between firms is often very limited, except in the case of simple subcontractors. However, when one takes into account the production of collective goods by local institutions and often the local authority, it can be seen as evidence of relative territorialization, with positive effects after a decade or more: infrastructures, relations with research, training of the labour force, marketing, support to start-ups, creation of a milieu with rules and norms. There has been some relatively successful economic development in Rennes, Montpellier, Nancy-Metz, Strasbourg, Lyon—in regional capitals that have benefited from the economic dynamic of the 1980s, and where both political and scientific elites promoted the science park in a voluntarist way. Cases of remarkable failure to achieve anything have also been noted, for instance in Bordeaux and Marseilles (Bruhat 1990).

It is interesting to note how large technological firms (Thomson, HP, Sony, France Telecoms) have invested in some research centres in science parks in order to benefit from the public research and some potential transfers. That has led in some cases, for instance in Rhône-Alpes, to the relative autonomy of these plants and research centres from their headquarters, and processes of territorialization which slowly are producing some effects.

Economists in IREPD (University of Grenoble) have studied the Grenoble miracle and its limits (Bernardy de Sigoyer and Boisgontier 1988; Chanarron, Perrin, and Ruffieux 1988). Again, all started in the 1960s with the deconcentration of state-owned plants and research centres (CENG, INPG). This then led to the creation of the first French science park, the ZIRST in Meylan, a new technology cluster. That was the result of vigorous mobilization of local public and private actors (a new left mayor, university leaders and local entrepreneurs) within a stimulating milieu, which had been running for several decades. It now includes a dozen branches of well-known firms (from Hewlett Packard to Matra), and about seventy SMEs. Critics have pointed to the low level of co-operation between firms and the incapacity of many of them to grow, sometimes a clear strategy of the owners. There are about 3,000 jobs in ZIRST, but inter-firm co-operation has remained rather low, and cases of SME development not so common. IREPD researchers have demonstrated that in Grenoble it was largish international firms (Hewlett-Packard and Merlin-Gerin for instance) rather than SMEs that had long-term productive relations with local institutions and centres of research. Rousier (1997) have in particular stressed the fact that large firms use science parks to get information on research and development, which they then use in a different context. That also emerged from research on science parks in Rennes and Montpellier. The limited success of Grenoble ZIRST is also the consequences of the industrial Meccano discussed earlier. Restructuring strategies for major firms (Thomson, for instance) have also led to erratic investment and disinvestment which have blocked the development of a local productive system (Salais and Storper 1993).

By contrast, Sophia-Antipolis, created from nothing in the late 1960s by the French state, seems now to enjoy remarkable growth. Once seen as completely isolated from its locality, it is now slowly becoming more embedded. Examples of co-operation between firms and of institutionalization of collective action to produce competitive collective goods (training, infrastructure) are appearing.

Science parks therefore illustrate the obstacles to the emergence of autonomous and integrated local economies in France—the remaining domination of large firms and the strength of professional networks outside a particular local economy—but also processes of local institutionalization to produce competitive collective goods.

Conclusion: What Happens Next to Local Economies in France?

France is clearly looking for a 'post-dirigiste identity' (Levy 1999) that is less national. Obviously French firms are also part of processes of Europeanization and globalization. At the same time, we have tried to give evidence of local dynamism and the making of modes of governance of local economies. In most cases, it is not a case of local versus global or private versus public, but of combination. What is common in most of our stories is a modernization and development of SMEs and collective forms of mobilization of business leaders to produce the collective competition goods they need. If we follow our governance framework, we see fewer hierarchies and more networks, networks of firms both within and beyond the locality. French economic space was (still is) highly institutionalized, and the macro-variables of growth are to some extent standardized (labour costs, qualifications, level of infrastructures). In the metropolization model, firms tend to limit risks and increase their room for manoeuvre by moving to the large urban region, as cost differences with the rest of the country are not so important (Veltz 1996). In other words, the national production of many collective goods has made less relevant the question of local economies. Nevertheless, by contrast with the old model, competition goods seem to be produced more by market relations within networks of firms. But we also see associations of entrepreneurs. Last but not least, the transformation of state agencies, and therefore state regulation, is interesting. They play an active role in the local production of collective competitive goods in various ways, from the most irrelevant to the most effective in co-operation with firms. That also reflects the relative rise of supply side policies.

Two risks are particularly obvious in the French case. The first is the lack of co-ordination after the reorganization of the state (Salais and Storper 1993; Boyer 1997). Evidence of emerging modes of governance of local economies is only a partial story. On the one hand, large firms go global and therefore increasingly play with different rules and constraints. On the other hand, and this is a point which is nearly always forgotten, the rise of private capital is becoming an important feature of the economy. Arnaud, Pinault, Bolloré, Lagardère, Bouygues and others are building important stakes. SMEs and the local economies are another part of the equation.

This chapter has emphasized the uncertainties and contradictory trends of territorialization and de-territorialization. This question of co-ordination points to the role of some local or regional modes of governance to mobilize SMEs and local economies towards exports and markets (Hollingsworth and Boyer 1997). Two things appear crucial in the French case. Most important is to examine emerging modes of governance, which are more or less structured. Second, starting from firms, we need to examine the relative territorialization of networks and forms of co-ordination between various kinds of public actors, business associations and firms. Original combinations seem to be in the making in many places, forming the base of new governance of regional economies. Emerging local governance through the institutionalization of the production of collective goods and their impact on economic performance is the crucial point to examine. Some fragmentary evidence has been provided in this chapter. It is also a remarkable example of rapid, bottom-up learning by doing, dynamism, and some interesting successes and promises. It may lead to a revival of French SMEs and some local economies. In our view, it symbolizes the lack of co-ordination of the French economy, but perhaps also its diversity, dynamism, relative territorial embeddedness, and yet another deep silent pragmatic change.

However, beyond the optimistic scenario about the dynamic governance of local economies in France, there is a pessimistic view, which is not just about co-ordination. Those emerging modes of governance might also lead to rent-seeking behaviour. Instead of conquering new markets, some SME entrepreneurs may rather look for protection and support, not using opportunities to expand but rather to stagnate. Examples of clientelism towards firms also provide some evidence that this may occur. As shown in this chapter, there are some historical precedents. Local modes of governance may be in the making in different places, but to what extent do they mobilize towards the right objectives?

The diversity of kinds of local economies suggest that the current phase of restructuring of French capitalism is to some extent the story of de-statization of the French economy (only in part of course: see Schmidt 1996; Cohen, Hart, and Simmie 1997). On the one hand issues of mergers and global large firms are essential, as the transformation of Renault, Lyonnaize-Dumez, Air Liquide, Péchiney, Matra and the banks would suggest. On the other hand, the changing scale of those firms and the restructuring of state intervention draws a new framework of opportunities, constraints, risks under which some modes of governance of local economies are being restructured. By contrast to what would have been expected from a neo-institutionalist account, French industry has been reorganized in a way which is far away from the old model. Most authors point to this remarkable rapid change—and to the risks associated with weak co-ordination. Here we have rather stressed first the local and regional dynamism, and second the diversity of models in the making.

In the late 1960s few would have imagined that state investments and local mobilization in old French provincial cities would lead to the remarkable dynamics of regional cities in the 1980s. It may be the case that France is facing another silent revolution: beyond the national champions and major firms, the mobilization of associations, new local, regional and state public policies, the making of regional modes of governance mark a new era for SMEs. Several authors have mentioned the failure of new modes of governance of local economies in France. Our conclusion is more nuanced and more optimistic. However, beyond some well-known cases, because of the strength of existing models and hierarchies, changes will take time to materialize and to produce clear outcomes.

6

Great Britain: Falling through the Holes in the Network Concept

COLIN CROUCH AND HENRY FARRELL

British economic development has long exhibited strong regional patterns and contrasts. The UK shares with France a characteristic not possessed by Germany or Italy: the contemporary weakness of its major regional centres, so that the capital cities (London and Paris) and the regions surrounding them (the so-called Home Counties in south-east England and the Île de France) dominate. Post-industrial society, with its tendency to concentrate up-market services growth in a few chosen metropolitan centres capable of becoming global cities, has intensified this ancient process that was temporarily interrupted by industrialism. South-east England (excluding Greater London itself) is the only region in the UK to have an average per capita income above the European Union mean, but it is itself the richest region in the EU. Although Greater London contains within it the City of London, one of the biggest concentrations of wealth on the planet, and many other extremely rich areas, the mean income for Londoners in general is below the EU mean.

The Midlands and North continue, as during the initial decades of industrialization, to have the main concentrations of manufacturing industry. However, because population and new economic activity are becoming increasingly concentrated in south-east England, London, and neighbouring areas (the southern part of East Anglia and north-eastern parts of the South-West), a good deal of industrial production takes place there, including many dynamic branches. (Table 6.1 gives an indication of the distribution of population, regional contributions to gross domestic product, and changes in population over the past two decades.) All this has considerable implications for the formation of local production systems in Britain, as we shall see below.

The Geographical Distribution of Manufacturing in Great Britain

British official statistics provide data on employment according to geographical units known as Travel to Work Areas (TTWAs), which seek to identify local

TABLE 6.1. Regional Distributions of Population and GDP, UK, 1981–97 (numbers in 000s)

| | Total population | | | | | | % change, 1981–97 | Contribution to GDP 1997 | Ratio GDP:pop. 1997 |
| | 1981 | | 1991 | | 1997 | | | | |
	number	per cent	number	per cent	number	per cent			
Greater London	6,806	12.08	6,890	11.92	7,122	12.07	−0.07	15.10	1.25
South-East	7,245	12.86	7,679	13.28	7,959	13.49	4.91	15.90	1.18
East Anglia	4,854	8.61	5,150	8.91	5,334	9.04	4.94	9.20	1.02
South-West	4,381	7.77	4,718	8.16	4,876	8.26	6.29	8.10	0.98
West Midlands	5,187	9.20	5,265	9.11	5,321	9.02	−2.04	8.40	0.93
East Midlands	3,853	6.84	4,035	6.98	4,156	7.04	3.01	6.70	0.95
Yorks. and Humber.	4,918	8.73	4,983	8.62	5,037	8.54	−2.19	7.60	0.89
North-West	6,940	12.32	6,886	11.91	6,884	11.67	−5.27	10.60	0.91
North	2,636	4.68	2,603	4.50	2,594	4.40	−6.02	3.60	0.82
Wales	2,813	4.99	2,891	5.00	2,927	4.96	−0.63	4.10	0.83
Scotland	5,180	9.19	5,107	8.83	5,123	8.68	−5.55	8.30	0.96
Northern Ireland	1,538	2.73	1,601	2.77	1,675	2.84	4.00	2.30	0.81
Total	56,351	100.00	57,808	100.00	59,008	100.00		100.00	

Source: Annual Abstract of Statistics (various years).

labour markets based on analysis of actual journeys to work.[1] Appendix Table 6.1 shows the distribution of TTWAs in terms of the overall proportions of their employed populations working in manufacturing industry. The biggest concentrations are in the Midlands, especially the west, classic heartland of the British small-firm engineering industry and home of the original industrial districts described by Alfred Marshall (1919). Also important are the old industrial centres of north-west England, Yorkshire and Humberside, and (south) Wales. However many principal cities, including former major northern industrial centres like Glasgow, Manchester and Newcastle, have moved so far towards either tertiarization or economic decline, or a combination of both, that they fall below the national mean for industrial employment (10.58 per cent). Meanwhile some smaller cities in prosperous, previously non-industrial areas are above that mean (e.g., Cheltenham, Gloucester and other towns in south-west England, and some in East Anglia).

Unfortunately, available statistics do not provide a precise breakdown by TTWA for services sectors. Even if our research concentrates on manufacturing, some data on business services are important to a study of local production systems, the viability of which may often depend on the availability of services. We present, in Table 6.2, the *regional* distribution of firms and their turnover in the main services industries. With the exception of transport and education, these have distributions heavily skewed towards London and the South-East, for both numbers of firms and their turnover. Often this indicates the registered headquarters of businesses, which then have extensive networks in the country overall, but nevertheless it demonstrates the concentration in the South-East of at least headquarters offices of these services.

Table 6.3 presents the regional distribution of the main branches of manufacturing, drawing attention to particularly strong or weak concentrations. Greater London has a strong concentration of the printing and publishing industries and particularly low concentrations of all basic industries as well as metal working. South-east England has strong concentrations of office equipment (which includes computing) and precision equipment and is also weak in basic industries. These two regions therefore are the only ones to have strong concentrations of the 'knowledge-rich' sectors, with the exception of East Anglia (also publishing and printing), the South-West (precision equipment), and Scotland (office equipment). The West Midlands concentrates the whole metal production chain as well as other basic industries relevant to manufacturing. The East Midlands and, to a lesser extent, north-west England, focus mainly on textiles and clothing. Other regions do not have strong profiles.

---

[1] The definition of these areas is revised from time to time, as work travel patterns change. The data in this chapter are based on the labour force survey carried out in 1996. The map of TTWAs was revised in 1998, resulting in several changes. This chapter refers to the pre-1998 boundaries. The data produced by the National Statistical Office do not cover Northern Ireland. The province is also not covered by the system of TECs and LECs from which we have drawn much of our qualitative data. This chapter is therefore a study of Great Britain, not of the whole United Kingdom.

TABLE 6.2. Distribution of Services Enterprises, UK, 1997

	Transport services		Post and telecomm.		Financial services		Professional		Education	
	number per 1,000	turnover per 1,000	number per 1,000	turnover per 1,000	number per 1,000	turnover per 1,000	number per 1,000	turnover per 1,000	number per 1,000	turnover per 1,000
Greater London	2.34	0.149	0.42	0.018	1.49	0.533	21.66	0.455	0.31	0.026
South-East	3.29	0.099	0.50	0.012	0.54	0.110	23.14	0.262	0.40	0.021
East Anglia	3.51	0.091	0.37	0.006	0.35	0.061	13.99	0.110	0.34	0.024
South-West	2.85	0.034	0.31	0.003	0.35	0.062	14.58	0.118	0.32	0.028
West Midlands	2.48	0.032	0.32	0.005	0.29	0.037	10.78	0.136	0.28	0.023
East Midlands	3.54	0.048	0.34	0.003	0.28	0.021	12.26	0.120	0.32	0.021
Yorks. and Humb.	3.15	0.053	0.22	0.003	0.22	0.024	9.86	0.117	0.24	0.027
North-West	2.63	0.053	0.28	0.004	0.33	0.038	11.73	0.127	0.23	0.023
North	2.56	0.060	0.18	0.005	0.13	0.023	7.74	0.102	0.24	0.028
Wales	3.12	0.026	0.22	0.001	0.21	0.021	9.05	0.062	0.28	0.026
Scotland	2.22	0.053	0.19	0.003	0.32	0.128	9.93	0.101	0.25	0.028
Northern Ireland	2.46	0.050	0.16	0.001	0.20	0.014	6.34	0.050	0.11	0.001
Total	**2.81**	**0.073**	**0.33**	**0.007**	**0.52**	**0.117**	**14.73**	**0.192**	**0.30**	**0.024**

Note: Number per 1,000 = number of enterprises per 1,000 of employed population.
Turnover per 1,000 = Annual business turnover per 1,000 of employed population (£m).

Source: Authors' calculations based on Business Monitor 1997.

TABLE 6.3. Percentage of Employed Population Engaged in Manufacturing by Region and Branch, Great Britain, 1996

Branch	English regions									Wales	Scotland
	Greater London	South-East	East Anglia	South-West	West Midlands	East Midlands	Yorkshire & Humberside	North-West	North		
Total employees	3,648,519	3,875,479	820,694	1,786,724	2,174,143	1,456,309	1,877,107	2,355,043	1,076,255	971,450	1,989,822
15. Food and drink	*0.68*	*1.05*	**3.90**	2.10	2.02	2.80	**3.21**	2.29	2.22	1.99	2.58
17. Textiles	0.14	0.14	0.19	0.33	0.55	**3.00**	**1.90**	1.60	0.57	0.50	1.11
18. Wearing apparel	0.42	*0.20*	0.23	0.28	0.69	**1.84**	0.76	0.86	1.07	0.75	0.76
19. Leather and footwear	0.08	*0.04*	0.24	0.23	0.14	**0.86**	0.13	0.22	0.15	0.10	0.07
20. Wood products (excl. 36)	*0.16*	0.30	0.46	0.41	0.42	0.49	0.51	0.35	0.52	0.48	0.51
21. Pulp and paper products	*0.18*	0.52	0.82	0.48	0.36	0.61	0.62	**1.07**	0.65	0.85	0.54
22. Publishing, printing, etc.	**2.62**	1.73	**2.02**	1.50	1.07	1.55	1.62	1.14	0.88	0.98	0.98
23. Petrol, gas, energy	0.04	0.15	0.00	0.05	0.02	0.05	0.14	**0.41**	**0.71**	0.17	0.09
24. Chemicals	*0.61*	1.04	1.00	0.63	0.75	1.57	1.40	**2.10**	**2.18**	1.11	0.77
25. Rubber and plastics	*0.34*	0.89	1.38	1.08	**1.85**	1.28	0.99	1.25	1.36	1.42	0.68
26. Non-metal mineral products	*0.14*	0.37	0.55	0.50	**1.99**	1.00	0.81	0.62	0.66	0.69	0.42
27. Base metals	*0.08*	0.20	0.26	0.24	**1.61**	0.70	1.36	0.28	1.13	**2.26**	0.31
28. Metal products (excl. 29)	*0.66*	1.50	1.48	1.66	**4.86**	2.51	2.72	1.98	2.30	1.76	1.59
29. Machinery and equipment	*0.42*	1.79	**2.74**	1.81	**3.04**	2.69	2.27	1.71	2.43	1.40	1.26
30. Office equipment	*0.12*	**0.39**	0.22	0.27	0.22	0.21	*0.07*	*0.08*	*0.07*	0.20	**0.42**
31. Electrical goods	*0.34*	0.88	0.57	0.69	**1.34**	0.83	0.70	0.98	1.03	**1.26**	0.71
32. Radio, TV, etc.	*0.21*	0.82	0.75	0.79	0.38	0.50	0.28	0.35	0.79	**1.72**	0.77
33. Medical, precision, etc. goods	0.36	**1.35**	0.84	1.12	0.57	0.50	0.39	0.45	*0.34*	0.76	0.75
34. Motor vehicles	0.36	0.81	0.87	0.77	**3.38**	0.97	0.82	0.96	1.11	1.56	*0.23*
35. Other vehicles	*0.09*	0.64	0.47	**1.62**	0.51	1.06	0.42	0.88	**1.34**	0.73	0.90
36. Furniture and other products	0.45	0.77	0.94	0.77	1.12	**1.33**	**1.33**	0.95	0.96	**1.41**	*0.33*

Note: **Bold type** indicates proportions more than one standard deviation above mean. *Italic type* indicates proportions more than one standard deviation below mean.
Source: Authors' own calculations based on data supplied by National Statistical Office.

Small Firms in British Manufacturing

It is difficult to study small firms in the British economy because of deficiencies in official statistics. There are no statistics identifying numbers of individual *firms*, only different physical *units*, which may be branches of large firms, individual buildings of a large enterprise, or taxation units. (For example, if a firm chooses to make separate tax returns for its manual and non-manual employees, that firm will count as two units, even though they are both fully part of one operation.)

Industrial Districts

We shall first attempt to identify industrial districts as defined by the Italian researchers who first drew attention to the concept (see Burroni and Trigilia, this volume). Italian data take 250 employees as the maximum number for a small enterprise. Unfortunately that threshold is not used in British data, which have instead a cut-off point of 200. We therefore use a unit with 200 employees or fewer as our definition of a small or medium-sized enterprise (SME), bearing in mind that a unit does not necessarily identify a firm.

A second question concerns the level of specificity of a branch of industrial activity at which an industrial district can be said to exist. The two-digit categories of industrial classification indicate broadly defined industries. Sometimes a specialism may be at these levels, but in other cases it will exist at the more precisely defined three- or four-digit levels (e.g., footwear, machine tools, medical equipment, or computers). We here consider both. A list of branches and sub-branches used in the following analysis will be found in Appendix Table 6.2.

There is a further problem, mentioned by Michael Porter (1998). Firms co-operating in an innovative production cluster may well be located across quite different industrial sectors, so that for example, plastics and measuring instrument industries can provide highly specific inputs for firms in biotechnology. It is very difficult to identify such cases in an analysis based on conventional branch statistics. We shall however be alert to such possibilities.

In analysing the British data we need to take account of the fact that the proportions of overall employment represented by even two-digit industries are usually extremely small. The national TTWA mean for proportion of all employment in manufacturing is only 10.58 per cent. Fundamental to the concept of an industrial district is the idea that a particular branch of industry is so important in a town or district that the formal and informal institutions of the district are heavily influenced by those of the branch, which is fundamental both to Marshallian 'atmosphere' and to the ability of the industry to mobilize political and other public sources of local collective competition goods. It is difficult to know what threshold of employment needs to be passed for this to be the case, but it seems highly unlikely that employment concentrations of around 1 or 2 per cent would achieve it. We shall here take the arbitrary and probably too low figure of

5 per cent, but shall also give attention to cases between 2.5 per cent and 5 per cent where they concern sub-branches (three- to four-digit industries).

There is next the question of the minimum number of firms needed to produce a district. Some of the British cases are so small that only four or five units are involved—and units data exaggerate the number of actual firms. We again need to make an arbitrary decision, but here we are helped by a rule of the British National Statistical Office, which on grounds of privacy prohibits publication of data which might enable the identification of an individual establishment. This is defined as meaning concentrations of twenty or fewer units in any one TTWA. By considering as potential districts only those above this level we can satisfy the legal requirement and also place a threshold under our estimation of industrial districts.

Finally we must consider the possibility that an industrial district overlaps the boundaries of a TTWA. We shall deal with that here by treating as one district adjacent TTWAs which individually satisfy the other criteria. If the individual districts have twenty units or fewer, but together have twenty or more, we include that combined district.

We therefore operationalize the concept of industrial district in the British case to mean a TTWA (or set of adjacent TTWAs) which has:

1. an above average concentration of its employed population working in manufacturing industry;
2. an above average concentration of its employed population working in small (200 or fewer employees) manufacturing units;
3. an above average concentration of its employed population working in such units within one or more sub-branch (i.e., three- or four-digit industry) (subsidiarily within one or more branch (i.e., two-digit industry));
4. at least 5 per cent of its employed population working in that branch or sub-branch (subsidiarily, between 2.5 per cent and 5 per cent in a sub-branch);
5. more than twenty employing units within the branch or sub-branch and within the size range.

Table 6.4 and Figure 6.1 list all districts that pass these criteria. They show that industrial districts are found mainly in 'traditional' products (food and drink, textiles, some clothing and footwear), with a second concentration in metal goods and engineering. The only cases to fall outside this range are a weak (below 5 per cent) one in ceramics and one in chemicals. The regional pattern is similarly highly focused: isolated parts of Scotland for certain traditional pre-industrial products; the East Midlands, Yorkshire and Scotland for textiles and associated clothing industries; the West Midlands and Yorkshire for metal goods and engineering. There are no districts at all in the southern part of the country. There are also none in northern England or *industrial* Scotland, and only one in Wales. There are several cases of districts formed from adjacent TTWAs, but none where the number of units in each individual TTWA was twenty or less.

The most concentrated districts, in the sense of being sub-branches, are the pre-industrial, mainly Scottish, ones. With the exception of fish processing, all are

★ Food and drink   ⋈ Chemicals
● Textiles and clothing   + Metal goods
⊙ Leather and footwear   × Engineering

FIGURE 6.1. Industrial Districts, Great Britain, 1996

what would be called in Italy 'made in Italy' goods: quality *artigiano* products with a well-known association with their place of origin. Several other Scottish TTWAs would also have qualified for inclusion, particularly in the textile and garment branches, but the number of units involved was twenty or below.

TABLE 6.4. Industrial Districts, Great Britain, 1996

Branch	Sub-branch	West Midlands	East Midlands	Yorkshire & Humberside	North-West	Wales	Scotland
Food and drink (15)	151						**Peterhead (6.73)** **Keith (21.14)**
	1,520		Gainsborough (6.88)				Galashiels (6.71)
	1,591		*Gainsborough (4.03)*				Kilmarnock (5.44)
Textiles (17)		Leek (8.34)	Leicester (5.33)	Huddersfield (7.34) Keighley (6.93)	Rochdale (10.36) Pendle (4.9) Accrington (4.87)		
	171 175 177	*Kidderminster (3.57)*		*Huddersfield (2.60)*	*Rochdale (3.09)*		**Hawick (18.12)**
Clothing (18)	182		*Leicester (3.49)* *Leicester (3.32)*				
Leather, footwear (19)	1,930		**Wellinborough (7.99)** *Kettering (2.62)*				
Chemicals (24)	241				Widnes (9.78) *Widnes (3.06)*		
Mineral products (26)	262	*Stoke (3.13)*					
Metal goods (28)		Dudley (10.77) Walsall (9.63) Ludlow (7.75) Wolverhampton (6.12) Coventry (4.95)		Sheffield (4.94)	Rochdale (5.89)	Aberdare (7.86)	
	285 287				*Rochdale (2.56)*	*Aberdare (3.51)*	
Engineering (29)		Ludlow (5.82)	Gainsborough (6.09)	Keighley (7.00)			

Note: **Bold type**: sub-branches more than 5% of employed population. Roman type: branches with more than 5% employed population.
Italic type: sub-branches with > 2.5% to 5% employed population.
Source: Authors' own calculations based on data supplied by National Statistical Office.

Some of the other districts also date back to early industrial or pre-industrial times: the East Midlands, Yorkshire and Scottish textile areas; carpets in Kidderminster; ceramics in Stoke. Birmingham remains, as Alfred Marshall found it, at the centre of an extensive West Midlands small-firm metal goods region, though the city itself is today too diversified to be characterized as essentially a metal manufacturing city.

Only two areas have specialisms in more than one industry: Keighley in Yorkshire and Rochdale in Lancashire. Both have concentrations in textiles, with Keighley also having a presence in engineering and Rochdale in metal goods.

Concentrated Clusters

So far we have sought industrial districts as defined in the Italian literature. The more general concept of 'cluster' suggests something looser: a tendency for firms in similar types of business to locate close together, though without having a particularly important presence in an area. The tendency to concentrate suggests that there are gains from shared location and therefore collective competition goods, but we might not expect local public institutions to be concerned about the industry. All industrial districts will be examples of clusters, but not all clusters will form industrial districts.

In order to identify a concentrated cluster we need to note where activity is concentrated in particular TTWAs, irrespective of the relative weight of the activity within the area. The measure of above-mean concentrations in TTWAs of employment in small firms within a (sub-)branch would give us this datum, though for the cluster concept there is no need to limit attention to areas with above-mean levels of manufacturing in general. We need a measure of greater concentration than above the mean since there must by definition be many such cases, even if they do not really indicate clusters. This can be done by taking cases outside a specified range of standard deviations above the mean. With the exception of a few examples (printing, general engineering, furniture) most sub-branches are found in only a minority of districts. The modal value for the majority of sub-branches is usually zero, and the median and mean are often very close to zero. These characteristics of the statistical distributions of sub-branches require a high threshold for measuring exceptional concentrations. Data analyses which can assume normal distributions frequently uses 1.5 standard deviations above or below the mean as the threshold for identifying outliers or extreme cases. Given the characteristics of our data we shall use three standard deviations above the mean. In fact, virtually all sub-branches included at least one case at or beyond this level of concentration.

In order to identify as many potential cases as possible, we pursue the following procedure. All cases where sub-branches achieve the specified level are examined. If they have fewer than the required twenty-one units, we consider that TTWA along with any neighbouring TTWAs with a similar high concentration. If the two together contain more than twenty units, it is included as a district covering more than one TTWA.[2] If an individual TTWA has fewer than twenty-one units in the sub-branch in which it has a concentration of employment of the specified size, but has more than twenty units in the branch of which that sub-branch is a part,[3] we count it as a 'weak' case of a concentration, even if the overall level of the branch within the district is not particularly high. The rationale for this is that a small number of firms specializing within a sub-branch may draw on a wider community of collective competition goods available in the wider branch. Neighbouring TTWAs each having the required sub-branch concentration but lacking individually the required number of units at either sub-branch or branch level but reaching that level together for the branch will also be included as weak cases of clusters extending over more than one TTWA.

We therefore operationalize the concept of a concentrated cluster in the British case to mean a TTWA (or set of adjacent TTWAs) which has:

1. a concentration of its employed population working within one or more sub-branches equal to or greater than three standard deviations above the national mean for that sub-branch;
2. more than twenty employing units within the sub-branch and in the size range.

We operationalize a 'weak' cluster to mean a TTWA (or set of adjacent TTWAs) which has:

1. a concentration of its employed population working within one or more sub-branches equal to our greater than three standard deviations above the national mean;
2. more than twenty employing units within the wider branch of which that sub-branch forms a part, and in the size range.

Table 6.5 and Figure 6.2 list all clusters identified by this process. The industrial districts already identified appear, but in addition we can now identify the following.

Food and Drink. There is an additional weak general alcohol district in Scotland (Edinburgh). There are other food and drink concentrations elsewhere in Britain, but none covers more than twenty units.

Textiles, Clothing and Footwear. There are several examples, some of them geographically quite extensive and including some industrial districts. First, there are two extensive textile clusters. The largest, based on woollens, covers several TTWAs across West Yorkshire and extends into Lancashire in the North-West,

---

[2] We also consider as districts covering more than one TTWA cases which include TTWAs all or some of which have individual concentrations of more than twenty units.

[3] In more detail, the following procedure is followed. In the case of a concentration at a four-digit level sub-branch we take as the branch the relevant three-digit level; in the case of a concentration at a three-digit level sub-branch we take as the branch the relevant two-digit level.

with its centre in Huddersfield; this cluster embraces several stages of manufacture and extends into related engineering sectors. We can now see that the strong engineering cluster identified later in the table in the Bradford and Huddersfield area is in fact the manufacture of textile machinery. A second is concentrated on a different part of Lancashire and exists mainly at later stages of the production chain. It too is connected to a local textile machinery cluster in the Blackburn and Rochdale area. (Rochdale's engineering district also specializes in textile machinery.) There is a further strong, small textile sector in Kidderminster in the West Midlands, and a weak one in the Western Isles off the coast of Scotland.

Clothing is solely concentrated in the East Midlands, though the two locations (the relatively small one in Alfreton and the much larger one in Leicester) are geographically distinct. Although the main emphasis of the Leicester clothing industry is wearing apparel (sub-branch 1824), there are large numbers of small units in other sub-branches too. In our analysis of industrial districts, Leicester also appeared as a general case within the related textile sector, though no sub-branch appears here as a concentrated cluster. As with the Lancashire and Yorkshire textile areas, Leicester also supports a strong textile machinery cluster.

The main footwear cluster is also in the East Midlands, though in a different area, and has already been identified as an industrial district. There are also many small units in other leather-related industries in the area. There is a smaller footwear concentration in Accrington, itself part of the Lancashire textile cluster, and a leather cluster in Walsall that seems unrelated to footwear.

Printing and Publishing. Two clusters integrate publishing and printing: one containing a large number of firms, especially book publishers, in the Oxford/ Bicester area in the South-East; and another containing far fewer firms but covering an extensive geographical area in Suffolk. There are some smaller clusters in either one or the other industries elsewhere, but most of these are weak, or concentrated in the miscellaneous part of the printing industry, or do not spread across both industries. There is a weakness in our methodology here. Printing is one of a small number of branches which has small firms in large numbers doing local work almost everywhere. It is therefore possible for a weak cluster to appear in our data when there is a very small number of units in a very specialized sector (say bookbinding) backed by a large number of general job-bing printers who in fact have little connection with the specialized cases. These may well not be 'real' clusters.

It is notable that, with the exception of a general printing cluster in Keighley, a small weak one in Scarborough, and another small weak one in Stoke, all these cases, and certainly all examples of publishing clusters, are found in the southern regions: South-East, East Anglia, South-West. While both these are traditional, pre-industrial industries, publishing in particular is also an advanced 'knowledge industry'.

Finally there are strong clusters producing audio- and video-materials in the London region. It is extremely difficult for any sub-branch of manufacturing to

TABLE 6.5. Areas of Small-Unit Concentrated Specializations, Great Britain, 1996

Branch and sub-branch	English regions				
	Greater London	South-East	East Anglia	South-West	West Midlands
Food and drink					
1520					
1591					
Textiles					
1712					
1713					
1725					
1730					
1740					
1751					**Kidderminster 30**
1754					
1771					
1772					
Clothing					
1823					
1824					
Leather and footwear					
1920					**Walsall 75**
1930					
Publishing and printing					
2211		**Oxford/ Bicester 100**	Suffolk 22	Cheltenham 38	
2213			Peterborough 41	Bath 57	
2215		Hitchin/ Bedford 60		Gloucester 22	
2222		**Bicester 25**	**Thetford 28**	**St Austell 21 Stroud 61**	
2223			Sudbury 27	Bodmin 31	
2224		T. Wells 213			
2225					**Stoke 25**
2231	**London/ Heathrow 201**				
2232	**London 35**				
Chemicals					
2413					
2521					
2522					
2523		Hitchin 42			Malvern 23
2524		Banbury/ Bicester 27			
Mineral products					
2621					**Stoke 135**
2626					**Stoke and district 23**
Metal production					
2710					
2722					**Walsall 22**
2730					
2741					**Birmingham 25**

	English regions			Wales	Scotland
East Midlands	Yorkshire & Humberside	North West			
					Peterhead 25 Edinburgh 21
					Keith 35
	Huddersfield 31 **(also strong in all 172)** West Yorkshire/ Lancashire 44				Western Isles 44
	Huddersfield 49	**Lancashire 46** **Lancashire 77**			
		Lancashire 89			Hawick 22
Leicester 172 **Leicester 202** **(also strong in** **all 177)** Alfreton 21 **Leicester 319** **(also strong in** **all 182)**					
Wellingborough/ **Kettering 113** **(also strong in** **all 19)**		**Accrington 60**			
	Keighley 38				
	Scarborough 21				
		Widnes 34 Rochdale 33			
Alfreton 34 Corby 23	Rotherham 32	Burnley 24			
	Sheffield/ **Rotherham 24**				
	Sheffield 22				

TABLE 6.5. (*Continued*)

Branch and sub-branch	English regions				
	Greater London	South-East	East Anglia	South-West	West Midlands
Metal goods					
2811					
2840					**Dudley/Walsall/ Wolverhampton 231**
2851					**Dudley/Walsall/ Wolverhampton 214**
2852					
2861					
2862					**Walsall 65**
2863					**Walsall 41**
2871					Burton 41 Hereford 24 Telford 42
2872					
2874					**Wolverhampton 33** Worcester 28
Engineering					
2914					
2921					Stoke 70
2922				Stroud 23	
2923					
2940					**Coventry 118**
2954					
2955					
2956					
Electrical equipment					
3220		**Guildford/ Newbury/ Reading 64**	Huntingdon 31		
Precision equipment					
3310				Stroud/ Cirencester 32	
3320		**Hitchin/ Cambridge 133**[*]			
3330					
3340					
Motor vehicles					
3410					Telford 26
3420					
Aircraft and spacecraft					
3530		**Bournemouth 29**			
Furniture					
3611				Blandford 21	
3612		Chichester 28			
3613		Worthing 47			Kidderminster 32
3614		**Andover 22**			
3622		**Medway 26**			**Birmingham 263**

Note: **Bold type**: cases meeting both the employment concentration and the quota of 21 or more units in the sub-branch indicated.

Roman type: cases meeting the employment concentration in the sub-branch indicated, but the quota of 21 or more units only in the next widest sub-branch.

[*]Hitchin is classified as within the South-East, Cambridge within East Anglia.

	English regions		Wales	Scotland
East Midlands	Yorkshire & Humberside	North West		
Alfreton 22				
	Keighley 47			
			Aberdare 23	**Irvine 36**
	Sheffield 50 **Sheffield 107**			
	Hull 35	Blackburn 24 Wirral 45		
Alfreton 26				
		Rochdale 42		
	Huddersfield 26			
	Calderdale 40			
Leicester 38	**Bradford/** **Huddersfield 45**	**Blackburn/** **Rochdale 23** Accrington/ Rochdale 49		
Alfreton 27 Loughborough 24				
	Chesterfield 27			
			Wrexham 25	
Wellingborough 29				
Alfreton 31		Blackburn 55 Pendle 31	**South-East Wales 35**	
	Calderdale 55			
Newark 48	Barnsley 26		**South-East Wales 48**	

Source: Authors' own calculations based on data supplied by National Statistical Office.

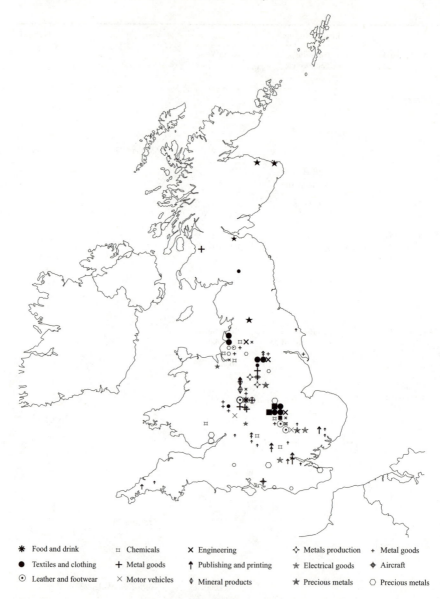

✳	Food and drink	⌑	Chemicals	✕	Engineering	✧	Metals production	+	Metal goods
●	Textiles and clothing	+	Metal goods	↑	Publishing and printing	★	Electrical goods	✦	Aircraft
☉	Leather and footwear	✕	Motor vehicles	◆	Mineral products	★	Precious metals	○	Precious metals

FIGURE 6.2. Areas of Small-Unit Concentrated Specializations, Great Britain, 1996

acquire statistical prominence in a service-oriented metropolis the size of London, but audio-materials passed our thresholds in both London and Heathrow, and video-materials in London. These very small sub-branches do not do so in any other part of the country. We have here the manifestation in manufacturing of the London cultural and entertainment sectors.

Chemicals and Minerals. The chemical industry is dominated by large corporations. There are a few cases of small-unit clusters, but they are all of the weak form: aggregates of between twenty-three and forty-two units are reached only by summing across the whole chemicals sector. The clusters that do exist are spread across most of England, with the exception of the South-West, East Anglia and the North-West.

The minerals-based industries produce just one strong cluster: the ceramics one already identified in Stoke, with some spread into the surrounding areas. This is part of the original heartland of industrial England, a world-famous historic production centre.

Metals and Engineering. This is the core of any industrial economy: the chain which stretches from the production of iron, steel and other metals, through various stages of metal forms and goods, to engineering products and machine construction. Much of this activity is dominated by very large production units, but there is room for smaller ones. The original centre for the production of basic steel, also famous for the specialized metal goods sub-branches of cutlery and tools, was Sheffield. It remains the sole British centre for small-unit production in cutlery.

The metals production concentration in Birmingham is in fact for the manufacture of gold. As such it relates to a different cluster altogether from this primarily ferrous set of industries, being linked to the city's jewellery district, which will be considered below.

Metal goods production is concentrated, as it has been since the nineteenth century, on the West Midlands, partly in Birmingham but mainly in the surrounding conurbation of Coventry, Dudley, Walsall and Wolverhampton. Large numbers of autonomous units continue to operate here. There are some other concentrations of metal goods, but apart from the isolated case of Irvine in Scotland, they are all weak. They are confined to Yorkshire, Lancashire, and the individual towns of Alfreton in the East Midlands and Aberdare in Wales. There are no clusters in the South or extreme North of England, and virtually nothing in Scotland or Wales.

The virtual disappearance of the engineering industry from the British small-firm economy, especially in the Midlands, is striking. There are just two main groups. First are textile machinery-making clusters attached to the textile and clothing industries of the East Midlands, Lancashire and Yorkshire; and there is a strong concentration of machine tools in the city of Coventry. Machinery industries tend to relate to their customer industries. In Coventry most work for the motor vehicle industry in the area. (Our data were collected before the crisis affecting the main motor industry firm, Rover, in spring 2000.) With the exception of the weak and isolated case of Stroud in the South-West (a town in fact located closer to the West Midlands than to most of the South-West), all other cases lie in a few locations within the same central band of England that has dominated this account: Coventry, Leicester, Bradford/Huddersfield, and Blackburn/Rochdale.

Electrical and Precision Equipment. There is a concentration of television transmitting equipment manufacturers around the adjacent Guildford, Newbury and Reading TTWAs to the south and west of the large Heathrow TTWA. There are some isolated concentrations of the same industry in East Anglia and the East Midlands.

The manufacture of precision equipment is one of those cases referred to by Porter (1998): activities ancillary to research-based and high-tech activities, such as medical equipment and measuring instruments. The existence of a large number of units in this branch in and to the immediate south of Cambridge is therefore significant. This is the centre of the bio-tech and computing research sector based mainly on the University of Cambridge (Lawson *et al.* 1996; Keeble *et al.* 1997; Swann, Prevezer and Stout 1998). The precision goods firms in Hitchin, Letchworth and Cambridge itself are probably among the suppliers of this rapidly growing but not yet goods-producing branch. Examples of this industry elsewhere are weak and widely scattered.

It should be noted that all but two examples of these two high-value-added industries (electrical goods and precision equipment) are located in the South-East and East Anglia.

Transport Equipment. The motor vehicle industry uses a large number of suppliers. Some of these will appear under other industries, and their connection will be lost. The Coventry machine-tool makers are one example; others may exist in textiles and plastics. Nevertheless, within the relevant branch there is a statistical sub-branch for motor-vehicle parts. Its very marginal appearance in Table 6.5 suggests that it does not cluster, at least in Britain. There are only three cases, all weak: Telford, which is close to the motor industry heartland; and Wellingborough and Wrexham, which are not.

The aircraft industry produces a strong cluster: at Bournemouth on the south coast.

Furniture and Other Consumer Goods. The furniture industry is like printing. Most towns have a number of firms in the general branch, which leads our methodology to exaggerate the importance of weak cases. As with printing, there are a number of such clusters spread across the country. More worthy of attention are the strong groupings in Newark and running across a number of TTWAs in south-east Wales.

The only other sector within the consumer goods branches to display a cluster is jewellery, with a small concentration in Medway, and a very large one in Birmingham—linked, as noted, to a gold-producing sector in the same city. The cluster is in fact an industrial district within the city, highly concentrated, with a large number of autonomous small firms, and dating back to the nineteenth century.

Concentrated Clusters: Conclusions. With some exceptions, concentrated clusters of small production units in British manufacturing have a strong geographical structure. Certain nineteenth-century legacies continue in their traditional heartlands in the North and Midlands: textiles and textile machinery in Lancashire, Yorkshire and Leicester; clothing around Leicester; shoes in nearby Kettering and Wellingborough; steel, cutlery and tools in Sheffield; metal goods in the Dudley, Wolverhampton and Walsall parts of the Birmingham conurbation; jewellery in Birmingham itself; machine tools in nearby Coventry. Also traditional are the isolated Scottish specialisms in woollen goods, alcohol and fish.

Publishing in Oxford is also traditional and pre-industrial, since it dates back 500 years. But it is also among the high-value-added and technology-related clusters found solely in southern England, primarily in the South-East and East Anglia: publishing and printing, including audio- and video- materials; various kinds of electrical and precision equipment; aircraft.

Large parts of the country are almost or entirely without clusters, and these tend to be the poorest parts. Although the southern regions have never been strongly industrial and are now mainly engaged in services activities, almost all knowledge-based manufacturing clusters were found there. The extreme North, most of Scotland and Wales, and the southern part of the South-West have no clusters of consequence at all.

Finally, these findings confirm the main current theories of clustering (e.g. Scott 1999): it involves both traditional craft goods and certain kinds of high-tech products. Different though they might seem to be, they both provide scope for firms capable of frequent adaptation and innovation based on knowledge of changing demands—whether those of fashion or of science.

Simple Clusters

When firms within an industry form concentrated clusters, there are probably important competition goods available. A cluster might however also have a weaker meaning: if there are potential gains from proximity for those engaged in similar operations, we might expect small firms within a specialized area of production which are located near each other to enjoy potential advantages over more isolated firms, even if these gains do not result in exceptional concentrations. To identify such groups we need only identify area of specialism, geographical location, and number of firms. To maintain our focus on proximity among specialized firms we consider solely sub-branches and individual TTWAs. We retain our usual size threshold of more than twenty units. We therefore operationalize the concept of a simple cluster to mean a TTWA that has more than twenty employing units within a four- or three-digit sub-branch.

A very simple factor will play a large part in determining the location of clusters: the higher the working population within a TTWA, the more likely is it to have more than twenty firms in any one sub-branch. Although this is obvious, it contains an important point: firms in high-population areas do stand a better chance of avoiding isolation (Huggins 1997). Therefore, the more that populations within a given territory are concentrated, the more difficult will it be for firms located outside such concentrations to take advantage of any collective competition goods that are available. We have excluded the London region from this part of our analysis, as it is so large that almost all sub-branches are represented by large numbers of units there. We should however bear this in mind, as it adds to the advantages flowing to firms located in and around the capital city.

We also exclude certain sub-branches: those which obviously serve very local markets (e.g., bakeries, suppliers of goods for the construction industry, and suppliers of wood); and those which are defined in a residual, general way and therefore do not constitute true specialist sub-branches (e.g., general printing, general engineering).

Table 6.6 presents the simple clusters identified after taking account of these exceptions. Cases which we have already discussed as individual districts or concentrated clusters reappear, and we see the importance within some sub-branches of some large cities which did not show in previous analyses because, even though they might have large concentrations of firms in a particular industry, these accounted for only a small proportion of the city's diversified workforce. We can now also identify some clusters that were only vaguely apparent before. Particularly interesting is a series in medical, process control, optical and other forms of precision equipment, as well as electrical and electronic equipment, in a belt of towns circling London, mainly lying outside the M25 London orbital motorway: Aylesbury and High Wycombe, Guildford, Hertford, Reading, Oxford, Watford. This connects with the smaller group linking the 'M25 belt' to Cambridge in East Anglia already identified as a concentrated cluster. Also within these areas are to be found all except one of the computing industry clusters identified (the exception is Manchester).[4]

Two points are notable here: (1) very little activity in these high-tech sectors is to be found outside the South-East, and were we to have taken London and Heathrow into account this concentration would have appeared even larger; and (2) these clusters are identifiable only at this weak level, which suggests that they are not supported by strong local institutions, and it is possible that the firms involved do not make much use of the networks potentially available to them, otherwise the clustering would be more concentrated.

The role of large cities is evident. The clusters we have identified are heavily concentrated in Birmingham, Coventry (and the area around these two), Leicester, Nottingham, Manchester, Newcastle, Leeds, Sheffield, Edinburgh, Glasgow, and of course Greater London. The medium-sized cities in the M25 belt are not large, but their proximity to London is important. Many industrial sub-branches in, for example, various forms of engineering, have more units concentrated there than in those parts of the country where they are more central to

---

[4] The literature often refers to the 'M4 corridor' of high-tech firms running alongside the eastern parts of the motorway linking London to the South-West. This overlaps a little with our observations (e.g., Oxford, Reading, and eventually Bristol), but the weight of our evidence stresses more the entire ring around London with, if anything, an emphasis to the north-east rather than due west.

the local economy. (Clearly, had we been able to study services sectors, we would have found an even more intense imbalance favouring London and the South-East.) We should again note the virtual absence of clusters in the northern region of England, Wales, and most of Scotland.

Our general finding that economic activity in Britain is subject to clustering is corroborated by recent work by Bennett, Graham and Bratton (1999). They plotted the geographical location of every registered company in Britain, and found a strong tendency for firms to be concentrated in groups within 20 km distance of each other. Their data enabled them to take account of business services firms as well as manufacturing, and they attribute an important role to the location of these in determining the location of firms in manufacturing and other services sectors. However, they considered firms of all sizes, so we cannot tell to what extent their results relate to the issue of small-firm dynamism. Further, they did not take account either of branch or sub-branch of activity, but just firms in general. This clearly limits the extent to which their results can be seen as confirming the role of collective competition goods, except those of a very general nature.

Given this, it is surprising that Bennett *et al.* 1999 conclude that, because the clusters they observe overlap heavily in a broad band running from the South-East to Lancashire and Yorkshire, there are no problems of isolation or disadvantages in being remote from the South-East for firms in the greater part of the English land mass. (They do acknowledge problems of remoteness for firms in the far North and South-West of England and in Scotland and Wales.) It seems to us that it is not possible to draw such a conclusion until branches and sub-branches of activity have been examined. Our own analysis of these suggests a considerably segmented geography, which may well inhibit the flows of contact and access to services which Bennett *et al.* see linking enterprises across most of England.

Systems of Governance

So far we have merely identified empirical clusters; what modes of governance might sustain them? To answer this we use both the existing secondary literature and the annual Economic Assessments that county councils, Training and Enterprise Councils (TECs) and Scottish Local Enterprise Companies (LECs) are required to produce for their areas.

Industrial Districts: Past, Present and Potential

We can probably assume that, as we move from industrial districts via concentrated clusters to simple clusters, we move from strong patterns of governance rooted in formal and informal associations and reciprocities to more market-sustained ones. In the British case this also seems to involve a movement from

TABLE 6.6. Areas of Small-Unit Simple Clusters, Great Britain (excluding Greater London, general goods, and those primarily for local markets), 1996

Sub-branch	South-East		East Anglia	South-West	West Midlands	
	'M 25 towns'	Rest of region			Birmingham area	Rest of region
Food and drink						
1513					Du (22)	
1520						
1542				Bl (31)		
1591						
Textiles						
1712						
1730						
1740	Wa (25)	Sn (23)			Bi (50)	
		Sd (26)				
1751						Ki (30)
1760						
1771					Co (32)	
1772						
Clothing						
1810						
1821					Bi (23)	
1822	Wa (55)	Sd (40)			Bi (155)	
					Co (55)	
					Du (123)	
					Wa (39)	
					Wo (68)	
1823					Bi (28)	
					Co (29)	
Leather and footwear						
1910					Wa (34)	
1920					Wa (75)	
1930						
Paper						
2112						
2121		Sd (21)		Bl (23)	Bi (29)	
					Du (21)	
2123	He (22)					
Publishing and printing						
2211	Ay (41)	Mi (21)	Ca (67)	Bl (28)	Bi (34)	
	Cr (58)	Po (24)		Pl (25)		
	He (27)	Sd (33)				
	Ox (94)					
	Re (35)					
	Tu (46)					
	Wa (70)					
2212	Cr (23)				Bi (37)	
2213	Cr (47)	Br (25)	Ca (36)	Bl (32)	Bi (28)	
	He (22)	Sd (21)				

East Midlands	Yorkshire & Humberside		North-West		North	Scotland
	Bradford Leeds area	Rest of region	Manchester area	Rest of region		
No (45)			Ma (22)			
		Gr (41)				Ab (45)
		Hu (31)				
						Pe (25)
						Ke (35)
	Br (23)					
	Ha (31)					
Le (113)	Br (43)		Bo (31)			
No (62)	Ca (28)		Ma (46)			
	Ha (49)					
Le (40)	Br (37)		Ac (27)	Li (27)	Ne (28)	Gl (42)
No (72)	Ha (26)		Bo (67)	Pr (22)		
	Le (29)		Ma (106)	Wn (24)		
	Wa (33)					
Le (70)						
No (23)						
Le (172)						
No (22)						
No (38)			Ma (61)			
Le (22)						
			Ma (26)	Li (23)		
De (32)	Br (28)		Bl (40)	Pr (32)	Ne (34)	Gl (50)
Le (252)	Ca (22)		Bo (44)			
No (92)	Ha (23)		Ma (151)			
	Le (74)		Ro (33)			
Al (21)			Ma (42)			
No (74)						
Le (83)						
We (81)			Ma (29)			
Ke (32)			Ac (60)			
Le (56)						
Nr (33)						
			Ma (22)	Li (25)		
Le (26)						
			Ma (48)			
			Ma (40)			
Le (23)			Ma (55)			Ed (45)
						Gl (26)
			Ma (49)			
	Le (21)		Ma (27)			Ed (21)
						Gl (24)

TABLE 6.6. (*Continued*)

Sub-branch	South-East		East Anglia	South-West	West Midlands	
	'M 25 towns'	Rest of region			Birmingham area	Rest of region
Publishing and printing (cont.)						
	Ox (41)					
	Re (26)					
	Sl (25)					
	Tu (22)					
	Wa (58)					
2223					Bi (21)	
2224	Ay (29)	Sd (31)		Bl (21)	Bi (40)	
	Wa (34)					
Chemicals						
2416					Bi (21)	
2430					Bi (23)	
Plastics						
2521					Bi (30)	
Mineral products						
2612					Bi (40)	
					Du (27)	
2621						St (135)
2625						St (64)
2630						St (25)
2663		Sd (21)			Bi (21)	
Metal production						
2710					Du (21)	
2722					Bi (28)	
					Du (33)	
					Wa (22)	
2732					Du (24)	
2741					Bi (25)	
2742					Du (22)	
2744					Bi (30)	
2745					Bi (26)	
2751					Du (28)	
2754					Bi (28)	
Metal goods						
2811	Me (24)	Sd (21)		Bl (32)	Bi (70)	
					Bi (47)	
					Du (70)	
					Wa (46)	St (26)
					Wo (21)	
2812	Wa (24)	Sd (27)		Bl (22)	Du (53)	
					Wa (27)	
2840	He (22)	Sd (25)			Bi (149)	
					Co (29)	
					Du (123)	
					Wa (69)	
					Wo (39)	
2851	Wa (30)				Bi (148)	
					Co (33)	
					Du (94)	
					Wa (67)	
					Wo (53)	
2861						
2862	Ay (58)	Po (22)			Bi (169)	
	Cr (21)	Sd (37)			Co (60)	
	He (33)				Du (104)	

	English regions					Scotland
East Midlands	Yorkshire & Humberside		North-West		North	
	Bradford Leeds area	Rest of region	Manchester area	Rest of region		
Le (30)	Le (26)		Ma (40)			
			Ma (33)			
			Ma (24)			
			Ma (32)			
			Ma (23)		Ne (22)	
Re (21)						
No (31)	Br (29) Le (24)	Hu (33) Sh (24)	Bo (31) Ma (51)	Li (33) Wn (25)	Ne (29)	Ab (24) Gl (36)
	Le (24)		Ma (52)	Li (23)		Gl (37)
No (24)		Sh (33)	Ma (40)		Ne (22)	
Le (26) No (24)		Sh (32)	Bo (25) Ma (54)			Gl (26)
Le (42)		Sh (50) Sh (107)	Ma (49)			

TABLE 6.6. (*Continued*)

Sub-branch	English regions					
	South-East		East Anglia	South-West	West Midlands	
	'M 25 towns'	Rest of region			Birmingham area	Rest of region
2863					Wa (65) Wo (25) Bi (35)	
2873					Wa (41) Bi (29)	
2874					Du (22) Bi (71) Du (86) Wa (27) Wo (33)	
Engineering						
2912					Bi (33)	
2913					Bi (21)	
2914					Bi (24)	
2922	He (21)	Sd (28)			Bi (61) Du (77) Wa (25)	
2923	Me (32) Sl (21) Wa (27)	Sn (21) Sd (21)			Bi (80) Du (50) Wa (22)	
2932						
2940	Ay (37) He (51) Me (23) Sl (25) Wa (48)	Sd (38)		Bl (32) Po (23)	Bi (212) Co (118) Du (87) Wa (73) Wo (32)	
2953					Bi (28)	
2954						
2956	He (33) Sl (24) Wa (28)	Po (22) Sn (21)		Bl (21)	Bi (63) Co (22) Du (42) Wa (29)	St (36)
Computers						
3002	Gu (23) Ox (22) Sl (39) Wa (31)		Ca (36)		Bi (35)	
Electrical equipment						
3110	Gu (28)				Bi (30)	
3120	Cr (23) Wa (25)				Bi (31) Du (26)	
3150					Bi (41)	
Electronic equipment						
3210	Gu (33) He (36) Hi (21) Re (21) Sl (23)	Po (28) Sd (28)	Ca (26)		Bi (31)	

| | English regions | | | | | Scotland |
| East Midlands | Yorkshire & Humberside | | North-West | | North | |
	Bradford Leeds area	Rest of region	Manchester area	Rest of region		
			Ma (22)			
Le (23) No (28)	Br (31)	Sh (22)	Ma (53)	Li (32) Wn (23)	Ne (25)	Gl (30)
Le (29) No (32)			Ma (57)			Gl (43)
		Hu (21) Yo (28)		Pr (24)		
Le (66) No (37)	Ca (34) Le (29)	Sh (50)	Ma (69)	Li (27)	Ne (22)	Gl (27)
Le (38) No (23)	Br (29)		Ma (24)			
Le (39) No (28)	Le (29)	Sh (24)	Bo (21) Ma (48)			Gl (23)
			Ma (34)			
	Le (21)		Ma (27) Ma (32)			Gl (26)
			Ma (32)			
			Ma (30)			

TABLE 6.6. (*Continued*)

Sub-branch	English regions		East Anglia	South-West	West Midlands	
	South-East					
	'M 25 towns'	Rest of region			Birmingham area	Rest of region
3220	Wa (30) Gu (39) He (26)	Sd (22)	Ca (21)		Bi (21)	
3230	Wa (27) Ay (24) Gu (32) He (21) Re (25) Wa (42)	Sd (37)	Ca (31)			
Precision equipment						
3310	Ay (28) Gu (28) He (29) Me (28) Ox (25) Wa (36)	Br (31) Sn (21) Sd (33)	Ca (26)	Bl (24)	Bi (72)	
3320	Br (31) Ch (25) Gu (53) He (60) Hi (45) Me (27) Ox (55) Re (40) Sl (47) Tu (29) Wa (81)	Mi (40) Po (32) Sn (50) Sd (49) Wo (34)	Ca (88)	Bt (32) Bl (49) Po (43) Sw (22)	Bi (73) Co (30) Du (27) Wa (23)	St (25)
3340	Wa (32)					
Motor vehicles						
3410					Bi (26) Co (31)	
3420						
3430	Wa (25)	Sd (24)			Bi (95) Co (37) Du (39) Wa (27)	
Other transport equipment						
3511	Me (22)	Co (22) Go (24) Is (25) Sn (69) Sd (34)		Pl (24) Po (34)		
3512		Sn (34)				
3520				Bl (43)		
3530	Gu (40) He (22) Wa (35)	Sd (22)	Ca (26)	Bo (29) Bt (29)	Bi (30) Co (24)	
Furniture						
3611	Ay (39)				Bi (31) Du (61)	
3612	Ay (24) He (28)	Sd (32)		Bl (22)	Bi (51)	
3613	Wa (26)					

English regions						Scotland
East Midlands	Yorkshire & Humberside		North-West		North	
	Bradford Leeds area	Rest of region	Manchester area	Rest of region		
			Ma (22)			
Le (25)	Le (23)		Ma (38)			
No (38)	Le (38)	Sh (43)	Bo (33) Ma (76)	Li (43)		Gl (34)
Le (25) Nr (21) No (32)	Br (27) Le (37)	Sh (23)	Bo (28) Ma (91)	Li (31) Wl (25)	Ne (21)	Ab (28) Ed (22) Gl (32)
			Ma (22)			
			Ma (23)			
Le (21)	Br (24)	Hu (23)	Ma (41)			
		Hu (26)			Ne (23)	Ab (24)
			Ma (53)	Wl (22)		
No (44)			Bo (35) Ma (35)			
Le (37)	Le (29)		Ma (44)			
			Ma (28)			

TABLE 6.6. (*Continued*)

Sub-branch	South-East		East Anglia	South-West	West Midlands	
	'M 25 towns'	Rest of region			Birmingham area	Rest of region
Other consumer goods						
3622	Me (26)	Sd (26)			Bi (263)	
3640					Bi (24)	
3661					Bi (33)	

Key:						
Ay = Aylesbury	Br = Brighton	Ca = Cambridge	Bo = Bournemouth	Bi = Birmingham	Ki = Kidderminster
Ch = Chelmsford	Co = Colchester		Bl = Bristol	Co = Coventry	St = Stoke
Cr = Crawley	Go = Gosport		Bt = Bridport	Du = Dudley	
Gu = Guildford	Is = Isle of Wight		Pl = Plymouth	Wa = Walsall	
He = Hertford	Mi = Milton Keynes		Po = Poole	Wo = Wolverhampton	
Hitchin	Po = Portsmouth		Sw = Swindon		
Me = Medway	Sd = Southend				
Ox = Oxford	Sn = Southampton				
Re = Reading	Wo = Worthing				
Sl = Slough					
Tu = Tunbridge Wells					
Wa = Watford					

traditional to 'advanced' sectors. As Porter (1998) and Scott (1999) have recently argued, the idea that because a product is 'traditional' its industry must be out-moded is misleading. Very standard or basic items can be designed, made and marketed in innovative ways; clothing and ceramics are both major cases in point. Burroni and Trigilia (this volume) show that in Italy many districts making traditional products continue to be dynamic and are found in dynamic areas of the country. Meanwhile, in that country and in Germany (Glassmann and Voelzkow, this volume) there are districts in more 'modern' industrial sectors, which is not the case in Britain. But how dynamic in fact are the traditional districts and concentrated clusters? This is difficult to determine, but we might achieve some kind of proxy for this by considering the relative success in international trade of a branch. Are British industrial districts engaged in activities where the country has a strong record in international competition or a weak one? We know that the products of the strongest districts—Scotch whisky, Scottish craft-made woollen garments, and high-quality shoes from Northamptonshire—do occupy valuable niches as goods of recognized quality. But there are very few of these.

Table 6.7 enables us to make a wider statistical assessment. The import penetration index calculates the strength of imports in relation to home consumption and exports for a given branch; the higher the figure the higher the level of import penetration. In 1996 the broad branches within which most British industrial districts were found (17, 28 and 29) ranked 9th, 18th and 11th respectively in terms of important penetration: either moderate or (in the case of metal goods) low levels. Unfortunately these data were not produced for several years in Britain, so it is difficult to estimate change over time. The series was

	English regions						Scotland
East Midlands	Yorkshire & Humberside		North-West		North		
	Bradford Leeds area	Rest of region	Manchester area	Rest of region			
Le (21)		Sh (34)				Gl (22)	
Al = Alfreton	Br = Bradford	Gr = Grimsby	Ac = Accrington	Li = Liverpool	Ne = Newcastle		Ab = Aberdeen
De = Derby	Ca = Calderdale	Hu = Hull	Bl = Blackburn	Pr = Preston			Ed = Edinburgh
Ke = Kettering	Ha = Harrogate	Sh = Sheffield	Bo = Bolton	Wn = Wigan			Gl = Glasgow
Le = Leicester	Le = Leeds	Yo = York	Ma = Manchester	Wl = Wirral			Ke = Keith
No = Nottingham	Wakefield		Ro = Rochdale				Pe = Peterhead
No = Northam							
Re = Retford							
We = Wellingborough							

Source: Authors' own calculations based on data supplied by National Statistical Office.

restarted in 1993, so it is possible to estimate change over a three-year period. Import penetration declined slightly in textiles, increased slightly in metal goods and was static in engineering. Although it is not possible to separate the particular performance of either small units or more precisely specified sub-branches within this general picture, it seems that British industrial districts are in neither particularly dynamic nor particularly failing troubled branches.

A second measure of international performance of a branch is to take the ratio of exports to imports, ignoring domestic consumption of home production. Unfortunately data for this use international calculations based on products rather than industrial branches, so only approximate connections can be made to the industrial branch coding we have been using. Here both the textile and metal goods branches appear much weaker than according to the former measure. Machinery manufacture within the engineering industry has a positive trade balance and an export performance above the national mean, but there were only three relatively small and scattered cases of districts within this general area. Here it is possible to track change over a longer period. Performance in textiles and metal goods has improved and by more than the national mean, while machinery (engineering) has deteriorated. There is therefore some convergence among branches, but again the results are inconclusive.

Evidence from the various districts and clusters is similarly ambiguous concerning quality. Several of the complexities are revealed by closer study of the large textile and clothing cases. The main forms of governance seem to be a combination of the large customer firms (Baker 1993), the market advantages of

TABLE 6.7. International Trade Performance of Economic Branches, Great Britain, 1991 and 1996

Import penetration index

Branch	1993	1996	% change	1996 rank
15	17	20	17.65	17
17	37	36	-2.70	9
18	47	49	4.26	4
19	50	56	12.00	1
20	37	33	-10.81	13
21	28	31	10.71	14
22	5	6	20.00	20
24	31	35	12.90	11
25	21	22	4.76	16
26	15	16	6.67	18
27	61	46	-24.59	5
28	15	16	6.67	18
29	35	35	0.00	11
30	56	53	-5.36	2
31	31	38	22.58	8
32	48	52	8.33	3
33	37	44	18.92	6
34	41	41	0.00	7
35	28	29	3.57	15
36	35	36	2.86	9

Export/import ratios

Branch	1991	1996	% change	1996 rank
Food*	0.45	0.47974	5.64	3
Beverages	1.54	1.37435	-10.55	15
Textiles	0.63	0.67117	6.71	5
Clothing and footwear	0.42	0.49759	18.05	4
Wood products	0.14	0.20428	43.52	1
Paper	0.42	0.46568	10.90	2
Chemicals	1.26	1.20047	-4.37	13
Plastics	0.70	0.74766	6.71	8
Iron & steel	1.15	1.11141	-3.32	12
Non-ferrous metals	0.77	0.70544	-8.56	7
Metal goods	0.86	0.94207	9.02	10
Mechanical machinery	1.24	1.22721	-1.40	14
Electrical machinery	0.86	0.91791	6.68	9
Scientific, etc goods	1.04	1.08157	3.77	11
Road vehicles	0.84	0.70064	-16.33	6
Other transport goods	1.57	1.47515	-6.25	16
All	0.88	0.91092	3.31	

Source: Annual Abstract of Statistics (various years).

proximity (Godley 1996; Winterton and Barlow 1996), and a distinctive form of community reciprocity. Most firms work for the big retail chains based in London, which maintain arm's length contract exchanges with them. (Our data were collected before the crisis affecting the largest of these retailers, Marks and Spencer, since 1999.) They do not develop the 'tutorial' relations which Japanese firms have with their suppliers. Firms working for these retailers do not have much opportunity to explore individual niches on the model of flexible special-ization, and must compete on cost. However, a number of studies suggest that low cost has been combined with high skill in order to retain competitiveness. This paradoxical combination has been made possible through a strong form of community reciprocity.

This refers to the solidarity and trust relations extant among the Pakistani and Bangladeshi immigrants and their descendants who play an important part in these industries, in particular in the strong textile and clothing industrial district around Leicester. Although this district is an old one, many of the firms in it today are owned by immigrants, who often come from textile and clothing industrial districts in their countries of origin, and who have traditions of self-employment and the management of small businesses: 4.4 per cent of Leicester's Asian population are self-employed, compared with 2.1 per cent of whites (Leicester County Council 1983). The patriarchal Islamic family system makes possible the flexible use of family labour in a manner not easily achieved with normal labour contracts (Allen and Wolkowitz 1987; Phizacklea 1990). It is notable that these industries are among the few branches of manufacturing to have a large female labour force in most societies. This particular family form, combined with racism in the sur-rounding British society, makes it difficult for these workers to leave their industry. Wages are low (Baker 1996; Taplin 1996). Authors disagree over whether these structures involve reciprocity and community strength (Ram 1994, 1996) or ethnic and gender exploitation (Coyle 1992; Leman 1992; Phizacklea 1992; Baker 1993; Kabeer 1994; Lloyd 1997). In fact the two are not necessarily incompatible. Certainly this family system provides a collective competition good.

The other main city of the East Midlands, Nottingham, was also a pre-industrial textile and clothing town, based on lace-making. It is now too diverse to be considered a clothing city, but there is a textile and clothing district, still organized around the site of the old Lace Market. It comprises a network of small firms, largely engaged in quality production (Toterdill 1992). Nottinghamshire County Council, the local TEC, and the firms have organized a 'Fashion Col-lective' to assist with co-operative marketing and exhibiting (Nottinghamshire County Council 1997), providing direct services on the Emilian-Romagnan model (Zeitlin 1996). However, in her comparative study of Nottingham and Prato, Garmise (1997) argued that this help was vitiated by the funding arrangements of UK central government, which required the county and city councils to compete with each other. The city was also forced by its need to increase income to assist the building of office blocks at the expense of the clothing district. In contrast with Prato, she also found that the centralization of government in the UK seemed to rob the locality, including local associations, of capacity for autonomy and direction of change (ibid.: 191).

Known as 'the Potteries', the ceramics area around Stoke was in the nineteenth century one of the most perfect examples of an industrial district. Our data show that over 100 small units still survive. Some of the brand names of the region are famous, and this is a 'made in England' industry. Although there has been a considerable number of mergers and take-overs, there has also been considerable growth in the numbers of small enterprises (Rowley 1994:135). Some authors (Imrie 1989) see evidence of flexible specialization here, while others (Rowley 1989, 1994) argue that most of this has been in down-market, low-skilled production rather than quality niches. The local TEC reports that small firms have found it difficult to invest individually in new technology, and have therefore lost ground in the more skill-intensive and sophisticated areas of ceramic production (Staffordshire TEC 1997). Overall, the non-metallic mineral products sector in Staffordshire, which is dominated by ceramics, saw the loss of 6,500 jobs in the 1991–93 period, while the number of employers in the 11–25 employee size band fell by almost 40 per cent (ibid.).

Similarly, the Northamptonshire shoe and leather industry lost 60 per cent of its employees between 1971 and 1991, losing another 1,500 jobs between 1991 and 1993 (Northamptonshire TEC 1996). In the Sheffield cutlery and tools clusters, complex interaction between firms had almost vanished by the early 1970s, as more and more of the production process became internalized within particular firms (Hayter and Patchell 1993). This change coincided with the long-term decline of the steel industry in the city.

Similar problems afflict the hand-crafted glass industry in Sunderland, which had had an important local presence since the eighth century, but which did not appear at all in our statistics (Sunderland TEC 1998). Many firms are too small to provide either the training required for hand-blowing glass or the international marketing required to establish export niches. It has not been possible to establish joint training or marketing systems, and while a National Glass Centre may be established in the area, this is expected to be little more than a tourist attraction.

There is too much evidence of survival, of local specialization, and of commercial strength in these accounts to justify the very negative conclusions of many observers concerning the state of small-firm clusters in Britain. There are certainly some important quality niches. On the other hand the prevailing impression is of under-used potentiality for exploiting possibilities of networking, caused either by aspects of government policy or by other sources of failure. In several cases collective goods have sustained competition on the basis of low wages rather than the pursuit of innovative quality. Large customer firms also seem mainly to insist on low prices rather than on up-grading quality. The small manufacturing firms that exist in Britain today have survived downturns that saw many others go bankrupt. They are therefore tough and resilient, but inclined to look to themselves and their suppliers rather than beyond. This is seen particularly strongly in the still extensive Birmingham-based metal goods industry. This has a long tail of weakly performing small companies, with low levels of capital, old production methods and heavy dependence on large corporations in a motor industry that is itself in difficulties (Birmingham Economic Information Centre 1998). They seem not to take advantage of opportunities for either sharing best practice among themselves or using business support agencies (ibid.: 3).

Geographically isolated areas, particularly in Scotland, which have economies dominated by small firms because transport networks are poor, are in a different position. They are more inclined (or constrained) to seek out collective competition goods and develop community forms of governance and associationism (Boyle 1993; MacLeod 1996). Further, the relevant development authorities, and in particular the Highlands and Islands LECs, seem to be more locally embedded, and more focused on indigenous small-firm-based development than their equivalents in England. In addition to the strong Scottish districts that appeared in our statistics, there are other smaller examples of co-operative local activity, which appear to be able to reproduce themselves, and to provide collective goods, either through producer initiatives or the involvement of public or semi-public bodies. For example, the unique high-quality yarn provided by seaweed-eating sheep in North Ronaldsay in the Orkney Islands is marketed communally. While this used to be done informally by North Ronaldsay Community Council, it is now being managed more formally through a company, Yarn from North Ronaldsay, which handles the collection, marketing and transporting of fleeces (Orkney Enterprise 1996). In Dumfries and Galloway, the LEC has a partnership with the Forestry Contracting Association and a Sawmill Assistance Scheme, which together allow it to provide services to the locally important timber industry (Dumfries and Galloway Enterprise 1997). Both the relevant trade association and the responsible LEC have been involved in joint initiatives to help the troubled textile industry in the Scottish Borders area (Scottish Borders Enterprise 1996).

Often however the population base is simply too small to produce an industry of significant size (e.g., the small concentration of food products and some high-tech activities in North Yorkshire (North Yorkshire TEC 1996) and small firms in Cumbria (Cumbria TEC 1997)).

Serendipitous Local Collective Goods

South-east England contained several empirically observable clusters in advanced, high-value-added sectors, but with the exception of the Oxford/ Bicester publishing and printing cluster, most seemed to be only simple clusters. It is notable that, while part of the contemporary 'knowledge industry', publishing and printing in Oxford is also a pre-industrial cluster. It is also strongly connected to the presence of some large publishing firms in the area, particularly Oxford University Press. These do not so much act as customer firms as reinforce a market form of governance. The presence of the large firms attracts practitioners of the various skills used in the industries, which then attract small firms seeking to use the same skills. The Suffolk publishing and in particular printing cluster is possibly related to the nearby presence of Cambridge University Press.

However, the role of universities in both these cases, as well as their place (and especially Cambridge) within science-based clusters, indicate the possibility of another form of governance of local production systems: the existence of a major non-market institution which is itself sustained by a heavily regulative structure of some public kind. Its own relative immunity from market fluctuations enables such an institution to provide stability for certain competition goods, in particular knowledge resources. Because such types of governance are indirect and unplanned they have a diversity of substantive forms, and can be called seren-dipitous governance.

One might expect the unconscious nature of this form to result in further under-exploitation of potential networks, and there is evidence of this. Helen Lawton-Smith (1997) has presented clear evidence of small-firm networking in high-tech sectors in both Cambridge and Oxford, but shows the universities' role to be very passive and indirect. (In fact, she sees a difference, with Cambridge having had more of a conscious policy. It is notable that it was only around that city that our statistical analysis detected evidence of a high-tech cluster.) Keeble *et al.* (1996a and b) found that 60 per cent of high-tech firms in these areas reported close contacts with other firms in the locality, mainly involving supply, services or research collaboration. Entrepreneurial spin-offs and continuing scientific interactions, partly routed through university channels, were also important (ibid.). Firms in these sectors need of course to be engaged in international and remote exchanges, but they report that the combination of global contacts and more intensive local interactions is important to them (Lawson *et al.* 1996).

There also seems to be some differentiation according to sector. Garnsey, Galloway and Mathis (1994)—who found that the Cambridge cluster does not have the highly developed institutional framework that Italian districts do—argue that firms in the instrumentation and biotechnology sectors seem more likely to have networks, and also comment on the dynamic cluster in ink jet printing and associated technologies (see also Garnsey and Alford 1994). Many firms sought to help suppliers through early payment, equipment transfers and giving business when order books were low. Most interestingly, it would appear from Garnsey and Alford's work that the phenomenon goes beyond a simple aggregation of bilateral relationships—there is evidence of an embryonic community-based enforcement system, in which general norms and the reputations of individual firms play an important part. There seem to be relatively low levels of oppor-tunism as a result, which makes co-operation between firms easier, allowing them, for example to enjoy significant economies of scale through the use of joint suppliers (ibid.).

We have already remarked above on the difficulty in identifying high-tech sectors, as they are not often involved in direct production, or even if they are in production they are not identifiable through the concepts used in official statistics. In some cases it is possible to get round this last problem through supplementary sources. For example, Oxfordshire County Council, aware of the existence of a bio-technology cluster within and around its borders that was completely unrecognizable from standard statistics, carried out a survey of firms to discover its size and character. It found a clear cluster, but not necessarily engaged in direct manufacturing. One reason why Oxford and Cambridge show up more clearly than several other areas of this kind is that for historical reasons these cities have unusually large universities given the size of the surrounding population, enabling university-based economic activity to stand out more easily within statistics. There is also evidence of clusters in information technology and biotechnology in the Scottish 'Silicon Glen', the Edinburgh (Lothian and Edinburgh Enterprise Ltd. 1998; Midlothian Council/Lothian and Edinburgh Enterprise nd) and Glasgow (Glasgow Development Agency 1997) areas. These clusters were not observable from our statistics,[5] but probably rely on competition goods provided by the local university and science park infrastructure.

One can also include in this category of serendipitous collective good production the presence of large media corporations, which stimulate a mass of small independent producers and subcontracting firms (e.g., in Cardiff around the BBC and Wales-based private television firms (South Glamorgan TEC 1997)). This is not just a case of supplier networks around a large corporation: where British terrestrial television is concerned, this can be regarded as the indirect product of a form of governance structure. Legislation both limits the holdings of firms owning combinations of television and press media, and stipulates some involvement of small firms in the sector. Airports can produce similar results: heavy regulation provides protection from extreme instabilities of competition and some guarantee of permanence, helping small firms to grow up around airport activities (Manchester TEC 1997).

A further striking example of such a regime in a high-tech, SME-based sector is Formula One motor racing engineering and design, a small niche in which the UK is dominant. Production is based on small and medium-sized firms, concentrated in a broad regional arc, running from Southampton through Oxford and Northamptonshire to Cambridge (Henry, Pinch, and Russell 1996; Pinch and Henry 1999a and b). In fact, the industry only just failed to make our criteria for statistical significance as a concentrated cluster in one TTWA. Near the centre of the zone is the Silverstone racing circuit in South Northamptonshire (Northamptonshire TEC 1996). This concentration seems likely to grow with the creation of an advanced technology park adjacent to the circuit. It should be noted that again this area is within the M25 belt. The very nature of the industry

---

[5] It will be recalled that Scotland as a whole did have an exceptional concentration of employment in the office equipment industry, nowadays dominated by computers (Table 6.3), but this was not observable in any of our data on *small* units. This is consistent with the argument of Turok (1993), who found that Silicon Glen was dominated by large inward investors without local supply chains.

requires a high degree of regulation—technological progress has to be limited in order to maintain the sport's long-term viability (Henry, Pinch and Russell 1996). There also appears to be a high degree of mobility between firms—employees move readily from one to another so that informal relations often supplement competition between rivals, and a body of diffuse, localized knowledge has been built up which helps cement the local industry's international dominance (Pinch and Henry 1999a and b).

There is a high degree of local authority involvement in the governance and further development of the cluster—to promote a European network of racing circuits and local authorities to exchange best practice, promote joint ventures, research and development, promote spin-off technology, and fight off the threat of Asian competition (Northamptonshire TEC 1996). Although the Formula One industry seems a strange one to provide an example of local rootedness, it seems that the importance of a key geographical location, together with the gains from tacit knowledge in a rapidly changing field, and the overall constraints of a regulatory structure, do in fact make this possible.

The existence of roads and other means of transport linking areas to ports and other important supply routes can serve the role of serendipitous governance, both attracting firms to an area and then retaining them, though such clusters are then likely to remain without internal co-ordination possibilities. The M25 zone identified above is one such example. Others include a small area of advanced engineering in southern Somerset alongside the A303 (Somerset TEC 1997), and similar specialisms in the same region in industrial estates in Yate, located close to the M4 and M5 motorways (WESTEC 1996). Although this role of transport links can be analysed by standard economics as a market process, the decision to build and maintain the network in particular locations stands outside the market and provides the stability of a form of governance.

Finally, it should be noted that London itself serves as a vast form of serendipity which cannot be understood by market forces alone. The emergence and maintenance of a capital city as an entirely exceptional location results from a mass of political and other decisions taken over a period of centuries and constantly reinforced by further path-dependent decisions today. This is the case of both London and Paris, as well as some other capitals largely in developing countries. A different politics has produced the very different urban structures of Germany, Italy, Spain, the USA and some other states.[6] Keeble (1998) has argued that the strong recent growth of the East Anglian regional economy owes nothing to government regional policy, as it occurred during a period when government was ideologically opposed to economic intervention. But the only regional policies that were stopped were those directed at poorer regions. The mass of government actions which sustain the centrality of the capital continued, and it was the increased pressure which this placed on London and the South-East

---

[6] Even if geographically small countries are dominated by their capitals, the small overall size of the territory reduces the implications for those relatively remote from the centre. Whether a state's territory is large or small is itself of course a result of political decisions.

which increased the attractiveness of East Anglia as a cheaper and greener location, as Keeble himself (ibid.) acknowledges.

Large-Firm Dominated Regions

Many parts of the country remain dominated by large firms, with no evidence of small firm clustering. For example, relatively low-productivity big firms dominate the Yorkshire and Humberside region (Yorkshire and Humberside TECs 1996). The pharmaceuticals industry is strongly established, but involves bulk production of standard products by large plants, lacking the science- and innovation-based network infrastructure that appears alongside the dynamic parts of this industry. West Wales similarly remains dependent on large firms (West Wales TEC 1998). We have also seen above how some small-firm clusters are sustained by large customer corporations. This is partly the case for the West Midlands metal industry (dependent on the motor industry), though there is also considerable autonomy in that sector (Marshall, M. 1990). Textiles and clothing in the East Midlands and elsewhere are heavily dependent on a few large retailers, though the governance regime of the region is a combination of this and the ethnic minority character of many of the firms.

It was partly in an attempt to change the arm's-length contract relations of large customers, which seemed to devitalize local entrepreneurship, that British governments during the 1980s encouraged Japanese and later Korean direct investment (Amin and Tomaney 1991). It was hoped that plants such as the Nissan complex in Sunderland and other Japanese investments in South Wales and Swindon would acclimatize local firms to advanced production techniques, and that close collaboration between buyers and subcontractors would disseminate best practice. Furthermore, just-in-time production techniques, with their emphasis on close proximity of subcontractors, would bind the incoming firms to the local economy.

This policy has had mixed results. Cooke and Morgan (1998: ch. 6), two leading specialists in business networks who have particular expertise in South Wales, have high expectations of the Japanese motor-industry firms there. Oliver and Wilkinson (1992) report that Japanese firms investing in the UK do appear to be bringing many of their manufacturing practices with them. Munday, Morris and Wilkinson (1995) note the creation of some sub-contracting complexes and of stable supply linkages for some firms, though they also found that Japanese subsidiaries' activities in Wales mostly involved low-value-added inputs requiring little complex collaboration. Okamuro (1997) reports the growth of long-term relations between inward investing Japanese motor manufacturers and their suppliers, the second and third tiers of which were predominately small firms according to our definition (ibid.: 140). However, most of these suppliers were located in the existing West Midlands cluster, and not within the areas of inward-investment themselves. Our own statistical survey above found no evidence of a cluster of motor components units in any of these areas. Similar negative results are reported for Scotland's Silicon Glen (Turok 1993). Phelps, Lovering and Morgan (1998) considered that inward investment was in fact putting local institutions under considerable strain, while Lovering (1999) is sceptical whether there are any positive effects on local economies.

There is some evidence of a general emulation effect from Japanese investors, pushing British firms towards closer and more collaborative supply relationships. Morris and Imrie (1992) found, despite considerable initial scepticism, that firms in certain sectors in the UK are moving closer to obligational contracting with genuine bonds of trust, in order to emulate what is perceived to be international best practice. Some examples which predate the Japanese influence can also be found in the aerospace sector, and in particular the privatized monopoly firm British Aerospace (BAe). This dominates the economy of west Lancashire (LAWTEC 1997), where many small firms are dependent on it. Both BAe and Rolls Royce also have had a long-established presence in the Bristol region, which has produced a small cluster of small contracting firms (WESTEC 1996), but there is no evidence of any development of relational contracting, of much direct interaction between firms in Bristol (Boddy and Lovering 1986), or of activities in aerospace having helped jump-start high-value-added activities in other sectors in Lancashire, which scores below the national average on a number of important economic indicators (Lancashire County Council 1997).

However, British Aerospace has recently provided a clear example of quasi-hierarchical governance assisting in the solution of quite general collective good problems. The company found state-provided education and training inadequate to its needs, and has decided to create its own 'virtual university', offering training and education up to PhD level (Hampshire TEC 1998). The initiative will be open to employees, partner companies and the supplier base, and will involve partnership with other academic institutions (British Aerospace 1998). However, this solution reflects British Aerospace's unusual position of dominance—it forms so large a part of the relevant sector that, in the absence of an adequate response from government, it makes sense for it to solve the problem itself. Most buyer firms are nowhere near so dominant, and restrict themselves to less far-reaching initiatives. It is notable that the initiative originated in Hampshire, the site (in Bournemouth TTWA) of the only aerospace cluster identified in our statistics—and part of the South-East.

Policy-Stimulated Clusters

This argument leads us to consider other cases where there seems to be inter-action between government policy and formal or informal types of co-operation among SMEs. In most such cases it is difficult to say whether the policy of public or quasi-public agencies has had a measurable impact. In some areas there is clearly local debate among public authorities and local business elites over the desirability of a stronger governance model, but these generally remain at the aspirational level. In areas with deeply rooted economic problems, one might expect greater awareness of the need for a strategic response and less reliance on market forces. And in some troubled parts of the country, such as Sheffield and Tyneside, this appears to be true (Shutt and Pellow 1998).

Most of the available evidence is of policy efforts to promote co-operation, rather than evidence of co-operation itself. It is thus difficult to measure the level of policy success. There is also controversy as to whether local economic development in the UK involves genuine partnership, or whether business elites have replaced local authorities as the key actors in the development process. There is evidence of genuine and comprehensive partnership, despite continuing differences of interest between actors, in Sheffield, where the local authority remains the most important actor (Lawless 1994, 1996). The same appears to be true of Bristol (Bassett 1996). However, in Manchester, the local development agenda appears to have been dominated by a self-perpetuating group of important businessmen (Peck and Tickell 1995).

A further problem of evaluation is that European- and national-level funding schemes stress the need for 'partnership', which gives local bodies an incentive to exaggerate the degree of co-operation taking place in order to secure the funds. There is evidence of activity to encourage inter-firm co-operation in districts receiving these funds, but little discussion of its effectiveness. For example, much of the Hereford and Worcester area is eligible for EU Objective 5b funding or Regional Selective Assistance. Public and private organizations have combined to create a Rural Strategy Partnership to seek to reverse rural decline, but so far it is difficult to perceive any concrete economic results (Hereford and Worcester County Council *et al.* 1997). The area has had some success with inward investment, attracting over 130 foreign firms. These have, however, simply established branches in the district. There is no evidence of relational supplier networks. There seems slightly more evidence of activity in Gloucestershire, where again the county council has sought to take advantage of various EU funding opportunities (Gloucestershire Labour Market Information Unit 1997). There are clusters of small firms in metal products, printing and publishing, wood and furniture, some of which were identified in our statistics. However, no research seems to have been conducted on whether these exhibit any internal governance modes.

Similar accounts of public policy attempts but little response can be found in Calderdale and Kirklees (in Yorkshire) and in County Durham and Darlington. In the former a primarily manufacturing economy has a high presence of SMEs, concentrating mainly on textiles and clothing, but also in machinery, furniture and chemicals (Calderdale and Kirklees TEC 1997). There has been some growth of these firms in recent years, but it remains a relatively poor area. Public authorities and business elites are seeking a local strategy, but are having diffi-culty in agreeing on whether to concentrate on developing particular localities, or to co-operate in setting up a regional inward investment strategy. Similar problems have been reported in a number of other areas (Tickell, Peck and Dicken 1995). In County Durham there is evidence of county council activity seeking to co-ordinate the local economy and organize its overseas representation, but the area remains dominated by large firms (County Durham and Darlington TEC 1998).

Many of the same problems apply to assessing the impact of TECs and LECs on the governance of small firm co-operation in their local areas of responsibility. While the vast majority of TECs seem to have some form of sector-specific activity (CRG 1996), it is hard to assess how active they have been in promoting relations between firms. Robert Huggins (1997) reports that 90 per cent of TECs surveyed in his research report had started up at least one network of firms in their area, and that 71.4 per cent intended to introduce new initiatives aimed at improving networking between firms in their localities. However, he notes that they tended to be vague about the specifics of these initiatives, and that the figures suggest that TECs have been unsuccessful by their own measure in setting up networks. Analysis of TEC and LEC economic reports and other documents tends to confirm this assessment. Many TECs report having set up 'clubs' of business-people in various sectors, or with particular interests. However, these clubs often appear to be little more than means through which the TECs can target their policy and information services for particular sub-groups of the business population, with little scope for real governance. Some TECs and LECs also provide collective competition goods such as joint marketing of goods and joint stands at trade fairs.

There are however some instances where public policy may have had an appreciable and important impact on local economic development. Shutt and Pellow (1998) discuss efforts by the North Tyneside Council and Tyneside TEC to emulate Emilia-Romagna through the encouragement of inter-firm co-operation and the provision of 'real services' (Brusco 1992). This has taken the form of a Real Service Centre and a number of initiatives in different sectors encouraging firms to work together. It is notable that most of the joint ventures take the form of limited companies in which each participating firm supplies a director. While the authors accept that it is still too early to assess the success of this policy, it does seem to have encouraged some genuine instances of inter-firm co-operation.

Perhaps more substantive in terms of positive results for the local economy is another case discussed by Shutt and Pellow (1998), the creation of a media cluster in Sheffield. The city, faced with massive redundancies in steel and engineering, decided to create a Cultural Industries Quarter in 1981. Despite initial scepticism and indeed derision from critics who refused to believe that a declining industrial city could create a culture industry *ab novo*, the strategy has had some successes, producing at least one internationally acclaimed film, *The Full Monty*. There is a cluster of some 140 firms in the Quarter. Glasgow, a city with a similar history of severe decline of traditional large-scale industry, has had a similar success in becoming a centre for film and other media industries (Glasgow Development Agency 1997).

Market-Driven Clusters

Meanwhile, important clusters in relatively advanced economic sectors continue to exist outside any of the forms of governance described above. These are mainly in south-east England. Apart from the important serendipitous role played by the existence of London as an elaborately maintained capital city, they seem to be held together solely by market forces.

For example, there is the previously mentioned concentration of television transmitting equipment manufacturers in Guildford, Newbury and Reading TTWAs. This is among a number of looser agglomerations—in electronics, precision-engineering, bio-tech, computer software, and telecommunications—within the wealthy area running from the London conurbation to purely rural areas (Surrey TEC and Surrey County Council 1996). These industries require concentrations of rather specialized skills, which are most likely to be found in such a region, with a very large population base, high general educational level, and many higher education institutions.

This area runs into another concentration of high-tech, export-oriented SMEs around the so-called 'growth pole' of Gatwick Airport, the M2 motorway and the A233. This experienced decline during the first half of the 1990s (Coopers and Lybrand n.d.). The firms in this area and sector are described as 'footloose', and there has been a loss of inward investment as well as out-migration from previous inwardly investing firms. The area has had one of the highest 'death rates' of firms in the UK (ibid.). By 1998 the local economy had bounced back, with new inward investment and job growth, but still on the basis of a relatively undeveloped local infrastructure (Sussex Enterprise 1998). This conforms to the familiar British pattern of alternating brief periods of growth and set-back, with little being done to establish infrastructures for more sustained development. Even in industries that approximate to the diversified quality production or flexible specialization models, such as the bespoke engineering industry, there appears to be little inter-trading or networking among firms in these south-eastern areas (Surrey TEC and Surrey County Council 1996).

The South London TEC (SOLOTEC 1996) identified clusters in the paper, publishing and printing chain, and noted that its local industry seemed to be more clustered than the rest of the London economy. However, it also noted that little or nothing was being done to develop the co-operative potential of these, and that the firms involved depended mainly on domestic markets and were not developing areas of potential growth. It also noted a lack of co-ordination between firms and local educational institutions in the provision of workforce skills (ibid.: 12).

Similarly, Simmie (1997a), in an examination of innovation among high-technology firms in Hertfordshire (to the north of London), found little evidence of local supply-side links. What there were tended to involve low-level support services such as cleaning. Henry (1992) also found little evidence of a localized production complex in Hertfordshire. It is interesting to note that the existing advanced engineering and other high-tech activities in this area seem to be stagnating, in favour of Oxford, Cambridge and parts of London, where there is a better infrastructure of research support (Hertfordshire TEC 1997).

One of the earliest cases to appear in the academic literature was the North London furniture industry discussed by Best (1990). He compared this industry with its Italian opposite number, and showed how the latter developed co-operative solutions while British firms responded with intensified and in the end mutually destructive competition. Today the North London TEC (1996) reports that small furniture firms still exist in the area, but there is no evidence that they have solved the problem of co-operative activity. More generally, in an overall national survey Curran and Blackburn (1994) present a negative account of the possibilities for local co-operation between firms in the UK.

Nevertheless, Keeble and others' analysis of the results of the 1995 Cambridge University ESRC Centre for Business Research Survey suggests that service firms in the South-East are over twice as likely as their counterparts in peripheral regions to report collaborative arrangements with other companies (Keeble *et al.* 1996b). Manufacturing firms in the South-East are also more likely to have such arrangements than those in the periphery. The most likely interpretation of this finding is that it is far easier for firms in this region to find collaborative partners, given the relative concentration of activity (see our analysis above of simple clusters, and also Bryson, Wood and Keeble 1993). The South-East has a far higher population of firms in high-value-added sectors where co-operation of certain kinds (R&D, joint marketing, and so on) is likely to be more lucrative. Thus, *ex ante*, firms in this region have more opportunities and reasons to engage in co-operation than their counterparts elsewhere.

Government Policy and the Collective Action
Question in British Business

Jonathan Zeitlin (1995) noted the importance of both industrial districts and regional agglomerations in late nineteenth-century Britain, arguing that the economy of this era was actually dominated by industrial districts. These began to lose their dynamism before the First World War, and large firms became decisively more important between the late 1940s and 1970s. In Zeitlin's account, the decisions of national-level state policy-makers played a crucial role in accelerating the decline; a story similar to that told for France by Aniello and Le Galès elsewhere in this volume.

The fact that British industrialization was unprecedented, slow, and for a long time entirely unanticipated meant that, quite apart from any ideological pre-ferences for *laissez faire*, industrial development was not initially an important objective of government policy. It only became so, from the 1920s onwards, in the face of the need to assist areas suffering from industrial decline, an emphasis that continued even in the successful years of the 1950s. Irrespective of political ideology or phase in economic development, industrial policy in the UK has usually been about rescue, support and subsidy in the face of crisis. It has rarely been concerned with innovation and new activities. Exceptions to this, such as the experiments with indicative planning in the 1960s, and the Industrial Reorganization Corporation of the mid-1970s, have been brief and eventually unsuccessful. Regional economic policy has similarly focused on assisting regions with problems by allocating funds and strengthening infrastructure. Meanwhile, dynamism has moved south towards London. The South-East in turn made its own demands for infrastructural support to help it accommodate rapid growth and to protect its physical environment, often negating the assistance being given to other regions.

Meanwhile, small firms have had a problematic role in British economic thinking. The political rhetoric of the Conservative Party has favoured them as sources of enterprise and independence, but in practice Conservative governments have done little for them (Assimakopoulou 1998). The Labour Party has normally been either hostile or indifferent. The British economy is one of the most concentrated in the capitalist world, in part due to the legal framework of company ownership, which has long favoured hostile take-over activity. Further, the country has never developed a legal framework favouring the equivalents to *artisan*, *artigiano* or *Handwerker*, which terms have no exact English equivalent. 'Artisan' is archaic, while 'craftsman' carries the burden of the arts and crafts and the specifically anti-industrial arguments of William Morris and his school. In this context small firms have not been seen as possessing particular skills in or approaches to industrial production. Policy towards them has concentrated on easing their taxation position and assisting them with access to investment funds.

Assimakopoulou (ibid.) argues that changes in British policy towards small firms from the 1980s onwards were primarily ideological. First, the neo-liberal Conservative governments of Margaret Thatcher linked small-firm creation to the instilling of entrepreneurial spirit. Also, the initial desire of the Conservatives to revive British industrialism was eventually replaced by the belief that Britain needed a post-industrial economy, and that nothing needed to be done to address the problems of entrepreneurs in manufacturing. As Assimakopoulou stresses, the main policy concern was small-firm *creation* rather than survival. All these factors combined to steer policy away from infrastructural supports to assist the survival of small companies.

The Labour Party was coping with the problem of long-term opposition in this period. It fell back on its local government base, and tried to develop local enterprise strategies based on the limited actions available to local government. This did lead to the party creating links with small business interests for the first time in its history, and may have had long-term implications for its *rapprochement* with the private sector in general. However, little came directly from these policies. There was considerable mistrust between Labour and business, and matters were not helped by the determination of the Conservative government to disrupt what was being achieved. The Greater London Council was abolished while it was developing its Greater London Enterprise Board; business leaders in Sheffield encountered government disapproval of their willingness to join a consensus pact for the area with the Labour city council.

By the late 1980s the search for a specifically *industrial* economic revival which had been an unsuccessful object of policy for many years seemed to have become first impossible, and then unnecessary. The economy discovered a new capacity for dynamism and in particular for job creation both in both knowledge-based service sectors such as financial services, and low-skill ones like hotels and restaurants. The absence of an *artigiano* skill base and set of associated infrastructural supports valuable to small firms in much of manufacturing and high-value-added services is less relevant to many of these service sectors. Problems of financial access have been eased by the rapid growth of venture capital facilities within the UK economy. Therefore, while industrial production has not shaken off its historical sources of weakness, and many of these have in fact worsened, small firms have had a new opportunity to thrive within certain services.

Nonetheless, certain ideas connected to networks and inter-firm co-operation in manufacturing began to enter central government thinking in the early 1990s and to produce new policies, surviving the change to a Labour government in 1997, albeit with some new emphases. The story is still unfolding at the time of writing. The policy milieu remains confused. The terms 'network' and 'net-working' may themselves be responsible for much of the confusion, since they are difficult to define precisely. Public policy seems to have decided that inter-firm networks are a 'good thing', but there is not much awareness that their forms will depend on their governance institutions.

Regional Development, TECs, and Networking as a Policy Goal

The starting-point for the new direction came during the 1980s, when the government attributed many of the economic problems of Scotland and northern England to a lack of 'entrepreneurial culture' (Amin and Tomaney 1991; Danson 1995a). Culture had a special, Hayekian, meaning in this context. A long history of state subsidy and support was considered to have robbed people in these areas of an entrepreneurial spirit *that would otherwise exist*. Without such obstacles, it was assumed that entrepreneurial *individuals* would emerge, each acting on his or her own, providing an example to aspiring business people. The role of institutions and social context was seen solely as the negative ones produced by government intervention. Policy thus aimed at creating the role model of the dynamic entrepreneur (Amin and Tomaney 1991).

Urban development corporations were created to regenerate urban areas by stimulating property development (Imrie and Thomas 1993). These were dominated by business people appointed by central government, sidelining elected local government authorities which tended to be dominated by the Labour Party and considered to be hostile to entrepreneurship. Existing regional economic development institutions, such as the Welsh Development Agency (WDA) and the Scottish Development Agency (SDA), were changed.

The Welsh Development Agency (WDA) was founded in 1976, and has since pursued the aims of promoting economic renewal and improving the environment (Morgan 1997b). However, its subsequent history has been somewhat erratic; while it has been subject to sustained and frequently justified criticism, it has also been directly involved in interesting and innovative attempts to promote inter-action and co-operation between firms and other actors in its ambit. It has sought to encourage inward investment, especially from Japanese manufacturers. The WDA had its autonomy substantially curtailed in the 1990s after public con-troversy over spending irregularities (ibid.).

Scotland has a history of public–private partnerships (Boyle 1993), and the Scottish Development Agency (SDA), founded in 1974, built upon this legacy. Like other development authorities in the UK, it sought to attract inward investment, but it also provided collective competition goods to Scottish firms, and sought to identify business actors' collective interests and thus build net-works of firms, brokering, for example, fora for collaboration in the financial services and woollen industries (Moore 1995). In 1991 the Scottish Development Agency and Training Agency merged to become Scottish Enterprise (Danson, Lloyd, and Newlands 1989; Boyle 1993). The new agency's perception of its role was very strongly guided by the government view of Scotland's 'anti-enterprise culture'. This led to the Business Birth-Rate Enquiry and consequent Business Birth-Rate Strategy which sought to foster entrepreneurialism by paying atten-tion to disadvantaged groups who lacked the social support and financial backing to start up businesses (Danson 1995a). It emphasized networks, but between individuals rather than small firms: the shallowness of Scots' personal networks was seen as one of the factors contributing to their apparent lack of entrepre-neurialism (McNicoll 1995; for a critique of this set of assumptions, see Whittan and Kirk 1995). Policy measures included the creation of LINC Scotland, which aims to bring potential entrepreneurs and 'angels' (i.e., counsellors) together, the provision of counselling sessions and the organization of shows to attract potential entrepreneurs. Whether this set of strategies has had beneficial results is difficult to assess.

Scottish Enterprise has also sought to attract inward investment. This policy is not without its problems (Turok 1993), and although various LECs claim that an important aspect of their work with inward investors is encouraging them to develop local sourcing (e.g., Fife Enterprise 1997), it is not clear whether there has been real success in this; certainly our statistical analysis did not confirm any important presence of small firms in these districts—or in areas of England and Wales subject to similar policies.

A different approach is Enterprise Ayrshire's strategy of encouraging Industry Groups among SMEs, which can promote shared activities such as joint mar-keting in an area with many economic weaknesses (Enterprise Ayrshire 1999).

Success is reported from the engineering and textile sectors; other Industry Groups include food and drink and tourism. A number of other LECs have been encouraging such groups, sometimes known as 'export clubs', among the SMEs of their areas (e.g., Scottish Borders Enterprise 1996). Other Scottish agencies seem to concentrate on working with a selected group of individual companies, agency and firm trying together to improve performance (Dunbartonshire Enterprise 1997). This is more like a local version of a French 'national champions' strategy than a cluster-oriented approach.

At national level a further stage in policy development was the establishment in 1991 of eighty-two Training and Enterprise Councils (TECs) in England and Wales and twenty-three Local Enterprise Companies (LECs) in Scotland. These became the key agencies through which public policy for network creation operated (for more detail see Crouch, Finegold and Sako 1999: ch. 6). They replaced all existing structures for organizing and supervising government policy for advanced skill creation, and at the same time administered schemes for assisting the young and adult unemployed. Their primary role was vocational training, but in several cases TECs and LECs found that firms were less interested in training than in a wider enterprise encouragement role. TECs found it difficult to recruit persons from small and medium-sized firms (Bennett and McCoshan 1993: 187–8; Vaughan 1993) and services sectors (ibid.). This latter is consistent with the general finding that TEC activity has been stronger in older manufacturing areas than in those dominated by the new tertiary economy. In their subsequent activities TECs have made much more progress in their relations with large, geographically concentrated corporations than with small companies (Vickerstaff and Parker 1995).

Their members have been drawn primarily from the business community, but rarely hold representative positions in business organizations. There were no necessary links to local government or trade unions. In practice however most have included persons from local government in their board membership (Richardson 1993). In some cases trade union leaders have also been significant figures within TECs. In particular, in cities in the declining industrial areas of northern England unions, local government and local employers have grouped together in projects for economic revival, and TECs have played an important part as the meeting-point for much of this activity. Government eventually had second thoughts about the desirability of cutting TECs off from local organized business. It began instead to seek institutional thickness, and looked to local chambers of commerce to become partners of the TECs, eventually even encouraging their merger with TECs to provide 'one-stop shops' for business services. A policy that had begun with a purely individualist approach to entrepreneurship ended by advocating mergers between state agencies and private representative bodies.

It has been an innovation in British industrial history to have a whole class of mixed public/private agencies dedicated to seeking to promote business co-operation. Almost every TEC report and local economic assessment we surveyed reported initiatives of this kind. Particularly active examples include the Wiltshire and Swindon Economic Partnership (Wiltshire County Council 1998), and the Nottingham Fashion Collective discussed above. TECs were expected to encourage networks with the assistance of the Business Links programme of the government, but despite initial optimism (Grayson 1996), confused priorities and lack of resources prevented this from developing a substantial role (Shutt and Pellow 1998).

The Development of a Regional Tier of Government

Meanwhile important developments have been taking place in economic policy institutions at a sub-state level above that of the TEC and LEC districts and local government. Britain has never had a democratic regional tier of government. Sometimes, as in the 1960s, advisory councils of persons in designated regions have been appointed by central government to provide a regional 'voice'. During the 1980s however government increasingly recognized a need for increased competence for *itself* at the regional level in order to attract inward investment and EU funds. In 1994, the Conservative government established Government Offices for the Regions (GORs), groups of civil servants co-ordinating government business in each region, but with no formal (and often no informal) involvement of groups or authorities within the region. As the Centre for Urban and Regional Development Studies at the University of Newcastle on Tyne put it, GORs are regional 'outposts' of national government (Select Committee on Environment, Transport and Regional Affairs 1999a).

The Labour government which took office in May 1997 introduced elected parliaments and regional/national governments to replace the special territorial ministries for managing affairs in Scotland and Wales. It also restored the concept of an elected council to govern Greater London as a whole. This left the rest of England—the bulk of Britain—without such a level, an anomalous position but one difficult to rectify in the absence of any strong demand for democracy in the regions at the popular level.

The government's strategy has been to clarify the role of the GORs; to appoint new Regional Development Agencies (RDAs) for the English regions; and to encourage the latter to work closely with both the GORs and the voluntary regional chambers which have been developing spontaneously in England. These last are not chambers of commerce, but non-elected assemblies of local governments and other important institutions in the regions; they have no powers. The RDAs have been established as public institutions, appointed by ministers and having public responsibilities, but continue the TEC tradition of being 'business-led'—the chairman and several members of each RDA come from private business backgrounds. There is also strong formal representation from local government, and a token trade union (formally 'employee interest') presence.

The primary task of RDAs is to further the economic development of their region. Small-firm development and co-operation were mentioned explicitly in the policy documents establishing them, and they are being asked to establish Regional Supply Offices to develop supply chains. It is at present too early to say how this aspect of their role will develop, and what implications it would then have for the governance of small-firm local economies. While the DETR guidance encourages regions to identify and seek support for local clusters, it is unclear what policy instruments might be used for this. Further, as the Federation of Small Businesses has pointed out, RDAs are likely to find it much easier to establish contacts with a few large retail superstores and clearing banks than with a mass of small firms (Select Committee on Environment, Transport and Regional Affairs 1999b).

Much of the politics of RDAs will be dictated by their triangular relations with the GORs and the Chambers, and their implied links to central and local government respectively. Particular victims will be the TECs, which will be wound up and their competences passed to a smaller number of less local new authorities for steering post-16 education. As observers at the University of Newcastle on Tyne noted (Select Committee on Environment, Transport and Regional Affairs 1999a), without such a shift, the RDAs would have neither resources nor authority to implement the policies which they might decide are needed for their areas. However, abolition of the TECs means both a step back from localism and a further major institutional change in an area where stability and interaction over a number of years are most likely to be important in building up the trust which is necessary for co-operation.

Conclusions

These emerging patterns of formal government relationships to local economies relate in interesting ways to the established models of types of governance. They are partly examples of state-led governance, in that most of the ideas and policies are developed by central government, which keeps a tight rein on funding and strategic ideas. However, this is not *dirigiste* in the sense of seeking to impose a particular pattern of industrial development, apart from the encouragement of inward investment (which then in turn becomes a form of governance through the hierarchies and supplier networks of individual large firms). The state leans very heavily on the business world to provide personnel and ideas. To some extent therefore one might argue that the governance regime remains largely market driven, but this would ignore the bundle of initiatives for encouraging behaviour not immediately determined by market incentives. If British central government power is used against any interests, it is those of local government. If the English regions acquire political competences, they will probably be at the expense of the local rather than the central level. The history of the TECs suggests this. At first established as agencies of central government without reference to local authorities but having developed such connections informally, they are now being absorbed upwards to the new regional level.

There are also elements of informal associational governance in the British context, in the encouragement of networks and co-operative initiatives, though we might doubt whether the British understanding of networks really amounts to a mode of governance. This is particularly the case as the capacity of local government to play an active role in such networks seems to be increasingly weakened.

Most modes of governance are therefore to be found within British local production systems. In general, and with the exception of some Scottish districts, we find that the stronger the local system, the more traditional the product, and the closer to the English Midlands it is located. Clusters in knowledge-rich industries are more weakly structured and found overwhelmingly in the South-East. Systems based on relations with external customer firms tend to compete on low labour costs rather than quality niches. There is considerable evidence of under-exploitation of the potential capacity of networks, sometimes due to their serendipitous nature.

If one governance regime dominates, it is the centripetal power of London. As more and more of the country's dynamism becomes concentrated there, the South-East, and neighbouring parts of other regions, so population flows to it, increasing its political and economic weight and thereby increasing its power further. At its heart rests partly a highly centralized national state, and, increasingly important, the City of London, centre of the financial sector and increasingly the most dynamic sector of the economy. Since our study has concentrated on manufacturing we have been unable to comment on what is in fact the country's biggest single industrial district, comprising a mass of firms, large and small, linked together through many different kinds of relation, in very close geographical proximity and making considerable use of tacit knowledge collective competition goods. Like the publishing and printing sector around Oxford, the City is at once mediaeval and a twenty-first-century knowledge-based sector. It also has both geographical and institutional connections to the UK government unrivalled by any sector of manufacturing or other services. By looking at links between clusters of small firms and their local governments in Britain without looking at relations between the City and Whitehall, we have probably been considering Hamlet without the prince.

	English Regions				
Greater London	South-East		East Anglia	South-West	West Midlands
Heathrow 10.06	Sittingbourne and Sheerness	25.83	Haverhill 41.04	Chard 46.83	Uttoxeter and Ashbourne 43.4
London 8.19	Bicester	23.95	Beccles and Halesworth 38.49	Stroud 35.31	Walsall 37.1
	Banbury	23.26	Thetford 35.49	Torrington 35.16	Telford and Bridgnorth 36.6
	Hitchin and Letchworth	23.23	Sudbury 32.85	Tiverton 32.90	Dudley and Sandwell 33.4
	Andover	23.05	Wisbech 32.30	Yeovil 30.19	Stoke 32.1
	Portsmouth	21.66	Diss 27.44	Cinderford and Ross-on-Wye 28.03	Leek 31.8
	Isle of Wight	19.67	Huntingdon and St Neots 24.19	Trowbridge and Frome 28.01	Kidderminster 31.2
	Hertford and Harlow	18.44	Fakenham 24.13	Chippenham 26.83	Burton-on-Trent 30.9
			Newmarket 23.73	Falmouth 26.74	Wolverhampton 28.9
	Chelmsford and Braintree	18.19	King's Lynn and Hunstanton 22.52	Blandford 24.68	Ludlow 27.1
	Watford and Luton	17.87	Peterborough 21.09	Shaftesbury 24.59	Hereford and Leominster 25.9
	Southend	17.55	Lowestoft 20.10	Bideford 24.33	Coventry and Hinckley 25.6
	Milton Keynes	17.36	Bury St Edmunds 19.03	South Molton 24.13	Evesham 23.1
	Bedford	17.04	Cambridge 16.93	Poole 23.06	Birmingham 23.1
	Aylesbury and Wycombe	16.75	Norwich 16.58	Bridgwater 22.62	Whitchurch and Market Drayton 22.0
	Gosport and Fareham	16.50	Cromer and North Walsham 16.43	Cheltenham 21.82	Oswestry 21.1
	Basingstoke and Alton	16.42	Ipswich 13.92	Redruth and Camborne 20.99	Worcester 21.0
	Medway and Maidstone	16.25	Great Yarmouth 13.48	Swindon 20.57	Rugby and Daventry 20.2
	Southampton	15.88	Woodbridge and Leiston 12.88	Barnstaple and Ilfracombe 20.28	Malvern and Ledbury 20.1
	Thanet	15.68		Plymouth 20.28	Stafford 19.9
				Okehampton 20.23	Warwick 17.
	Dover and Deal	15.61		Launceston 19.61	Shrewsbury 12.2
	Chichester	15.15		Gloucester 19.49	
	Colchester	14.96		Honiton and Axminster 17.58	
	Worthing	14.90		Wareham and Swanage 17.31	
	Slough	14.81		Devizes 16.48	
				Wells 16.39	
	Ashford	14.72		Bridport 16.32	
	Harwich	14.65		Totnes 15.85	
	Eastbourne	14.32		St Austell 15.85	

	English Regions							Wales		Scotland	
t Midlands		Yorkshire and Humberside		North-West		North		Wales		Scotland	
reton and shfield	44.64	Scunthorpe	35.52	Pendle	44.75	Bishop Auckland	41.64	Neath and Port Talbot	36.52	Annan	47.15
·by	37.62	Calderdale	33.33	Blackburn	38.63	Whitehaven	38.41	Blaenau Gwent and Abergavenny	35.17	Hawick	43.20
xton	35.76	Keighley	32.53	Burnley	35.55	Barrow-in-Furness	30.52	Wrexham	34.44	Girvan	35.78
·by	31.57	Huddersfield	31.21	Oldham	34.08			Bridgend	33.80	Kelso and Jedburgh	33.73
nsborough	31.56	Bradford	28.25	Accrington and Rossendale	33.34	Hartlepool	30.41	Pontypridd and Rhondda	31.35	Bathgate	30.16
ughborough d Coalville	31.17	Malton	28.02			Sunderland	29.64	Shotton, Flint and Rhyl	31.32	Keith	30.03
llingborough d Rushden	31.15	Thirsk	27.27	Rochdale	28.72	Workington	28.87	Newport	30.02	Irvine	27.41
rksop	31.07	Rotherham and Mexborough	26.30	Wigan and St Helens	28.48	Stockton-on-Tees	26.48	Aberdare	29.57	Fraserburgh	27.27
cester	28.92	Barnsley	26.20	Crewe	27.84	Berwick-on-Tweed	23.35	Merthyr and Rhymney	29.08	Greenock	26.32
ttering and arket Harborough	28.89	Grimsby	25.39	Widnes and Runcorn	27.50	South Tyneside	22.12	Newtown	27.83	Alloa	25.82
alding d Holbeach	27.54	Castleford and Pontefract	25.36	Macclesfield	27.10	Carlisle	21.79	Llanelli	26.76	Buckie	25.14
lton Mowbray	25.86	Wakefield and Dewsbury	25.22			Durham	21.33	Pontypool and Cwmbran	26.04	Forfar	24.94
						Middlesbrough	20.72			Kilmarnock	24.75
esterfield	25.77	Bridlington and Driffield	23.21	Clitheroe	26.14	Darlington	19.71	Welshpool	23.33	Lockerbie	24.59
wark	25.20	Goole and Selby	22.70	Northwich	21.80	Newcastle-upon-Tyne	17.98	Llandrindod Wells	20.83	Dunfermline	24.27
rncastle and arket Rasen	24.14	Sheffield	21.93	Bolton and Bury	20.47	Kendal	16.12	Machynlleth	18.15	Falkirk	24.23
antham	23.58	Hull	21.05	Wirral and Chester	19.11	Morpeth and Ashington	15.72	Lampeter and Aberaeron	16.70	Lanarkshire	23.80
ttingham	22.97	Scarborough and Filey	19.93	Preston	18.21	Penrith	14.83	Porthmadoc and Ffestiniog	16.56	Kirkcaldy	23.57
aford	22.94	Skipton	19.17	Manchester	16.84	Alnwick and Amble	11.78	Llandeilo	16.08	Cumnock and Sanquhar	23.28
mford	21.76	Doncaster	18.47	Blackpool	16.57	Hexham	11.77	Haverfordwest	14.74	Peterhead	23.26
								Swansea	14.30	Arbroath	22.76
ansfield	20.62	Pickering and Helmsley	18.05	Warrington	16.23	Windermere	2.88	Monmouth	14.30	Galashiels	22.36
uth and ablethorpe	20.62	York	16.27	Liverpool	13.55	Keswick	2.74	Cardigan	14.29	Campbeltown	19.40
rthampton	20.16	Leeds	16.21	Lancaster and Morecambe	12.89			Fishguard	13.69	Berwickshire	19.36
tford	19.28	Whitby	14.18					Cardiff	13.56	Brechin and Montrose	18.87
ston	16.67	Ripon	13.48					Bangor and Caernarfon	11.69	Elgin	18.36
atlock	15.63	Northallerton	9.26					Denbigh	11.24	Huntly	18.23
egness	15.23	Settle	9.11					Dolgellau and Barmouth	8.59	Ayr	18.22
ncoln	14.68	Harrogate	8.40					Pwllheli	7.96	Dundee	17.63
		Richmondshire	6.33					Brecon	6.17	Peebles	17.38
								South Pembrokeshire	5.54	Invergordon and Dingwall	14.77

APPENDIX Table 6.1. (*Continued*)

Greater London	South-East		East Anglia	South-West		West Midlands
				English Regions		
	Hastings	14.26		Newton Abbot	15.42	
	Newbury	14.20		Bodmin and Liskeard	15.10	
	Oxford	14.03		Weston-s.-Mare	14.43	
				Bristol	14.38	
	Winchester and Eastleigh	12.57		Cirencester	12.99	
	Tunbridge Wells	12.27		Torbay	12.92	
	Brighton	12.23		Bath	12.65	
	Clacton	12.02		Minehead	12.55	
	Crawley	11.88		Bournemouth	11.93	
	Guildford and Aldershot	11.23		Bude	11.41	
	Folkestone	11.22		Salisbury	10.83	
	Reading	8.82		Dorchester and Weymouth	10.64	
	Canterbury	8.56		Dartmouth and Kingsbridge	10.33	
				Taunton	10.31	
				Warminster	8.93	
				Newquay	8.72	
				Exeter	8.12	
				Penzance and St Ives	6.31	
				Helston	5.93	
				Truro	4.00	

Source: Authors' own calculations based on data supplied by National Statistical Office.

	English Regions			Wales		Scotland	
East Midlands	Yorkshire and Humberside	North-West	North				
				Conwy and Colwyn	4.68	Haddington	14.10
				Aberystwyth	4.03	Lochaber	13.92
				Carmarthen	1.80	Glasgow	13.89
						Newton Stewart	13.59
						Dumbarton	13.33
						Dumfries	13.30
						Thurso	13.20
						Blairgowrie and Pitlochry	12.83
						Banff	11.38
						Stewartry	11.06
						Wick	10.30
						Aberdeen	10.24
						Crieff	10.12
						Inverness	9.75
						Orkney Islands	9.74
						Stranraer	9.48
						Edinburgh	9.13
						North East Fife	8.95
						Western Isles	8.91
						Stirling	8.84
						Shetland Islands	8.68
						Dunoon and Bute	8.53
						Badenoch	8.11
						Forres	6.35
						Islay/Mid Argyll	6.34
						Perth	5.23
						Oban	4.88
						Skye and Wester Ross	4.43
						Sutherland	4.43

15: Food and drink
1513 Production: meat & poultry meat products
1520 Processing/preserving of fish
1542 Manufacture of refined oils and fats
1591 Manufacture of alcoholic beverages

17: Textiles
1712 Preparation/spinning: wool-type fibres
1713 Preparation/spinning: worsted-type fibre
1725 Other textile weaving
1730 Finishing of textiles
1740 Manufacture of made-up textile articles
1751 Manufacture of carpets and rugs
1754 Manufacture of other textiles nec
1760 Manufacture of knitted/crocheted fabrics
1771 Manufacture of knitted/crocheted hosiery
1772 Manufacture: knitted/crocheted pullovers

18: Clothing
1810 Manufacture of leather clothes
1821 Manufacture of workwear
1822 Manufacture of other outerwear
1823 Manufacture of underwear
1824 Manufacture of other wearing apparel nec

19: Leather goods
1910 Tanning and dressing of leather
1920 Manufacture of luggage, handbags, etc
1930 Manufacture of footwear

21: Pulp and paper
2112 Manufacture of paper and paperboard
2121 Manufacture of corrugated paper, etc

22: Publishing and printing
2211 Publishing of books
2212 Publishing of newspapers
2213 Publishing of journals and periodicals
2215 Other publishing
2222 Printing nec
2223 Bookbinding and finishing
2224 Composition and plate-making
2225 Other activities related to printing
2231 Reproduction of sound recording
2232 Reproduction of video recording

24: Chemicals
2413 Manufacture: other inorganic chemicals
2416 Manufacture of plastics in primary forms
2430 Manufacture of paints, varnishes, etc

25: Rubber and plastics
2521 Manufacture of plastic plates/sheets, etc
2522 Manufacture of plastic packing goods
2523 Manufacture of builders' ware of plastic
2524 Manufacture of other plastic products

26: Mineral products
2621 Manufacture of ceramic household articles
2625 Manufacture of other ceramic products
2626 Manufacture of refractory ceramic products
2630 Manufacture of ceramic tiles and flags
2663 Manufacture of ready-mixed concrete

27: Basic metals
2710 Manufacture of basic iron/steel, etc
2722 Manufacture of steel tubes
2731 Cold drawing
2732 Cold rolling of narrow strip
2741 Precious metals production
2742 Aluminum production
2744 Copper production
2745 Other non-ferrous metal production
2751 Casting of iron
2754 Casting of other non-ferrous metals

28: Metal products
2811 Manufacture of metal structures and parts
2812 Manufacture of builders' carpentry, etc
2840 Forging, pressing, stamping, etc
2851 Treatment and coating of metals
2852 General mechanical engineering
2861 Manufacture of cutlery
2862 Manufacture of tools
2863 Manufacture of locks and hinges
2871 Manufacture of steel drums, etc
2872 Manufacture of light metal packaging
2873 Manufacture of wire products
2874 Manufacture of fasteners, etc

29: Metal machinery
2912 Manufacture of pumps and compressors
2913 Manufacture of taps and valves
2914 Manufacture of bearings, gears, etc
2921 Manufacture of furnaces/furnace burners
2922 Manufacture: lifting/handling equipment
2923 Manufacture of ventilation equipment, etc
2940 Manufacture of machine tools
2953 Manufacture of machinery for food, etc
2954 Manufacture of machinery for textile, etc
2955 Manufacture of machinery for paper, etc
2956 Manufacture: other special machinery nec

30: Office machinery
3002 Manufacture of computers, etc

31: Electrical equipment
3110 Manufacture: electric motors/ generators
3120 Manufacture: elect. distrib. apparatus

3150 Manufacture of lighting equipment, etc

32: Electronic Equipment
3210 Manufacture of electronic valves, etc
3220 Manufacture of TV/radio transmitters, etc
3230 Manufacture of TV/radio receivers, etc

33: Precision equipment
3310 Manufacture of medical/surgical equipment, etc
3320 Manufacture of instruments for measuring, etc
3330 Manufacture of industrial process control equipment
3340 Manufacture of optical instruments, etc

34: Motor vehicles
3410 Manufacture of motor vehicles
3420 Manufacture of motor vehicles' bodies, etc
3430 Manufacture of parts for motor vehicles

35: Other transport
3511 Building and repairing of ships
3512 Building and repairing of pleasure boats, etc
3520 Manufacture of railway/tramway vehicles
3530 Manufacture of aircraft and spacecraft

36: Furniture and other consumer goods
3611 Manufacture of chairs and seats
3612 Manufacture: other office/shop furniture
3613 Manufacture of other kitchen furniture
3614 Manufacture of other furniture
3622 Manufacture of jewellery nec
3640 Manufacture of sports goods
3661 Manufacture of imitation jewellery

Note: Branches and sub-branches listed are those used in Tables 6.4, 6.5, and 6.6.
nec = not elsewhere classified.

7

Conclusions: Still Local Economies in Global Capitalism?

COLIN CROUCH AND CARLO TRIGILIA

The preceding chapters have assessed the role of local production systems (LPSs) in manufacturing industries in four large European countries. These systems comprise geographical areas of economic specialization in which small and medium-sized enterprises (SMEs) are particularly important, in terms of numbers of both productive units and employees. LPSs exist where there are either particular competitive advantages for participation by clusters of SMEs as opposed to large corporations, or where such clusters at least stand as good a chance as large firms. Small firms may work through a more or less intense co-operation among themselves, or with larger firms located in the same area, or by making use of local facilities provided by governmental or other external agencies—or a combination of all three. These possibilities exist in sectors that share two characteristics. First, the production process is divisible into a number of different levels, each giving scope to specialized firms; second, product markets are fragmented and variable over time and space, giving advantages to niche rather than mass producers.

As is mentioned in the Introduction, in the last two decades an extensive literature has discussed the role of LPSs. In the 1980s, a more optimistic view prevailed. It was assumed that the search for flexibility and quality, typical of post-Fordist models of economic organization, would enhance their role. In the ensuing decade, a more pessimistic analysis was put forward. It was argued that the increasing globalization of the economy would bring about a demise of LPSs, under pressure from new global firms. New technologies—both in production and in communications—would foster the search for lower labour costs by assembling components made in different locations. This trend, in turn, would bring about a de-territorialization of production at the expense of local networks of specialized SMEs. At the same time, huge investments, necessary to run the new global firms and to control an increasingly volatile market, would reduce their role.

A New Approach

There were three main flaws in this debate. First, the definition of LPSs was not clear and was not used consistently. Local systems were usually identified with industrial districts, and it was assumed that they were characterized by similar models of governance, which produced rich local collective competition goods. Second, the rise or demise of local systems was generally predicated on the basis of anecdotal and scattered evidence, based on stories of local success or decline. Finally, predictions of the incapacity of either large corporations or LPSs to adapt to changing circumstances failed to anticipate the innovative capacities of entrepreneurship. The national studies in this volume try to overcome these shortcomings.

The Diversity of Local Production Systems

Taking advantage of a rich theoretical and empirical literature, we have tried to define more precisely the different forms that LPSs can show. Therefore we distinguish among the following types:

(i) *Industrial districts*: LPSs characterized by strong horizontal integration among autonomous SMEs concentrated in local areas and specialized in particular sectors (in both capital and consumer goods). We also call these systems 'networks of small and medium-sized firms'. Only a limited number of these firms have access to the final market, most being 'stage firms', specialized in a certain stage of production or in the production of a particular component or service. In districts, competition occurs between subcontracting firms with the same specialization, while co-operation—especially in design, technical innovation and finance—takes place between 'stage firms' and customer firms.

(ii) *Networked firms*: where large customer firms whose operative units are involved in relatively stable, and more or less intense, subcontracting relations with SMEs localized in the same territorial system. Networked firms are specialized in flexible production of consumer or capital goods, both in more traditional or modern sectors, and rely on external collaborations to increase flexibility and reduce costs of innovation. However, they are able to exercise a stronger control over the market.

(iii) *Empirical clusters of small and medium-sized firms*: local concentrations of SMEs that are also specialized in one or more sectors with fragmented and unstable markets. However, this type is characterized by a lower level of horizontal integration in comparison to industrial districts, and by a less stable and institutionalized collaboration with large customer firms located within or outside the local system. A greater number of local small firms work for the final market than in the previous types.

All these forms based on the widespread presence of small firms are different from local systems characterized by one or more traditional large firms (for instance, the 'one company town' model). The old Fordist firms of mass production used to dominate local economies through the prevailing role of hierarchy as a form of governance: they internalized most productive stages and the production of economic services, such as training, and even that of social services for their workers. As has been illustrated in the Introduction, a peculiar feature of LPSs based on small firms is their dependence on some forms of collective provision of competition goods. Small units cannot produce by themselves all the input in terms of goods and services that they need to compete (information on technology and markets, training, infrastructure, and so on). Therefore, a rich supply of tangible and intangible local competition goods is particularly important for these systems. This is why Alfred Marshall (1919) pointed to the role of external economies and to the 'industrial atmosphere', a concept that has been crucial to the understanding of industrial districts and local economies (Becattini 1979a and b, 2000; Brusco 1989; Pyke, Becattini and Sengenberger 1990). However, we stress that not only might the supply be variable, but it might also be produced in different ways, that is by different models of governance based on particular mixes of market, state, hierarchy, community and associations.

Beyond the Anecdotal Approach

By means of these analytical tools, our national chapters have tried to go beyond the case-study literature and shed light systematically on the variety of LPSs in the four countries that have been studied, both in terms of productive organization and of governance. Using travel-to-work-area data, they have also aimed at assessing more systematically the diffusion of local economies based on small firms in each country and their change over time. The main results can be summarized in the following terms:

(i) LPSs show a greater variety in our countries than one could expect on the basis of the literature on small-firm development and industrial districts. The district is just one model of LPS. It is particularly important in Italy, as one could expect, but is much less widespread in other countries. However, other types are present and more or less diffuse in all our countries. In addition, it is notable that not only are industrial districts not the sole form of local system, but the governance of these systems shows a wide variety of models.

(ii) National political economy seems a crucial independent variable that influences both the types of local productive organization and their governance models. However, it is interesting that some more general patterns of relationship between these two phenomena emerge and hold across national borders (we shall return to these later).

(iii) Over time there has not been a decline in the role of LPSs, as had been foreseen by some studies of the 1990s, but neither has there been a general rise, as one might have expected on the basis of the more optimistic view of the 1980s. In Britain and France the role of systems based on small firms is more modest than in Italy and Germany. However, such systems seem to be rising in importance in Britain and France, as well as in Italy. Germany is the country where some systems based on networked firms seem more at risk under the pressure of globalizing trends in production. In general, however, rather than being an interlude, swept away by globalization, local systems based on SMEs seem a stable component of the economy in developed countries, able to co-exist with rather than surrender to the new large global firms. For this reason, they can also be seen as an effective resource for fostering local economic development.

(iv) In all our countries, as is clearly shown by Rodríguez-Pose (Chapter 2), economic dynamism in general has had a strong territorial component in the last two decades. Between the late 1970s and the 1990s economic development has been concentrated away from the regions of old industrialization and mass production (steel, shipbuilding, car industry, and so on). The regions that showed higher growth rates were characterized by low initial levels of employment and value added in manufacturing (in the 1970s), and by an ensuing increase in both indicators. Contrary to what one could expect, it was not services but manufacturing that was the most important component in economic growth. LPSs based on small firms have played a crucial role in this dynamism, both in large urban areas and in more peripheral regions. Therefore, a new economic geography has emerged and the national studies in this volume outline the new borders of dynamism and decline.

Analysing Entrepreneurship

Claims made during the European recession of the early 1990s that local systems had lost their capacity for change and adaptation seem therefore to have been falsified. This should not surprise us, as true risk-taking entrepreneurship depends on doing the unexpected. Firms will be willing to take risks if they see opportunities for temporarily making larger than normal profits by extracting rents. In a competitive environment with low barriers to entry, which is the situation of most small firms, possibilities to do this are likely to appear only when a firm can do something new, which is, for a while, not easily imitated. Adaptations to the operation of an LPS itself will be examples of such unanticipated changes.

This Schumpeterian model of innovation based on surprise is bound by definition to confound the predictions of social scientists and financial analysts. There are other types of innovation, which are more compatible with the paradigm of contemporary economic theory, in which conduct is governed by perfect knowledge and a perfect capacity to respond to rational expectations. Here it must be assumed that all firms equipped with appropriate knowledge will simultaneously make the same innovation. Rents will be possible only if there are barriers either to access to the high level of knowledge assumed by the theory or knowledge or to implementing the anticipated innovations. Both usually favour access by large firms only.

Among the factors that determine which innovations attempted by small firms succeed will be the luck and personal skill of the entrepreneurs, and it is that combination which is usually understood by entrepreneurship. The concept of LPSs points however to a further, more sociological factor. This is what we have called here the availability of local collective competition goods: factors in the social environment of firms which provide them with resources for innovation *which do not enter their cost structures*, and therefore produce external local economies. Take for example two firms making shoes. The first exists in isolation from other firms in and around that industry. For capacity to innovate it may depend on buying advice from external design consultants. The second firm exists in close proximity to other shoemakers, as well as firms producing shoe-making equipment and others marketing shoes. From interaction and discussion within this environment it becomes informed, and informs others, of new pos-sibilities in design and sales, without paying anything. Or it is located in an area where specialized resources are available from public agencies, associations, a local university, or some other source which either deliberately or serendipitously provides such goods either free of charge or at a very reduced cost. *Ceteris paribus*, it has cost advantages over the isolated firm.

Of course, the *ceteris paribus* clause will not always apply. The particular district in which the second firm is situated may be one that has been left behind by recent developments in its industry, or the firms in it may be suspicious of each other and unwilling to engage in discussion. Or the consultants used by the isolated firm may be particularly good; perhaps they are themselves part of a specialized district of consultants, benefiting from their own collective compe-tition goods and able to pass on the advantages of these to remotely located clients.

Also, in many sectors giant firms continue to have overwhelming advantages, as the continuing trend towards mergers, take-overs and strategic alliances shows. Earlier writers on flexible specialization and post-Fordism overlooked the capacity, demonstrated during the 1990s, of large firms to learn from post-Fordist developments. Many have now turned themselves into complex amalgams of quasi-autonomous cost centres, or concentrated on their core business and con-tracted out many of their activities, in order to capture many of the advantages of small firms. At one time it even seemed that the resurgence of LPSs in the 1980s was just an interval while the large firms restructured themselves (Trigilia 1992a). We now know that this was not the case, but neither did the large-firm model fail to adapt. Both small and large firms have taken academic observers by surprise.

It is important not to exaggerate the role of LPSs, and also not to romanticize them as a nostalgic refuge from modernity. This was the mistake made by the British craft tradition in the later nineteenth century. Also, as Veltz (1996) has pointed out, and as studies of the Italian industrial districts have clearly shown, there is often more conflict than cosy communitarianism at work in sustaining them. Krätke's (1997) useful model of local economies cited by Le Galès and Voelzkow in the Introduction presents a serious structure of production system, region, infrastructure and geographical location, not a Romantic escape.

We do however insist on drawing attention to the continued viability of LPSs in a wide range of sectors, for a number of reasons. First, entrepreneurial SMEs can be a valuable source of autonomous dynamism for localities which might otherwise become heavily dependent on easily withdrawn external sources, whether public authorities or large enterprises (Cooke and Morgan 1998). Second, the strong current tendency for several high-technology sectors to develop through geographical clusters demonstrates the continuing and possibly enhanced value of this form of organization (Storper 1997; Swann, Prevezer and Stout 1998; Scott 1999). Third, there is a tendency for economic and political elites to seek 'one best way' of economic organization, towards which they gravitate to the detriment of other forms. At present this tendency strongly favours multinational enterprises quoted on stock exchanges and owned mainly by institutional investors who insist on the maximization of shareholder value. Exclusive pursuit of this model could destroy the foundations of other important sources of entrepreneurial activity and economic dynamism, in both developed and backward areas. We shall return later to these policy implications.

Countries and Types of Local Production Systems

The research shows clear-cut differences in the diffusion of various types of LPSs in our countries (see Table 7.1). Both in Britain and France the presence of local systems remains limited. This is particularly true for industrial districts, which in these countries (and Germany) appear more as survivors of the past than as new developments. Districts can be found in isolated areas and in 'traditional' sectors (such as textiles, clothing, footwear, food and drink, ceramics, furniture) but also in 'modern' (e.g., machinery or precision goods) and high-tech ones. (The distinction between traditional and advanced sectors may be misleading because it underestimates the role of innovation in products and processes that characterizes traditional sectors (Porter 1998; Scott 1999).) In some cases, innovation also entails a blending of old and new technology, as in the case of computer-based machinery. These districts usually specialize in small-scale quality production that takes advantage of growing niches in the national and international markets for such goods.

In Britain and France, however, the most interesting developments seem to take the shape of networked firms and above all of empirical clusters. The former are more important in France and are related to the restructuring of large firms which were originally located outside Paris, in regional centres, under the pressure of central planning by the French state (examples can be found in the car industry, electrical appliances, aeronautics). Some of these networks, however, suffered from the search for more favourable costs on the part of large customer firms. New empirical clusters of SMEs developed as a result of the attempt by small and medium subcontracting units to adjust and survive. Local and regional governments often strengthened this trend, but also sustained the growth of micro-clusters in other areas.

France appears today as offering more scope to local autonomy than the UK. As Aniello and Le Galès make clear (Chapter 5), although French Fordism was

TABLE 7.1. Local Production Systems and Models of Governance

Country	Types of LPSs	Diffusion	Models of Governance	Trend
Italy	Industrial districts	High	Community, state (local), associations	Stable
	Networked firms	High	Hierarchy, associations, community	Increasing
	Empirical clusters	High	Market, community, associations	Increasing
Germany	Old industrial districts	Low	Community, state (regional), associations	Stable
	Networked firms	High	Hierarchy, market, state (regional), universities, and research centres	Decreasing
	Empirical clusters	High	Market, state (regional), universities, and research centres	Decreasing
France	Old industrial districts	Low	Community, state (local), associations	Stable
	Networked firms	Low	Hierarchy, market, state (central)	Increasing
	Empirical clusters	Low	Market, state (local), universities, and research centres	Increasing
Britain	Old industrial districts	Low	Community, state (local), associations	Stable
	Networked firms	Low	Hierarchy, market, state (central)	Stable
	Empirical clusters	High	Market, universities, and research centres	Increasing

strongly state-directed—far more than in the UK—as a result the state did itself provide collective competition goods. These were then localized via the local *notables* who play such an important role in negotiating between political centre and periphery. Despite the 'killing' of local systems during *les trente glorieuses* (1945–75), local networks remain in place and are now beginning to act autonomously as the old model collapses. As in Germany, regional government has been very important in establishing policy access for SMEs; small firms find it impossible to talk to central government, while purely local government often lacks resources or expertise in economic policy. As a result of the earlier suppression, there are now few examples of LPSs as such, and, as Aniello and Le Galès show, these become anomalies requiring special explanation. This does not mean, however, that there is no economic geography in France. There are strong regional patterns to development, and also tendencies for growth to cluster in particular ways. Large urban agglomerations seem increasingly to be the focus of new industrial dynamism. Also, following the establishment of limited regional government, regional capitals, where political capacities for providing governance at local level can be generated, have begun to generate clusters.

In the UK relations between customer firms and small-scale suppliers seem mainly to take a simple contract form, with few examples of stronger relations developing. Attempts to encourage a different approach through the role of Japanese inward investment have not yet produced results strong enough to be detectable in Crouch and Farrell's survey (Chapter 6) of the statistical data.

Until the very recent devolutions of government to Scotland and Wales, the UK has been the only country in our group to lack important intermediate levels of this kind, while local government has had more and more of its powers removed. As Crouch and Farrell show, central government has tried to fill the gap with agencies which can relate to local firms, but these have lacked local embeddedness and expertise, and have had limited life spans. Formal business associations, outside a small number of industries, have never been strong. It has been an economy dominated by large corporations, whose relations with suppliers are of a pure market type; such SMEs as have existed have tended not to be dynamic and in any case have found it difficult to overcome rivalries in order to co-operate.

In both Britain and France there is another important source of clustering among small firms. It is connected to high-tech sectors in urban areas, especially around London and Paris, where universities and public and private research centres are located and where educated and highly skilled labour is available. The role of LPSs is therefore modest, though new forms of economic dynamism are developing, especially in the shape of empirical clusters of SMEs.

Italy and Germany have in common a tradition of strong diffusion of LPSs based on SMEs. However, there are also great differences in the variety of local clusters. In Germany, a crucial and almost unique role is played by large networked firms with complex chains of subcontractors. This is the traditional form that economic development has taken in the last decades, especially in Southern Germany: 'diversified quality production' in various sectors such as the car industry, electrical appliances, electronics and machinery. But Glassmann and Voelzkow (Chapter 4) point to the serious problems that networked firms have been facing in recent years. Globalization is undermining well-established chains of collaboration between large customer firms and SMEs because of the search for lower costs and the tendency to de-localize some stages of production.

Glassmann and Voelzkow challenge conventional wisdom by showing not only that the Baden-Württemberg economy is not so distinctive within Germany as many authors have claimed, but that it is *Land* and local government institutions, universities and other research institutes, rather than local associations, which are the main actors. They perform in even and equal ways throughout at least the territory of the former western Federal Republic. This uniformity of a strong form of public provision seems similar to France. There is, however, a major difference in that, whereas French industrial policy deliberately tried to break local specialized SME economies, the decentralized, federal character of German public power serves to strengthen them. More or less standard institutional packages are delivered by autonomous local actors. There is considerably less interaction among firms than in the Italian cases (see also Grote 1997, who reached similar conclusions using the different research technique of network analysis).

However, Germany cannot be reduced to a single model. There are some industrial districts, though mainly in small corners of traditional craft production, which are not at the heart of the German economic model. Business associations and *Kammern* play a role, especially in vocational training. Further, the industrial relations system is also engaged in local economic governance in that it provides a strong shared framework among firms. Many SMEs simply take advantage of the collective facilities provided by the public research infrastructure, forming empirical clusters around these facilities but with little horizontal interaction.

Italy is the well-known country of industrial districts. This type of LPS is particularly widespread here both in traditional and modern sectors. This is not the result of a coherent government policy, but almost the opposite: it has often been the incapacity of the Italian state which has led local groups to find their own solutions to the problem of creating collective goods (Trigilia 1997). However, this is not the same as a flight from an incompetent public sphere into individualization, but the discovery of alternative forms of collective provision.

The growth of industrial districts was especially concentrated in the 1970s and 1980s. In the ensuing period they restructured. Horizontal co-operation became more formalized. In many cases, new leading firms emerged and new, more institutionalized forms of collaboration with subcontracting units developed. Trends towards the de-localization of some stages of production—especially the simplest ones, more sensitive to labour costs—also took place. Overall, industrial districts continued to grow and thrive, but their performance was out-paced by that of newly developing networked firms, especially in some sectors. During the 1990s there was no significant growth of new districts, while new examples of the networked firm pattern did emerge, especially in the North-East and in sectors such as textiles and clothing, footwear, spectacles and furniture, but also in machinery and engineering. Another interesting trend that characterized the Italian situation was the significant growth of new empirical clusters of SMEs, both in the backward regions of the South and in areas close to the old centres of Fordist production. However, contrary to what is happening in France and Britain, Italian clusters are less specialized in high-tech products and more concentrated in the traditional sectors of 'made in Italy' goods.

To some extent the four countries appear as pairs: Germany and Italy; France and the UK. Rodríguez-Pose (Chapter 2) shows how both Germany[1] and Italy

---

[1] This is unlikely to change with the shift of the German capital from Bonn to Berlin. With the exception of the Nazi interlude, previous forms of united Germany (1870–1914, 1918–33) were both strongly federal.

have a diversified urban geography, with important provincial cities rivalling the capitals. London and the Home Counties, Paris and the Île de France, on the other hand, monopolize disproportionate shares of their respective countries' urban dynamism. He also shows that, while industrial districts had no guarantee of manufacturing success during the 1990s, they were spared the worst of decline, which was concentrated on those industrial cities that did not follow a district model. The most advantageous urban-industrial pattern seemed to be a combination of diffused urban concentrations and districts. Such patterns seem to have maximized interaction between the innovation and high education levels typical of large cities with the collective competition goods of the districts.

Types of Local Production System and Models of Governance

Despite all differences among our countries, there are certain broad patterns in the relation between types of LPSs and models of governance, which hold across national borders and deserve some comments (see Table 7.1). These models constitute, not pure examples of the forms of governance analysed in the Introduction by Le Galès and Voelzkow, but various combinations of these. We call these combinations 'models' of governance to distinguish them from the 'forms'. We shall examine the models typical of the three types of LPS identified above.

Industrial Districts

Industrial districts seem to be connected, in all our countries, to the richest supplies of local collective competition goods. This is due to two main factors. First, the limited size of productive units makes them especially dependent on external economies. Second, this general feature is reinforced, for instance in comparison to empirical clusters, by the stronger horizontal integration of the productive process. This requires a higher degree of co-operation among firms and between entrepreneurs and workers. Therefore, intangible components of competition goods, in terms of both cognitive and normative resources, become particularly important. The former are related to 'tacit knowledge' and conventions which may speed up and improve the productive process (Becattini and Rullani 1993). The latter are connected to trust. An extensive division of labour potentially increases transaction costs, and this problem cannot be solved by means of market arrangements alone. In other words, a problem of incomplete contracts arises with the increase in horizontal integration. This is why industrial districts usually rely on a rich endowment in terms of social relations (or social capital) and on stronger local identities that sustain such social networks. But local social capital is also important in collective terms, as a property that shapes relationships between collective actors such as interest organizations and local or regional governments. These relations affect the more formalized supply of tangible collective competition goods (information on markets and technologies, education and training, physical infrastructure).

Therefore, in all our cases, industrial districts tend to be governed by a combination of forms in which community (or reciprocity), associations, and local or regional governments have a major role and work together. We could also call this model of governance 'neo-localist regulation'.[2] Our findings do not therefore support the views of those writers on social capital (Putnam 1993; Fukuyama 1995) who would set patterns of reciprocity *against* the role of formal associations or political authorities (Trigilia 1999).

Of course, there are differences, both across and within countries, in the capacity of governance models to provide an adequate supply of competition goods. This is a crucial variable for the future of districts. On the one hand, globalization creates opportunities for wider market niches in consumer goods and machinery, connected to flexible and quality production. On the other hand, it undermines systems of production which are more dependent on low costs—especially low labour costs—and are menaced by the newly industrializing countries. Therefore, the capacity to produce collective competition goods to upgrade the quality of production, and better to use human and social capital as competitive resources, is crucial for industrial districts in developed countries. As far as they are able to proceed along this path, there is no reason to think that this type of LPSs is bound to perish under the pressure of new global firms.

Empirical Clusters

Empirical clusters can be found in more traditional sectors where labour costs are particularly important, but also in more modern and innovative ones. These systems are less dependent on a rich supply of local competition goods, precisely because they are less horizontally integrated than districts. There is a lower degree of co-operation among local units and therefore a more limited reliance on intangible forms of such goods (e.g., tacit knowledge and trust). Sheer agglomeration creates some external economies, in terms of availability of skilled labour or physical infrastructure. This outcome can be determined by the presence in the area of one or more larger firms in traditional or innovative sectors and/or of public institutions such as important universities and research centres. In fact, the origins of these clusters may be traced—directly or indirectly—to the role of such institutional actors in the local area, while in the case of industrial districts long-lasting craft traditions—not eroded by mass production—are usually more important.

Within this general framework one can understand why the model of governance is more based on market exchanges than on community and reciprocity, and on hierarchy and state policies (local and national) more than on associations.

---

[2] This does not mean that the public resources that are deployed are only local. They can also be regional or central, but their provision takes place through a localist regulation in which co-operation and mobilization on the part of local private and public actors is crucial (Trigilia 1986a).

Obligational and associational relations require time to develop, or require previous strong identities. But this is not the case for most empirical clusters that have recently emerged. This type of LPS seems to be growing in our countries. It is the way through which new forms of economic dynamism tend to appear in local areas. However, one can assume that to consolidate their role in the national and international markets, these systems too have to improve the quality and distinctiveness of their production through an increase of their tangible and intangible external economies.

Consolidation will entail a move towards more structured networks, which can strengthen the role of SMEs through co-operation among themselves and/or with larger firms and public institutions. In other words, one can assume that only some empirical clusters will succeed and become more structured, by moving towards either the district form or the network centred on large firms. This does not mean that empirical clusters will become less important, but it is likely that volatility will be higher for these systems. Many clusters will appear as a Schumpeterian form of innovation in the post-Fordist era—especially in new sectors and where new technologies and processes are experimented—but only a few will survive without consolidating their role.

The Networked Firm

The role of large customer firms with wide networks of subcontractors has been particularly important in the restructuring of large companies in Europe. This adjustment has been a way out of Fordism and a path to seize the new opportunities opened up for flexible and quality production, but with higher volumes and higher control of the market than industrial districts, isolated small firms or poorly integrated empirical clusters. Networked firms have developed in various sectors in textiles and clothing as well as in the car industry, electronics and machinery. In this local system too the need for collective competition goods is lower than in industrial districts, but it is not negligible. Large customer firms provide by themselves some collective goods as club goods for their collaborators (especially technological information and advice and financial assistance). However, they need expert partners as subcontractors at various levels and these can grow only in an external environment which provides some basic collective goods in terms of training, information and physical infrastructure.

In this framework the role of hierarchy is more important in the governance, but it may be mitigated by other forms, such as public policies or community and associations, which make SMEs less dependent on the customer firms. Relational contracting and specific agreements between large companies and small subcontractors can be seen as a way of reducing the role of market exchanges—which may be less effective for flexible and quality production—without directly relying on internal integration and hierarchy. Of course, the power of large firms is higher and may influence the choices and the organization of small units more than in other LPSs. However, this power can be limited in so far as other forms of governance that provide collective competition goods are available in the local area and may strengthen the autonomy of SMEs. These can be related to the role of local associations or of community, such as in Italy, or to the role of associations and regional government, as in Germany.

As a consequence, the LPSs based on networked firms face a specific dilemma. The more that hierarchy and the market regulate the system, they run the risk of impoverishing local sources of skills, making small firms more dependent and less innovative. On the other hand, to the extent that LPSs are able to produce collective competition goods, their chances are less tied to the choices and the success of customer firms. In this case the border between networked firms and industrial districts becomes more blurred. This is probably the reason why Italian industrial districts and German networked firms have often been considered similar, but this may also be the reason for the greater variability in the forms of governance of systems based on networked firms even within national borders.

Analysing Modes of Governance of Local Economies

The diversity within and between national experiences which we have identified, together with the implicit and possibly even unconscious structure of some governance systems, suggests that we are here dealing with important underlying, emergent social processes and not just objects of policy. We therefore need to look behind the identified empirical forms and seek out some underlying social characteristics. We shall do this by looking at three abstract dimensions of institutions: endogeneity versus exogeneity; procedural rules versus substantive provision; formality versus informality. The three variables relate to different dimensions of interaction. The endogeneity/exogeneity variable relates to where the rules are made; substance/procedure refers to their content; formality/ informality concerns how they are implemented.

Different forms of governance may be analysed as different combinations of these three, enabling us to see scope for considerable diversity in types of governance institutions and also to gain access to the fundamental processes underlying their empirical characterizations. For example, associations and communities differ from each other in degree of formality of organizational structure, but are similar in that they both involve direct participation by members from the economic sector concerned. The state and the market differ very clearly from each other, but both normally exclude participants from direct involvement in shaping rules.

The Endogeneity/Exogeneity Continuum

The extent to which the governance of an LPS is constructed and conducted within (i.e., *endogenous* to) the local community or imposed from without (*exogenous*) forms an important theme within the literature. The more endogenous a system the more it requires extensive co-operation among the participants, since there is no external regulation. In exogenous systems this obligation is exchanged

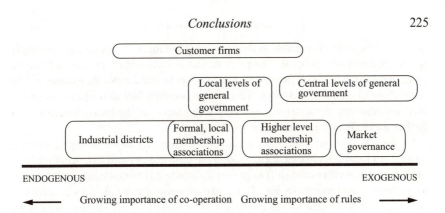

FIGURE 7.1. Forms of Governance of Local Economies:
The Continuum of Endogeneity/Exogeneity

for one to obey rules imposed by an external source of governance. Figure 7.1 indicates some typical positions along the continuum.

In the extreme endogenous case—probably never found in reality—the controllers of the firms *constitute* the co-operative system, and enforce its rules by either mutual consensus or a mass of small sanctions, both achieved through frequent interpersonal interaction and direct community or even family control. It is sometimes thought that local communities achieve conformity by a consensus reached through dialogistic processes alone. This ignores the scope for the masses of small sanctions, running across whole areas of life and including family members as well as the individuals directly involved, which are possible in small communities (Farrell 2000). In the simplest case, we assume that individual firms within the local economy are unitary actors. In a more complex and realistic model the positions of different persons and groups within short managerial hierarchies of small firms, industrial relations within firms and family relations also need to be considered. It is not necessarily the case at all that a highly participative system for heads of firms will also provide opportunities for participation by employees or other family members (Lauridsen forthcoming). There will also often be situations where an elite or leading figures within a community take a dominant part in organizing business affairs (as with the *impannatori* in Prato). This reduces the tough constraint of universal participation in management of the system required by extreme endogeneity, but at the cost of hierarchy within the local business community.

Further along the continuum we find formal, town- or district-level associations. The job of managing collective competition goods then becomes delegated to representatives and professional staff, relieving individual entrepreneurs further from the task of direct engagement and of the need to cultivate co-operative relations among each other. They can simply make use of the facilities provided without much mutual interaction, though in the case of local associations there is likely to be considerable interaction between ordinary members and those responsible for running the association. A further gain might come in improved quality of the collective goods as those responsible for them become increasingly specialized and professional. The price of this is increasing remoteness between firms and source of goods provision, partly offset by the accessible location of the latter close to the local economy. This in turn becomes lost as we move to higher level membership associations. At every step control of the local context moves further away from direct actors at local level.

So far we have assumed only a move to exogeneity in the sense of moving away from local governance forms *within* the business community. Another form of exogeneity involves the shift to governance external to that community, that is to general government levels. Here participation by local entrepreneurs is reduced to their general role as citizens, and we might expect—though we cannot be certain—that in general this becomes more remote as the locus shifts from locality towards nation-state.

A networked customer firm regulating its suppliers is also exogenous to them, but there can be diversity in the extent of this. Such a firm might offer degrees of interaction and mutual co-operation to suppliers in shaping the system, or it might work with them through pure market contract relations, embedding requirements for product quality, delivery dates, use of technology, and so on, in the contract terms.

In extreme exogeneity the governance system is managed by an entirely inaccessible external authority, which possesses coercive force. Examples would be a non-democratic state, an international organization, or a monopolistic purchasing firm. Firms concentrate on their economic activities without concern for their relations with each other or for delivery of collective goods. However, if an institution is completely exogenous, it may have little concern for sustaining and advancing the specific conditions of success of local economies, and may instead impose general national rules that allow no scope for local particularities, as has often been the case with the French state. Further, if actors from the external organization do in fact become endogenous to a particular local system, this becomes a breach of the conditions of the governance system and therefore a form of corruption.

On this continuum the market is located somewhere *towards* the extreme exogenous end but not *at* it. As systems of governance, markets provide an elaborate framework of rules based on property rights, laws governing contracts, the sale of goods and services, credit mechanisms, currencies and the mechanisms for sustaining them, and systems of sanctions. These latter involve both the sanctions of profit and loss by which the market mechanism rewards success and punishes failure, and also the legal and other regulations that enforce the property, contract, credit and currency regimes. Market systems vary in type and can hence occupy a limited range of positions on the continuum, though always towards the exogenous pole. The purer the market the more exogenous it is. Less pure markets might come under the influence of actors within a local economy, as when local banks develop links with business communities and allocate credit in a manner that shows understanding of local needs. A 'purer' market form would require such a bank to operate in an arm's length manner, giving no more preference to a local firm than to one remotely located.

Pure markets do not occupy the extreme point of exogeneity because, as North (1990) has observed, political authorities which are entirely autonomous of the society in which they are located are likely to show disrespect for property rights and therefore break one of the fundamental requirements of true markets. Therefore the most appropriate form of government for the development of free-market capitalism is one which is responsible to the general class of property owners (and probably not responsible to other, non-propertied classes, who may have an interest in restraining the rights of capital). This places the optimal conditions for markets at a subtle empirical point within the continuum: sufficiently endogenous to be committed to the rights of property owners, but no more. Given our current concern with the geography of governance, this raises the further question of the geographical level at which 'society' exists in the above formulation. Economic and sociological theory, both notoriously silent on the matter of defining society, implicitly give that task to the state. The state normally defines property rights and their juridification in precise detail.

The system of sovereign nation-states managing their own economic systems, which had played a core role in the origins of capitalism, became an obstacle to further development. Differences of legal and political regime, not to mention outright mercantilism and protectionism, impeded and distorted international trade. Gradually, international agreements have established core elements of supranational economic legal frameworks. At their most extensive these take the form of the General Agreement on Tariffs and Trade, consolidated into an international governance regime in the form of the World Trade Organization during the 1990s. At world-regional level groups of countries began to form joint regimes embodying more detailed degrees of uniform regulation, of which the European Union is by far the most advanced. As a result, the nation-state is losing its position as the main level for the definition of legal regimes of market governance.

This process is important for the endogeneity/exogeneity continuum. So long as nation-states remain the highest level at which democratic politics operate, moves to transnational levels of economic governance mark new moves towards the exogeneity end. In a longer historical perspective, this possibly restores the governance of the capitalist economy to the kind of position it had in the pre-democratic period.

Finally, we should note that the endogeneity/exogeneity continuum is not a true monotonic index but a synthetic one, as it comprises a variety of different elements. As we have now seen, a move from endogeneity to exogeneity can mean a move of geographical level, or a change of institutional type.

The Procedure/Substance Continuum

This continuum concerns the kinds of facility provided by the governance mechanism. Procedural mechanisms provide and administer only the framework

FIGURE 7.2. Forms of Governance of Local Economies:
The Continuum of Procedure/Substance

of rules by which competition goods are allocated to enterprises. Procedural ones provide such goods directly.

Assume that a particular economic activity is possible only if the producer has access to a certain piece of equipment, ownership of which is uneconomic for an individual small enterprise. Examples include a combine harvester needed by small farmers; a research facility needed for development of a complex new product such as an aero-engine; or a testing facility needed to monitor clinical trials of a new medical treatment. How might such a good be acquired?

There are several possibilities. Contracting firms might emerge which are able to make economies of scale by hiring out use of the production good to large numbers of firms. This requires the purely procedural governance mechanism of the market and administration of rules for hiring (i.e., an aspect of normal contract law). Alternatively, a number of firms might amalgamate (or be taken over by one of their number), making possible adequate economies of scale to justify purchase of the tool. This demands a partly procedural form of governance (the market rules permitting the amalgamation); and partly substantive (within the hierarchy of the new large firm there is direct allocation of the facility). Third, a group of producers might purchase the good jointly and share use of it. This requires primarily substantive governance, as the group directly allocates access rights; but hiring charges reflecting market values (procedural governance) are probably also involved. Finally, a public authority might buy the good and make it available to identifiable members of the group free of charge or at a subsidized cost. This would be a purely substantive form of governance; introduction of true market pricing in allocation would introduce a procedural component. As we can see from some of these examples, in addition to the pure types there can be mixes.

Figure 7.2 indicates the positions of certain empirical cases along this continuum. At the most procedural level, the authority just sustains and enforces the rules. This does not necessarily imply a purely passive role; there can be a proactive approach, where rules are frequently re-examined and reshaped in order to secure improved competitive advantage for the actors concerned. Here the market does represent the extreme case of the most procedural possible form of governance, in that all which is provided is a framework of the kinds of action which are permissible, together with a system of legal redress for dealing with disputes.

Moving away from the procedural pole we encounter situations where governance takes the form of regulating the criteria which permit actors to enter the local market. This is still highly procedural: There is no direct selection of the individuals who may participate, merely legislation of the criteria they must meet. And all that is provided is access to a set of market procedures. For example, where the name of a location of production is generally known as a mark of quality—as with French and Italian wine growers—a governance mechanism assumes the task of deciding the criteria which a producer must meet in order to use it. The place name is the competition good. The governance regime does not produce it; it merely decides the rules by which an individual firm can regard itself as belonging to the place. It will be a further move along the continuum if the governance mechanism also facilitates the provision of some services to ensure that the substantive qualities of the place are maintained or enhanced.

Towards the substantive end of the continuum we encounter such phenomena as the ownership of shared plant by groups of small producers, or the maintenance of technological universities serving local industry. Within intermediate stages of this direct provision access to the services is on the basis of a market charge, or possibly a subsidized one. Further towards the extreme substantive pole, the facility is provided as a club good: free of charge or for a subsidized fee provided the actor is a member of the designated group (as with a stable circle of suppliers to a networked firm). Finally, at the most substantive end, the governance institution might engage in direct provision itself.

The Formality/Informality Continuum

Finally, rules of governance can vary in their degree of formality. At one extreme they can be implicit, unwritten, diffuse, with no formally established procedure for enforcement. At the other extreme are codified rules with clear channels of enforcement and arrangements for agreeing contracts.

This is closely related to the kind of trust that the parties to arrangements have in one another. All acts of exchange where there is a more than trivial time delay between the execution of the two sides of the bargain require some type of trust. There can be direct interpersonal trust based on actual knowledge of the other's likely behaviour; here regulation of the extreme informal kind will be both possible and necessary.[3] One intermediate position is the case of institutional trust based on the expectation that the other party will be subject to diffuse sanctions from its own associates if it defects (Farrell 2000). This still accepts considerable informality, but the rules must be sufficiently formal for it to be clear to the relevant third parties when they have been broken. Finally, at the other extreme is the minimal kind of trust embedded in the expectation that it will

---

[3] Possible, in the sense that only where there is direct personal knowledge of this kind are parties to a contract likely to risk the lack of recourse to external sanctions involved; necessary, in that only the dense web of interactions characteristic of informal rules is likely to sustain interpersonal trust.

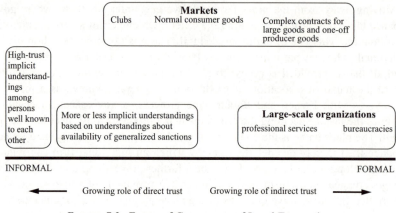

FIGURE 7.3. Forms of Governance of Local Economies:
The Continuum of Informality/Formality

be possible to enforce the law of contract in the case of defection. Here there is no necessary trust in the other party at all, but in the official apparatus of law enforcement, which requires highly formal rules.

Figure 7.3 shows the relevant continuum. It will be noted that the market, far from being a pure form, both occupies a mid-point on this continuum and can be internally varied. It can range from the provision of club goods to precisely defined legal contracts. At the extreme informal end of the continuum are implicit understandings among actors personally known to each other. Formal public or corporate bureaucracies are most likely to require high levels of formality. Extreme informality is characteristic of industrial districts.

Combining the Continua

Figure 7.4 combines the three continua, indicating the positions of the main institutional forms of governance identified in this study. We have stressed the possibility of a diversity of positions across the space defined by the continua. But one could also hypothesize tendencies towards grouping in particular spaces. In particular, theories of the growth and rationalization of capitalism would predict a move towards the procedural/exogenous/moderately formal area, as it is here that pure markets are to be found.[4] Such a combination would maximize *anonymity*. It is a fundamental contention of orthodox neo-institutionalism that this is the characteristic of the extension of markets which opens up the full possibilities of exploiting trading opportunities and improved efficiencies

---

[4] There are alternative hypotheses. For example, predicting a change along a diagonal running between procedural/endogenous/informal and substantive/exogenous/formal implies a movement away from local community regulation as collective competition goods are more directly provided. This could occur with growing professionalism, relevant expertise being seen as residing in higher levels (geographical or institutional). The classic French model resembled this.

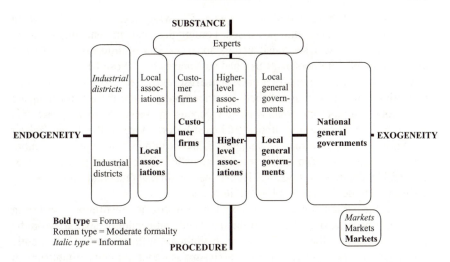

FIGURE 7.4. Forms of Governance of Local Economies: The Combined Continua

(North 1990). Anonymity becomes possible as governments establish the legal and institutional framework of a capitalist order. Exogenous governance which has established and maintains a structure of procedural market rules and moderate formality makes possible complex trade among actors who are total strangers to each other and do not have interpersonal trust. Orthodox neo-institutionalist accounts of economic history thus describe the gradual transcendence of economies based on close and substantive co-operation among communities of producers by impersonal but enforced frameworks of market rules, property rights and recognized currencies. These facilitate in their turn the emergence of many other institutions that further the process: banks, limited liability companies, stock exchanges, insurance systems.

Post-Fordist theories assert the opposite: by claiming the general superiority of the industrial district model and flexible specialization they predict an efficiency-improving move towards the substantive/endogenous informal area. This opens the dispute between orthodox and other forms of neo-institutionalist theory.

Anonymity, Reputation and Trust in the Expansion of Exchange

In orthodox neo-institutionalist accounts of the development of capitalism (North 1990; Greif 1999), economic institutions assume the burden of trust that partners to exchanges otherwise need to vest in each other. Provided I can trust the efficacy of the currency of the realm, the banking system, and the law of contract, I can enter into an economic exchange with you even though I know nothing about you beyond the bare details necessary to ensure that I could enforce the law of contract against you.

The growth of these institutions is seen as following an earlier period in which groups of producers who possessed community and mutual interpersonal knowledge (i.e., who sustained endogenous systems of informal governance making possible interpersonal trust) had advantages over those who lacked these characteristics. Institutions of impersonal trust and external state or state-like regulation had not been established. In other words, where there is no adequate exogenous system of governance an endogenous one serves *faute de mieux*. It is as the institutions to sustain impersonal trust become formed that those *lacking* in community begin to reap advantages, as they can now trade among far more extensive groups and can make more rationalistic calculations of profit and loss, unbound by community loyalties. Human personality, at one point important to a capacity to trade, becomes a limit to its scope.

This is the particular position occupied by orthodox neo-institutional writers in relation to neo-classical theory on the one hand and economic sociology on the other. They regard the sociological or institutional infrastructures of economic exchange (factors neglected by neo-classicism) as important in the establishment of the complete equipment of a true capitalist market, but once this has been achieved they can be taken for granted and no longer perform an active role. For economic sociology this is never the case. Both the maintenance of and change and development in this infrastructure remain a matter of constant importance and intellectual interest (Trigilia 1998).

In the process of transcending endogenous institutions, the gains from community do not *disappear*; but are *transcended* by the superior capacity of anonymous exogenous, procedural and largely formal institutions. A role for endogenous structures in making possible transactions would therefore remain valid for any points within the total universe of potential exchanges not (or at least not yet) covered by adequate exogenous institutions. Given the capacity of market actors to seek out new opportunities for trade, while governance and regulatory systems tend to move more slowly,[5] it is likely that the capacity of entrepreneurs to out-pace formal structures will be endemic and continuing within dynamic economies, and not just a once-and-for-all process of market-making during a general history of modernization.

This means that, once a given set of exogenous governance mechanisms has been established, new gains might be had by developing endogenous relations within them to facilitate new market opportunities. These might in turn be transcended by the construction of further exogenous institutions, which formalize their achievements. This dialectical process might continue indefinitely. Particularly at moments of rapid change, new knowledge and new networks are frequently appearing and will not be entirely captured by existing formal

---

[5] Almost by definition, a governance mechanism to regulate a new form of economic behaviour must appear after the behaviour itself. Further, revisions to forms of governance usually require some discursive and formal process before they can be implemented. Further delays still are likely to be caused by interest conflicts over the desirability of regulation, and by technical difficulties in establishing the most appropriate form.

arrangements. There will therefore usually be scope for gains to be made by supplementing what can be achieved through formal and impersonal procedures with 'insider' contacts and knowledge.

The idea of reputation, that is knowledge of the past performance of parties to a transaction, can be considered in this context. This is a relatively weak form of trust. It can mean two rather different things. By trusting a firm's reputation one might simply be trusting the accumulated experience of past customers; or one might be trusting the fact that the firm cares about its future reputation. By definition reputation breaks the anonymity rule which is a major achievement of formal, procedural exogeneity. Assume a transaction between A and B. The reputation of A becomes important whenever knowledge available to B at the moment when commitment is made is inadequate to ensure B that an acceptable deal has been made. This is likely to be the case with all transactions beyond the very simplest; a car may break down in a manner unpredictable at point of sale; an apple may be rotten in a manner invisible from the outside; an after-sales service system necessary to adequate maintenance of a product may collapse. (See Akelov's famous discussion of the problem of buying a 'lemon'.)

Purely exogenous and procedural systems of redress can provide some help with these issues, through for example building quality terms into contracts; but requirements for precision and specificity of product requirements in a context of rapid innovation cannot easily be met through standardized norms. At this point neo-classical theory offers the flexibility and incentives to good quality and rapid response to customers which are encouraged by the market. Producers have to retain customers and sustain reputations for good products. This requires and assumes repeated transactions: customers return frequently to the same supplier to buy the same or similar goods, which already marks some compromise with the anonymity ideal.

In purely anonymous markets individual customers make purchases only rarely and the only communications among actors are those of market signals; purchasers have no means of informing each other of the fact that a particular supplier has poor-quality goods. Imagine a game in which a large number of purchasers have to choose to buy a product once from any one of a number of suppliers. Prices are displayed and the goods may be visually inspected by the purchasers, but they are unable to communicate information to another player about qualities of the goods that they discover after purchase. Purchasers will be reluctant to buy. Suppliers will therefore reduce their prices to the point where some potential customers are willing to take a risk in making purchases. More risk-averse purchasers may themselves be willing to start buying if they observe that those who have bought the goods seem to experience no problems.

This is an inferior solution for suppliers and customers alike, especially where the customers are firms producing goods in rapidly changing markets, where knowledge based on past observation becomes outdated. Customer firms face a choice between risking buying faulty components or machines and losing time while waiting for the less risk-averse to take their chance. Suppliers have to keep their prices very low, as the risk premium remains high. Both sets of parties therefore have an incentive to break the anonymity condition. Customers have an incentive to communicate directly with each other concerning the reputations of the suppliers; suppliers and customers have incentives to communicate to establish knowledge of each other's practices. If the purchasers are themselves intermediate consumers, sharing information with each other, that is, with potential competitors, requires trust.

As transactions become more complex and commitments within them more extensive, so actors have an interest in becoming maximally known, because this increases the likelihood that trust will be placed in them. For example, our capacity to act as a customer is increased by making known more facts about ourselves: cheques, credit cards, bank references. Similarly, suppliers will want to advertise a willingness to take back defective goods, provide after-sales service, and so on.

Dynamic firms must be expected to take a highly pro-active approach to reputation- and trust-building, not only through such devices as advertising, but also in attempts to construct bonds with customer- and supplier-firms. This is therefore not an odd residual corner of business practice, but one likely to be at the forefront of innovation. All these instances are covered by Hirschman's (1970) concept of loyalty: attempts to prevent exit by imbuing customers with a sense of bond that should outweigh the cost-benefit position of any transaction. In the case of Williamsonian transactions, attempts will be made to establish informality and community-type bases of norms in order to cut the costs of elaborate formal procedures.

There are however transaction costs in establishing the close personal relations which informal relations require for trust purposes in order to reduce transaction costs. This is why informality usually depends on the *prior existence* of community, as the Italian industrial district research shows. In this way informality becomes a local collective competition good.

From such an understanding of why persons engaged in pure business relations ostensibly adequately covered by the existence of well-developed markets and an elaborate law of contract still find it useful to develop interpersonal relations and trust, one can derive the whole system of business contacts, social gatherings, network-building, Rotary and other clubs, and freemasonry that constitute the social world of entrepreneurs in most parts of the world. Such systems are always fraught with problems. Without them certain opportunities for forms of interaction will be lost. With them there is the risk of confidence trickery and corruption. We may take the example of business gifts. It is completely normal for firms to make small gifts to customer firms and suppliers, for example at Christmas time. It is a process well understood by social anthropology and plays a part in generally sustaining networks and interpersonal relationships, a generalized thanks for past custom and an indication of a hope that the relationship will continue. But the thanks and the intimations for the future might become more specific and tied to particular past or future transactions. And the gifts might grow in size from being small tokens to being substantial items. At a certain, but often indistinct, point the combination of specificity and size ceases to be a gift and becomes corruption. Company rules and systems of law will attempt to define at what point corruption can be said to exist, but sociologically it is difficult to make a clear definition.

The slide from gift to corruption is a particularly dramatic example of the problem of personal relations within market ones. The two follow contradictory logics, the former rewarding loyalty and an absence of constant calculation of profit and loss, the latter having no place for the former and requiring the latter. According to orthodox neo-institutional theory, the relationship between interpersonal relations and efficiency will be an inverted U-curve. Initially increases in the personal quality serve to resolve information and trust problems. After a certain point however the relationship is developed for its own sake, and the pursuit of efficiency gains is sacrificed to it. (A clear example would be where supplies continue to be bought from a subcontracting firm even though they are declining in quality, because of a personal friendship which has developed between the supplier and the customer firm's purchasing officer.) In practice, however, this turning point might not be clear, particularly in situations where relationships need to be 'serviced' in order to sustain longer-term co-operation. (Examples would be temporary tolerance of adjustment inefficiencies in a supplier by a Japanese motor firm; or 'goodwill gestures' carried out by firms towards each other within the framework of an industrial district.)

Conclusions

Social relationships are like political interventions in their economic consequences. Sometimes they can serve efficiency goals by strengthening the quality of participation in the market; at other times they merely provide protection from the market. Neo-classical and neo-liberal economics try to solve this dilemma by excluding both the social and the political from economic transactions, a priori regarding the losses that result from their misuse as more significant than the gains which come from their appropriate use. Others try to distinguish theoretically between weak ties (good) and strong ties (bad) (Granovetter 1985; Grabher 1993); or between social bonds that constitute social capital and those which produce a *mafia* (Putnam 1993). It is doubtful whether anything so systematic can be achieved; more detailed and careful analyses are needed (Bagnasco 1999; Piselli 1999; Trigilia 1999).

There is a further moral hazard as actors try to reduce the costs of information gathering and rely on secondary reputation and trust. Imagine a situation in which customers know that within a universe of available suppliers of a particular type of good there is an x per cent chance of randomly finding one who will meet a certain standard of quality; but that among suppliers who are members of sub-set A the chance is considerably higher than x. If carrying out more rigorous searches to find a high-quality good is costly or time-consuming, it becomes rational to choose a supplier from that sub-set, even if the character of the class is external to the conditions of production and supply (e.g., membership of a particular ethnic group). The ecological fallacy involved here is the price of not seeking more specific information, and provides scope for the confidence trickster. If the risks of being tricked are high, customers may need to invest more heavily in these information costs—which membership of a prior community might provide implicitly and therefore more cheaply.

According to strict neo-classical theory, in a world of perfect markets none of all this would be necessary because there would be perfect information. Orthodox neo-institutionalists are able to establish a more realistic condition: where public authorities have developed an adequate institutional structure it will not be necessary to have perfect information. Such a structure includes the legal and other mechanisms which are required to make markets work, and implies repeated returns to policy-making by the authorities to remedy abuses, stop loopholes and make innovations to make markets work as experience, technical change, further extensions of markets, and so on, indicate need for improvement. However, given the dynamic character of capitalism and the way in which it spreads to engage more and more activities in a global system of exchanges, even in a perfectly efficient system institutional and regulatory structures will always be behind the action. While the gaps are being covered there is scope for more informal mechanisms and structures to develop to fill the spaces. This is not a task that can be considered complete at a certain point in history, but one likely to be permanent and infinite. In the practical case, perfect efficiency cannot be assumed; in these cases the scope for endogenous and substantive mechanisms to play a role becomes even more extensive.

The present moment in economic history is paradoxical. On the one hand, the theoretical and ideological dominance of neo-classical economics together with the homogenization induced by certain aspects of global competition suggest that there should be convergence on a single 'best way'. On the other hand, globalization itself creates the incentive to find and exploit the advantages of particular and inimitable niches in order to avoid the most obvious forms of homogenizing competition. This can well include the emphasis of points of endogeneity, substantive provision of collective competition goods, and informality. Globalization and the Internet are currently bringing us closer to the neo-classical paradigm, where actors all over the world have access to all the information that science can provide about products, processes, consumers and markets. In such a situation there are great competitive advantages for groups of producers who informally exchange information that has just emerged from their recent experience and which cannot yet be found on anyone's web site.

If central government or international economic policy pursue too strongly the policy remedies of neo-classicism, they run the risk of destroying local competitive capacities of this kind. The evidence from local economic govern-ance suggests the advantages of a Popperian and Schumpeterian as opposed to a neo-classical approach to economic dynamism and innovation: Popperian, in the sense that no single best means of securing an end is envisaged, but diversity in permanently continuing experiment encouraged; and Schumpeterian, in the sense that entrepreneurship is seen as a disruptive and unpredictable force, not the out-working of static economic laws.

The question of the optimum basis for a governance mechanism in a local economy is therefore undetermined. Each form of governance will also have its characteristic weaknesses: for markets, the lack of any actor capable of exploiting strategic opportunities; for community interactions and hierarchies the weakness of strong ties; for governmental agencies the absence of either community links to the business community or the market's disciplines. It is not surprising that the empirical *models* of governance that we have found in place in each of our countries did not correspond to simple theoretical *forms*. One must always remember that, unlike the technological and engineering rationalities that inspired the concept of path dependency (North 1990), socio-economic systems are complex and rarely embody one over-riding logic or ideal type. If the logic of one component of their identity has run into the ground, another aspect may well be able to innovate further. Sometimes, though of course not necessarily, the sheer existence of the clash of forms can produce creative change.

REFERENCES

Abdelmalki, L. and Courlet, C. (1997), *Les Nouvelles Logiques du Développement: Globalisation vs. Localisation*. Paris: l'Harmattan.

Abelshauser, W. (1984), *Der Ruhrkohlenbergbau seit 1945: Wiederaufbau, Krise, Anpassung*. Munich: Beck Verlag.

Aglietta, M. (1977), *A Theory of Capitalist Regulation: The US Experience*. London: New Left Books.

AIMVER and DATAR (1998), 'Etudes sur les coopérations locales inter-entreprises'. Paris: DATAR, mimeo.

Alacevich, F. (1999) (ed.), *L'Agenda del Lavoro: Processi in Atto e Problemi in Discussione nel 1998*. Firenze: Edizioni CUSL.

Albert, M. (1991), *Capitalisme contre Capitalisme*. Paris: Le Seuil.

Allen, S. and Wolkowitz, C. (1987), *Home Working: Myths and Realities*. Basingstoke: Macmillan.

Alvergne, C. (1997), *Vingt Cinq Ans d'Évolution de l'Industrie et des Territoires Français*. Paris: l'Harmattan.

Amendola, C. (1988), *La Dynamique Économique de l'Innovation*. Paris: Economica.

Amin, A. (1989), 'Flexible Specialization and Small Firms in Italy: Myths and Realities', *Antipode*, 21: 1, 13–34.

—— (1993), 'The Globalization of the Economy. An Erosion of Regional Networks?' In Grabher (ed.), q.v.

—— (1994) (ed.), *Post-Fordism: A Reader*. Oxford: Blackwell.

—— (1999), 'An Institutional Perspective on Regional Economic Development', *International Journal of Urban and Regional Research*, 23: 365–78.

—— and Robins, K. (1990a), 'The Re-Emergence of Regional Economies? The Mythical Geography of Flexible Accumulation', *Environment and Planning D, Society and Space*, 8: 1, 7–34.

——, —— (1990b), 'Industrial Districts and Regional Development: Limits and Possibilities'. In Pyke, Becattini, and Sengenberger (eds.), q.v.

—— and Thrift, N. (1992), 'Neo-Marshallian Nodes in Global Networks', *International Journal of Urban and Regional Research*, 16: 571–87.

——, —— (1994) (eds.), *Globalization, Institutions and Regional Development in Europe*. Oxford: Oxford University Press.

—— and Tomaney, J. (1991), 'Creating an Enterprise Culture in the North East? The Impact of Urban and Regional Policies in the 1980s', *Regional Studies*, 25: 5, 479–87.

Anastasia, B. and Coro, G. (1996), *Evoluzione di un' Economia Regionale: Il Nordest dopo il Successo*. Portugruaro: Nuovo Dimensione Ediciclo.

Anderson, J. (1992), *The Territorial Imperative: Pluralism, Corporatism, and the Economic Crisis*. Cambridge: Cambridge University Press.

Ardenti, R. and Vrain, P. (1995), *L'Emploi dans les PME: Rapport du Centre d'Études de l'Emploi pour la DARES*. Paris: Ministère des Affaires Sociales.

Armstrong, H. W. (1995), 'An Appraisal of the Evidence from Cross-sectional Analysis of the Regional Growth Process within the European Union'. In Armstrong and Vickerman (eds.), q.v.

Armstrong, H. W. and Vickerman, R. W. (eds.), *Convergence and Divergence among European Regions*. London: Pion.

Arocena, J. (1983), *La Création d'Entreprise, un Enjeu Local*. Paris: La Documentation Française.

—, Paul-Cavallier, M. and Richard, P. (1984), *Initiative Locale et Développement*. Paris: Centre d'Études Sociologiques.

—, Bernoux, P., Minguet, G., Paul-Cavallier, M., and Richard, P. (1982), *La Création d'Entreprise, Une Affaire de Réseaux*. Paris: Centre d'Etudes Sociologiques.

Asheim (1997), 'Learning Regions in a Globalised World Economy: Towards a New Competitive Advantage of Industrial Districts'. In S. Conti and M. Taylor (eds.), *Interdependent and Uneven Development: Global-Local Perspectives*. Aldershot: Ashgate.

Assimakopoulou, Z. (1998), *The Development of Small Business in Britain, 1970–1900: Politics and Policies*. Florence: Unpublished Ph.D. Thesis, European University Institute.

Audretsch, D. B. and Feldman, M. P. (1996), 'R&D Spillovers and the Geography of Innovation and Production', *American Economic Review*, 86: 3, 630–40.

— and Vivarelli, M. (1996), 'Firms Size and R&D Spillovers: Evidence from Italy', *Small Business Economics*, 8: 249–58.

Aydalot, P. (1986), *Milieux Innovateurs en Europe*. Paris: Gremi.

— and Keeble, D. (1988), *High Technology Industry and Innovative Environments: The European Experience*. London/New York: Routledge.

Bagnasco, A. (1977), *Tre Italie: La Problematica Territoriale dello Sviluppo Italiano*. Bologna: Il Mulino.

— (1988), *La Costruzione Sociale del Mercato*. Bologna: Il Mulino.

— (1997), 'Un Nord-Ovest di Cespugli', *Il Sole 24 Ore*, 2/12/1997.

— (1999), 'Teoria del capitale e *polital economy* comparata', *Stato e Mercato*, 3.

— and Le Galès, P. (2000a), 'Introduction: Cities in Europe, Local Societies and Governance'. In Bagnasco and Le Galès 2000b (eds.), q.v.

—, — (2000b) (eds.), *Cities in Contemporary Europe*. Cambridge: Cambridge University Press.

— and Sabel, C. (1995) (eds.), *Small Firms in Europe*. London: Pinter.

Bahnmüller, R. and Bispinck, R. (1995), 'Vom Vorzeige- zum Auslaufmodell? Das Deutsche Tarifsystem zwischen Kollektiver Regulierung, Betrieblicher Flexibilisierung und Individuellen Interessen'. In Bispinck, R. (ed.), *Tarifpolitik der Zukunft. Was wird aus dem Flächentarifvertrag?* Hamburg: VSA-Verlag.

Baker, P. (1993), 'Production Restructuring in the Textiles and Clothing Industries', *New Technology, Work and Employment*, 8: 1, 43–55.

— (1996), 'Reactive Restructuring in Textiles and Clothing'. In Taplin and Winterton (eds.), q.v.

Barro, R. J. (1991), 'Economic Growth in a Cross-Section of Countries', *Quarterly Journal of Economics*, 106: 407–43.

— and Sala-I-Martín, X. X. (1991), 'Convergence across States and Regions', *Brookings Papers on Economic Activity*, 1: 107–82.

Bassett, K. (1996), 'Partnerships, Business Elites and Urban Politics: New Forms of Governance in an English City?', *Urban Studies*, 33: 3, 539–55.

Baudry, B. (1995), *L'Économie des Relations Interentreprises*. Paris: La Découverte.

Bauer, M. and Cohen, E. (1981), *Qui Gouverne les Groupes Industriels*. Paris: Editions Seuil.

Becattini, G. (1979a), 'Dal Settore Industriale al Distretto Industriale: Alcune Consider-azioni sull'Unità d'Indagine dell'Economia Industriale', *Rivista di Economia e Politica Industriale*, 1, 7–21.

—— (1979b) (ed.), *Modelli Locali di Sviluppo*. Bologna: Il Mulino.

—— (1987) (ed.), *Mercato e Forze Locali: Il Distretto Industriale*. Bologna: Il Mulino.

—— (1989), 'Riflessioni sul Distretto Industriale Marshalliano come Concetto Socio-Economico', *Stato e Mercato*, 25, 111–28.

—— (1990), 'The Marshallian Industrial District as a Socio-Economic Notion'. In Pyke, Becattini, and Sengenberger (eds.), q.v.

—— (1991), 'The Industrial District as a Creative Milieu'. In Benko and Dunford (eds.), q.v.

—— (1997) (ed.), *Il Distretto Industriale (1943–1993): Prato, Storia di una Città 4*. Florence: Le Monnier.

—— (2000), *Il Distretto Industriale*. Turin: Rosenberg and Sellier.

—— and Rullani, G. (1993), 'Sistema Locale e Mercato Globale', *Economia e Politica Industriale*, 80, 70–83.

Bechtle, G. and Lang, C. (1996), 'Die Grenzen Eines Erfolgreichen Innovationsmusters im Baden-Württembergischen Maschinenbau'. In Braczyk and Schienstock (eds.), q.v.

——, —— (1999), *Risikosteuerung bei Innovationsprozessen im Internationalen Region-alvergleich: Baden-Württemberg und Emilia-Romagna. Endbericht*. Munich: Institut für Sozialwissenschaftliche Forschung e.V. ISF München.

Beckouche, P. (1996), *La Nouvelle Géographie de l'Industrie Aéronautique*. Paris: L'Harmattan.

—— (1999), *Pour une Métropolisation Raisonnée: Diagnostic Socio-Économique de la Région Parisienne*. Paris: La Documentation Française.

Bellandi, M. (1987), 'Il Distretto Industriale Secondo Marshall'. In Becattini (ed.), q.v.

—— and Trigilia, C. (1991), 'Come Cambia un Distretto Industriale: Strategie di Riaggiustamento e Tecnologie Informatiche nell' Industria Tessile di Prato', *Economia e Politica Industriale*, 70, 121–52.

Belussi, F. (1987), *Benetton: Information Technology in Production and Distribution*. Sussex: University of Sussex Occasional Paper No. 25.

—— (1992) (ed.), *Nuovi Modelli di Impresa: Gerarchie Oganizzative e Impresa Rete*. Milano: Angeli.

—— (1996), 'Local Systems, Industrial Districts and Institutional Networks: Towards a New Evolutionary Paradigm of Industrial Economics', *European Planning Studies*, 4: 1–15.

—— (1997), 'Il Divano in Pelle fra Artigianato e Post-Fordismo', *Il Sole 24 Ore*, 24/2/ 1997.

Benko, G. (1990), *La Dynamique Spatiale de l'Economie Contemporaine*. Paris: Edition de l'Espace Européen.

—— and Dunford, M. (1991) (eds.), *Industrial Change and Regional Development*. London/New York: Belhaven Press.

—— and Lipietz, A. (1992) (eds.), *Les Régions qui Gagnent: Districts et Réseaux*. Paris: PUF.

——, —— (1999) (eds.), *La Richesse des Régions*. Paris: PUF.

Benko, G., Dunford, M., and Heurley, J. (1997), 'Districts Industriels. Vingt Ans de Recherche', *Espaces et Sociétés*, 88–89, 305–27.

Benetton (1996), *Benetton Annual Report*. Treviso.

Bennett, R. J., Graham, D. J., and Bratton, W. (1999), 'The Location and Concentration of Business in Britain: Business Clusters, Business Services, Market Coverage and Local Economic Development', *Transactions of the Institute of British Geographers*, 24: 393–420.

— and McCoshan, A. (1993), *Enterprise and Human Resource Development: Local Capacity Building*. London: Paul Chapman.

Bergeron, L. (1998), *L'Industrie du Luxe en France*. Paris: Oldie Jacob.

— and Bourdelais, P. (1998) (eds.), *La France N'est-elle pas Douée pour l'Industrie?* Paris: Belin.

Bergmann, E. M., Maier, G., and Tödtling, F. (1991) (eds.), *Regions Reconsidered: Economic Networks, Innovation, and Local Development in Industrialized Countries*. London: Mandell.

Bernardy de Sigoyer, M. and Boisgontier, P. (1988), *Grains de Technopôle*. Grenoble: Presses Universitaires de Grénoble.

—, — (1996), *La Technopôle. Une Certaine Idée de la Ville*. Paris: L'Harmattan.

Beslay, C., Grossetti, M., Taulelle, F., Salles, D., Guillaume, R., and Daynac, M. (1998), *La construction des systèmes locaux*. Paris: L'Harmattan.

Best, M. (1990), *The New Competition*. Oxford: Polity.

Bianchi, P. and Gualteri, G. (1990), 'Emilia-Romagna and Its Industrial Districts: The Evolution of a Model'. In Leonardi and Nanetti (eds.), q.v.

Birmingham Economic Information Centre (1998), *The Birmingham Economic Review and Prospects 1998*. Birmingham: Birmingham Economic Information Centre.

Boch, R. (1997), 'The Rise and Decline of Flexible Production: The Cutlery Industry of Solingen since the Eighteenth Century'. In Sabel and Zeitlin (eds.), q.v.

Boddy, M. and Lovering, J. (1986), 'High Technology Industry in the Bristol Sub-Region: The Aerospace/Defence Nexus', *Regional Studies*, 20: 3, 217–31.

Bonamy, J. and May, N. (1994), *Services et Mutations Urbains*. Paris: Antropos Economica.

Bonazzi, G. (1995), *Il Tubo di Cristallo: Modello Giapponese e Fabbrica Integrata alla Fiat Auto*. Bologna: Il Mulino.

Borrás-Alomar, S., Christiansen, T., and Rodríguez-Pose A. (1994), 'Towards a "Europe of the Regions"? Visions and Reality from a Critical Perspective', *Regional Politics and Policy*, 4: 1–27.

Borraz, O. (1997), *Gouverner une ville*. Rennes: Presses Universitaires de Rennes.

Bottazzi, G. (1990), 'I Sud del Sud: I Divari Interni al Mezzogiorno e il Rovesciamento delle Gerarchie Spaziali', *Meridiana*, 10: 114–18.

Bourdonnec, Y. (1996), *Le Miracle Breton*. Paris: Calmann-Levy.

Boyer, R. (1986), *La Théorie de la Régulation: Une Analyse Critique*. Paris: Éditions La Découverte.

— (1989), *New Directions in Management Practices and Work Organisation: General Principles and National Trajectories*. Paris: OECD.

— (1990), *The Regulation School: A Critical Introduction*. New York: Columbia University Press.

— (1997), 'French Statism at the Crossroads'. In Crouch and Streeck (eds.), q.v.

Boyer, R. (1998), 'La Spécificité de l'Industrie Française en Quête de Théories: Essor et Crise d'une Variante Étatique du Modèle Fordiste (1945–1995)'. In Bergeron, L. and Bourdelais, P. (eds.), q.v.

—— (2000), 'Polity in the Era of Global Finance: Recent Debates in Regulation Theory', *International Journal of Urban and Regional Research*, 24: 1.

—— and Saillard, Y. (1995) (eds.), *Théorie de la Régulation, Etat des Savoirs*. Paris: La Découverte.

Boyle, R. (1993), 'Changing Partners: the Experience of Urban Economic Policy in West Central Scotland 1980–90', *Urban Studies*, 30: 2, 309–24.

Braczyk, H.-J., Cooke, P., and Heidenreich, M. (1998) (eds.), *Regional Innovation Systems: The Role of Governance in a Globalized World*. London: UCL Press.

—— and Schienstock, G. (1996) (eds.), *Kurswechsel in der Industrie. Lean Production in Baden-Württemberg*. Berlin/Cologne: Kohlhammer.

——, ——, and Steffensen, B. (1996), 'Die Regionalökonomie Baden-Württembergs: Ursachen und Grenzen des Erfolgs'. In Braczyk and Schienstock (eds.), q.v.

Brenner, N. (1998), 'Global Cities, Global States: Global City Formation and State Territorial Restructuring in Contemporary Europe', *Review of International Political Economy*, 5. 1, 1–37.

British Aerospace (1998), *British Aerospace Founds Its Virtual University*. London: British Aerospace.

Bruch-Krumbein, W., Hellmer, F., and Krumbein, W. (1997), *Neues in Sachen Industriepolitik? Mythen und Empirische Realitäten*. Göttingen: Regionale Trends Schriftenreihe des Instituts für Regionalforschung an der Universität Göttingen, No. 12.

Bruhat, T. (1990), *Les Technopôles en France*. Paris: La Documentation Française.

Brusco, S. (1982), 'The Emilian Model: Productive Decentralisation and Social Integration', *Cambridge Journal of Economics*, 6: 167–84.

—— (1989), *Piccole Imprese e Distretti Industriali: Una Raccolta di Saggi*. Turin: Rosenberg and Sellier.

—— (1990), 'The Idea of the Industrial District: Its Genesis'. In Pyke, Becattini, and Sengenberger (eds.), q.v.

—— (1992), 'Small Firms and the Provision of Real Services'. In Pyke and Sengenberger (eds.), q.v.

Bryson, J., Wood, P., and Keeble, D. (1993), 'Business Networks, Small Firm Flexibility and Regional Development in UK Business Services', *Entrepreneurship and Regional Development*, 5: 3, 265–77.

Bucaille, A. and Costa de Beauregard, B. (1988), *Pmi: Enjeux Régionaux et Internationaux*. Paris: Economica.

Büchtemann, C. F. and Kuhlmann, U.-W. (1996), 'Internationalisierungsstrategien deutscher Unternehmen: Am Beispiel von Mercedes-Benz'. In Meil, P. (ed.), *Globalisierung Industrieller Produktion. Strategien und Strukturen, Ergebnisse des Expertenkreises 'Zukunftsstrategien'*. Frankfurt: Campus.

Burroni, L. (1999a), 'Mutamenti nell'Organizzazione Produttiva della Terza Italia: Una Comparazione tra Veneto e Toscana', *Sviluppo Locale*, 11, 33–67.

—— (1999b), 'Regolazione Locale nelle Regioni della Terza Italia', *Sviluppo Locale*, 12, 5–43.

Business Monitor (1997), *Size Analysis of UK Businesses*, PIX 1003. London: HMSO.

Button, K. J. and Pentecost, E. J. (1995), 'Testing for Convergence of the EU Regional Economies', *Economic Inquiry*, 3, 664–71.

Calderdale and Kirklees TEC (1997), *Economic and Labour Market Assessment 1996/97*. Calderdale: Calderdale and Kirklees TEC.

Camagni, R. P. (1991) (ed.), *Innovation Networks: Spatial Perspectives*. London/New York: Belhaven Press.

Casanova, J. C. and Levy-Leboyer, M. (1991) (eds.), *Le Capitalisme en France*. Paris: Gallimard.

Castells, M. (1989), *The Informational City: Information Technology, Economic Restructuring and the Urban-Regional Process*. Oxford: Blackwell.

— (1996), *The Rise of the Network Society*. Oxford: Blackwell.

— and Hall, P. (1994), *Technopoles of the World: The Making of 21st Century Industrial Complexes*. London/New York: Routledge.

CEDEFOP (1995), *Vocational Education and Training in the Federal Republic of Germany*. Luxembourg: Office for Official Publications of the European Communities.

Censis (1998), *Distretti Industriali, Infrastrutture e Servizi per la Logistica*. Rome: Censis.

CEPME (1991), *Dix Ans d'Évolution des pme-pmi*. Paris: CEPME.

CEREM-FORUM (1998), *L'Émergence d'Oligopoles en Réseau Fondé sur la Connaissance*. Paris: Commissariat Général au Plan.

Champion, T., Mønnesland, J., and Vandermotten, C. (1996), 'The New Regional Map of Europe', *Progress in Planning*, 4: 1–89.

Cheshire, P. C. and Carbonaro, G. (1995), 'Convergence–Divergence in Regional Growth Rates: An Empty Black Box?' In Armstrong and Vickerman (eds.), q.v.

— and Gordon, I. R. (1996), 'Territorial Competition and the Predictability of Collective (In)action', *International Journal of Urban and Regional Research*, 20: 383–400.

—, — (1998), 'Territorial Competition: Some Lessons for Policy', *Annals of Regional Science*, 33: 321–46.

Cieply, S. and Hancké, B. (1999), 'Le Financement des PME dans Leur Espace de Transaction: le Relâchement de l'Hypothèse de Rationnement du Crédit', *Revue Internationale des PME*, 11: 4, 237–52.

Cohen, E. (1989), *L'Etat-Brancardier*. Paris: Calmann-Lévy.

— (1992), *Le Colbertisme High-Tech*. Paris: Hachette/Pluriel.

— (1996), *La Tentation Hexagonale*. Paris: Fayard.

Cohen, J., Hart, D., and Simmie, J. (1997) (eds.), *Recherche et Développement Régional, Travaux Franco-Britanniques*. Paris: Presses de la Sorbonne.

Colletis, G., Courlet, C., and Pecqueur, B. (1990), *Les Systèmes Industriels Localisés en Europe*. Paris: l'Harmattan.

Cooke, P. (1992), 'Regional Innovation Systems: Competitive Regulation in the New Europe', *Geoforum*, 23: 365–82.

— (1995) (ed.), *The Rise of the Rustbelt*. London: UCL Press.

— (1996), 'The New Wave of Regional Innovation Networks: Analysis, Characteristics and Strategy', *Small Business Economics*, 8: 159–71.

— (1997), 'Regions in a Global Market: The Experiences of Wales and Baden-Württemberg', *Review of International Political Economy*, 4: 349–81.

— and Morgan, K. (1990), *Learning through Networking: Regional Innovation and Lessons of Baden-Württemberg. Regional Industrial Research Report No. 5*. Cardiff: University of Wales.

—, — (1994a), 'The Network Paradigm: New Departures in Corporate and Regional Development', *Environment and Planning D: Society and Space*, 11: 543–64.

Cooke, P. and Morgan, K. (1994b), 'Growth Regions Under Duress: Renewal Strategies in Baden-Württemberg and Emilia Romagna'. In Amin and Thrift (eds.), q.v.

—, — (1998), *The Associational Economy: Firms, Regions and Innovation*. Oxford: Oxford University Press.

—, —, and Pires, A. R. (1984), 'Productive Decentralization in Three European Regions', *Environment and Planning A*, 17: 527–54.

Coopers and Lybrand (n.d.) *Sussex Chamber of Commerce, Training and Enterprise: Stage 1 Summary Report: Key Issues and Trends*. London: Coopers and Lybrand.

Coriat, B. (1995), 'France, un Fordisme Brisé et Sans Successeur'. In Boyer and Saillard (eds.), q.v.

— and Taddéi, B. (1993), *Enterprise France (Made in France)*. Paris: Le Livre de Poche.

County Durham and Darlington TEC (1998), *County Durham and Darlington Economic Assessment (1997–98)*. County Durham and Darlington TEC.

Cour des Comptes (1995), *Vue d'ensemble annuaire*. Paris: Cour des Comptes.

Courault, B. (1992), *Les transformations du système choletais*. In Ganne (ed.) (1992b), q.v.

— and Parat, E. (1998), 'Textile Habillement, Distribution: une Filière Pilotée par l'Aval', *Lettre du Centre d'Études de l'Emploi*, 28.

—, — (2000), 'Les PME de l'habillement à Roanne et Cholet, une dynamique de l'emploi à rebours de l'histoire', *Lettre du Centre d'Études de l'Emploi*, 54.

—, Parat, E., and Trouvé, P. (2000) (eds.), *Les dynamiques de PME. Approches internationales*. Paris: Centres d'Etude de l'Emploi/PUF

Courlet, C. and Pecqueur, B. (1992), 'Les Systèmes Industriels Localisés en France, un Nouveau Modèle de Développement'. In Benko and Lipietz (eds.), q.v.

—, — and Soulage, B. (1994) (eds.), *Industrie, Territoire et Politiques Publiques*. Paris: L'Harmattan.

Coyle, A. (1992), 'Sex and Skill in the Organization of the Clothing Industry'. In McDowell, L. and Pringle, R. (eds.), *Defining Women: Social Institutions and Gender Divisions*. Oxford: Blackwell.

CRG (1996), *Report: TECs' Sector-Specific Activities*. Report submitted to Department for Education and Employment (London: DfEE).

Crouch, C., Finegold, D., and Sako, M. (1999), *Are Skills the Answer?: The Political Economy of Skill Creation in Advanced Industrial Countries*. Oxford: Oxford University Press.

— and Streeck, W. (1997) (eds.), *Political Economy of Modern Capitalism: Mapping Convergence and Diversity*. London/Beverly Hills: Sage.

Cumbria TEC (1997), *Cumbria Economic and Labour Market Assessment*. Cumbria TEC.

Curran, J. and Blackburn, R. (1994), *Small Firms and Local Economic Networks: The Death of the Local Economy?* London: Paul Chapman.

Damette, F. (1995), *La France en Villes*. Paris: La Documentation Française.

Danson, M. W. (1995a), New Firm Formation and Regional Economic Development: An Introduction and Review of the Scottish Experience, *Small Business Economics*, 7: 2, 81–7.

— (1995b) (ed.), *New Firm Formation and Regional Economic Development*. London: Routledge.

—, Lloyd, M., and Newlands, D. (1989), '"Scottish Enterprise": Towards a Model Agency or Flawed Initiative?', *Regional Studies*, 23: 6, 557–63.

DATAR (1986), *Guide du Developpement Local*. Paris: Syros-Alternatives.

DATAR (1990), *Vingt Technopoles: Un Premier Bilan*. Paris: La Documentation Française.
— (1997), *Grandes Entreprises et Appui au Développement Local*. Paris: La Documentation Française.
Davezies, L. (1995), 'L'inégalité spatiale en France'. In Savy, M. and Veltz, P. (eds.), *Economie globale et réinvention du local*. La Tour d'Aigues: DATAR/Editions de l'Aube.
— (1998), 'L'Autre Main Invisible: La Part Hors-Marché de l'Économie des Régions et des Villes', *Pouvoirs Locaux*, 37, 45–57.
Decoster, E. and Tabaries, M. (1997), 'Système Régional d'Innovation et Système Productif Francilien: Les Réseaux d'Innovation'. In Cohen, Hart, and Simmie (eds.), q.v.
Dei Ottati, G. (1992), 'Fiducia, Transazioni Intrecciate e Credito nel Distretto Industriale', *Note Economiche*, 1/2, 1–30.
— (1995), *Tra Mercato e Comunità: Aspetti Concettuali e Ricerche Empiriche sul Distretto Industriale*. Milan: Angeli.
— (1996), 'La Recente Evoluzione Economica dei Distretti Industriali Toscani', *Sviluppo Locale*, 2–3: 92–124.
DETR [Department of the Environment, Transport and the Regions] (1999), *Regional Development Agencies, Regional Strategies*. London: DETR.
Diamanti, I. (1996), *Il Male del Nord: Lega, Localismo, Secessione*. Rome: Donzelli.
DiGiovanna, S. (1996), 'Industrial Districts and Regional Economic Development: A Regulation Approach', *Regional Studies*, 30: 4, 373–86.
Doeringer, P., Terkla, D., and Topakian, G. (1987), *Invisible Factors in Local Economic Development*. Oxford: Oxford University Press.
Dosi, G. (1988), 'Sources, Procedures and Microeconomic Effects of Innovation', *Journal of Economic Literature*, 26: 1120–71.
Dumfries and Galloway Enterprise (1997), *Annual Report and Accounts 1996–1997*. Dumfries: Dumfries and Galloway Enterprise.
Dunbartonshire Enterprise (1997), Playing Our Part: Dunbartonshire Enterprise Annual Report and Accounts 1996/1997. Dunbarton: Dunbartonshire Enterprise.
Dunford, M. (1990), 'Theories of Regulation', *Environment and Planning D: Society and Space*, 8: 297–321.
— (1991), *Rhone-Alpes in the 1990s. Special report no. 2165*. London: Economist Intelligence Unit.
— and Benko, G. (1991) (eds.), *Industrial Change and Regional Development: The Transformation of New Industrial Spaces*. London: Belhaven Press.
— and Kafkalas, G. (1992) (eds.), *Cities and Regions in the New Europe*. London: Pinter.
Dupont, M. J. and Francois, J. P. (1998), 'L'Industrie Française Fortement Pénétrée par les Capitaux Étrangers'. In SESSI (1998b), q.v.
Dupuy, C. (1991), *L'Urbanisme des Réseaux. Théories et Méthodes*. Paris: Armand Colin.
— and Gilly J.-P. (1991), 'Toulouse et les Dynamismes Intra-Régionaux de Midi-Pyrénées', *Revue Géographique des Pyrénées et du Sud-Ouest*, 62.
—, — (1993) (eds.), *Industrie et Territoires en France*. Paris: La Documentation Française.
—, — (1997) (eds.), *Midi-Pyrénées. Dynamisme Industriel et Renouveau Rural*. Paris: La Documentation Française.
Eberlein, B. (1996), 'French Center-Periphery Relations and Science Park Development: Local Polity Initiatives and Intergovernmental Policymaking', *Governance*, 9: 4, 351–74.

Engel, C. (1993), 'Regionen in der EG. Rechtliche Vielfalt und integrationspolitische Rollensuche', *Gutachten im Auftrag der Staats- und Senatskanzleien*.

Enterprise Ayrshire (1999), *Challenge for the Millennium: Enterprise Ayrshire Strategy 1996–1999*. Ayr: Enterprise Ayrshire.

Evette, T. and Lautier, F. (1994), *De l'Atelier au Territoire: Le Travail en Quête d'Espaces*. Paris: L'Harmattan.

Farrell, H. (2000), *The Political Economy of Trust: Cooperation between Machine Producers in Industrial Districts in Italy and Germany*. Washington, DC: Unpublished Ph.D. Thesis, Georgetown University.

Fife Enterprise (1997), *Working for Fife: Annual Report and Accounts 1996/1997*. Fife: Fife Enterprise.

Fourcade, C. (1987) (ed.), *Industries et Régions*. Paris: Economica, Collection ADEFI-GRECO.

—— (1991), *Petite Entreprise et Développement Local*. Paris: Eska.

Francfort, I., Osty, F., Sainsaulieu, R., and Uhlade, M. (1995), *Les Mondes Sociaux de l'Entreprise*. Paris: Desclées de Brouwer.

Freschi, A. C. (1993), 'Istituzioni Politiche e Sviluppo Locale nella Terza Italia', *Sviluppo Locale*, 1, 71–118.

Fridenson, P. and Straus, A. (1987), *Le Capitalisme Français: Blocages et Dynamismes d'une Croissance*. Paris: Fayard.

Friedrichs, J., Häußermann, H., and Siebel, W. (1986) (eds.), *Süd-Nord-Gefälle in der Bundesrepublik?* Opladen: Westdeutscher Verlag.

Fringant, V. J. (1997), 'La Reconversion des Industries de Défense en Gironde', mimeo.

Fukuyama, F. (1995), *Trust: The Social Virtues and the Creation of Prosperity*. London: Hamish Hamilton.

Gaffard, J.-L. (1990), *Economie Industrielle de l'Innovation*. Paris: Précis-Dalloz.

Ganne, B. (1983), *Gens du Cuir ... Gens du Papier ... Transformations d'Annonay Depuis les Années 1920*. Paris: Editions du CNRS.

—— (1990), *Industrialisation Diffuse et Systèmes Industriels*. Geneva: Institut International d'Études Sociales de Genève.

—— (1992a), 'Place et Évolution des Systèmes Industriels Locaux en France. Economie Politique d'une Transformation'. In Benko and Lipietz (eds.), q.v.

—— (1992b) (ed.), *Développement Local et Ensemble des PME, Rapport du Groupe de Travail PIRTEM*. Paris: CNRS.

—— (1995), 'France: Behind Small and Medium Size Enterprises Lies the State'. In Bagnasco and Sabel (eds.), q.v.

—— (1997), 'Politiques Publiques Industrielles et Système d'Aide aux PME Depuis 25 Ans', *Espaces et Sociétés*, 88–9, 259–97.

—— (2000), 'PME, Districts et Nouvelles Territorialités'. In Courault, Parat, and Trouvé (eds.), q.v.

Garlichs, D., Maier, F., and Semlinger, K. (1983) (eds.), *Regionalisierte Arbeitsmarkt- und Beschäftigungspolitik*. Frankfurt am Main/ New York: Campus.

Garmise, S. (1997), *Institutional Networks and Industrial Restructuring: Local Institutions towards the Textile Industry in Nottingham and Prato*. London: Unpublished Ph.D. Thesis, University of London.

Garnsey, E. and Alford, H. (1994), 'Innovative Interaction: Supplier Relations among New Technology-Based Firms'. In Oakey, R. (ed.), *New Technology-Based Firms in the 1990s: Volume II*. London: Paul Chapman.

Garnsey, E., Galloway, S. C., and Mathis, S. H. (1994), 'Flexibility and Specialization in Question; Birth, Growth and Death Rates of Cambridge New Technology-Based Firms', *Entrepreneurship and Regional Development*, 6: 1, 81–107.

Garrett, G. (1998), *Partisan Politics in the Global Economy*. Cambridge: Cambridge University Press.

Gertler, M. S. and Rutherford, T. D. (1996), 'Regional-Industrial Networks and the Role of Labour'. In Staber, Schaefer, and Sharma (eds.), q.v.

Giaccaria, P. (1999), *Competitività e Sviluppo Locale: Produrre Valore a Torino*. Milan: Franco Angeli.

Gilly, J. P. and Pecqueur, B. (1995), 'La Dimension Locale de la Régulation'. In Boyer and Saillard (eds.), q.v.

—— and Wallet, F. (2001), 'Proximités, Hybridation et Gouvernance Locale, le Cas des Processus de Gouvernance Industrielle', *International Journal of Urban and Regional Research*.

Glasgow Development Agency (1997). *Annual Report and Accounts 1996–1997*. Glasgow: Glasgow Development Agency.

Glassmann, U. (1999), 'Der Einfluß von Internationalisierungsstrategien auf die baden-württembergische Zulieferindustrie: Das Beispiel Mercedes-Benz'. In Eckardt, A., Köhler, H.-D., and Pries, L. (eds.), *Global Players in lokalen Bindungen. Unternehmensglobalisierung in soziologischer Perspektive*. Berlin: edition sigma.

Gloucestershire Labour Market Information Unit (1997), *The Economy of Gloucestershire 1997*. Gloucester: Gloucestershire Labour Market Information Unit.

GLYSI (1992), *Développement Local et Ensemble de PME. n. 6/1992 (Contrat PIRTTEM)*. Lyon: GLYSI.

Godley, A. (1996), 'The Emergence of Mass Production in the UK Clothing Industry'. In Taplin and Winterton, q.v.

Gorgeu, A. and Mathieu, R. (1995a), *Recrutement et Production au Plus Juste: Les Nouvelles Usines d'Équipment Autonomobile en France*. Paris: Centre d'Étude de l'Emploi.

——, —— (1995b), 'Stratégies d'Approvisionement des Grandes Firmes et Livraisons Juste à Temps: Quel Impact Spatial?', *L'Espace Géographique*, 3, 245–59.

——, —— (1996), 'L'Assurance Qualité Fournisseur de l'Industrie Automobile Française', *Revue d'Economie Industrielle*, 75: 1, 223–38.

——, ——, and Pialoux, M. (1998), *Organisation du Travail et Gestion de la Main-d'Oeuvre dans la Filière Automobile. Dossier 14*. Paris: Centre d'Études de l'Emploi.

Grabher, G. (1993) (ed.), *The Embedded Firm: On the Socioeconomics of Industrial Networks*. London/New York: Routledge.

Granovetter, M. (1985), 'Economic Action and Social Structure: The Problem of Embeddedness', *American Journal of Sociology*, 3: 481–510.

Grayson, D. (1996), 'United Kingdom: A—The Business Links Programme'. In OECD (ed.), *Networks of Enterprises and Local Development: Competing and Co-operating in Local Productive Systems*. Paris: OECD.

Green, N. (1998), *Du sentier à la Avenue: la confection et les immigrés', Paris—New York, 1880–1980*. Paris: Seuil.

Greffe, X. (1984), *Territoires en France: Les Enjeux Économiques de la Décentralisation*. Paris: Economica.

—— (1988), *Décentraliser Pour l'Emploi*. Paris: Economica.

Gregersen, B. and Johnson, B. (1997), 'Learning Economies, Innovation Systems and European Integration', *Regional Studies*, 31: 479–90.

Greif, A. (1999), 'Impersonal Exchange and the Origins of Markets: From the Community Responsibility System to Individual Legal Responsibility in Pre-Modern Europe'. In Aoki, M. and Hayami, Y. (eds.), *Communities and Markets*. Oxford: Oxford University Press.

Grossetti, M. (1995), *Science, Industrie et Territoire*. Toulouse: Presses Universitaires du Mirail.

—— and Gilly, J. P. (1993), 'Organisations, Individus et Territoires, le Cas des Systèmes Locaux d'Innovation', *Revue d'Économie Régionale et Urbaine*, 3.

Grote, J. R. (1997), *Regionale Vernetzung: Interorganisatorische Strukturdifferenzen regionaler Politikgestaltung. Working Paper No. 23*. Mannheim: Mannheimer Zentrum für Europäische Sozialforschung, AB III.

—— (1998), *The Political Ecology of Regionalism. State–Society Relations in Nine European Regions*. Florence: Unpublished Ph.D. Thesis, European University Institute.

Guegan, J.-C. and Rousier, N. (1989), *Sur l'Organisation Territoriale de l'Industrie Française*. Grenoble: IREPD.

Hall, P. (1993), 'Forces Shaping Urban Europe', *Urban Studies*, 30: 883–98.

Hall, P. A. (1986), *Governing the Economy: The Politics of State Intervention in Britain and France*. Oxford: Oxford University Press.

Hampshire TEC (1998), *Local Economic Assessment*. Hampshire TEC.

Hancké, B. (1997), *Modernisation without Flexible Specialisation: How Large Firm Restructuring and Government Regional Policies Became the Step Parents of Autarchical Regional Production Systems in France. WZB, Discussion paper FS I 97-304*. Berlin: Wissenschaftszentrum Berlin.

—— (1998a), *Industrial Restructuring and Industrial Relations in the European Car Industry: WZB Discussion Paper FS I 98-305*. Berlin: Wissenschaftszentrum Berlin.

—— (1998b), 'Trust of Hierarchy, Changing Relationships between Large and Small firms in France', *Small Business Economics*, 11: 3, 237–52.

—— (2001), 'Many Roads to Flexibility, How Large Firms Built Autarchic Regional Production Systems in France', *International Journal of Urban and Regional Research*.

—— and Soskice, D. (1996), *Coordination and Restructuring in Large French Firms: Working Paper FS I 96-303*. Berlin: Wissenschaftszentrum Berlin.

Harrison, B. (1994a), 'The Italian Industrial Districts and the Crisis of the Cooperative Form'. In Krumbein, M. (ed.), *Ökonomische und Politische Netzwerke in der Region. Beiträge aus der Internationalen Debatte*. Münster/ Hamburg: Lit.

—— (1994b), *Lean and Mean: The Resurrection of Corporate Power in an Age of Flexibility*. New York: Basic Books.

Harrison, R. T. and Leitch, C. M. (1995), 'Whatever You Hit Call the Target: An Alternative Approach to Small Business Policy'. In Danson (ed.), q.v.

Harvey, D. (1985), *The Urbanization of Capital*. Oxford: Blackwell.

—— (1989), *The Conditions of Postmodernity*. Oxford: Blackwell.

Hassel, A. (1999), 'The Erosion of the German System of Industrial Relations', *British Journal of Industrial Relations*, 37: 3, 483–505.

Hassink, R. (1992), *Regional Innovation Policy: Case-studies from the Ruhr-Area, Baden-Württemberg and the North East of England*. Utrecht: Faculty of Geographical Sciences, University of Utrecht.

Hassink, R. (1993), 'Regional Innovation Policies Compared', *Urban Studies*, 30: 1009–24.

Hayter, R. and Patchell, J. (1993), 'Different Trajectories in the Social Divisions of Labour: The Cutlery Industry in Sheffield, England, and Tsubame, Japan', *Urban Studies*, 30: 8, 1427–45.

Hayward, J. (1986), *The State and the Market Economy: Industrial Patriotism and Economic Intervention in France*. Brighton: Wheatsheaf Books.

—— and Shalom, E. (1995) (eds.), *Industrial Enterprise and European Integration*. Oxford: Oxford University Press.

Heidenreich, M. (1996), 'Beyond Flexible Specialization: The Rearrangement of Regional Production Orders in Emilia-Romagna and Baden-Württemberg', *European Planning Studies*, 4: 4, 401–19.

—— and Krauss, G. (1998), 'The Baden-Württemberg Production and Innovation Regime: Past Successes and New Challenges'. In Braczyk, Cooke, and Heidenreich (eds.), q.v.

Heinze, R. G. and Voelzkow, H. (1997) (eds.), *Regionalisierung der Strukturpolitik in Nordrhein-Westfalen*. Opladen: Westdeutscher Verlag.

——, ——, and Hilbert, J. (1992), *Strukturwandel und Strukturpolitik in Nordrhein-Westfalen*. Opladen: Budrich & Leske.

Hellmer, F., Friese, C., Kollros, H., and Krumbein, W. (1999), *Mythos Netzwerke. Regionale Innovationsprozesse zwischen Kontinuität und Wandel*. Berlin: edition sigma.

Helmstädter, H.-G. (1996), 'Regionale Struktur und Entwicklung der Industriebeschäftigung: Konzentration oder Dekonzentration?', *Seminarbericht der Gesellschaft für Regionalforschung*, 37, 75–104.

Henry, N. (1992), The New Industrial Spaces: Locational Logic of a New Production Era?, *International Journal of Urban and Regional Research*, 16: 3, 375–96.

——, Pinch, S., and Russell, S. (1996), 'In Pole Position? Untraded Interdependencies, New Industrial Spaces and the British Motor Sport Industry', *Area*, 28: 1, 25–36.

Hereford and Worcester County Council, Chamber of Commerce Training and Enterprise Hereford and Worcester, and Central England TEC (1997), *Hereford and Worcester County—Economic Assessment 1997*. Hereford: Hereford and Worcester County Council.

Herrigel, G. B. (1989), 'Industrial Order and the Politics of Industrial Change: Mechanical Engineering'. In Katzenstein, P. J. (ed.), *Industry and Politics in West Germany*. Ithaca, New York: Cornell University Press.

—— (1993a), 'Power and the Redefinition of Industrial Districts. The Case of Baden-Württemberg'. In Grabher (ed.), q.v.

—— (1993b), 'Large Firms, Small Firms, and the Governance of Flexible Specialization'. In Kogut, B. (ed.), *Country Competitiveness. Technology and the Organizing of Work. New York*. Oxford: Oxford University Press.

—— (1994), 'Industry as a Form of Order'. In Hollingsworth, Schmitter, and Streeck (eds.), q.v.

—— (1996a), 'Crisis in German Decentralized Production: Unexpected Rigidity and the Challenge of an Alternative Form of Flexible Organization in Baden Württemberg', *European Urban and Regional Studies*, 3: 33–52.

—— (1996b), *Industrial Constructions. The Sources of German Industrial Power*. Cambridge: Cambridge University Press.

—— (forthcoming) *De-Regionalization, Re-Regionalization and the Transformation of Manufacturing Flexibility: Large Firms and Industrial Districts in Europe*.

Hertfordshire TEC (1997), *Local Economy Assessment for Hertfordshire 1997*. Hemel Hempstead: Hertfordshire TEC.

Hilbert, U. (1991) (ed.), *Regional Innovation and Decentralisation. High Tech Industry and Government Policy*. London/ New York: Routledge.

Hirsch, J. P. and Minard, P. (1998), ' "Laissez Nous Faire et Protégez Nous Beaucoup": Pour une Histoire des Pratiques Institutionnelles dans l'Industrie Française (XVIIIème-XIXème siècle)'. In Bergeron and Bourdelais (eds.), q.v.

Hirschman, A. (1970), *Exit, Voice and Loyalty: Responses to Decline in Firms, Organisations and States*. Cambridge, Mass.: Harvard University Press.

Hirst, P. and Thompson, G. (1996), *Globalisation in Question: The International Economy and Possibilities for Governance*. Cambridge: Polity Press.

—— and Zeitlin, J. (1991), 'Flexible Specialisation vs. Post-Fordism: Theory, Evidence and Policy-Implications', *Economy and Society*, 20: 1, 1–56.

——, —— (1997), 'Flexible Specialization: Theory and Evidence in the Analysis of Industrial Change'. In Hollingsworth and Boyer (eds.), q.v.

Hollingsworth, J. R. and Boyer, R. (1997) (eds.), *Contemporary Capitalism. The Embeddedness of Institutions*. Cambridge: Cambridge University Press.

——, Schmitter, P. C., and Streeck, W. (1994a), 'Capitalism, Sectors, Institutions and Performance'. In Hollingsworth, Schmitter, and Streeck (1994b) (eds.), q.v.

——, ——, —— (1994b) (eds.), *Governing Capitalist Economies: Performance and Control of Economic Sectors*. New York/Oxford: Oxford University Press.

Holwegler, B. D. and Trautwein, H.-M. (1998), *Beschäftigungswirkung der Internationalisierung. Eine Studie Aus- und Einfließender Direktinvestitionen der Metall- und Elektoindustrie im Raum Stuttgart*. Stuttgart-Hohenheim: mimeo.

Hoppe, A. and Voelzkow, H. (1999), 'Raumordnungs- und Regionalpolitik in der Bundesrepublik Deutschland. Rahmenbedingungen, Entwicklungen und Perspektiven'. In Holtmann, E. and Ellwein, T. (eds.), *50 Jahre Bundesrepublik Deutschland. Rahmenbedingungen Entwicklungen Perspektiven*. Opladen: Westdeutscher Verlag.

Hudson, R. (1997), 'Regional Futures: Industrial Restructuring, New High Volume Production Concepts and Spatial Development Strategies in the New Europe', *Regional Studies*, 31: 467–78.

Huggins, R. (1997), *Local Business Co-operation and Training and Enterprise Councils: The Development of Inter-firm Networks*. Cardiff: Center for Advanced Studies in the Social Sciences, University of Wales.

Imrie, R. (1989), 'Industrial Restructuring, Labour and Locality: The Case of the British Pottery Industry', *New Technology, Work and Employment*, 21: 3–26.

—— and Thomas, H. (1993), 'Urban Policy and the Urban Development Corporations'. In Imrie and Thomas (eds.), *British Urban Policy and the Urban Development Corporations*. London: Paul Chapman.

INSEE-SIRENE (1999), *INSEE Première No. 650*, June, 1.

Ismayr, W. (1997), 'Das politische System Deutschlands'. In Ismayr (ed.), *Die politischen Systeme Westeuropas*. Opladen: Leske & Budrich.

ISTAT (1996), *Rapporto Annuale: La Situazione del Paese 1995*. Rome: ISTAT.

—— (1997), *I Sistemi Locali del Lavoro 1991*. Rome: ISTAT.

—— (1999), *Censimento intermedio dell' industria e dei servizi*, http://cens.istat.it.

Jackman, R. W. (1987), 'The Politics of Economic Growth in the Industrial Democracies, 1974–1980: Leftist Strength or North Sea Oil?', *Journal of Politics*, 49: 242–56.

Jalabert, G., Laborie, J. P. *et al.* (1993), 'Une Spécialisation: Toulouse et le Secteur Aéronautique et Spatial'. In Sallez (ed.), *Les Villes, Lieux d'Europe*. La Tour d'Aigues: Editions de l'Aube/DATAR.

Jenny, F. and Weber, A.-P. (1976), *L'Enterprise et les Politiques de Concurrence: Ententes, Cartels, Monopoles*. Paris: Editions d'Organisation.

Jessop, B. (1995), 'The Regulation Approach, Governance and Post-Fordism', *Economy and Society*, 24: 307–33.

— (1998), 'The Rise of Governance and the Risks of Failures: The Case of Economic Development', *International Social Science Journal*, 155, 25–49.

Jobert, B. and Muller, P. (1987), *L'État en Action*. Paris: PUF.

Kabeer, N. (1994), 'The Structure of "Revealed Preference": Race, Community and Female Labour Supply in the London Clothing Industry', *Development and Change*, 25: 2, 307–22.

Keating, M. (1997), 'Is There a Regional Level of Government in Europe?' In Le Galès and Lequesne (eds.), q.v.

— (1998), *The New Regionalism in Western Europe: Territorial Restructuring and Political Change*. Northampton (Mass.): Edward Elgar.

— and Loughlin, J. (1996) (eds.), *The Political Economy of Regionalism*. London: Frank Cass.

Keeble, D. (1996a), *Small Firms, Innovation and Regional Development in Britain in the 1990's*. Cambridge: ESRC Centre for Business Research, University of Cambridge Working Paper No. 42.

— (1996b), *SMEs and Inter-Firm Networks in Britain*. Cambridge: ESRC Centre for Business Research, University of Cambridge.

— (1998), *Local Economic Development and Dynamics: The East Anglian Case*. Cambridge: ESRC Centre for Business Research, University of Cambridge Working Paper No. 96.

—, Lawson, C., Lawton-Smith, H., Moore, B., and Wilkinson, F. (1997), *Internationalisation Processes, Networking and Local Embeddedness in Technology-Intensive Small Firms*. Cambridge: ESRC Centre for Business Research, University of Cambridge Working Paper No. 53.

Keller, B. (1993), *Einführung in die Arbeitspolitik*. Munich: Oldenbourg.

Kerst, C. and Steffensen, B. (1995), *Die Krise des Baden-Württembergischen Maschinenbaus im Spiegel des NIFA-Panels. Arbeitsbericht No. 49*. Stuttgart: Akademie für Technikfolgenabschätzung.

Kilper, H. and Lhotta, R. (1995), *Föderalismus in der Bundesrepublik Deutschland*. Opladen: Leske & Budrich.

Klönne, A., Borowczak, W., and Voelzkow, H. (1991), *Institutionen Regionaler Technik-förderung. Eine Analyse in Ostwestfalen-Lippe und im Östlichen Ruhrgebiet*. Opladen: Westdeutscher Verlag.

Knodt, M. (1998), *Tiefenwirkung europäischer Politik. Eigensinn oder Anpassung regionalen Regierens?* Baden-Baden: Nomos.

Krafft, A. and Ullrich, G. (1993), *Chancen und Risiken regionaler Selbstorganisation. Erfahrungen mit der Regionalisierung der Wirtschaftspolitik in Nordrhein-Westfalen und Niedersachsen*. Opladen: Leske & Budrich.

Krätke, S. (1991), 'Cities in Transformation: The Case of West Germany'. In Benko and Dunford (eds.), q.v.

Krätke, S. (1997), 'Une Approche Régulationniste des Études Régionales', *L'Année de la Régulation*, 1: 263–98.

Kristensen, P. H. (1992), 'Industrial Districts in West Jutland, Denmark'. In Pyke and Sengenberger (eds.), q.v.

Krugman, P. (1991), *Geography and Trade*. Cambridge, MA: MIT Press.

Kuisel, R. (1984), *Le Capitalisme et l'État en France*. Paris: Gallimard.

Laine, F. and Rieu, C. (1999a), *La Diversité Industrielle des Territoires: INSEE Première No. 630*.

——, —— (1999b), *Le Tissu Productif Régional: Diversité et Concentration: INSEE Première No. 630*.

Lallement, M. (1999), *Les Gouvernances de l'Emploi*. Paris: Desclées de Brouwer.

Lancashire County Council (1997), *Lancashire 1998: An Economic Situation Report*. Manchester: Lancashire County Council.

LATTS (1998), *Globalisation et Territorialisation des Groupes Industriels. Rapport RR 9818*. Paris: DATAR.

Lau, D. (1997), *Sektorale Räumliche Konzentration und Ihre Bedeutung für die Industriepolitik*. Baden-Baden: Nomos.

Lauridsen, A.-L. (forthcoming), *Industrial Relations and Industrial Districts in Denmark and Italy*. Florence: Unpublished Ph.D. Thesis, European University Institute.

Lawless, P. (1994), 'Partnership in Urban Regeneration in the UK: The Sheffield Central Area Study', *Urban Studies*, 31: 8, 1303–24.

—— (1996), 'The Nature of Urban Partnership in Sheffield in the mid 1990's: A Documentary Analysis'. Sheffield: Centre for Regional Economic and Social Research, Sheffield Hallam University, Urban and Regional Development Series Paper No: UR 19. 96.

Lawson, C., Moore, B., Keeble, D., Lawton-Smith, H., and Wilkinson, F. (1996), *Inter-Firm Links between Regionally Clustered High-Technology SMEs: A Comparison of Cambridge and Oxford Innovation Networks*. Cambridge: ESRC Centre for Business Research, University of Cambridge, mimeo.

LAWTEC (1997), *LAWTEC Economic and Labour Market Assessment 1996/97*. Manchester: LAWTEC.

Lawton-Smith, H. (1997), 'National Laboratories and Regional Development: Case Studies from the UK, France, Belgium'. In Simmie (1997b) (ed.), q.v.

Lay, G. (1996), 'Regionalspezifisch Angepaßtes Technologiemanagement als Schlüssel zur Wettbewerbsfähigkeit Baden-Württembergischer Firmen'. In Braczyk and Schienstock (eds.), q.v.

Lazzaroto, M., Moulier-Boutang,Y., Negri, A., and Santilli, G. (1990), *Des Entreprises pas Comme les Autres. Benetton en Italie et le Sentier à Paris*. Paris: Editions Publisud.

Le Galès, P. (1987), 'Les Politiques de Développement Local'. In Wachter (ed.), q.v.

—— (1993), *Politiques Urbaines et Développement Local en France et en Grande-Bretagne*. Paris: L'Harmattan.

—— (1994), 'Regional Economic Policies: An Alternative to French Economic Dirigisme?', *Regional Policy and Politics*, 4: 3, 72–91.

—— (1997), 'Government and Governance of Regions in Europe: Structural Weaknesses and New Mobilisations'. In Le Galès and Lequesne (eds.), q.v.

—— (1998), 'Regulation and Governance in European Cities', *International Journal of Urban and Regional Research*, 22: 482–505.

Le Galès, P. and Lequesne, C. (1997) (eds.), *Regions in Europe: The Paradox of Power*. London: Routledge.

Leicestershire County Council (1983), Survey of Leicester. Leicester: Leicestershire County Council.

Lehmbruch, G. and Schmitter, P. C. (1982) (eds.), *Patterns of Corporatist Policy-Making*. Beverly Hills/London: Sage.

Leman, S. (1992), 'Ethnicity, Technology and Local Labour Markets in the Clothing Industry of Northern England', *Urban Anthropology*, 21: 2, 115–36.

Leonardi, R. and Nanetti, R. (1994) (eds.), *Regional Development in a Modern European Economy: The Case of Tuscany*. London: Pinter.

Lescure, M. (1996), *PME et Croissance Économique, l'Expérience des Années 1920*. Paris: Economica.

—— (1999), 'Small and Medium Size Industrial Enterprises in France 1900–1975'. In Odaka, K. and Sawai, M. (eds.), *Small Firms, Large Concerns: The Development of Small Business in Comparative Perspective*. Oxford: Oxford University Press.

Levy, J. (1999), *Tocqueville's Revenge*. Cambridge, MA: Harvard University Press.

Levy-Leboyer, M. (1996), *Histoire de la France Industrielle*. Paris: Larousse.

Lloyd, C. (1997), 'Microelectronics in the Clothing Industry: Firm Strategy and the Skills Debate', *New Technology, Work and Employment*, 12: 1, 36–47.

Locke, R. (1995), *Remaking the Italian Economy*. Ithaca: Cornell University Press.

—— (1996), 'The Composite Economy: Local Politics and Industrial Change in Contemporary Italy', *Economy and Society*, 25: 483–510.

Lompe, K. (1996), *Regionalisierung als Innovationsstrategie. Die VW-Region auf dem Weg von der Automobil- zur Verkehrskompetenzregion*. Berlin: edition sigma.

—— and Blöcker, A. (1997), 'Die Region als Politisch-Ökonomisches Handlungsfeld: Chancen und Risiken der Umsetzung des Südostniedersächsischen Entwicklungsmodells "Von der Automobil- zur Verkehrskompetenzregion"'. In Bullmann, U. and Heinze, R. (eds.), *Regionale Moderinsierungspolitik. Nationale und Internationale Perspektiven*. Opladen: Leske & Budrich.

López-Bazo, E., Vayá, E., Mora, A. J., and Suriñach, J. (1999), 'Regional Economic Dynamics and Convergence in the European Union', *Annals of Regional Science*, 33: 343–70.

Lothian and Edinburgh Enterprise Ltd. (1998), *About People: Lothian and Edinburgh Enterprise Limited Annual Report 1997/98*. Edinburgh: Lothian and Edinburgh Enterprise Ltd.

Lovering, J. (1995), 'Creating Discourses Rather Than Jobs: The Crisis in the Cities and the Transition Fantasies of Intellectuals and Policy Makers'. In Healy, P. *et al.* (eds.), *Managing Cities: The New Urban Context*. Chichester: Wiley.

—— (1999), 'The Inadequacies of the "New Regionalism"', *International Journal of Urban and Regional Research*, 23: 379–95.

Lundvall, B.-Å. (1992) (ed.), *National Systems of Innovation: Towards a Theory of Innovation and Interactive Learning*. London: Pinter.

—— and Johnson, B. (1994), 'The Learning Economy', *Journal of Industry Studies*, 1: 23–42.

MacLeod, G. (1996), 'The Cult of Enterprise in a Networked, Learning Region? Governing Business and Skills in Lowland Scotland', *Regional Studies*, 30: 8, 749–55.

Maddison, A. (1995), *Monitoring the World Economy: 1920–1992*. Paris: OECD.

Maier, H. E. (1989), 'Industrieentwicklung und Industriepolitik in Baden-Württemberg. Überlegungen zu den Institutionellen Voraussetzungen Differenzierter Qualitäts-produktion'. In Hucke, J. and Wollmann, H. (eds.), *Dezentrale Technologiepolitik?* Basel: Birkhäuser.

Maillat, D. (1995), 'Territorial Dynamics, Innovative Milieus and Regional Policy', *Entrepreneurship and Regional Development*, 7: 157–65.

— and Perrin, J.-C. (1993), *Entreprises Innovatrices et Développement Territorial.* Neuchatel: GREMI-EDES.

—, Quevit, M., and Senn, L. (1993), *Réseaux d'Innovation et Milieux Innovateurs: Un Pari pour le Développement Regional.* Neuchatel: GREMI-EDES.

Malecki, E. J. (1994), Entrepreneurship in Regional and Local Development, *International Regional Science Review*, 16: 119–53.

Manchester TEC (1997), *Economic Assessment 1996–1997.* Manchester: Manchester TEC.

Marshall, A. (1919), *Industry and Trade*. London: Macmillan.

— (1920), *Principles of Economics*. London: Macmillan.

Marshall, M. (1990), 'Regional Alternatives to Economic Decline in Britain's Industrial Heartland: Industrial Restructuring and Local Economic Intervention in the West Midlands Conurbation'. In Stöhr, W. (ed.), *Global Challenge and Local Response: Initiatives for Economic Regeneration in Contemporary Europe.* London: Mansell.

Maskell, P. (1998), 'Low-Tech Competitive Advantages and the Role of Proximity: The Danish Wooden Furniture Industry', *European Urban and Regional Studies*, 5: 99–118.

— et al. (1998) (eds.), *Competitiveness, Localised Learning and Regional Development: Specialisation and Prosperity in Small Open Economies.* London: Routledge.

— and Malmberg, A. (1999), 'The Competitiveness of Firms and Regions: Ubiquification and the Importance of Localized Learning', *European Urban and Regional Studies*, 6: 9–26.

McNicoll, A. (1995), 'Social Networking—A Comparative Behavioural Study between Would-Be Entrepreneurs in Scotland and Boston, Massachusetts'. In Danson (1995b) (ed.), q.v.

Meldolesi, L. (1998), *Dalla Parte del Sud*. Bari: Laterza.

— and Aniello, V. (1998), 'L'Italia Che Non C'è, Quant'è, Dov'è, Com'è', *Rivista di Politica Economica*, 8–9.

Mériaux, O. (1999), *L'Action Publique Partagée: Formes et Dynamiques Institutionelles de la Régulation Politique du Régime Française de Formation Continue.* Grenoble: Unpublished Ph.D. Thesis, Institut d'Études Politiques.

Michan, F. and Segrestin, D. (1990), *L'Emploi, l'Enterprise et la Société*. Paris: Economica.

Midlothian Council, Lothian and Edinburgh Enterprise (n.d.) *Economic Strategy for Midlothian*. Edinburgh: Lothian and Edinburgh Enterprise.

Minguet, G. (1985), *Naissance de l'Anjou Industriel*. Paris: L'Harmattan.

— (1993), *Chef d'Entreprise dans l'Ouest*. Paris: PUF.

Molle, W. and Boeckhout, S. (1995), 'Economic Disparity under Conditions of Integration: A Long Term View of the European Case', *Papers in Regional Science*, 74: 105–23.

Moore, C. (1995), 'Scotland and the SDA'. In Rhodes (ed.), q.v.

Morgan, K. (1997a), 'The Learning Region: Institutions, Innovation and Regional Renewal', *Regional Studies*, 31: 491–503.

— (1997b), 'The Regional Animateur: Taking Stock of the Welsh Development Agency', *Regional and Federal Studies*, 7: 2, 70–94.

Morris, J. and Imrie, R. (1992), *Transforming Buyer–Supplier Relations*. London: Macmillan.

Morvan, Y. (1996), 'L'excellence des Territoires... Ou la Nécessaire Organisation des Systèmes Productifs Locaux', *Cahiers Economiques de Bretagne*, 1.

— and Marchand, M. J. (1994), *L'Intervention Économique des Régions*. Paris: LGDJ Montchrestien.

Moulaert, F. (1996), 'Rediscovering Spatial Inequality in Europe: Building Blocks for an Appropriate "Regulationist" Analytical Framework', *Environment and Planning D: Society and Space*, 14: 155–79.

— and Swyngedouw, E. (1989), 'A Regulation Approach to the Geography of Flexible Production Systems', *Environment and Planning D: Society and Space*, 7: 327–45.

Muller, P. (1989), *Airbus, l'Ambition Européenne, Logique d'Etat, Logique de Marché*. Paris: L'Harmattan.

Müller-Jentsch, W. (1986), *Soziologie der Industriellen Beziehungen. Eine Einführung*. New York: Franfurt am Main.

— (1995), 'Auf dem Prüfstand: Das Deutsche Modell der Industriellen Beziehungen', *Industrielle Beziehungen*, 2: 1, 11–24.

Munday, M., Morris, J., and Wilkinson, B. (1995), 'Factories or Warehouses? A Welsh Perspective on Japanese Transplant Manufacturing', *Regional Studies*, 29: 1, 1–17.

Naschold, F. (1996), 'Jenseits des Baden-Württembergischen "Exceptionalism": Strukturprobleme der Deutschen Industrie'. In Braczyk and Schienstock (eds.), q.v.

Neitzel, M. and Schauerte, M. (1998), *Wir Bringen Ideen in Bewegung. Ein Bericht zu Branchentrends des Maschinenbaus in NRW*. Bochum: Metall im Dialog 2.

Nelson, R. (1993), *National Innovation Systems*. Oxford: Oxford University Press.

Niedersächsisches Ministerium für Wirtschaft, Technologie und Verkehr (1998), *Wirtschaftsbericht*. Niedersächsisches Ministerium für Wirtschaft, Technologie und Verkehr.

North, D. C. (1990), *Institutions, Institutional Change and Economic Performance*. Cambridge: Cambridge University Press.

North London TEC (1996), *Quarterly Research and Economic Development Bulletin January 1996*. London: North London TEC.

North Yorkshire TEC (1996), *The York and North Yorkshire Economic and Labour Market Assessment*. North Yorkshire TEC.

Northamptonshire TEC (1996), *Northamptonshire Economic and Labour Market Assessment—1996*. Northampton: Northamptonshire TEC.

Nottinghamshire County Council (1997), *Economic Development Review: Nottinghamshire 1997*. Nottingham: Nottinghamshire County Council.

OCDE (1996), *Réseaux d'Entreprises et Développement Local*. Paris: OCDE.

Ohmae, K. (1990), *The Borderless World*. New York: Harper.

— (1995), *The End of the Nation State: The Rise of Regional Economies*. New York: The Free Press.

Okamuro, H. (1997), 'Impacts of the Japanese Investment in the UK on the Local Supplier Relationship', *Hitotsubashi Journal of Economics*, 38: 2, 167–82.

Oliver, N. and Wilkinson, B. (1992), *The Japanisation of British Industry*. Oxford: Blackwell.

Olson, M. (1971), *The Logic of Collective Action. Public Goods and the Theory of Groups*. Cambridge, MA: Harvard University Press.

Orkney Enterprise (1996), *Fifth Annual Report (1995/96)*. Orkney: Orkney Enterprise.

Paolazzi, L. and Moussanet, M. (1992), *Gioielli, Bambole e Coltelli*. Milan: Angeli.

Parat, E. (1998), *La Filière Textile-Habillement-Distribution*. Paris: Centres d'Études de l'Emploi.

—— and Courault, B. (1998), 'Les PME de l'Habillement à Roanne et Cholet: Une Dynamique de l'Emploi à Rebours de l'Histoire'. In Courault, Parat, and Trouvé (eds.), q.v.

Peck, J. A. and Tickell, A. (1994), 'Searching for a New Institutional Fix: The After-Fordist Crisis and Global-Local Disorder'. In Amin (ed.), q.v.

——, —— (1995), 'Business Goes Local: Dissecting the Business Agenda in Manchester', *International Journal of Urban and Regional Research*, 19: 1, 55–78.

Pecqueur, B. (1996a), *Le Développement Local: Mode ou Modèle?* Paris: Syros-Alternatives.

—— (1996b), *Dynamiques Territoriales et Mutations Économiques*. Paris: Syros/ L'Harmattan.

—— (2000), *Le Développement Local*. Paris: Syros-Alternatives.

Perulli, P. (1998) (ed.), *Neoregionalismo: L'Economia-Arcipelago*. Turin: Bollati Boringhieri.

Phelps, N. A., Lovering, J., and Morgan, K. (1998), 'Tying the Firm to the Region or Tying the Region to the Firm? Early Observations on the Case of LG in South Wales', *European Urban and Regional Studies*, 5: 2, 119–38.

Phizacklea, A. (1990), *Unpacking the Fashion Industry: Gender, Racism and Class in Production*. London: Routledge.

—— (1992), 'Jobs for the Girls: The Production of Women's Outerwear in the UK'. In Cross, M. (ed.), *Ethnic Minorities and Industrial Change in Europe and North America*. Cambridge: Cambridge University Press.

Picchieri, A. (1998) (ed.), *La Regionalizzatione delle Politiche Industriali: Il Caso Rhône-Alpes*. Turin: Rosenberg and Sellier.

Pinch, S. and Henry, N. (1999a), 'Discursive Aspects of Technological Innovation: The Case of the British Motor-Sport Industry', *Environment and Planning A*, 31: 665–82.

——, —— (1999b), 'Paul Krugman's Geographical Economics, Industrial Clustering and the British Motor Sport Industry', *Regional Studies*, 33: 9, 815–28.

Piore, M. J. and Sabel, C. F. (1984), *The Second Industrial Divide: Possibilities for Prosperity*. New York: Basic Books.

PIRTTEM (1992), *Le District Industriel de la Vallée de l'Arve, Rapport PIRTTEM Développement Local et Ensemble de PME*. Lyon: PIRTTEM.

Piselli, F. (1999), 'Capitale Sociale: Un Concetto Situazionale e Dinamico', *Stato e Mercato*, 3, 395–418.

Planque, B. (1983), *Innovation et Développement Régional*. Paris: Economica.

Porter, M. (1991), *Nationale Wettbewerbsvorteile. Erfolgreich Konkurrieren auf dem Weltmarkt*. München: Droemersche Verlagsanstalt.

—— (1998), *The Competitive Advantage of Nations: With a New Introduction by the Author*. London: Collier Macmillan.

Pratt, A. C. (1997), 'Production Values: From Cultural Industries to the Governance of Culture', *Environment and Planning A*, 29: 11, 1911–17.

Puhlmann, K., Bechinka, U., and Wolf, W. (1996), *Sichtsweisen und Handlungsstrategien des LVI im Hinblick auf Regionale Innovationsprozesse*. Stuttgart: Akademie für Technikfolgenabschätzung in Baden-Württemberg, Working Paper No. 55.

Putnam, R. D. (1993), *Making Democracy Work: Civic Traditions in Modern Italy*. Princeton, NJ: Princeton University Press.

Pyke, F. and Sengenberger, W. (1992) (eds.), *Industrial Districts and Local Economic Regeneration*. Geneva: International Institute for Labour Studies.

—, Becattini, G., and Sengenberger, W. (1990) (eds.), *Industrial Districts and Inter-Firm Co-operation in Italy*. Geneva: International Institute for Labour Studies.

—, Sengenberger, W., and Cossentino, F. (1996) (eds.), *Local and Regional Response to Global Pressure: The Case of Italy and Its Industrial Districts*. Geneva: International Labour Organization.

Quah, D. (1996), *Regional Convergence Clusters across Europe*. London: Centre for Economic Performance, Working Paper No. 1286.

Rabelloti, R. and Schmitz, H. (1999), 'The Internal Heterogeneity of Industrial Districts in Italy, Brazil and Mexico', *Regional Studies*, 33: 97–108.

Ram, M. (1994), *Managing to Survive: Working Lives in Small Firms*. Oxford: Blackwell.

—— (1996), 'Unravelling the Hidden Clothing Industry: Managing the Ethnic Minority Garment Sector'. In Taplin and Winterton (eds.), q.v.

Raveyre, M. F. and Saglio, J. (1984), Les Systèmes Industriels Localisés: Éléments pour une Analyse Sociologique des Ensembles de PME Industriels, *Sociologie du Travail*, 2.

Regini, M. and Sabel, C. F. (1989) (eds.), *Strategie di Riaggustimento Industriale*. Bologna: Il Mulino.

Rerat, F. (1990), 'Le textile à Roanne, Logiques de développement d'un système industriel localisé', *Dossier de recherche du centre d'étude de l'emploi*.

—— and Courault, B. (1992), *Les PME en Milieu Local: Dossier n.48*. Paris: Centre d'Étude de l'Emploi.

Rhodes, M. (1995) (ed.), *The Regions and the New Europe. Patterns in Core and Periphery Development*. Manchester/New York: Manchester University Press.

Richardson, W. (1993), 'Employers as an Instrument of School Reform? Education–business "compacts" in Britain and America'. In Finegold, D., McFarland, L., and Richardson, W. (eds.), *Something Borrowed, Something Blue? A Study of the Thatcher Government's Appropriation of American Education and Training Policy*, Part 2, *Oxford Studies in Comparative Education* 3, 1.

Richter, G. (1987), *Stuttgart Problemregion der 90er Jahre? Gefährdungen der Arbeitnehmer durch Umstrukturierungen in der Metallindustrie im Wirtschaftsraum Stuttgart*. Stuttgart: IMU-Institut Studien 7.

Rodríguez-Pose, A. (1998), *Dynamics of Regional Growth in Europe*. Oxford: Oxford University Press.

—— (1999a), 'Convergence or Divergence? Types of Regional Responses to Socio-Economic Change in Western Europe', *Tijdschrift voor Economische en Sociale Geografie*, 90: 4, 363–78.

—— (1999b), 'Innovation Prone and Innovation Averse Societies: Economic Performance in Europe', *Growth and Change*, 30: 1, 75–105.

Ronit, K. and Schneider, V. (1997), 'Organisierte Interessen in Nationalen und Supranationalen Politökologien—Ein Vergleich der G7-Länder mit der Europäischen Union'. In von Alemann, U. and Wessels, B. (eds.), *Verbände in Vergleichender Perspektive: Beiträge zu Einem Vernachlässigtem Feld*. Berlin: edition sigma.

Ronneberger, K. (1995), 'Von High-Tech Regionen lernen?', *Jahrbuch Sozialwissenschaftliche Technikberichterstattung. Schwerpunkt: Technik und Region*. Berlin: edition sigma.

Ross and Cromarty Enterprise (1996), *Growing Businesses, Developing People, Strengthening Communities. 5th Annual Report, 1995–1996.* Ross and Cromarty: Ross and Cromarty Enterprise.

Roualdes, D. (1997), *La Restructuration des Grands Établissements Industriels: INSEE Première No.512.*

Rousier, N. (1997), 'Internationalisation et Développement des Technopoles: Grenoble et les Réseaux Internationaux'. In Cohen, Hart, and Simmie (eds.), q.v.

Rowley, C. (1989), 'The British Pottery Industry: A Case of Industrial Restructuring, Labour and Locality', *Environment and Planning A*, 24: 1645–90.

—— (1994), 'The Illusion of Flexible Specialization: The Case of the Domesticware Sector of the British Ceramics Industry', *New Technology, Work and Employment*, 9: 2, 127–39.

Rudzio, W. (1996), *Das Politische System der Bundesrepublik Deutschland.* Opladen: Leske & Budrich.

Rullani, E. (1998), 'Dal Fordismo Realizzato al Postfordismo Possibile: La Difficile Transizione'. In Rullani and Luca (eds.), *Il Postfordismo: Idee per il Capitalismo Prossimo Venturo.* Perugia: Etas Libri.

—— and Romano, L. (1998) (eds.), *Il Postfordismo: Idee per il Capitalismo Prossimo Venturo.* Perugia: Etas Libri.

Russo, M. (1985), 'Technical Change and the Industrial District: The Role of Inter-Firm Relations in the Growth and Transformation of Ceramic Tile Production in Italy', *Research Policy*, 14: 329–43.

Sabel, C. F. (1989), 'Flexible Specialization and the Re-emergence of Regional Economies'. In Hirst, P. and Zeitlin, J. (eds.), *Reversing Industrial Decline? Industrial Structure and Policy in Britain and Her Competitors.* Oxford: Berg.

—— and Zeitlin, J. (1989), 'Historical Alternatives to Mass Production: Politics, Markets, and Technologies in Nineteenth Century Industrialization', *Past and Present*, 108: 133–76.

——, —— (1997a), 'Stories, Strategies, Structures: Rethinking Historical Alternatives to Mass Production'. In Sabel and Zeitlin (eds.), q.v.

——, —— (1997b) (eds.), *World of Possibilities: Flexibility and Mass Production in Western Industrialization.* Cambridge: Cambridge University Press.

——, Herrigel, G., Deeg, R., and Kazis, R. (1989), 'Regional Prosperities Compared: Massachusetts and Baden-Württemberg in the 1980s', *Economy and Society*, 18: 4, 374–404.

Sala-I-Martin, X. X. (1996), 'Regional Cohesion: Evidence and Theories of Regional Growth', *European Economic Review*, 40: 1325–52.

Salais, R. and Storper, M. (1993), *Les Mondes de Production.* Paris: Editions de l'École des Hautes Études en Sciences Sociales.

Sassen, S. (1991), *The Global City: New York, London, Tokyo.* Princeton, NJ: Princeton University Press.

Sauer, P. (1991), *Kleine Geschichte Stuttgarts: Von der Reichsgründung bis Heute.* Stuttgart/Berlin/Köln: Kohlhammer.

Savy, M. and Veltz, P. (1993) (eds.), *Les Nouveaux Espaces des Entreprises.* La Tour d'Aigues: Editions de l'Aube/DATAR.

Saxenian, A. L. (1994), *Regional Advantage: Culture and Competition in Silicon Valley and Route 128.* Cambridge, MA: Harvard University Press.

Sayer, A. (1989a), 'The "New" Regional Geography and Problems of Narrative', *Environment and Planning D: Society and Space*, 253–76.

—— (1989b), 'Postfordism in Question', *International Journal of Urban and Regional Research*, 13: 4, 666–95.

Scharpf, F. W. (1997), *Globalisierung als Beschränkung der Handlungsmöglichkeiten Nationalstaatlicher Politik*. Köln: MPIfG Discussion Paper 97/1.

——, Reissert, B., and Schnabel, F. (1976), *Theorie und Empirie des kooperativen Föderalismus in der Bundesrepublik*. Kronberg: Ts. Scriptor.

Schmidt, V. (1990), *Democratizing France*. Cambridge: Polity Press.

—— (1996), *From State to Market? The Transformation of Business in France*. Cambridge: Cambridge University Press.

Schmitter, P. C. and Lehmbruch, G. (1979) (eds.), *Trends Towards Corporatist Intermediation*. Beverly Hills/London: Sage.

Schmitz, H. (1992), 'Industrial Districts: Model and Reality in Baden-Württemberg, Germany'. In Pyke and Sengenberger (eds.), q.v.

Scott, A. J. (1988a), 'Flexible Production Systems and Regional Development: The Rise of New Industrial Spaces in North America and Western Europe', *International Journal of Urban and Regional Research*, 12: 2, 171–86.

—— (1988b), *New Industrial Spaces: Flexible Production Organization and Regional Development in North America and Western Europe*. London: Pion.

—— (1992), 'The Collective Order of Flexible Production Agglomerations: Lessons for Local Economic Development Policy and Strategic Choice', *Economic Geography*, 68: 219–33.

—— (1996), 'Regional Motors of the Global Economy', *Futures*, 28: 391–411.

—— (1999), *The Regional World*. Oxford: Oxford University Press.

—— and Storper, M. (1986) (eds.), *Production, Work, Territory: The Geographical Anatomy of Industrial Capitalism*. London: Allen & Unwin.

——, —— (1992a), 'Le Développement Régional Réconsideré', *Espaces et Sociétés*, 66–67: 7–38.

——, —— (1992b), 'Regional Development Reconsidered'. In Ernste, H. and Meier, V. (eds.), *Regional Development and Contemporary Industrial Response*. London: Bellhaven Press.

Scottish Borders Enterprise (1996), *Annual Report and Accounts 1995/1996*. Scottish Borders Enterprise.

Select Committee on Environment, Transport and Regional Affairs (1999a), *Memorandum by the Centre for Urban and Regional Development Studies (CURDS), University of Newcastle on Tyne to Select Committee on Environment, Transport and Regional Affairs*. London: House of Commons.

Select Committee on Environment, Transport and Regional Affairs (1999b), *Memorandum by the Federation of Small Businesses to Select Committee on Environment, Transport and Regional Affairs*. London: House of Commons.

Semlinger, K. (1993), 'Economic Development and Industrial Policy in Baden-Württemberg: Small Firms in a Benevolent Environment', *European Planning Studies*, 1: 435–63.

—— (1995), 'Industrial Policy and Small-Firm Cooperation in Baden-Württemberg'. In Bagnasco and Sabel (eds.), q.v.

—— (1996), 'Industrial-district-Politik in Baden-Württemberg—zwischen Neubesinnung und Neuanfang'. In Braczyk and Schienstock (eds.), q.v.

SESSI (1996), *L'Industrie dans les Régions*. Paris: Ministère de l'Industrie des Postes et des Télécommunications.

——(1998a), *L'Habillement*. Paris: Ministère de l'Economie, des Finances et de l'Industrie.

——(1998b), *Industrie Française et Mondialisation*. Paris: Ministère de l'Economie, des Finances et de l'Industrie.

——(1999a), *L'État des PMI*. Paris: Ministère de l'Economie, des Finances et de l'Industrie.

——(1999b), *L'Industrie dans les Régions*. Paris: Ministère de l'Industrie des Postes et des Télécommunications.

Sforzi, F. (1993), 'Il Modello Toscano: un Interpretazione alla Luce delle Recenti Tendenze'. In Leonardi and Nanetti (eds.), q.v.

——(1995a), 'Sistemi Locali e Cambiamento Industriale in Italia', *Geotema*, 2, 42–54.

——(1995b), 'Il Cambiamento Economico nel Sistema Urbano Italiano'. In Dematteis, G. and Bonavero, P. (eds.), *Il Sistema Urbano Italiano nello Spazio Unificato Europeo*. Bologna: Il Mulino.

Shonfield, A. (1965), *Modern Capitalism*. Oxford: Oxford University Press.

Shutt, J. and Pellow, N. (1998), *Industrial Clusters and LED Business Support: Contrasting Strategy Evidence from the North of England*. Leeds: European Regional Business and Development Unit Working Paper No. 6, Leeds Business School, Leeds Metropolitan University.

Simmie, J. (1997a), 'The Origins and Characteristics of Innovation in Highly Innovative Areas: the Case of Hertfordshire'. In Simmie (1997b) (ed.), q.v.

——(1997b) (ed.), *Innovation, Networks and Learning Regions?* London: Regional Studies Association/Jessica Kingsley Publishers.

SOLOTEC (1996), *South London Economic Assessment 1996*. London: SOLOTEC.

Somerset TEC (1997), *Somerset TEC Economic Bulletin*. Taunton: Somerset TEC.

South Glamorgan TEC (1997), *Economic Outlook: Cardiff and the Vale of Glamorgan*. Cardiff: South Glamorgan TEC.

Staber, U. (1996a), 'Accounting for Variations in the Performance of Industrial Districts: The Case of Baden-Württemberg', *International Journal of Urban and Regional Research*, 20: 299–316.

——(1996b), 'Networks and Regional Development: Perspectives and Unresolved Issues'. In Staber, Shaefer, and Sharma (eds.), q.v.

——, Shaefer, N. V., and Sharma, B. (1996) (eds.), *Business Networks: Prospects for Regional Development*. Berlin/New York: de Gruyter.

Staffordshire TEC (1997), *The Changing Face of Staffordshire: Staffordshire Market Analysis 1997–98*. Staffordshire TEC.

Statistisches Bundesamt (1998), *Statistisches Jahrbuch für die Bundesrepublik Deutschland*. Wiesbaden: Metzler-Poeschel.

Statistisches Landesamt Baden-Württemberg (1994). *Berichte des Statistischen Landesamtes Baden-Württemberg 1991–1994: Statistische Berichte Produzierendes Gewerbe, Bergbau und Verarbeitendes Gewerbe*. Stuttgart: Statistisches Landesamt Baden-Württemberg.

Steinbeis-Stiftung (1997), *Wir Machen Innovationen Schneller: Bericht 1997*. Stuttgart: Fischer Druck GmbH.

Sternberg, R., Behrendt, H., Seeger, H., and Tamasy, C. (1996), *Bilanz eines Booms—Wirkungsanalyse von Technologie- und Gründerzentren in Deutschland*. Dortmund: Dortmunder Vertrieb für Bau- und Planungsliteratur.

Stoffaës, C. (1991), 'La Restructuration Industrielle'. In Casanova and Lévy-Leboyer (eds.), q.v.

Storper, M. (1992), 'The Limits to Globalization: Technology Districts and International Trade', *Economic Geography*, 68: 60–93.

——(1995a), 'Regional Technology Coalitions: An Essential Dimension of National Technology Policy', *Research Policy*, 24: 895–911.

——(1995b), 'The Resurgence of Regional Economies, Ten Years Later: The Region as a Nexus of Untraded Interdependencies', *European Urban and Regional Studies*, 2: 3, 191–221.

——(1997), *The Regional World*. New York: Guilford Press.

—— and Harrison, B. (1992), 'Flessibilità, Gerarchia e Sviluppo Regionale: La Ristrutturazione Organizzativa dei Sistemi Produttivi e le Nuove Forme di Governance'. In Belussi (ed.), q.v.

—— and Salais, R. (1998), *Worlds of Production. The Action Frameworks of the Economy*. Cambridge, MA: Harvard University Press.

—— and Scott, A. J. (1992) (eds.), *Pathways to Industrialization and Regional Development*. London: Routledge.

Streeck, W. (1991), 'On the Institutional Conditions of Diversified Quality Production'. In Matzner, E. and Streeck, W. (eds.), *Beyond Keynesianism. The Socio-Economics of Full Employment*. Aldershot: Brookfields.

——(1994), 'Staat und Verbände: Neue Fragen. Neue Antworten?' In Streeck (ed.), *Politische Vierteljahresschrift (Special Issue: Staat und Verbände)*. Opladen: Westdeutscher Verlag.

——(1997), 'German Capitalism: Does It Exist? Can It Survive?' In Crouch and Streeck (eds.), q.v.

—— and Schmitter, P. C. (1985), 'Community, Market, State—and Association? The Prospective Contribution of Interest Governance to Social Order'. In Streeck and Schmitter (eds.), *Private Interest Government: Beyond Market and State*. London, Beverly Hills: Sage.

——, Hilbert, J., Van Kevelaer, K.-H., and Weber, H. (1987), *Steuerung und Regulierung der Beruflichen Bildung. Die Rolle der Sozialpartner in der Ausbildung und Beruflichen Weiterbildung in der Bundesrepublik Deutschland*. Berlin: edition sigma.

Sunderland TEC (1998), *Business Concerns. TECniques*. Sunderland: Sunderland TEC.

Surrey TEC and Surrey County Council (1996), *An Economic Audit of Surrey 1996: Surrey's Focus on the Future*. Guildford: Surrey TEC/Surrey County Council.

Sussex Enterprise (1998), *Realising Our Potential: The Sussex Economy 1997–1998*. Brighton: Sussex Enterprise.

Svimez (1999). *Rapporto 1999 sull'Economia del Mezzogiorno*. Rome: Svimez.

Swann, G. M. P., Prevezer, M., and Stout, D. (1998), *The Dynamics of Industrial Clustering: International Comparisons in Computing and Biotechnology*. Oxford: Oxford University Press.

Swyngedouw, E. (1997), 'Neither Global nor Local: "Glocalisation" and the Politics of Scale'. In Cox, K. R. (ed.), *Spaces of Globalisation: Reasserting the Power of the Local*. New York/London: The Guilford Press.

Taplin, I. M. (1996), Introduction. In Taplin and Winterton (eds.), q.v.

—— and Winterton, J. (1996) (eds.), *Restructuring within a Labour-Intensive Industry: The UK Clothing Industry in Transition*. Aldershot: Avebury.

Taylor, P. J. (2000), 'World Cities and Territorial States under Conditions of Contemporary Globalization', *Political Geography*, 19: 5–32.

TECSA Consultants (1997), *Les Systèmes Productifs Localisés et Leur Identification en France*. Paris: DATAR.

Teisserenc, P. (1994), *Les Politiques de Développement Local*. Paris: Economica.

Tickell, A., Peck, J., and Dicken, P. (1995), 'The Fragmented Region: Business, the State and Economic Development in North West England'. In Rhodes (ed.), q.v.

Töpfer, A. (1998), *Die Restrukturierung des Daimler-Benz Konzerns 1995–1997: Portfoliobereinigung, Prozeßoptimierung, Profitables Wachstum*. Neuwied/Kriftel: Luchterhand.

Toterdill, P. (1992), 'The Textiles and Clothing Industry: A Laboratory of Industrial Policy'. In Geddes, M. and Benington, J. (eds.), *Restructuring the Local Economy*. London: Longman.

Touati, P.-Y. (1989), *Le Capital-Risque Régional et Local en France*. Paris: Syros-Alternatives.

Tranie, B. (1995), *L'Equation du Développement Local*. Paris: Association Racine.

Trigilia, C. (1986a), *Grande Partiti e Piccole Imprese: Comunisti e Democristiani nelle Regioni a Economia Diffusa*. Bologna: Il Mulino.

—— (1986b), 'Small-Firm Development and Political Subcultures in Italy', *European Sociological Review*, 2: 3, 161–75.

—— (1990), 'Work and Politics in the Third Italy's Industrial Districts'. In Pyke, Becattini, and Sengenberger (eds.), q.v.

—— (1992a), 'Italian Industrial Districts: Neither Myth nor Interlude'. In Pyke and Sengenberger (eds.), q.v.

—— (1992b), *Sviluppo senza Autonomia: Effetti Perversi delle Politiche nel Mezzogiorno*. Bologna: Il Mulino.

—— (1997), 'Le Occasioni dello Sviluppo Locale'. In Bevilacqua, P. *et al.*, *Melfi, Gioia Tauro: Le Sfide dello Sviluppo*. Rome: Donzelli.

—— (1998), *Sociologia Economica*. Bologna: Il Mulino.

—— (1999), 'Capitale Sociale e Sviluppo Locale', *Stato e Mercato*, 3, 419–40.

Turok, I. (1993), 'Inward Investment and Local Linkages: How Deeply Embedded is Silicon Glen?', *Regional Studies*, 27: 5, 401–17.

Uhrich, R. (1987), *La France Inverse. Les Régions en Mutation*. Paris: Economica.

Unioncamere (1995), *Imprese e Istituzioni nei Distretti Industriali che Cambiano*. Milan: Angeli.

Vaughan, P. (1993), *TECs and Employers: Developing Effective Links, Part 1*. London: Employment Department, Research Series No. 12.

Vavakova, B. (1998), *La Science de la Nation: Les Paradoxes Politiques de la Logique Économique: Doctoral Thesis in Sociology*. Paris: Sciences-Po.

Veltz, P. (1996), *Mondialisation, Villes et Territoires*. Paris: PUF.

—— (1997), 'Les Villes Européennes dans l'Économie Mondiale'. In Bagnasco and Le Galès (eds.), q.v.

—— (2000a), *Le nouveau monde industriel*. Paris: Gallimard.

—— (2000b) *Métropolisation et Formes Économiques Émergentes*.

Vergeau, E. and Chabanas, N. (1997), *Le Nombre de Groupes d'Entreprises a Explosé en 15 Ans: INSEE Première No. 553.*

Vickerstaff, S. and Parker, K. (1995), 'Helping Small Firms: The Contribution of TECs and LECs', *International Small Business Journal*, 13: 4, 56–72.

Viesti, G. (1995), 'Lo Sviluppo Possibile: Casi di Successo Internazionale di Distretti Industriali nel Sud d'Italia', *Rassegna Economica*, 1, 119–39.

— and Bodo, G. (1997), *La Grande Svolta: Il Mezzogiorno d'Italia nell'Italia degli Anni Novanta.* Rome: Donzelli.

Vitols, S. (1996), *German Industrial Policy: An Overview.* Berlin: Discussion Paper, FS I 96-321, Wissenschaftszentrum Berlin für Sozialforschung.

Voelzkow, H. (1996), 'Der Zug in die Regionen. Politische Regionalisierung als Antwort auf die Globalisierung der Ökonomie', *Berliner Debatte INITIAL: Zeitschrift für Sozialwissenschaftlichen Diskurs*, 5: 68–78.

— (1997), *Governance of Regional Economies: An International Comparison. A Brief Project Description.* Cologne: Max-Planck-Institut für Gesellschaftsforschung.

— (1999), 'Die Governance Regionaler Ökonomien im internationalen Vergleich: Deutschland und Italien'. In Fuchs, G., Krauss, G., and Wolf, H.-G. (eds.), *Die Bindungen der Globalisierung Interorganisationsbeziehungen im Regionalen und Globalen Wirtschaftsraum.* Marburg: Metropolis.

Wachters, S. (1987) (ed.), *État, Décentralisation et Territoires.* Paris: L'Harmattan.

West Wales TEC (1998), *West Wales Annual Labour Market Assessment—Executive Summary 1997/98.* West Wales TEC.

WESTEC (1996), *WESTEC 1996 Labour Market Assessment.* WESTEC.

Whitley, R. (1993), *European Business Systems: Firms and Markets in their National Context.* London: Sage.

— (1998), 'Internationalisation and Varieties of Capitalism: The Limited Effects of Cross-National Coordination of Economic Activities on the Nature of Business Systems', *Review of International Political Economy*, 5: 3, 445–81.

— and Kristensen, P. H. (1996) (eds.), *The Changing European Firm.* London: Routledge.

Whittan, G. and Kirk, C. (1995), 'The Business Birth Rate, Real Services and Networking: Strategic Options'. In Danson (1995b) (ed.), q.v.

Williamson, O. E. (1975), *Markets and Hierarchies: Analysis and Antitrust Implications.* New York: The Free Press.

— (1985), *The Economic Institutions of Capitalism.* New York: Free Press.

— (1995), *The Mechanisms of Governance.* Oxford: Oxford University Press.

Wiltshire County Council (1998), *Wiltshire Business Facts.* Swindon: Wiltshire County Council.

Winterton, A. and Barlow, A. (1996), 'Economic Restructuring of UK Clothing'. In Taplin and Winterton (eds.), q.v.

Yorkshire and Humberside TECs (1996), *Shaping the Future: An Economic and Labour Market Assessment of Yorkshire and Humberside.* Yorkshire and Humberside TECs.

Zalio, P. P. (1999), *Grandes Familles de Marseille au Xxième Siècle.* Paris: Berlin.

Zeitlin, J. (1992a), 'Industrial Districts and Local Economic Regeneration: Overview and Comment'. In Pyke and Sengenberger (eds.), q.v.

— (1992b), 'The Third Italy: Inter-Firm Cooperation and Technological Innovation'. In Murray, R. (ed.), *Technology Strategies and Local Economic Intervention.* Nottingham: Spokesman Books.

Zeitlin, J. (1995), 'Why Are there No Industrial Districts in the United Kingdom?' In Bagnasco and Sabel (eds.), q.v.

—— (1996), 'The Clothing Industry in Transition'. In Taplin and Winterton (eds.), q.v.

Zysman, J. (1977), *Political Strategies for Industrial Order: State, Market and Industry in France*. Berkeley: University of California Press.

Index